DICKENS
AND POPULAR
ENTERTAINMENT

DICKENS

AND POPULAR ENTERTAINMENT

PAUL SCHLICKE

Department of English,
University of Aberdeen

London
ALLEN & UNWIN
Boston   Sydney

Allen & Unwin (Publishers) Ltd,
40 Museum Street, London WC1A 1LU, UK

Allen & Unwin (Publishers) Ltd,
Park Lane, Hemel Hempstead, Herts HP2 4TE, UK

Allen & Unwin, Inc.,
8 Winchester Place, Winchester, Mass. 01890, USA

Allen & Unwin (Australia) Ltd,
8 Napier Street, North Sydney, NSW 2060, Australia

First published in 1985

British Library Cataloguing in Publication Data

Schlicke, Paul
    Dickens and popular entertainment.
    1. Dickens, Charles, *1812–1870*—Criticism and interpretation
823′.8   PR4588

ISBN 0–04–800038–8

Library of Congress Cataloging in Publication Data

Schlicke, Paul.
    Dickens and popular entertainment.
    Bibliography: p.
    Includes index.
    1. Dickens, Charles, 1812–1870—Knowledge—Performing
arts. 2. Dickens, Charles, 1812–1870—Criticism and
interpretation. 3. Performing arts in literature. 4. Performing
arts—Great Britain—History—19th century. 5. Great
Britain—Popular culture. I. Title.
PR4592.P45S35 1985   823′.8   85–6024
ISBN 0–04–800038–8 (alk. paper)

Set in 10 on 11 point Bembo by Phoenix Photosetting, Chatham
and printed in Great Britain by Mackays of Chatham Ltd.

CONTENTS

This book is dedicated to my mother,
Hilda Hinckley Schlicke,
who did not live to see it completed,
and to my wife,
Priscilla Adelaide Schlicke,
who never thought she would live to see
the day it was completed.

PREFACE

From early childhood, when my father used to read *A Christmas Carol* aloud each year by the family fireside, I have been fascinated by Dickens as the greatest of all entertainers. My desire to account for this interest has evolved over many years into the present book, and the debts of gratitude which I have incurred along the way are many.

Dorothy Van Ghent's essay 'The Dickens world: a view from Todgers'' first taught me how Dickens could be both funny and profound. Philip Collins's books, articles and editions have shown me how deeply Dickens's concerns were rooted in their time, and Professor Collins's scholarship has provided a model worthy of emulation.

Long-suffering friends and colleagues have provided assistance of a more personal kind. For their encouragement, patience, faith and practical advice I am particularly grateful to Joe Ging, Elizabeth Grice, Liz Maclachlan, Robin MacLachlan, David Malcolm, Andrew Sanders, Michael Slater, George Speaight and Kathleen Tillotson.

My thanks also go to colleagues and students at the University of Aberdeen, especially to Robin Gilmour and Colin Milton, both of whom read early drafts of Chapters 4 and 5, and to Bob Lawson-Peebles, who read drafts of Chapters 1, 2, 3 and 6. Their constructive criticism has been challenging and helpful in more ways than I can say; the faults which remain are, of course, my own.

I am grateful to have had opportunities to test some of the ideas of the book in papers which I presented at the University of Kent, the University of Aberdeen, Wroxton College of Fairleigh Dickinson University, the University of Edinburgh, and the Aberdeen Literary Society.

For generous assistance with the research on which the book is based I wish to thank the librarians, archivists and staff of the following institutions: Aberdeen University Library, Aylesbury Central Library, Banbury Public Library, Birmingham Public Library, the Bodleian Library, the British Library, Buckingham

Public Library, the Dickens House Museum, the Guildhall Library, the Guildhall Record Office, Madame Tussaud's, Margate Central Library, the Mary Evans Picture Gallery, the Museum of London, Preston Central Library, Robert Gordon's Institute of Technology Library and School of Librarianship, Shrewsbury Public Library, the Society for Theatre Research, the Theatre Museum, the Tyne and Wear County Council Museums, the Victoria and Albert Museum, and Warwick Central Library.

Research was undertaken with financial assistance from the University of Aberdeen Fund for Travel Allowances annually between 1976 and 1984. Illustrations were gathered with the aid of a grant from the Carnegie Trust for the Universities of Scotland. I am pleased to acknowledge this generous support.

Illustrations are reproduced with permission from the Aberdeen University Library, the Bodleian Library, the Dickens House Museum, and the Guildhall Library. Details are given in the List of Illustrations. Quotations from the following volumes are made with permission of the Oxford University Press: *The Speeches of Charles Dickens* (1960) (ed.) K. J. Fielding; the Pilgrim edition of *The Letters of Charles Dickens*, Vols. 1 (1965) (eds.) M. House and G. Storey; Vol. 2 (1969) (eds.) M. House and G. Storey; Vol. 3 (1974) (eds.) M. House, G. Storey and K. Tillotson; Vol. 4 (1977) (ed.) K. Tillotson; Vol. 5 (1981) (eds.) G. Storey and K. J. Fielding; the Clarendon edition of *Oliver Twist* (1966) (ed.) K. Tillotson; the Clarendon edition of *The Mystery of Edwin Drood* (1972) (ed.) M. Cardwell; the Clarendon edition of *Dombey and Son* (1974) (ed.) A. Horsman; the Clarendon edition of *Little Dorrit* (1979) (ed.) H. P. Sucksmith; the Clarendon edition of *David Copperfield* (1981) (ed.) N. Burgis; the Clarendon edition of *Martin Chuzzlewit* (1982) (ed.) M. Cardwell; *Charles Dickens: The Public Readings* (1975) (ed.) P. Collins.

Finally, I am grateful to my research assistant, Debbie Esson, and to my typist, Barbara Rae, for help in the final stages of preparing the manuscript for the publisher.

University of Aberdeen
November 1984

LIST OF ILLUSTRATIONS

REFERENCES AND
ABBREVIATIONS

References to Dickens's novels are to the Clarendon Edition (Oxford, 1966–) for *Oliver Twist, Martin Chuzzlewit, Dombey and Son, David Copperfield, Little Dorrit* and *The Mystery of Edwin Drood,* and to the New Oxford Illustrated Dickens (London, 1947–58) for all other volumes. They are cited in the text by chapter number.

References to Dickens's periodicals are to the original bound editions. For attributions of articles in *Household Words* I have consulted Anne Lohrli, *'Household Words', a Weekly Journal 1850–59 Conducted by Charles Dickens: Table of Contents, List of Contributors and Their Contributions, Based on the 'Household Words' Office Book* (Toronto, 1973), and for articles in *All the Year Round* I have consulted Ella Ann Oppenlander, 'Dickens' *All the Year Round*: descriptive index and contributors list', PhD thesis, University of Texas at Austin, 1978.

AYR	*All the Year Round*
BH	*Bleak House*
BM	*Bentley's Miscellany*
BR	*Barnaby Rudge*
CB	*Christmas Books*, New Oxford Illustrated Dickens
CC	*A Christmas Carol*, in *CB*
DC	*David Copperfield*
Dolby	George Dolby, *Charles Dickens as I Knew Him* (London, 1885)
DS	*Dombey and Son*
Field	Kate Field, *Pen Photographs of Charles Dickens's Readings* (1868), rev. edn (London, 1871)
Forster	John Forster, *The Life of Charles Dickens* (1872–4), ed. J. W. T. Ley (London, 1928)

GE	*Great Expectations*
Grimaldi	*Memoirs of Joseph Grimaldi*, ed. 'Boz' (London, 1838)
HT	*Hard Times*
HW	*Household Words*
Kent	Charles Kent, *Charles Dickens as a Reader* (London, 1872)
LD	*Little Dorrit*
Mathews	Mrs [Anne] Mathews, *Memoirs of Charles Mathews, Comedian*, 4 vols (London, 1838–9)
MC	*Martin Chuzzlewit*
MED	*The Mystery of Edwin Drood*
MHC	*Master Humphrey's Clock*
MP	*Miscellaneous Papers*, ed. B. W. Matz, National Edition (London, 1908)
NN	*Nicholas Nickleby*
Nonesuch	*The Letters of Charles Dickens*, ed. Walter Dexter, Nonesuch Edition (London, 1938)
OCS	*The Old Curiosity Shop*
OMF	*Our Mutual Friend*
OT	*Oliver Twist*
PI	*Pictures from Italy*, New Oxford Illustrated Dickens
Pilgrim	*The Letters of Charles Dickens*, ed. Madeline House, Graham Storey *et al.*, Pilgrim Edition (Oxford, 1965–)
PP	*The Pickwick Papers*
Readings	*Charles Dickens: The Public Readings*, ed. Philip Collins (Oxford, 1975)
RP	*Reprinted Pieces*, New Oxford Illustrated Dickens
SB	*Sketches by Boz*, New Oxford Illustrated Dickens
Speeches	*The Speeches of Charles Dickens*, ed. Kenneth Fielding (Oxford, 1960)
TTC	*A Tale of Two Cities*
UT	*The Uncommercial Traveller*, New Oxford Illustrated Dickens
VCH	*The Victoria History of the Counties of England* (1900–)

CHAPTER 1

Introduction

Dickens and the Changing Patterns of Popular Entertainment

The fair in Hyde Park – which covered some fifty acres of ground – swarmed with an eager, busy crowd from morning until night. There were booths of all kinds and sizes, from Richardson's Theatre, which is always the largest, to the canvas residences of the giants, which are always the smallest; and exhibitions of all sorts, from tragedy to tumbling . . .

This part of the amusements of the people, on the occasion of the Coronation, is particularly worthy of notice, not only as being a very pleasant and agreeable scene, but as affording a strong and additional proof, if proof were necessary, that the many are at least as capable of decent enjoyment as the few. There were no thimble-rig men, who are plentiful at race-courses, as at Epsom, where only *gold* can be staked; no gambling tents, roulette tables, hazard booths, or dice shops. There was beer drinking, no doubt, such beer drinking as Hogarth has embodied in his happy, hearty picture, and there were faces as jovial as ever he could paint. These may be, and are, sore sights to the bleared eyes of bigotry and gloom, but to all right-thinking men who possess any sympathy with, or regard for, those whom fortune has placed beneath them, they will afford long and lasting ground of pleasurable recollection – first, that they should have occurred at all; and, secondly, that by their whole progress and result, at a time of general holiday and universal excitement, they should have yielded so unanswerable a refutation of the crude and narrow statements of those who, deducing their facts from the proceedings of the very worst members of society, let loose on the very worst opportunities, and under the most disadvantageous circumstances, would apply their inferences to the whole mass of the people.[1]

On 28 June 1838, England celebrated the coronation of its young

1

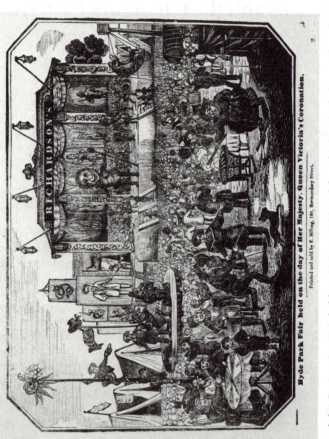

Hyde Park Fair held on the day of Her Majesty, Queen Victoria's Coronation.

Printed and sold by E. Billing, 195, Bermondsey Street.

Dickens visited the Coronation Fair held on 28 June 1838 and found it 'particularly worthy of notice' as proof that 'the many are at least as capable of decent enjoyment as the few'.

queen, but not all eyes were on the pomp of the official ceremonies. Her Majesty's most famous novelist, breaking off a characteristically energetic holiday in Twickenham and interrupting work on two novels in progress (he was writing both *Oliver Twist* and *Nicholas Nickleby* at the time, as well as editing *Bentley's Miscellany*), went instead to Hyde Park to witness the festivities of the common people. His brief account of the great fair, which lasted for nine days and 'attracted all the great exhibitions in the country with a whole army of minor showmen', appeared as the tailpiece to an article on the coronation in the *Examiner*.[2] Although what Dickens wrote consists of no more than a few lines of unsigned journalism, the lines which I have quoted above reveal plainly the fervour of his convictions about popular entertainment. His delight in the fair is abundantly clear, and he is stout in his support of the ordinary men and women who participate in the national occasion. He writes as a fascinated observer, with a ready eye for absurdity (the residences of the giants are 'the smallest') and an obvious familiarity with his subject (the residences of the giants are '*always* the smallest'). He recognizes the vulgarity of the scene but compares it favourably to more 'respectable' amusements and invokes the tradition of hearty English enjoyment, as recorded by Hogarth, as evidence of its time-honoured value. It is also apparent that he feels a distinct need to come to the defence of these popular celebrations. His attacks on the 'bleared eyes of bigotry and gloom' and his appeal to 'all right-thinking men' indicate the contentious nature of his subject and signal his readiness to enter the fray. In the early days of his career, at the very outset of the Victorian era, the amusements of the people were under attack from many directions, and Dickens, the great popular entertainer, was their champion.

His love of entertainment dated from childhood, and it was a lifelong commitment. From his schoolboy production of *The Miller and His Men* in a toy theatre, through the novels, amateur theatricals and public readings of his adulthood, Dickens devoted himself to providing entertainment for others. His friend and biographer John Forster noted a 'native capacity for humorous enjoyment' as one of his distinctive characteristics, and the eagerness with which he sought amusement is attested by the restless curiosity with which he wandered the streets of London, the avid frequency of his theatre-going, the urgent appeals to friends to join him in some new delight. His daughter Mamie wrote that, despite the delicacy and illness which afflicted Dickens as a youth, in his manhood sports were a 'passion' with him; he participated in bar-leaping, bowling and quoits, enjoyed cricket 'intensely' as a spectator, and organized field sports for local villagers in a meadow at the back of Gad's Hill Place.[3]

The forms of entertainment which he enjoyed most were essentially popular. He responded with unashamed pleasure to the circus and the pantomime, to sensational melodrama and the Punch and Judy show. Such entertainment, as distinct from élitist culture which demanded education, wealth and social position, was broad-based in its appeal, inexpensive and widely available.[4] As a journalist he watched it observantly; as a social reformer he applauded its benefits for the people; as a popular artist he shared its aims; and as a participant he wholeheartedly entered into the fun.

Entertainment was a subject Dickens wrote about often and, as we shall see in chapters which follow, it assumes central structural and thematic importance in three of his novels. More fundamentally, entertainment is linked inextricably with the nature of his art. His earliest fiction began in conscious imitation of popular literature of the day, and *Pickwick* became the publishing sensation of the nineteenth century. He was the most widely popular English writer since Shakespeare, and even as his artistry matured in depth and complexity he never abandoned the basic intention of providing his audience with amusement. His repeated advice to fellow-novelists was to take seriously the need to entertain readers; the avowed intention of his journalism was to transcend 'grim realities' by showing that 'in all familiar things . . . there is Romance enough, if we will find it out'. This declaration, like the command to his subeditor W. H. Wills – 'KEEP HOUSEHOLD WORDS IMAGINATIVE!' – stressed the appeal to man's innate sense of wonder and curiosity which it is the entertainer's purpose to arouse.[5] He made this appeal most directly when, in the final twelve years of his life, he turned largely away from fiction and journalism to appear in public as a reader of his work. Central to his role as an artist, integral with his social convictions, rooted in his deepest values, and a source of lifelong delight, popular entertainment reaches to the core of Dickens's life and work.

During the formative early years of his life, English popular entertainment was in a process of radical transformation. The old rural pastimes of the people, which had been benignly tolerated by the gentry as integral to a social stability based on traditional lifestyles, were increasingly eroded, and by the 1830s very little had emerged to take their place. The great urban fairs, having long since lost their commercial function, were susceptible to determined efforts to suppress them, and the greatest of them, Bartholomew Fair, was effectively put down by civic fiat in 1840. Rapid urbanization and population explosion eliminated open spaces which had formerly been used for leisure activities and gave the public house vital importance as a social centre. The rise of the factory system introduced a fundamental change in the conception of work, away from the variety of seasonal occupation to a regimented, mechanical system, even as the vast pool of cheap labour ensured that men, rather than machines, performed most of the tasks that were done. The hours and conditions of work were a source of seething discontent among the labouring poor, particularly in the industrial North, and legislative proposals for dealing with labour problems were put before Parliament year after year. There were a few gains: violent sports such as bull-baiting and cock-throwing had virtually disappeared by the 1820s, and the rise of railways in the 1830s made it increasingly possible for people to travel to permanent exhibitions and resort areas. Metropolitan exhibition-halls and minor theatres flourished, but not until after mid-century did music-halls, organized sports, public recreation facilities, Saturday half-holidays, and other possibilities for urban amusement arise. Most modern historians are convinced that the nadir of English popular culture was reached during the 1830s, the very time Dickens began writing about it.[6]

The decline of older forms of popular entertainment was only one aspect of the alteration of English society, which was entering a particularly dynamic phase in the 1830s. During these years England changed from a rural, agrarian-based economy to an urban, industrialized state, a shift most dramatically symbolized by the railway boom. Between the opening of the Liverpool and Manchester Railway in 1830 and the time Dickens was writing *The Old Curiosity Shop* in 1840, nearly 1,500 miles of track had been built in the United Kingdom and over 2,500 miles sanctioned, unavoidable evidence of the speed, power, size and disruption the new heavy industries were bringing.[7] Commerce and industry became heavily capitalized as never before; parliamentary life was altered by the Reform Act of 1832, and there was a host of new social legislation, most notably the Factory Act of 1833 and the New Poor Law of 1834. Ferment in religion (the Oxford Movement), in politics (Chartism), in economics (Mill's *Essays*, not published until 1844, were written around 1830), in social philosophy and history (Carlyle wrote *Sartor Resartus, The French Revolution* and *Chartism* in this decade) indicates only some of the pressures during this era. By the time Victoria came to the throne in 1837, a revaluation of manners, morals, thought and feeling was in full flood.

Popular amusements were inevitably caught up in the general movement of change. In the long term, there was a decisive shift away from gregarious, participatory activities towards large-scale spectator entertainments such as music-hall and professional sport. The most striking instance of this trend, which historians have referred to as the 'commercialisation of leisure', is the circus.[8] Philip Astley opened his circus at Westminster Bridge in 1769 with a modest show of horsemanship exercises, and during the nineteenth century his enterprise grew phenomenally in scope and grandeur, culminating late in the century under 'Lord' George Sanger's direction with extravaganzas such as *Gulliver's Travels*, which Sanger himself in all modesty described as

> . . . the biggest thing ever attempted by any theatrical or circus manager before or since. In the big scene there were on the stage at the time three hundred girls, two hundred men, two hundred children, thirteen elephants, nine camels, and fifty-two horses, in addition to ostriches, emus, pelicans, deer of all kinds, kangaroos, Indian buffaloes, Brahmin bulls, and, to crown the picture, two living lions led by the collar and chain into the centre of the group.[9]

Jerry's dogs in *The Old Curiosity Shop* pale rather, in comparison. Sanger himself provides the archetypal example of the commercialization of entertainment, graduating from a boy's exhibition of six white mice to his later orchestration of massive productions like the one described above. Inspired by Astley's, other circuses sprang up, consisting initially of little more than a few routines on horseback. The shows gradually became more elaborate and various, but wild beast acts were included only from the late 1830s and elaborate feats of daring after mid-century. A few modest circuses soldiered on until the end of the century, but the trend, in circus, in music-hall and in sport, was towards size and expense, culminating in the birth of the mass-entertainment industry in the early years of the twentieth century.

Transition, then, was the keynote during Dickens's lifetime. His writing registers the decline of old patterns and the difficulty of establishing new ones. He is concerned with the replacement of traditional kinds of leisure activities by new forms and, more centrally, with changing attitudes to entertainment. He is staunch in his resistance to pressures antagonistic to amusement, but he is also warmly supportive of forces for improvement. For example, he was an intimate adviser at the Theatre Royal, Covent Garden, during its management by his friend William Charles Macready, who endeavoured to improve the environment of the theatre by banishing prostitutes from it, and to raise the level of performance by insisting on proper rehearsals. Dickens's association with Macready's celebrated 1838 production of *King Lear* had direct consequences for his fiction.[10] He published articles in his journals circumstantially praising Madame Tussaud's waxwork museum for having become a 'national institution'; others noticing the worthy efforts of musical clubs to provide 'an emollient for brutal tastes', extolling the benefits of opening Kew Gardens and the British Museum to the public, comparing the licentiousness and riot of ancient May Days with the exhilarating May Day 1851, when British industry made possible a structure more wonderful than the palace Aladdin raised with his lamp, the Crystal Palace in Hyde Park.[11] Above all, his own career gives clear evidence of his positive response to trends of the day: he kept scrupulous watch on the financial value and audience appeal of his writings, and his decision to embark on the public readings which dominated his last years, under the management of a professional theatrical agency, represented a fulfilment of his earliest aspirations within the context of the emerging commercial circumstances.

But the fundamental point about Dickens's attitudes to popular entertainment, the fact which deeply colours his relationship to it, is that his attachment is rooted in the traditions of the past. There are two principal reasons why this is so. First, the values which he associates with entertainment have less to do with its increasing scale and commercialism than with the old communal patterns. For Dickens, entertainment was a locus for the spontaneity, selflessness and fellow-feeling which lay at the heart of his moral convictions. The human enjoyment by family and friends of shared amusements had meaning for him far above the aesthetic accomplishment of the professional entertainer impersonally exhibiting his skills before an anonymous audience. He was well aware of the vast difference in quality between entertainments, and both in his own work and in his response to that of others he strove determinedly for excellence. Nevertheless, it is abundantly clear from the evidence of his life and work that he found ample cause for delight in simple, lowly or even absurd entertainments; whether he laughed with or at the showmen, what mattered was that they provided amusement. In his writing he focused largely on the humble aspirations of individual showmen, earning their honest penny by bringing colour, novelty and amusement into people's lives; on the fraternal feelings of entertainment troupes, giving pleasure to themselves as they offered it to others; and especially on the needs of the solitary individual, struggling to alleviate the burdens of his or her life in imaginative release. Even when he deals with commercial entertainment, such as Crummles's strollers or Sleary's equestrians, Dickens concentrates less on the economic basis of their enterprises than on the feelings which motivate their work; he happily records the gusto and dedication with which they perform, he takes us offstage to glimpse the quality of their lives, and he singles out knots of spectators eager for gregarious pleasure. As a writer he cultivated a strong sense of personal relationship with his readers, and his public readings were motivated not only by the attraction of financial gain but also by the opportunity they provided for an even closer intimacy with his audience. His emphasis lay on participation, on carefree imprudence, on unaffected relaxation and release – age-old qualities of popular amusement, which were being substantially altered by the trend towards larger scale of organization, greater outlay in cost, and stricter attention to the clock.

The second and more compelling reason why Dickens favoured entertainments which reflected the older tradition was that his fascination was firmly established in his earliest childhood. His attachment to the first years of his life was the single greatest influence on his adult perspectives, and one quality of childhood which he particularly cherished was responsiveness to entertainment. That responsiveness was conditioned by innocence, awakened in wonder, and conducive to imagination. 'If we can only preserve ourselves from growing up, we shall never grow old,' he declared in *Household Words*, and his adult association of entertainment with childhood means that even when he contemplates the present or the future he is instinctively drawn to look back to childhood in order to explain and verify the authenticity of feelings aroused.[12] The temptation of such an outlook is to nostalgia, but at best the link with childhood gives his conception of popular entertainment a vital simplicity, as he affirms the importance of refusing to outgrow the purity of the child's spontaneous delight.

In his thinking about entertainment children are often included; childlike attitudes are encouraged, and the forms of entertainment which he personally finds most attractive are those which he encountered as a boy. The connection in his mind between entertainment and childhood led him to consider love of amusement to be a natural human inclination, which he believed, on the basis of close observation, most people would follow with good-humour and good will. His novels are full of characters who gaily seek pleasure at the first opportunity, and of others who depend on scraps of enjoyment to eke out otherwise bleak existence. Conversely, characters who oppose amusement are portrayed as misguided at best, villainous at worst, and they are invariably incomplete and frustrated in their own lives. The instinctive desire for amusement is the axiom with which the first issue of *Household Words* opened, when he announced, as an avowed purpose of the new periodical he was launching, that he 'would tenderly cherish that light of Fancy which is inherent in the human breast' and which 'can never be extinguished'.[13] It is also a central theme in *Hard Times*, where imaginative release into the realms of delight symbolized by the circus is seen as a human necessity, as basic as food and shelter. Denied healthy outlet for their sense of wonder, the children of Mr Gradgrind are blighted by his perverse philosophy. Dickens's point is emphatic, not merely that a better educational system would nurture happier children, but also that the attempt to root out every inclination which seeks to rise above Fact is to misunderstand human nature. Fancy is an inalienable attribute.

The stress on childhood and on the supreme value to be found in the life of the imagination is, as critics have often noted, Blakean, but it is also important to discriminate the strongly un-Blakean component of Dickens's conception of 'fancy'. Far from betokening a transcendence into some ideal state of contemplation, for Dickens fancy constituted the more mundane 'capacity of being easily pleased with what is meant to please us'.[14] This disposition includes a response to literary invention, of course – his love of the *Arabian Nights* and of *Robinson Crusoe* is a frequently sounded chord, and his own great accomplishment is literary – but it is also an eager curiosity for the sights to be found in everyday life, and an active willingness to enjoy recreations, shows, plays and other humble forms of truly popular entertainment. For Dickens the celebration of fancy is intimate with participation in the enjoyments of the common man.

The grounding of Dickens's attachment to popular entertainment in traditional patterns and in childhood has inevitable consequences. It gives a passionate intensity to his commitment to the values of entertainment and makes the depiction of amusements an important vehicle for conveying his social and moral concerns. On the other hand, it gives a distinctly dated quality to the entertainers in his fiction; even within the social context of nineteenth-century England, they seem vestiges of a previous era. The strolling actors in *Nicholas Nickleby* and the itinerant showfolk in *The Old Curiosity Shop* are struggling to survive in a culture indifferent to them at best; the circus performers in *Hard Times* exist more as idealized alternatives to pernicious attitudes than as actual representatives of the Victorian business of entertainment. Dickens has less to tell us about the directions entertainment was to take after he wrote than about reasons why it is an activity vital to the individual and to society; but, if his writing on the subject has limited usefulness as prophecy, it nevertheless provides us with some of the most exuberant prose that even he ever wrote, and it leads us into some of his essential preoccupations.

He held his convictions with tenacity and defended them with vigour because provision of entertainment for the people was highly controversial. Leisure had a diminishing place in the lives of a great many English men and women, and it had powerful enemies. The breakdown of small community relationships sharpened class differences and aroused the emerging middle classes to decry wholly lower-class amusements as vulgar licence. Increasingly earnest attitudes about the sanctity of work created suspicion of leisure of any sort, unnecessary to workers and costly to industrialists. Religion and recreation, so closely integrated throughout history, diverged sharply in the nineteenth century, competing for separate allegiance. Evangelical Christianity, dedicated single-mindedly to personal salvation, was a force inimical to worldly pleasures, and its spectacular rise in the late eighteenth and early nineteenth century made it the most formidable of antagonists to traditional community recreations.[15] The extreme wing of Evangelicalism was categorical in its denunciation of amusements, for no recreation could be innocent when idleness was seen as the occasion of evil. In the words of one prominent Sabbatarian leader:

> Nothing is to be done which is merely for amusement or for gain. To saunter in the public walks where the gay and worldly scene necessarily unfits the mind for devotion – to read the public journal, or other works which are not religious, to read and to write letters upon business, or any other common topics – to pay idle visits – to engage in frivolous conversation at home or elsewhere . . . must be contrary to the Christian's duty of the Lord's-day.[16]

Another went even further: 'Thousands have ascribed their religious declension, and subsequent ruin, to Sunday walks.'[17] These attitudes underpinned the Sabbatarian movement, an exceptionally well-organized pressure group, which sought moral reform through legislation. By means of widespread publicity, petition campaigns, and parliamentary bills, principal Sabbatarian organizations made themselves a force to be reckoned with, promoting restrictions on Sunday of drinking-hours, trade, travel, rights of assembly, postal delivery, band concerts in public parks, and all other activity which they deemed Godless. Separate but also powerful were the temperance movement, seeking variously to shorten drinking-hours, provide alternative attractions to drink, or prohibit its consumption altogether; and animal protection societies, dedicated to stamping out blood sports and other cruelty to animals. All of these groups were overtly hostile to traditional popular amusements and vocal in their attempts to suppress them. Although they were predominantly middle-class in membership, and although their activities were widely attacked for class bias (since the lower classes depended more upon public facilities and had less free time than their betters), all

'Animal Suffering' by Pierce Egan the Younger. The amusements of the people faced vigorous opposition, often more effective than that shown here.

received varying degrees of support from elements within the working class, who saw reform movements as potential means of improving their lot. The potency of these enemies of popular entertainment can hardly be overestimated. As one eminent social historian points out: 'Much larger social groups were more directly affected by restrictions on recreation and by limitations on drinking hours than by early nineteenth-century legislation on factory hours or poor relief.'[18]

Dickens responded to the pressures against leisure with stalwart defence and stinging satire. In addition to such well-known set pieces in his fiction as the description of the maddening boredom of an English Sunday (*LD*, I, 3) and the address to the Brick Lane Branch of the United Grand Junction Ebenezer Temperance Association by the canting drunkard Mr Stiggins (*PP*, 33), he used his journalism as a forum for the support of amusements for the people. From the early *Sunday under Three Heads*, which he wrote in the spring of 1836, just as *Pickwick* was under way, to the late 'Great Drunkery Discovery' which he assisted his son Charley to prepare for *All the Year Round* in 1869, less than a year before he died, he counterattacked against specific attempts to restrict the pleasures of the poor. His convictions about popular entertainment are a function of his social conscience.

Finally, Dickens's role as a popular entertainer contributes significantly to the development of his art. His career as a creative writer began with works in which he sought to tap familiar formulas of the day for providing amusement. In *Sketches by Boz* and in three of his first four novels, all written before the end of 1840, he sketched a number of scenes set in places of entertainment; he made a desire for amusement a primary motivation for several principal characters; and he included many entertainers, both amateur and professional, among his casts of characters. At the same time, his driving ambition and the critical success of his early work led him to conceive novels which would contain far more than ingredients for idle diversion. In the rapid maturing of his genius, he sought to combine seriousness of content and artistry of design, without foresaking the original aim of entertaining his readers. The direction which this progress took was away from entertainment as a major subject of his work to a thematic use of imagination – the 'fancy' which he saw as integral with a love of entertainment – as a key principle of his later fiction. With the notable exception of *Hard Times*, written in 1854, in his later career Dickens largely transferred his treatment of the amusements of the people from his novels to his periodicals, and his public readings became the principal outlet for his purpose to entertain.

The chapters which follow develop these approaches, moving between the social context and Dickens's art in an attempt to clarify the relationship between them. Chapter 2 focuses upon the importance of the child in Dickens's thinking about entertainment, and Chapters 3, 4 and 5 concentrate on the novels in which entertainers figure most prominently: *Nicholas Nickleby, The Old Curiosity Shop* and *Hard Times*. Chapter 6 deals with popular entertainment as it appears in Dickens's journalism, and Chapter 7 is concerned with the public readings. In his fiction, his journalism, his performances and his life, popular entertainment was of central importance. Recognition of that centrality is essential to an understanding of Dickens.

CHAPTER 2

Popular Entertainment and Childhood

The values which Dickens associated with popular entertainment – including spontaneity, freedom, fancy and release, as opposed to life-denying forces of hard-headedness and hard-heartedness – converged in the most important image in his art, that of the child. For Dickens, the child was being endowed with special capabilities of sensitivity, wonder and imagination, all of which found particularly congenial outlet in activities of play and amusement. Inheriting from Rousseau the conception of innocence as the natural state of childhood, Dickens was the first major novelist to place children at the centre of novels, and his achievement in doing so is one of his significant contributions to literature. In several works he focused his exploration of moral, social and psychological themes upon the image of the child, and in all of his fiction, as a number of critics have ably demonstrated, he makes a child's outlook integral to his artistic vision.[1] The eager curiosity and receptiveness to novelty and energy; the fascination with imitation and its problematic relation with reality; the sense of absurdity, in which delight and terror are never far apart – each of these vital components of his genius has its roots in his conception of childhood, and each finds particularly full expression in his concern with entertainment. For its intimate relationship with childhood alone, popular entertainment assumes central importance for an understanding of Dickens's art, and it can help us to discriminate certain attitudes which reveal more about life during his own childhood than about later developments in English society.

Dickens's lifelong predilection was for those forms of entertainment which he first experienced as a child, and his love of the circus, theatre and pantomime is consonant with his attachment to the values and experiences of childhood. Several of his best-known occasional pieces – 'Our School', 'Nurse's Stories', 'Birthday Celebrations', 'A Christmas Tree', 'Dullborough Town' – are autobiographical recollections of his happiest childhood days. In these essays he dwells with loving detail upon the simple festivities of a family

Christmas, the hopeful emotions of birthday parties, the excitement of bedtime stories. The fact that his childhood contained other, far less lighthearted events unquestionably made such moments all the more precious, and if memories of the tale of Captain Murderer and the dreadful mask at Christmas contain an edge of terror the softening distance of time transforms childish fear into delicious piquancy. Typical of the way in which Dickens integrates fear, sorrow or disaster into a complex evocation of childhood joys is his account of the white mice in 'Our School':

> The boys trained the mice, much better than the masters trained the boys. We recall one white mouse, who lived in the cover of a Latin dictionary, who ran up ladders, drew Roman chariots, shouldered muskets, turned wheels, and even made a very creditable appearance on the stage as the Dog of Montargis. He might have achieved greater things, but for having the misfortune to mistake his way in a triumphal procession to the Capitol, when he fell into a deep inkstand, and was dyed black and drowned.[2]

The entertainment comes to an end in death and blighted hopes, but the star performer is only a mouse after all, and the performance confined to a schoolroom. By adopting a tone which purports to take seriously the prospects and ultimate fate of the mouse, Dickens simultaneously authenticates the genuine fascination of the boys even as he gently mocks the intensity of their commitment to so trivial an activity. The circumstantial precision of the description indicates the hold the episode retains on Dickens's memory, even as an adult, and the aside about schoolmasters lightly extends the application of the vignette beyond mere amusement.

Convinced equally of children's inherent disposition to enjoy, and of the beneficent effects of entertainment upon them, Dickens was eager to preserve childhood pleasures, both in the memory of his own past and in his concern for present and future children. He was indignant at the thought of anyone tampering, as George Cruikshank did in his 'Frauds on the Fairies', with the direct appeal of children's entertainment, and the core of his indictment of parental disciplinarians such as Murdstone, Gradgrind and Mrs Joe was that they left no room for a child's natural graces to flourish. Opportunity for play was essential for every child: 'Play they must and play they will, somewhere or other, under whatsoever circumstances of difficulty' (*Speeches*, p. 272). One thinks, in this context, of the young Dickens, wandering back to his lodgings from the blacking warehouse and being 'seduced more than once' into a

CHRISTOPHER'S FIRST APPEARANCE IN PUBLIC.

'Christopher's First Appearance in Public' by John Leech. The values which Dickens associated with popular entertainment converged on the most important image in his art, that of the child.

16

show-van on a street-corner where, in company 'with a very motley assemblage', he saw 'the Fat Pig, the Wild Indian, and the Little Lady': his use of the definite article in itemizing these wonders registers the particular impression they made upon his youthful fancy.[3] Young David Copperfield, in similar circumstances, spends his moments of idleness away from Murdstone and Grinby's wandering across London Bridge to look over the balustrades at the sun shining on the water, or sitting down upon a bench by the river to watch coal-heavers dancing in an open space before a little public house (*DC*, 11). Such snatches of entertainment, Dickens makes clear, provide sustaining nourishment for the lonely, neglected child.

And because he perceived childhood as a state peculiarly responsive to the appeals of entertainment, he was eager to retain such attitudes in adulthood. His 1853 essay 'Where We Stopped Growing' is an explicit declaration of gratitude that he has not outgrown many of the pleasures he enjoyed as a child, but can still participate in them as an adult. This sentiment is echoed in his last complete novel, *Our Mutual Friend*, when Rumpty Wilfer, led out of his office and taken on a day's outing to Greenwich, allows his hair to be tousled like a little boy's and spends the afternoon building castles in air with 'the lovely woman'; he is so moved by the day's events that 'there was water in the foolish little fellow's eyes, but she kissed them dry' (*OMF*, I, 8). Particularly in his writings about Christmas, Dickens encouraged the sentiment that 'it is good to be children sometimes, and never better than at Christmas, when its mighty Founder was a child himself' (*CC*, stave 3). This is the lesson which Scrooge must learn from the three spirits, and one which Bob Cratchit acts upon the moment he leaves the counting-house, when he 'went down a slide on Cornhill, twenty times, in honour of its being Christmas Eve, and then ran home to Camden Town, as hard as he could pelt, to play at blindman's buff' (*CC*, stave 1). So, too, Mr Pickwick, sliding on the ice with his friends at Dingley Dell, keeps alive the Christmas spirit and remains eternally young at heart, even after he has been exposed to the shadows of the Fleet.

Dickens's advocacy of adult retention of the child's outlook is, of course, far from unequivocal; perhaps of all his 'holy innocents' only Mr Pickwick is accorded unqualified admiration by his creator, and the feckless Harold Skimpole stands as warning of the unprincipled selfishness to which childishness in adults is liable. Childlike indulgence is more often celebrated in Dickens's writing as holiday release, valuable precisely because it is a brief exception to the work, pain and responsibility of everyday existence. As we shall see, he defended leisure on Sunday because it gave respite from the toil of every other day of the week, and he championed Christmas as 'the only time . . . in the long calendar of the year, when men and women seem by one consent to open their shut up hearts freely' (*CC*, stave 1). Economic necessity and limited opportunities for entertainment and recreation meant that adults were less likely to be childlike than children were to become prematurely adult, and his fiction contains many poignant examples of children for whom life provides no amusement at all. His concern that adults cherish the joys of childhood was, in part, a plea that children should be enabled to do so.

As a consequence of his belief in the special attributes of the child, Dickens emphasizes the separation of its world from that of adults. This distance is signalled again and again in the novels: by the isolation of Oliver, David and Pip at crucial stages of their early lives; by the uncomprehending attitudes of Mr Dombey and Mr Gradgrind towards their children; by the secret retreat of Jenny Wren and Lizzie Hexam, far away from the dust-heaps and the river. His first-person narrators look back upon their younger days with keen awareness of how far they have travelled: David remarks of his boyhood reading that 'it is curious to me how I could ever have consoled myself under my small troubles (which were great troubles to me), by impersonating my favourite characters' (*DC*, 4), and Pip thinks of the helpless folly with which he set out to 'do all the shining deeds of the young Knight of romance, and marry the Princess' (*GE*, 29). Reflecting on his own childhood as well, for all the intimacy of his recollections, Dickens was under no illusion that they were other than recollections. Some scenes had disappeared completely, like Our School, swallowed up by the railway: 'Locomotives now run smoothly over its ashes.' Others took on new meanings, or lost their old power, as he matured; but all were sealed in the irrevocable past, where they were fixed and static, incapable of change save through the distortions of memory. Thus, Nurse's stories remain 'unchanged' with the passage of time; the image of his youngest Christmas experiences stands 'ever unalterable'.[4]

The sense of distance has important consequences not only for his depictions of childhood, but also for his outlook on entertainment. The perceived gap between the child's instinctive delight and the more consciously reconstructed sense of enjoyment of adults locates a principal impetus for his convictions about entertainment in the past, and makes this concern essentially backward-looking. He is urgent for better leisure opportunities in the present, but the source of his fervour and the forms which he is predisposed to favour come overwhelmingly from his childhood. Dickens, as is well known, was no naïve admirer of the past, but his feelings about his own past were notable more for tenacity than for flexibility. This makes him basically conservative about entertainment: his concern is less for innovations which may be possible in the altered circumstances of the future than for the traditions which were being eroded. Those traditions, having been first encountered in irretrievable childhood, take on for him the permanence of completed experience, to be treasured through memory in unchanging images. The contrast between past joys, sanctified by the associations of his earliest affections, and a less wonderful present, in which adult cares contaminate the purity of the child's response, adds an element of regret which flavours much of his writing about entertainment, and the idealization of childhood innocence inevitably creates a preference for simplicity and directness. In short, the conjunction of childhood and entertainment in Dickens's mind renders his writing liable not merely to deep conviction but also to nostalgia.

This is precisely the charge which Dickens's detractors over the years have levelled against him, and one which even some of his most thoughtful admirers have found in need of apology; that he was insufficiently engaged with the real culture and adult concerns of his time; that he substituted feeling for thought; and that his solution to the world's ills was a menu of Christmas pudding every day, in a Never-Never-Land populated – in Aldous Huxley's phrase – with 'gruesome old Peter Pans'.[5] Dickens's contemporary George Henry Lewes found little in the novels 'for the reader of cultivated taste', only 'overflowing fun' which required thoughtful men to respond 'like children at a play', and this conception of Dickens as no more than a 'great entertainer' (as F. R. Leavis called him, before being converted to the ranks of the faithful) has remained for over a century the popular image of the Inimitable.[6] Dickens's entertainment, in this view of the matter, is unsuitable for adult attention, and Edmund Wilson's classic defence of Dickens merely sidesteps the objection by locating his achievement elsewhere. A whole generation of critics following Wilson has explored the dark insights of the unhappy artist divided against himself; but, as Denis Donoghue astutely observed in the centenary year of Dickens's death, to praise Dickens by setting aside the comedy and the entertainment is to 'take Dickens not as we find him but as we improve him'.[7] While it is no doubt true that some of Dickens's journal writings about convivial amusements, particularly in the later Christmas stories, lack the artistic excellence of the great novels, it is also true that some of his most characteristic attitudes are found here; and, as it is the purpose of the present study to demonstrate, these attitudes are intimate with his stature. It seems to me possible to admire Dickens's positive achievements, his conscious artistry and his articulate convictions as well as his obsessions with the morbid and the irrational. To understand this writer who emerged out of the popular culture of the early nineteenth century it is essential to face squarely the entertainment in and of his work.

One of the most revealing writings in which Dickens looks directly at the amusements of his childhood is the 1860 sketch entitled 'Dullborough Town'. This essay was conceived as part of the series of personal reflections which he first published in *All the Year Round* and later collected in *The Uncommercial Traveller*, and it is among the best of several pieces in the series which draw upon his boyhood memories.[8] Written in the full maturity of his prose style, on subjects of lifelong interest, and infused with an intimate personal tone, *The Uncommercial Traveller* achieves the highest standards of Dickens's journalism, and it had crucial importance in the gestation of the supreme achievement of his genius, *Great Expectations*, for it was while he was working on papers for *The Uncommercial Traveller* that he hit upon a notion which, he announced excitedly to Forster, 'so opens out before me that I can see the whole of a serial revolving on it, in a most singular and comic manner'. This, Forster reports, was 'the germ of Pip and Magwitch'.[9] Certainly the mood and manner of the opening pages of that novel have the strongest affinities with *The Uncommercial Traveller*, and 'Dullborough Town' in particular, reminiscing from an adult's perspective with humour and pathos upon boyhood scenes in and around a country town, prefigures the posture of Pip's narrative.

The setting of 'Dullborough Town' is of the sort to which Dickens instinctively returns when thinking of boyhood. Like their creator, Oliver, Nicholas, David and Pip all grow up in small rural towns before making their way to London. Nicholas's birthplace, Dawlish, is located in Devonshire, and David's Blunderstone is in Suffolk, but Dickens thinks of them generically; as he says in *The Uncommercial Traveller*, 'Most of us come from Dullborough who come from a country town'. For five years of his boyhood Dickens himself lived near Rochester, and this town appears in his fiction sometimes under its own name and at other times under such aliases as Great Winglebury and Mudfog. The name Dullborough may have been suggested to him by its variant, 'Dulminster', which was portrayed in a sketch in *Household Words* in 1856 – although it is always possible, given Dickens's editorial methods, that this name, too, was his own invention. 'Early Days in Dulminster', written by a contributor unknown today save by his name, Browne, is, like 'Dullborough Town', cast as the reminiscence of an adult returning to the scenes of his childhood. Both articles set the remembered past around 1820, and their gaze includes subjects common to both –

bygone coaching days, the state of the theatre, a child's awareness of politics. But Browne's essay is less coherent and vivid that Dickens's own, and lacks altogether the firm narrative control – of a child's view mediated by adult perception – which distinguishes 'Dullborough Town'.

Through its setting, 'Dullborough Town' registers attitudes found as early in Dickens's work as the scenes of 'Our Parish' in *Sketches by Boz*, and as late as the streets of Cloisterham in *The Mystery of Edwin Drood*. But it also reflects the particular circumstances of Dickens's life in the months prior to its composition. In the aftermath of the breakdown of his marriage, Dickens plunged into a searching reassessment of his values and loyalties. He severed friendships, embarked upon the first of his public-reading tours, wound up *Household Words* and started a new periodical, *All the Year Round*, to take its place. He wrote a novel, *A Tale of Two Cities*, which questions the use of living, in a combination of self-disgust and self-pity. He soon moved permanently out of London and settled in rural Kent. By the spring of 1860, when he came to write 'Dullborough Town', in other words, a number of factors were converging which inclined him to look more favourably than ever on the amusements of his childhood: a dissatisfaction with his present life and a physical return to the place he had lived as a boy; a rejection of the metropolis, where he had spent most of his life from the age of 10, in favour of rural surroundings; and, with the purchase of Gad's Hill Place, a reaffirmation of his earliest imaginings. It was a house which he had first seen as a 'very queer small boy' living in Chatham, across the Medway from Rochester, and he had been told by his father that, if he worked hard, one day he might live there.[10] With its associations of Falstaff and of his own youthful dreams, the place was the most vivid of reminders of the conjunction of past and present in his own life.

'Dullborough Town' is presented as the description of a grown man's first return to 'the scene among which my earliest days were passed'. In real life, of course, Dickens had visited Rochester many times after his childhood, but the fiction heightens the contrast between old and new impressions, and gives immediacy to the reawakening of youthful associations. The distance in time, between his last experience of the town and his present visit, is stressed from the outset by the juxtaposition of the stagecoach by which he left Dullborough and the railway train by which he returns. When he left, it was 'in the days when there were no railroads in the land', and he travelled in solitary self-importance; on return, his portmanteau stamped and himself ticketed, he is 'cavalierly shunted' back to the town. This opening sets the mood for the dominant emphasis in the

21

sketch, on the discovery of change. He arrives full of 'tender remembrance' of the scenes of his youth, but soon finds that little remains as he knew it. The old playing-field is gone, swallowed up by the railway station; the coaching office, along with several houses on each side of it, has been knocked down to make way for a monstrous establishment for great rattling wagons; the theatre, largely converted to wine- and beer-vaults, is advertised To Let, 'and hopelessly so, for its old purposes'. There is a new Mechanics' Institute, but it is far from inspiring romantic associations: 'approached by an infirm step-ladder . . . it led a modest and retired existence up a stable-yard'. The one sight which he finds unaltered, the figure of the greengrocer, 'with his hands in his pockets and leaning his shoulder against the doorpost, as my childish eyes had seen him many a time', is indifferent to the visitor's reappearance, and it is not until the end of the day, in a chance encounter with an old schoolfellow, that he finds anything in Dullborough which has changed for the better.

Otherwise, the town has deteriorated sadly. He is appalled by the desecration of loveliness caused by the coming of the railway.

> The two beautiful hawthorn-trees, the hedge, the turf, and all those buttercups and daisies, had given place to the stoniest of jolting roads: while, beyond the Station, an ugly dark monster of a tunnel kept its jaws open, as if it had swallowed them and were ravenous for more destruction.   (*UT*, pp. 116–17)

The image is a child's fantasy of a mythical beast terrorizing the sacred homeland, but it expresses the actuality perceived by the adult, of a countryside made ugly in the pursuit of progress. Similarly, his recollection of the romantically named coach in which he rode, Timpson's Blue-Eyed Maid, contrasts starkly with 'No. 97', the severely utilitarian designation of the locomotive engine which brought him home; and the removal of the beautiful oval transparency in the coaching-office window by the proprietor of the wagon firm, Pickford, affects him as both a personal affront and a violation of principle: 'I felt that he had done me an injury, not to say an act of boyslaughter, in running over my childhood in this rough manner . . . Moreover, I felt that Pickford had no right to come rushing into Dullborough and deprive the town of a public picture.' The outrage is hyperbolically expressed, to show that the emotions originate with the child, but the adult's disappointment is genuine enough. Surveying with a 'heavy heart' the violated playground, the shut-up theatre and the dreary Mechanics' Institute, Dickens meditates upon the lost happiness of his childhood, and proceeds to generalize about entertainment. Inevitably from the perspective thus

CRICKET.

The youthful Yeomanry are in the field,—
Their tents are pitched, and every heart beats high
To join the friendly strife ;—their stoutest forts
Are slender wickets ;—all their entrenchments,
A popping and a bowling-crease ; their weapons,
Bats ;—their ammunition, a brace of balls,
In leathern and tight-fitting jerkins clad.

Dickens lamented the loss to 'progress' of open fields suitable for innocent recreation, and late in his life he sponsored field sports in the meadow behind Gad's Hill Place.

established, a sense of sadness and of loss colours his reflections.

In dispiriting contrast to the present, what he remembers most specifically about his childhood are the variety and abundance of opportunity to find entertainment, and the intensity with which he responded to it all. Buildings and vehicles and people and events all fed his youthful imagination; play with schoolmates turned into romantic adventure; a game of cricket promised the glories of battlefield (although in the event polite decorum prevailed); the theatre enacted struggles of life and death within touching distance of his seat in the stage-box; books offered glamorous roles for boys and girls to imitate. But now, in place of the wonder, colour and excitement, which he found everywhere as a child, the prosaic reigns. Part of the problem, he is quick to realize, involves his own perception: the town seems 'shrunken' from its former grandeur; the Corn Exchange, which he once envisaged as 'the model on which the Genie of the Lamp built the palace for Aladdin', appears now 'a mean little brick heap'; the Indian sword-swallower, who thrilled him as a boy, from his present perspective seems unlikely to have been an Indian and unlikely to have swallowed the sword. This change in himself, is indeed, the concluding thought of the essay.

> All my early readings and early imaginations dated from this place, and I took them away so full of innocent construction and guileless belief, and I brought them back so worn and torn, so much the wiser and so much the worse! (*UT*, p. 126)

But the problem is not simply his own faulty memory and diminished capacity for enjoyment. More important is the town's 'dull and abortive' attitude to entertainment. In the theatre, the only attraction for a long time has been a panorama, billed, with 'leaden import', as 'pleasingly instructive'; in the Mechanics' Institute, lectures are acts of aggression, in which the audiences are 'knocked on the head' and 'stunned' with information. There, even the most innocent diversions are 'masked' as educational, as when the song 'Coming through the Rye' is introduced 'with some general remarks on wheat and clover'. The refusal to admit that leisure should include relief and diversion has inevitable consequences: no mechanics belong to the Mechanics' Institute, and it is 'steeped in debt to the chimney-pots'. Throughout Dullborough, Dickens objects,

> I still noticed everywhere the prevalence, to an extraordinary degree, of this custom of putting the natural demand for amusement out of sight, as some untidy housekeepers put dust, and pretending that it was swept away. (*UT*, p. 123)

Recreation has been pushed aside by progress, and the picturesque replaced by the functional. And yet, because amusement is sought where it is to be found, the desire for entertainment continues to be catered to, albeit surreptitiously. As evidence, Dickens observes a tract in the Evangelical bookshop, in which the very denunciation of entertainment has the appeal of a stage performance.

> Looking in at what is called in Dullborough 'the serious bookseller's', where, in my childhood, I had studied the faces of numbers of gentlemen depicted in rostrums with a gaslight on each side of them, and casting my eyes over the open pages of certain printed discourses there, I found a vast deal of aiming at jocosity and dramatic effect, even in them – yes, verily, even on the part of one very wrathful expounder who bitterly anathematised a poor little Circus. (*UT*, p. 123)

Here, in the 'rostrums with a gaslight', Dickens detects an overtly theatrical setting for a stirring harangue which, in its 'wrathful' tones of anathema, has the polarized morality of melodrama. Just as his imagination turns mundane railways and wagons into exciting monsters, so, too, he ekes entertainment out of its denial.

This still vital capacity to search out amusement even in inauspicious circumstances prevents 'Dullborough Town' from ever becoming dull or gloomy in its writing, even as Dickens laments the loss of childhood joy, and ensures that the contrast between past and present never degenerates into simple dichotomy. As he looks around Dullborough he recognizes that not everything has changed for the worse: despite the predilections of the Mechanics' Institute, a healthy interest in travel, biography and fiction is recorded in its library returns; his former companions Joe Specks and Lucy Green, though older, are prosperous and contented, and *their* children remind the visitor so much of the days gone by that 'it quite touched my foolish heart'. Moreover, as the phlegmatic greengrocer reminds him, the town has an independent life of its own, and does not exist exclusively in a sealed chamber of an absent son's memory. Other of Dickens's writings which contrast past and present confirm such complexity of response: in *Dombey and Son* Stagg's Gardens is destroyed by the railway, but a new, more prosperous community emerges; in *Great Expectations* Pip has a strong inclination to return at last to the forge, but his growth to true maturity cuts off that step as regressive; and in the 1851 sketch 'Our Watering Place' the mere survival of pleasures from the past, with no new sources of vitality, leaves the town in a semi-moribund condition.

At the same time, the detailed evocation of the past in 'Dullborough Town', as in all of Dickens's best writing on childhood, makes it clear that even in remembrance the happiness was not unalloyed. As he says of his ride in Timpson's Blue-Eyed Maid, 'life [was] sloppier than I expected to find it'. The excitement of waiting on the lady who gave birth to four, or perhaps five, babies does not disguise the fact that all of them died, or that he 'disgusted' everyone present by refusing to contribute to a subscription on her behalf. At the cricket match, the excessive politeness of the competitors smacks of such adult hypocrisy that he dismisses them as 'sneaks'. In the theatre, there is an edge of delicious terror to the excitement, but also gross misapprehension, as in his childish discovery 'that the witches in Macbeth bore an awful resemblance to the Thanes and other proper inhabitants of Scotland; and that the good King Duncan couldn't rest in his grave, but was constantly coming out of it and calling himself somebody else'. Such ignorance is also evident in his conception of 'the Radicals' and in his credulity over the Indian sword-swallower. It is clear, then, that the past was no more perfect than the present is wholly deplorable.

Finally, the relation between childhood and age is harmonized, as it is in *A Christmas Carol, David Copperfield* and *Great Expectations*, by the mediating power of memory. As remembered scenes change shape before his eyes, the spectator realizes that distance has led to idealization: places and events were glamorous not because of intrinsic attractiveness, but because he made them so. With the loss of his own innocence some of the magic has gone, but his apprehension of the town has moved closer to reality. Far more important, his readjusted vision of the past makes him content with the present, putting him in a more charitable mood with the town, its inhabitants and himself. This is particularly true in the reunion with Joe Specks: the mutual recollection of shared memories not only revivifies the past, but also gives it meaningful relation with the present; it reconciles them to what is lost for ever, and disposes both of them to renewed affection for one another. They are able to speak openly 'of our old selves as though our old selves were dead and gone, and indeed indeed they were'; at the same time Specks 'illuminated Dullborough with rays of interest that I wanted and should otherwise have missed in it, and linked its present with the past, in a highly agreeable chain'. The repetition ('indeed indeed') underlines the fervour of his newfound contentment, and the imagery of light suggests that a properly adjusted attitude to the past both brightens and clarifies his living experience of the entire span of his life. Like *The Haunted Man*, 'Dullborough Town' shows why Dickens believes it so important to 'keep my memory green'.

Consideration of these matters has taken us beyond strict concern for popular entertainment, but their prominence in this sketch is indicative of how integrally entertainment is tied to other subjects of major importance in Dickens's writing. The link between entertainment and childhood helps to locate a matrix of values basic to his vision, and the perceived distance between the child's experience and that of the adult provides one measure for his perception of the limitations of prevalent attitudes towards amusement. The presence of entertainment within the scope of memory is an indication of the intensity of its hold upon Dickens, and his conception of the sustaining power of the innocent enjoyments of childhood for the grown man is, like Wordsworth's overflow of powerful emotion recollected in tranquillity, a pillar of his thought. Dickens's imaginative return to the entertainment of his childhood is, in short, conducive to a great deal more than nostalgia.

Nevertheless, for all the beneficent influence of the past upon the present, and the potential influence for present children in their future, the conjunction of childhood and entertainment in Dickens's mind did encourage a disposition to look to the past for images of entertainment. 'Dullborough Town' is symptomatic of the tendency, which occurs everywhere in his work. In his journals, he chronicles origins and developments of particular forms of popular entertainment; he records with pleasure the survival of old amusements, and examines the evolution of entertainment for improvements as well as losses. Emphatically, he is aware of the contemporary state of entertainment: week by week, as we shall see below, his journals offer detailed accounts of theatres, parks, exhibitions, circuses, waxworks, street minstrels, and so on; many of the articles are prompted by current events affecting the provision of entertainment both in London and in the country at large. But the values which he associates with even the most innovative developments invariably are drawn from those which we have seen in 'Dullborough Town': release for imagination, escape from dull routine, encouragement to fellow-feeling, remembrance of past pleasures – in short, the traditional, communal, gregarious values which predate the entertainment of the Industrial Revolution, and which stand often in sharp conflict with the assumptions underlying the emergent commercial, disciplined, large-scale forms. Nowhere is this association with the past more apparent than in his major fictional renderings of popular entertainment. In *Nicholas Nickleby* the strolling actors form an extended family; faced with the widespread decline of the provincial theatre, they emigrate to America. In *The Old Curiosity Shop* the itinerant showmen are seen as colourful relics from the past, and their willingness to violate bonds of friendship for financial gain is seen as a betrayal of the very basis of their vocation. In *Hard Times* Sleary's circus is the repository of human fellowship, emotional security and imaginative vitality; the commercial underpinnings of its existence are nowhere in evidence. In each case, as we shall see in the chapters that follow, the image of entertainment as a form of human value is a source of artistic achievement within the novel, but the reliance upon past models inevitably places a definite limitation on that achievement.

In centring his valuation of popular entertainment in the past, Dickens shares a tendency with other major Victorian novelists. George Eliot, whose knowledge of the popular customs and folk-lore of her native Warwickshire was so extensive that she is routinely cited by local historians as an authority on the subject, devotes a large portion of her 1859 novel *Adam Bede* to the festivities surrounding Arthur Donnithorne's birthday celebration.[11] The action is placed in 1799; the setting is a small rural community called Hayslope, and in the time of leisure between the hay and corn harvests people of all ranks gather for amusements which include races, challenges, speeches, prizes, food, drink and dancing, all in honour of the heir to the estate. The entertainment is conducted at the expense and under the patronage of the local gentry; the inter-mingling of ranks is delicately orchestrated; and the speeches by Mr Poyser and by Arthur vigorously defend the event as an emblem of the stable, hierarchical, rural community in which they live and work. In the course of the novel Arthur's seduction of Hetty radi-cally undermines the relations between classes, and as a result the entertainment comes to be seen as a colourful vestige of an out-moded social structure. Here George Eliot uses an image of old forms of entertainment in order to portray the collapse of the social system on which it depended.

Hardy, likewise, in *The Mayor of Casterbridge* (1886), draws upon traditional modes of entertainment as part of his evidence for the tragic failure of his protagonist, Michael Henchard, to survive in a changing society. In the opening scene of the book Henchard arrives at a rural fair, which, with its 'peep-shows, toy-stands, waxworks, inspired monsters, disinterested medical men who travelled for the public good, thimble-riggers, nick-nack vendors, and readers of fate' (ch. 1), is a scene rife with superstition and deceit; and when, in a fit of drunken discontent, he sells his wife, the setting contributes to our sense of his act as a barbaric practice alien to modern civili-zation. Hardy sees old-fashioned entertainments as repositories of vitality as well as of vice, however, and it is a poignant moment when, late in the book, Henchard's public fête is ruined by the elements. Situated in an open spot within ancient earthworks, offering age-old country sports such as greased poles, a greased pig and sack races, free of charge to all who care to come, Henchard's affair is unable to compete in the bad weather with Farfrae's more practical covered dancing pavilion, and the difference between their respective entertainments is a measure of the distance between the failed old man of giant passions and his successful but more limited modern antagonist.

In these novels George Eliot and Hardy, like Dickens, view the passing of traditional forms of entertainment with a complex vision, in which the sense of loss predominates. The birthday festivities in *Adam Bede* buttress the quasi-feudal authority of Arthur's irascible grandfather, but the spirited participation by the entire countryside provides a greater sense of human fellowship than is likely in the ominously named alternative from which Dinah comes, the industrial town Stoniton. The strong liquor and sharp dealing at Weydon-Priors incite Henchard to an unpardonable act, but the fair itself is the afternoon's holiday following an assembly in the morning for the sale of horses and sheep; as in *Far from the Madding Crowd* (1874), in which Oak seeks employment at a 'mop', or hiring fair, and Troy rides in the circus at a sheep fair, the occasion is an integral part of the rhythms of work and play within the seasonal activities of a rural area. The entertainment in these novels, that is to say, is deployed to symbolize an older social fabric, which is giving way to new conditions less congenial to the vital communal spirit and depth of feeling found in the central characters.

What these novelists do not give us, as Dickens does not, is an equally full depiction of the new types of entertainment which were emerging to cater to the changed conditions of modern, urban, industrial society. Even when Victorian authors portray a large, anonymous, commercially based entertainment such as the circus, the qualities which they choose to single out in it are its old-fashioned romance (as in the dashing Sergeant Troy's enactment of 'Turpin's Ride to York and the Death of Black Bess') or its humane idealism (Sleary's pronouncement that 'People mutht be amuthed'). That the developing alternative tradition of entertainment could lend itself to being seen as a microcosm of modern life is clear enough from twentieth-century examples. In the Scottish poet John Davidson's poem 'The Crystal Palace' (1908), for example, we find the following:

> Contraption, – that's the bizarre, proper slang,
> Eclectic word, for this portentous toy,
> The flying machine, that gyrates stiffly, arms
> A-kimbo, so to say, and baskets slung
> From every elbow, skating in the air.

Irreverent, we; but Tartars from Tibet
May deem Sir Hiram the Grandest Lama, deem
His volatile machinery best, and most
Magnific, rotary engine, meant
For penitence and prayer combined, whereby
Petitioner as well as orison
Are spun about in space: a solemn rite
Before the portal of that fane unique,
Victorian temple of commercialism,
Our very own eighth wonder of the world,
The Crystal Palace . . .
Colossal ugliness . . .
Tis nature's outcast . . .
They all pursue their purpose business-like . . .
Resigned habitués on every hand . . .
Like savages bewitched . . .
Victims, and not companions, of delight.[12]

Or in D. H. Lawrence's *Women in Love* (1921) there is the architect Loerke, who is making 'a great frieze for a factory in Cologne':

> It was a representation of a fair, with peasants and artizans in an orgy of enjoyment, drunk and absurd in their modern dress, whirling ridiculously in roundabouts, gaping at shows, kissing and staggering and rolling in knots, swinging in swing-boats, and firing down shooting galleries, a frenzy of chaotic motion.

Loerke explains his conception of the frieze to Gudrun:

> 'Art should *interpret* industry, as art once interpreted religion,' he said.
> 'But does your fair interpret industry?' she asked him.
> 'Certainly. What is man doing, when he is at a fair like this? He is fulfilling the counterpart of labour – the machine works him, instead of he the machine. He enjoys the mechanical motion, in his own body.'
> 'But is there nothing but work – mechanical work?' said Gudrun.
> 'Nothing but work!' he repeated, leaning forward, his eyes two darknesses, the needle-points of light. 'No, it is nothing but this, serving a machine, or enjoying the motion of a machine – motion, that is all. You have never worked for hunger, or you would know what god governs us.' (ch. 29)

In these examples modern forms of entertainment are used as hateful images of what their authors saw as wrong in contemporary life; the anonymous, mechanical motion in both cases mirroring the essential quality of life in modern industrial society. More recently, Samuel Beckett in *Waiting for Godot* (1952), John Osborne in *The Entertainer* (1957) and Trevor Griffiths in *Comedians* (1975) have each looked to the now declining traditions of the music-hall – of all Victorian forms of popular entertainment, the one which led most directly into the mass-entertainment industry – for images with which to assess their conviction of the failure of modern civilization. But for me the most complex and haunting image of popular entertainment seen as a microcosm of modern society is to be found in Carol Reed's film of the Graham Greene story, *The Third Man* (1949), in which the great wheel at the funfair in Vienna is used as the climactic meeting-place for Holley Martins and Harry Lime. The image of the wheel superbly conveys the anonymous, uncontrollable quality of life as envisaged in the film – the characters are mere cogs in a gigantic machine, impersonally whirled about, with no effective volition of their own, and looking down far beneath them they can feel no sympathy for the people who appear as no more than tiny dots – black flies – on the pavement below (Harry is involved in an adulterated penicillin racket). At the same time – and herein lies the superiority of the image to those cited above – the wheel is also a perfect image of the release, the excitement and the fun of entertainment at its best: Holley, with his boy's crush on Harry, joins him briefly once again in an exhilarating adventure, high above the earth, and yet safe in the knowledge that it is, after all, only a ride in an amusement park – much as Harry conceives his own money-making schemes. Third, the wheel, appearing in the narrative just at the moment before Harry, at the height of his success, is gunned down in a sewer, can hardly avoid carrying implications of the medieval trope of the Wheel of Fortune, which lifts Harry high above the rest of mankind, only to hurl him back down at last. In these complex ways, wholly integrated with one another and with the widest purposes of the film, the strategy of setting an episode of the plot in an amusement park releases symbolic meanings which brilliantly reflect Greene and Reed's vision of society. An image of entertainment, taken not from the old gregarious, communal tradition but from that of modern, commercial, impersonal leisure activity, serves as microcosm for the condition of man in modern civilization.

What I have been attempting to suggest by means of these twentieth-century examples is that the new pattern of entertainment which began to emerge during the Industrial Revolution is as open to complex artistic treatment as was the older tradition which was

31

dying out. This new pattern embodied new forms and new values, and it also bore more relation than the older model to the kind of social system which was developing in the nineteenth century and has continued to grow in the twentieth. Such images were unquestionably available to Dickens: he knew perfectly well of the developing commercial basis of popular entertainment, its increasing size, expense, discipline, and organization; in the circus and the music-hall he had two major types immediately at hand. As a professional entertainer himself, in his various capacities as author, editor and public reader, he struck hard bargains for his own financial rewards, and from occasional remarks he made – for example, about the appeal of pantomime and the thrill of dangerous entertainment (see Chapter 6 below) – it is clear that he recognized ways in which the new modes of popular entertainment directly reflected the society in which it existed. Dickens chose to focus primarily on the declining tradition, and for the good reason that it represented for him values which he believed essential to humanity; but in thus limiting his range he offered what was more in the nature of an *alternative* to the society in which he lived than an integral part of it. Rooted in the past, this choice was for conservatism; for preservation rather than innovation. Seen as an alternative, the choice was for radicalism; for replacement rather than integration. Either way the choice was pessimistic, made in the realization that the values he defended were not in accord with the prevailing attitudes of the age. That his presentation of entertainment in his fiction could nevertheless generate the marvellous gusto and comedy for which it is known and loved is testimony to his affection for the delights of entertainment; and that, despite its limitations, his artistic treatment of popular entertainment could generate such range, complexity and insight affirms the breadth of his vision and the excellence of his artistry. For readers today, as in the past, Dickens remains the great entertainer, whose novels contain, among their riches, splendid depictions of popular entertainment.

CHAPTER 3

Nicholas Nickleby
The Novel as
Popular Entertainment

Every good actor plays direct to every good author, and every
writer of fiction, though he may not adopt the dramatic form,
writes in effect for the stage.

> Charles Dickens, speech to the Royal
> General Theatrical Fund, 29 March 1858
> (*Speeches*, p. 262)

I

In the spring of 1838, shortly before the first number of *Nicholas
Nickleby* was issued, Dickens had his publishers, Chapman and Hall,
circulate a public statement concerning his new work. The 'proclamation' denounced the 'dishonest dullards' who had turned his
previous fiction to their own profit by 'wretched imitations', and
served warning against further plagiarism. From the earliest days of
Pickwick's fame an entire industry derivative of Dickens's creations
had sprung up, marketing illustrations, plays, songs and endless
varieties of merchandise, in addition to printed adaptations of the
novels. The speed and persistence of this proliferation testify to
Dickens's popular appeal: not only could he command a huge
readership for work produced under the imprint of his own
publishers, but inferior imitations by hands other than his own had
enormous selling power as well. There were, for example, at least
seven stage versions of *Pickwick* produced before Dickens finished
writing the final number, and it was claimed that penny-issue plagiarisms of *Pickwick* and of *The Old Curiosity Shop* sold in the region of
50,000 copies weekly. Unprotected by adequate copyright laws,
Dickens was justifiably exasperated, both by the reworking of his
own material over which he had no control, and by the profits which
accrued not to himself but to those who had stolen his ideas. Mere

protest, however, was inevitably no defence, and the *Nickleby* proclamation was utterly ineffectual in preventing further plagiarism of his works. As Louis James has shown, the hacks seized upon *Nickleby* the moment the first number appeared, and one of them, calling himself 'Bos', impudently issued a counter-proclamation.[1]

But if Dickens's pronouncement had no influence on those who were cashing in on his popularity it did give a clear indication of his conception of the kind of attraction he hoped his own work would have. In addition to attacking plagiarists, Dickens included a paragraph outlining his intentions in his forthcoming novel. In it he gave notice to the public

> . . . that in our new work, as in our preceding one, it will be our aim to amuse, by providing a rapid succession of characters and incidents, and describing them as cheerfully and pleasantly as in us lies; that we have wandered into fresh fields and pastures new, to seek materials for the purpose; and that, in behalf of Nicholas Nickleby, we confidently hope to enlist their heartiest merriment, and their kindliest sympathies.[2]

Nicholas Nickleby was to be, in a word, entertainment. By filling his book with humour and pathos, he hoped to arouse 'merriment' and 'sympathies', and he proposed to amuse his readers by constructing a fast-moving plot full of striking incidents and a multiplicity of boldly delineated characters. This was a plan well tested by the novelists he admired most – Fielding, Smollett and Scott – and one in constant use in the popular theatre of his own day. It was also the basis of his own phenomenal success with *Pickwick*, and he had every reason to be sanguine that the formula would work again in *Nickleby*.

As far as it goes, this statement of intention in the *Nickleby* proclamation is an accurate enough description of the novel which followed, but it is fascinating primarily for what Dickens does not say. In trying to attract readers for a work not yet published – indeed, a work largely yet to be written – Dickens omits any suggestion of polemical intention. The social satire upon the Yorkshire schools, which constitutes the first and most famous section of the novel, is quaintly alluded to here as 'wander[ing] into fresh fields and pastures new'; and the moral imperatives which drive the plot and propel hero and villain to their respective fates receive no mention at all. Yet Dickens had gone to Yorkshire two months earlier for the specific purpose of gathering material which would give his novel an urgent sense of purpose.[3] As a skilled journalist he identified an emotionally charged subject and rapidly collected the facts he needed to portray it in vivid detail; as a radical social critic he developed those facts into a ringing condemnation of a system of scandalous inhumanity. From its very inception *Nickleby* was, like *Oliver Twist*, a novel of crusading resolve. It was hardly simple entertainment.

The proclamation was not disingenuous, however; despite the horror and outrage directed at Dotheboys Hall, the portrait of Squeers and his household manifests the ebullience of Dickens's power to amuse. From the moment Squeers enters the novel in Chapter 4, Dickens's writing rises above bitter satire to rejoice in the transcendent lunacy of comic invention. There is more delight than indignation in the glimpse of Squeers inspecting the diluted milk of his hapless charges and crying, '"Here's richness!"'; in Mrs Squeers wiping her hands on a pupil's curly head to complete the ceremony of brimstone and treacle; in young Wackford sucking his fingers in an ecstasy of sated gluttony; and in Fanny pouring forth the unwittingly hilarious fury of a woman crossed in love, in her letter to the uncle of her betrayer. The reality of iniquity at Dotheboys Hall is emphatic, but simultaneously Dickens turns it into a fantasy peopled by outlandish ogres. Entertainment and moral conviction work together as comedy lifts the villainy into a sphere of ethical certainties, in which we can laugh heartily at the wickedness because we know it will be defeated. As in the melodrama which dominated the stage at the time, in *Nickleby* real problems are resolved in ideal solutions. Dickens's desire to make his fiction amusing was not a contradiction to the seriousness of his purpose; as we saw in the previous chapter, he was far from thinking entertainment a trivial matter, and to the end of his career it was an essential ingredient of his art. 'In *Bleak House*', he declared in the preface to that work, 'I have purposely dwelt upon the romantic side of familiar things'; in *Great Expectations*, he wrote to Forster, 'I have made the opening, I hope, in its general effect exceedingly droll'.[4] Such statements show him gauging the appeal he intended his work to have for his prospective audience, and he reaffirmed the sentiments of the *Nickleby* proclamation when, in the week he finished writing the novel, he composed a preface to it. After devoting most of this preface to comment on the factual basis of Squeers and of the Cheeryble brothers, he concluded by expressing to his readers the hope that he had 'contributed to their amusement'.[5]

I have been stressing Dickens's announced intentions to make *Nickleby* entertaining because he himself did so, and because the wish to entertain motivates all his fiction. Moreover, this aim was a crucial factor in determining the sort of art he was later to create in the full maturity of his genius. Starting out as an entertainer himself, he gravitated naturally to the subject of popular entertainment when choosing material for his books. His earliest works, *Sketches by Boz, Pickwick, Memoirs of Grimaldi, Nickleby* and *The Old Curiosity Shop* all included entertainment as a major component of his subject-matter; readers of these volumes recognized that he was covering familiar territory, not only in the rambling tale of high jinks, which he inherited from the works of Combe, Surtees and Hook, but also in the scenes from the entertainment world, which formed a staple aspect of Pierce Egan's popularity. (Dickens was soon eager to dissociate his name from Egan's, and when he was writing *Nickleby* he asked Frederick Yates 'not to compare Nicholas to Tom and Jerry' in advertising the stage adaptation of the novel.)[6] What was new about the entertainment in Dickens's work was not its use as subject-matter, but the quality of his writing, the vividness of the portrayals, and, increasingly, the insight into the subject. His desire to entertain never left him, but the function of entertainment in his fiction became more complex, and sometimes problematic, as his artistry matured. At first, in *Sketches by Boz* and in *The Pickwick Papers*, Dickens drew upon entertainment largely for its own sake, as a ready source of amusement; its presence took on new implications when, in *Nicholas Nickleby*, he tried to combine the cheerful delights of those earlier works with the social criticism of *Oliver Twist*; and in *The Old Curiosity Shop* he faced squarely the values which entertainment contained for his own art. Where entertainment was beguiling diversion in his earliest fiction, the buoyant vitality of Crummles lay athwart the official conclusions of *Nickleby*. But in *The Old Curiosity Shop*, after surveying the lot of the itinerant showmen along Nell's route to death and exorcizing the perversities of the Punch-and-Judy figure of Quilp, Dickens affirmed the life-enhancing possibilities of entertainment by making it the focus for the creative fancy of the novel's ultimate hero, Dick Swiveller. With *The Old Curiosity Shop* imagination supplanted entertainment to become the key source of value for Dickens, and the exploration of its necessity was to be a concern in all his later fiction.[7]

That his assessment in this novel satisfied his own creative needs is evident in the striking fact that the amusements which bulked so large in his work up to that point virtually disappear from his next five novels. In *Barnaby Rudge*, which ran serially immediately after *The Old Curiosity Shop* in *Master Humphrey's Clock*, Dickens opens with a description of the Maypole, a country inn redolent of the traditions of Merrie England, but the young hero of the story, Joe Willett, finds that he must flee its moribund pleasures in order to make any life of his own, and his creator, too, bids farewell to the showfolk he portrayed with such affection in *The Old Curiosity Shop*. Thereafter, in the novels which follow, the occasional street performer wanders by, Montague Tigg cultivates the acquaintance of an unsavoury man of the theatre named Mr Pip (*MC*, 28), Mr Toots spars with a pugilist who glories in the sobriquet of The Game Chicken (*DS*, 22), David Copperfield takes Peggotty to see a waxwork exhibition (*DC*, 33), and Mademoiselle Hortense goes for target practice to Trooper George's shooting gallery (*BH*, 24). The panoramic nature of Dickens's vision ensured that random entertainers and entertainments would inevitably appear as part of the cityscape of his novels, but it was not until he determined in 1854 to centre *Hard Times* on the pernicious effects of the denial of imagination that he once again found it appropriate to include entertainers on a large scale. Sleary's circus is a colourful representation of a major form of nineteenth-century popular entertainment, as Crummles's strolling players had been sixteen years earlier, but by this point in his career Dickens had so substantially developed the art of his fiction that the later entertainers take on symbolic weight as trustees of imaginative vitality to an extent quite beyond the possibilities of his earlier work. Sleary is thus finally less important as an entertainer than as a thematic figure within the structure of the novel; Crummles, lacking so coherent a function, owes his vitality far more to what he is than to what he represents. If we look to Dickens's later fiction for the highest sophistication of his artistry, it is to his earlier works that we must turn to discover how his concern with popular entertainment contributed to his development into the greatest English novelist.

II

Before turning to *Nickleby* we should remind ourselves just how central entertainment was to his first imaginative publications. Dickens's first published volume, *Sketches by Boz*, contains a high proportion of material devoted to entertainments, recreations and amusements, and the avowed aim throughout the work is to discover scenes which will provoke interest and delight. Composed initially as occasional pieces for magazines and newspapers, the sketches have the imaginative young journalist's characteristic lively observation and colourful detail, and from the outset Dickens thought of them as more than ephemeral diversion. His letters of the time reveal the commitment he invested in these essays, and years later he still recalled the 'fear and trembling' with which he dropped his 'first effusion' into the letterbox at the office of the *Monthly Magazine*.[8] Publicly a single claim was all he cared to make for the miscellany before it appeared: it was to be 'entertaining'. This was his 'modest' description in an advertisement which he inserted in the *Morning Chronicle* six days before *Sketches by Boz*, First Series, was published on 8 February 1836 by John Macrone ('I really can*not* do the tremendous in puffing myself,' he confided to his publisher).[9] The collection sold well enough to warrant a second edition six months later and a second series within a year, but by this time its success was eclipsed by that of *Pickwick*, and Dickens 'decidedly underrated' the *Sketches* afterwards, according to Forster.[10]

As a whole *Sketches by Boz* is dedicated to the proposition that amusement is to be found abundantly in everyday life. To this end, Dickens takes his readers on visits to a wide variety of places of entertainment, including public gardens ('Vauxhall Gardens by Day', 'London Recreations'), the circus ('Astley's'), the tavern saloon ('Miss Evans and the Eagle') and the theatre ('Private Theatres', 'The Misplaced Attachment of Mr John Dounce', 'Making a Night of It'). He chronicles the pleasures of family gatherings ('A Christmas Dinner'), festive celebrations ('The New Year'), formal assemblies ('Public Dinners'), boat outings ('The River,' 'The Steam Excursion') and just pottering in one's garden ('London Recreations'). He shows the comical misadventures of personages who aspire to become entertainers themselves ('Private Theatres', 'The Mistaken Milliner', 'Mrs Joseph Porter'), and casts cheerful ridicule upon misanthropes who grumble against amusement ('Mr Minns and His Cousin', 'The Bloomsbury Christening'). Above all, his narrative voice celebrates the enjoyment to be found simply by keeping one's eyes open to the world about. 'What inexhaustible food for speculation do the streets of London afford!' he exclaims in 'Shops and Their Tenants', and the disposition to indulge in this feast spurs him on. Repeatedly throughout the sketches he draws attention to the fascination of the commonplace: 'It is very generally allowed that public conveyances afford an extensive field for amusement and observation' ('Omnibuses'); 'One of the most amusing places we know is the steam wharf of the London Bridge' ('The River'); 'The stranger who finds himself in "The Dials" for the first time . . . will see enough to keep his curiosity and attention awake for no inconsiderable time' ('Seven Dials').

And lest his interest appear merely frivolous Dickens leavened the volume with a few sketches which examined scenes decidedly not entertaining. These were tales of degradation, abandonment and death, and Dickens's letters show that he set great store by them. Two, 'A Visit to Newgate' and 'The Black Veil', were composed specifically for the first collected edition, and a third, 'The Drunkard's Death', was written with 'great pains' for the second series, to appear in the final position in the sequence, 'to finish the Volume with *eclat*'.[11] Although privately he wrote to Catherine

Young Philip joins a School of Crossing Sweepers.

Dickens thought that amusement depended upon a disposition to respond positively to the wide variety of amusing scenes to be found everywhere.

Hogarth that visiting the prisons had supplied him with 'lots of anecdotes . . . some of them rather amusing', in the essays themselves he was explicit in rejecting amusement as an appropriate response.[12]

> They [a group of adolescent prisoners] were evidently quite gratified at being thought worth the trouble of looking at; their idea appeared to be, that we had come to see Newgate as a grand affair, and that they were an indispensable part of the show; and every boy as he 'fell in' to the line, actually seemed as pleased and important as if he had done something excessively meritorious in getting there at all. We never looked upon a more disagreeable sight, because we never saw fourteen such hopeless creatures of neglect, before.
>
> ('A Visit to Newgate', *SB*, p. 207)

Like the majority of the sketches, the dark essays were based on observation and inspired by 'curiosity' (*SB*, pp. 198, 274), but in disclaiming entertainment they stand in sharp contrast to the dominant mood of the book, and serve thereby to discriminate the morally acceptable range of experience conducive to pleasure.

The mood of amusement in *Sketches by Boz* is controlled by the principle that the fascination of everyday scenes has only to be recognized to be enjoyed. Pleasure is thus dependent on the disposition of the beholder; whether he be participant, spectator or entertainer himself, a person's enjoyment arises from his own readiness to respond to the abundance and variety of stimuli available. From this perspective, nothing is more ridiculous and self-defeating than wilful taciturnity, and no characters in the stories are made to look more absurb than Augustus Minns and Nicodemus Dumps, whose steadfast refusals to countenance gaiety lead to their discomfort and our amusement. Conversely, the truest delight is to be gained by looking about in a spirit of cheerful speculation. Nowhere is this more evident than in 'Meditations on Monmouth Street', in which imagination magically transforms a somnolent scene, as Dickens conjures up a fanciful pantomime of living characters while staring at second-hand clothing hung up for sale. The source of interest was, he believed, inherent in the scenes themselves; as he said in the preface to the first series, *Sketches by Boz* consisted of 'little pictures of life and manners as they really are'. Certainly much of the appeal of the sketches resides in this evocation of reality; again and again Dickens's first readers praised his writing for the vividness and accuracy with which he animated familiar sights. As one early reviewer put it, 'His excellence appears to lie in describing just what everybody sees every day'.[13] The air of reality depends crucially, of course, on the quality of Dickens's prose style and on his mediating presence as narrator in the sketches, genially guiding our attention to scenes of interest and pointing out colourful and amusing details. Modern commentators have insisted upon the artifice with which this impression of reality is created: Virgil Grillo, comparing Dickens to other sketch-writers of the 1830s, argues that *Sketches by Boz* is distinctive in the 'rhetorical relationship' which Dickens establishes with the reader in order to distil the 'essence' of a scene; Edward Costigan, persuasively demonstrating how conventions of contemporary theatre influence the shape of the sketches, proposes that Dickens offers 'a shared delight in the illusions that are part of reality'.[14] The dynamic interrelation of spectator and spectacle means that the quality of the experience is to be found, as Wordsworth proclaimed in 'Tintern Abbey', in 'what they half create,/And what perceive'.

As a consequence of these attitudes it follows that in *Sketches by Boz* entertainment is seen as an integral part of everyday life. It offers an extension of the fascination found in more mundane activity, differing only in that it caters specifically to amusement, whereas the pleasure derived elsewhere is generally incidental to the purported rationale of buying, selling, or getting from one place to another. Observing people going to the circus, theatre or fair, and the people who do the entertaining in those places, Dickens finds bustle, noise and absurdity, just as in more workaday situations. What he does not see to any significant extent is entertainment divorced from or in conflict with the social patterns he presents. Far from being compartmentalized into snatched moments, remote from the mainstream of daily existence, entertainment in *Sketches by Boz* releases in concentrated form the spectacle inherent virtually everywhere. As in *Sunday under Three Heads* (written and published during the months between the appearance of the first and second series of *Sketches*) and in his later work, *Sketches* shows that Dickens is well aware that for most people, most of the time, leisure activity can take place only on the one day in the week free from work, or on a rare special outing: visits to rural tea-gardens are Sunday treats; Greenwich Fair and the May Day parades occur annually; families choose the Easter or midsummer holidays to go to the circus. Likewise, he knows that many sources of entertainment are in a state of decay or actively threatened by hostile forces: Vauxhall Gardens has opened its gates by day in an attempt to recoup losses by extending its hours; May Day dancing is disappearing; and he himself has neglected to visit Greenwich Fair for years. But the emphasis falls elsewhere: Sunday tea-gardens are seen in relation to the daily pleasures of tending one's private garden; the opening of Vauxhall Gardens by day may tarnish the magic, but it opens new possibilities for witnessing balloon ascents; the decline of the sweeps' dancing is correlative to growing public awareness of the lack of romance in the life of the chimney sweep; crowds still flock to the circus and fair. Indeed, as John Butt and Kathleen Tillotson have shown, Dickens pointedly toned down overtly 'political' defence of recreation when he revised the sketches for volume publication.[15] Entertainment in *Sketches by Boz* is not a beleagured right in need of impassioned defence, but a pleasure among many to be observed and enjoyed.

Ready availability of amusement and the disposition to seek it out reappear in *The Pickwick Papers*, which Dickens began to write on 18 February 1836, just ten days after *Sketches by Boz*, first series, was published. In contrast to the collections of separate sketches, *Pickwick* is organized as a continuous story, but the episodic nature of the adventures – to say nothing of the interpolated tales – ensures that it has the random variety of entertainment which characterizes the previous work. In the opening pages Mr Pickwick's intention of 'extending his travels and consequently enlarging his sphere of observation' is announced (*PP*, 1), and the search for amusing novelty is at once established as the motive force behind the book's forward progress. In Chapter 2, Mr Pickwick and his companions set off for Rochester, and before they finally retire they have wandered to Bury St Edmunds, Ipswich, Bath, Bristol and Birmingham, with frequent intermediate stops along the way. To be sure, with the introduction of Sam Weller and the ensuing complications with Mrs Bardell, a more coherent, developing action emerges, and the dynamic interrelation of Mr Pickwick and Sam takes over as the centre of interest, but to the very end new scenes and new characters continue to appear, and the sheer abundance of spirited activity constitutes much of *Pickwick*'s attraction.[16]

As every student of Dickens knows, the book originated in a proposal from the artist Robert Seymour to draw a series of Cockney sporting scenes, which were to be accompanied by letterpress. It was a format of tested popularity, devised to promote amusement by portraying the misadventures of unskilled sportsmen in a spirit of broad ridicule and boisterous comedy. The publishers Chapman and Hall agreed to take on the project and approached Dickens to supply the text. Before the scheme even included Dickens, that is, the decision had already been reached that both the subject-matter and the purpose of the projected work would be popular entertainment. The situation changed rapidly as Dickens objected that he was 'no great sportsman' (preface to the 1847 edition); Seymour killed himself; Hablôt Browne was hired to replace the illustrator in a role subordinate to Dickens and, above all, Dickens's conception of Mr Pickwick developed. Nevertheless, Dickens continued to fill the work with amusing adventures, and he publicly reaffirmed the purpose of providing his readers with entertainment. At the conclusion of the tenth number (December 1836) he inserted an announcement in which he referred to himself as 'Mr Pickwick's Stage-Manager' and likened his position as author to that of the great showman John Richardson, thanking his audience for their favour and promising to 'keep perpetually going on beginning again, until the end of the fair'. 'Muster' Richardson had for decades commanded the prime sites of English fairgrounds with his gaudy theatre-booth performances, and Dickens elsewhere described his show as 'the very centre and heart of the fair'.[17] The comparison is a revealing indication of Dickens's notion of *Pickwick* as entertaining spectacle: vigorous fun rather than high art. By the time the book was finished he was taking his achievement more elegantly, invoking the precedent of 'some of the greatest novelists in the English language' to defend its variety of incidents, but even then he continued to claim entertainment as his guiding purpose: his object had been, he said, to present characters and incidents which were 'vivid . . . life-like and amusing' (preface to the 1837 edition).

The amusements in *Pickwick* are almost wholly participatory and convivial in nature, and underpin the book's gaiety. As in *Sketches by Boz*, formally constituted entertainment merges with a prevailing atmosphere of pleasure, and active engagement in pastimes predominates over passive spectating. Early in the book, for example, Mr Pickwick and his friends go to watch a display of military exercises, only to find themselves absurdly caught up in a bayonet charge, and leisurely admiration of the grand review quickly gives way to the broad farce of Mr Pickwick chasing his hat. Again, when the Pickwickians go with Mr Wardle to see the cricket match between All-Muggleton and Dingley Dell, they spend as much time eating, drinking and talking as they do observing the game, and it is an integral part of the occasion when the players from both sides gather with the spectators after the contest at the Blue Lion Inn for a banquet, complete with toasts, speeches, carousing, and cheerful camaraderie. Dickens presents the cricket less as a sporting engagement than as a communal ritual, in which traditional forms of gregarious interaction serve to affirm bonds of human fellowship. Mr Pickwick is not an anonymous spectator, impersonally witnessing the skills of professional players, but an active participant who shares fully in the sociable nature of the event. The emphasis is similar in the two shooting episodes. These scenes, closer than any others in the book to Seymour's original intention, depict the laugh able incompetence of Mr Winkle and Mr Tupman as sportsmen, but they also serve to affirm the comradely affection of Mr Wardle and the Pickwickians. Mr Pickwick does not carry a gun – indeed, on the second expedition he is conveyed by Sam in a wheelbarrow – but he enjoys the recreation as fully as the others, cuts as ridiculous a figure, and enters as heartily into the spirit of the activity. Throughout their travels Mr Pickwick and his friends seek out the convivial pleasures for which English inns had been justly famous for centuries; they attend balls, parties and jovial gatherings wherever they go, and when other sources of amusement momentarily flag they engage strangers in conversation and story-telling. All of these shared delights lend support to the popular image of Dickens which links his name so intimately with the festive spirit of Christmas, for the good-natured Christmas celebrations at Dingley Dell epitomize the fun of this novel.

Participation is the key to enjoyment in *Pickwick*, and reciprocally professional entertainment, in the figure of Mr Jingle, steps out of its magically enclosed world into the lives of the characters. For this strolling player all the world truly is a stage, and he exploits his skills as an actor for any audience sufficiently gullible to be taken in by the roles he plays. From his first entrance Jingle's existence is histrionic posturing: he steps forward anonymously during Mr Pickwick's fracas with the cabman to alter the course of action in that scene; upon arrival in Rochester he changes costume with comically chaotic results; for his appearance in Eatanswill he assumes the new name of Charles Fitz-Marshall. He upstages Dr Slammer and Mr Tupman in courtship, has a flair for the strong curtain-line, and when challenged strikes attitudes which freeze a scene into comic tableau. His loquacious staccato is a perpetually diverting stage patter, derived, as Earle Davis has shown, from the one-man 'At Home' performances of Charles Mathews the elder, which Dickens went to see 'whenever he played' for three or four years; Jingle himself gives the clue to his origins when he tells Dr Slammer that he is not to be found 'at home'.[18] Jingle's translation of role-playing from the stage into the audience is a chief source of merriment in the novel, and Dickens had ample reason for his confidence that the character would make 'a decided hit'.[19]

Jingle never actually appears in a theatre at all in the course of the novel, and his talent for duplicity hardly requires professional qualifications. Like subsequent rascals in Dickens's fiction, he relies on native wit to outface any situation; there is a positive vitality in the gleeful impudence with which he cuts in on Dr Slammer, and the gulls he deceives are either so spoony (Mr Tupman) or self-important (the Nupkinses) that they richly deserve comic deflation.

But because his unscrupulousness conflicts with Mr Pickwick's principled selflessness Dickens chastens the stroller in the end and consigns him to the Fleet Prison. This turnabout gives Dickens the opportunity to demonstrate once again the sunny benevolence of Mr Pickwick, who forgives Jingle and Job and finances their emigration to Demerara, but the punishment strikes a discordant note – very. It contrasts sharply with the final appearance of the book's other principal deceivers, Dodson and Fogg, who exit basking in complacent unrepentance, cheerfully noting down the particulars of Mr Pickwick's denunciation of them in evidence for future legal chicanery. Mere morality is quite alien to their integrity, as it had seemed with Jingle. Furthermore, the sight of Jingle ill and penitent, humbled in his wrongdoing, suggests a 'real' person beneath the poses, quite contrary to the impression created by his previous activities, in which performance was all. This raises unsettling questions about the morality of acting, by implying that role-playing is not gesture but imposture. These are doubts which recur in acute form in *Nickleby* when Dickens sends Crummles, like Jingle, off to the New World without even, in the latter novel, the excuse that it is an act of justice.

On the other hand, the expulsion of Jingle is consistent with the happy idealism of *Pickwick*, in which pastimes are seen as the vehicle for human affection. Genuine entertainment, in this view, brooks no self-seeking or mercenary considerations; it arises out of shared pleasures and contentments, and must reject anyone who cynically plays upon man's need for amusement. Dickens stated in his preface to the original edition that it was his hope that *Pickwick* would be an inducement for the reader 'to think better of his fellow men and to look upon the brighter and more kindly side of human nature', and this is the lesson Jingle learns in the Fleet. Dickens's vision of entertainment in this book is decidedly old-fashioned; it looks back to an imaginary model of social harmony, in which the commingling of people of different age, sex and rank is fostered by leisure activity. As we saw in Chapter 1, Dickens cherished this model of pre-industrial traditions for the concord it represented, and here, in combination with the amiable innocence of Mr Pickwick and supported by the evocation of the rapidly disappearing exhilaration of coaching days, popular entertainment is celebrated as a vital and readily accessible tonic for the human spirit. Its joys were never to be so secure again.

Dickens's second novel, begun when he was barely halfway through the writing of *Pickwick*, was conceived in an altogether different spirit. Entertainers are decidedly thin on the ground in the squalid workhouse, and in the criminal underworld the 'indifferent' singers and 'remote' piano at the Three Cripples public house do nothing to soften the 'cunning, ferocity, and drunkenness' which prevail there (*OT*, 26). Oliver finds scant amusement in his young life until, perversely, the warmth of Fagin's den provides him with his first real companionship, and the Jew's impersonation for his pupils of an old gentleman fearful of thieves moves Oliver to tears of laughter. Innocent enjoyment, found in such lavish abundance in *Sketches by Boz* and *The Pickwick Papers*, is here restricted to the isolated havens of Mr Brownlow and the Maylies, and the utter polarity of the polite and criminal worlds has led Graham Greene to describe Dickens's vision in *Oliver Twist* as Manichaean.[20] It forms no part of Dickens's concerns to present or explore the pastimes of curiosity-seekers in this novel, which is devoted instead to the satiric exposure of social evils and an affirmation of the 'principle of Good' surviving adverse circumstances.

Nevertheless, he is instinctively prepared to draw upon the conventions of popular entertainment and to exploit them for his own purposes in the book. In particular, as readers have long recognized, his intimate familiarity with the theatre of his day infuses his art at every level. The boldly contrasting scenes, exciting action, larger-than-life characters, and stylized speech and gesture are the very stuff of early nineteenth-century melodrama, and Dickens points directly to this influence when he invokes the precedent of theatrical usage in his famous image of streaky bacon, to defend the abrupt transitions of *Oliver Twist*.

> It is the custom on the stage: in all good, murderous melo-dramas: to present the tragic and the comic scenes, in as regular alternation, as the layers of red and white in a side of streaky, well-cured bacon.   (*OT*, 17)

He goes on to urge that this is an aspect of the 'mimic life of the theatre', and his readiness to see popular forms as a mirror of the real world says much about the roots of his artistry. Striving ambitiously to create a work of urgent social import and high moral purpose, he turns to the amusements of the people for a vigorous, direct and accessible vehicle. Dickens's inspiration comes not from the élite culture of philosophical abstraction, classical education, and aesthetic theory, but from the living tradition of tavern song, pulpit oration, newspaper rhetoric, chapbook sensation, and circus, street and stage performance. He is the great artist who draws his sustenance from popular entertainment.[21]

Because he was prepared to draw on these sources for the form of *Oliver Twist*, it is the more striking that he neglected them as subject-matter, when they had figured to so great an extent in *Sketches by Boz* and *Pickwick*. The reason is near at hand, particularly if we take seriously – as I think we must – Kathleen Tillotson's suggestion that *Oliver Twist* was the first of Dickens's novels to be conceived, although the second to be written.[22] As the novel which had been gestating in his mind since at least 1833, when he was 21, *Oliver Twist* would have taken shape for him as the inaugural test of his powers as an aspiring artist; with a subject of importance and a timeless theme, and with a free hand on his material from the outset, he would attempt to follow in the footsteps of his revered Fielding and create a 'prose epic' (*OT*, 15; in *BM* edition only). *Sketches by Boz* and *Pickwick* both began as journalism; they were written to provide appealing diversion, and the inclusion of scenes of entertainment was entirely appropriate to this purpose. That they became something more was testimony to Dickens's talents as a writer, but their limited aim did not, he must have felt, give scope for him to work at full stretch. *Oliver Twist* was to be different, and one mark of Dickens's more ambitious plans for this novel was what it did not include. At the beginning of his career as a novelist, I am suggesting, there was a division in his mind between seriousness in fiction and the imprudence of entertainment. (Comedy, of course, was another matter, as was the right to seek amusement.) As we have already seen, this caused a minor ambiguity in *Pickwick* when he tried to fit Jingle into that book's moral framework; Dickens avoided such difficulty in *Oliver Twist* by the simple expedient of leaving entertainment scenes out.

III

Dickens's ambitions for *Oliver Twist* met with immediate success. The plagiarists and the theatres pounced upon it at once, and before half of its serial parts had appeared the novel received considerable critical acclaim. In an otherwise grudging notice, which compared Dickens's fame to a skyrocket ('he has risen like a rocket, and he will come down like the stick'), Abraham Hayward wrote in the *Quarterly Review* for October 1837 that *Oliver Twist* showed 'much higher promise' than his previous work. Two months later George Henry Lewes, comparing Dickens's satire to that of Voltaire and Swift, called *Oliver Twist* 'a work pregnant with philosophy and feeling'.[23] But *The Pickwick Papers* was also being seen as more than a passing fancy; reviewers soon mentioned it in relation to the achievements of Cervantes, Fielding, Sterne, Smollett and Scott, and the prestigious *Westminster Review* saw *Pickwick* as evidence that 'the great and extensive popularity of Boz is the result, not of popular caprice, or of popular bad taste, but of great intrinsic powers of mind, from which we augur considerable future excellence'.[24] Having thus been accorded stature as well as popularity for both his serious novel and his work of entertainment, Dickens moved to consolidate his fame by combining the two modes in his next novel, *Nicholas Nickleby*. To recapture the sense of purpose which had impelled the Poor Law satire of *Oliver Twist* he turned to the notorious evils of the Yorkshire schools, and to renew the amusement provided by the depiction of an entertainer an entire company of strolling players followed upon the figure of Mr Jingle.

The strategy for the new novel prospered. Sales for the serial instalments of *Nickleby*, at nearly 50,000 copies, were higher by some 10,000 than for the monthly numbers of *Pickwick*.[25] Dotheboys Hall promptly entered English mythology as the archetypal bad school, and Crummles became an enduring favourite. Moreover, the decision to incorporate entertainment scenes was to prove of the utmost importance for the book's later critical fortunes. *Nicholas Nickleby* has worn less well than any other novel by Dickens, and modern critics, when they have bothered to look at *Nickleby* at all, have expressed grave reservations about many of the book's characters, its structure, and what have been seen as embarrassing lapses of tone. Such reputation as the book can be said to hold at present rests largely on its theatre figures. Writing in 1958, J. Hillis Miller called the scenes among the troupe of actors 'a critique of the way of life of all the characters' in the novel, and four years later Bernard Bergonzi modified this view of Crummles's company as a 'parody' of the main plot, arguing that 'the theatre represents the nearest equivalent to a central unifying metaphor that *Nickleby* has to offer'. More recently, in his influential introduction to the Penguin English Library edition of the novel (1978), Michael Slater, describing theatricality and role-playing as 'the living heart' of *Nicholas Nickleby*, has shown conclusively that, in addition to the Crummleses, 'nearly everyone else in this crowded book is playing a role'.[26]

Both in its own day and in ours, the essential theatricality of the novel has been demonstrated by its suitability for stage production. From as early as 1834, when J. B. Buckstone adapted 'The Bloomsbury Christening' for performance at the Adelphi Theatre, Dickens's writings were incessantly plundered for stageworthy characters and incidents, and Dickens customarily took a jaundiced view of the results.[27] But with Edward Stirling's dramatization of *Nickleby* he was delighted. To the incredulity of Forster, who considered the play an 'indecent assault' on the novel, Dickens praised it, and wrote to its producer, Frederick Yates, disclaiming any objection to an adaptation 'so admirably done in every respect'. In fact, not quite every respect won his admiration; Mrs Keeley, who played Smike in the production, later recalled that her sentimental lines about 'the pretty harmless robins' had moved Dickens to exclaim 'Damn the robins; cut them out'. Despite the robins, the play was a decided success, running at the Adelphi for nearly a hundred nights, a considerable achievement at a time when most new theatrical pieces sank without trace after only a week or two, and Stirling went on to write many further adaptations of Dickens's work, including a sequel to *Nickleby* entitled *The Fortunes of Smike*.[28] Well over a century later, in 1980, David Edgar constructed a two-part, nine-hour dramatization of the same novel for the Royal Shakespeare Company. Many professional theatre critics and academic commentators were unenthusiastic about the production, but it met with rapturous applause from audiences in London and New York, and was recorded as the first major arts programme for Britain's newly opened fourth television channel. The audiences were certainly right: in its exuberance, variety, comedy and pathos, the play was an exhilarating theatrical experience. Stage performance validated aspects of the book at which modern readers cavil; in particular, Roger Rees fleshed out the title role to an extent hard to imagine from Nicholas's presence on the page, and David Threlfall made the sorry figure of Smike genuinely moving. Bernard Levin assessed the production correctly when he wrote in *The Times* for 8 July 1980 that

> . . . not for many years has London's theatre seen anything so richly joyous, so immoderately rife with pleasure, drama, colour and entertainment, so life-enhancing, yea-saying, and fecund, so – in the one word which embraces all these and more – so Dickensian.[29]

But *Nicholas Nickleby* is theatrical in more than its potential for stage adaptation. In the text itself the conventions of the theatre permeate its form and characterization. Like *Oliver Twist, Nickleby* is organized on the 'streaky bacon' principle, with boldly contrasting scenes of comedy and sentiment. The main plot is a melodrama of heroes and villains, in which innocence is threatened, wickedness defeated and virtue rewarded. The action includes such stock play-acting situations as the comic man eavesdropping on a secret confer-ence, the helpless innocent recaptured by his oppressors, and, twice over, the brave young man interceding when he overhears the virtuous maiden's name impugned. Among the characters, Crummles's players are professionally engaged in the theatre, and their disposition to turn every opportunity into an excuse for acting reveals histrionic sensibility as their essential trait. When Mr Lenville undertakes to pull Nicholas's nose before the assembled company or when, with 'heart-rending' sobs, Mr Crummles personates the bride's father at Miss Petowker's wedding, the artifice of dramatic performance spills off the stage into private life, and the absurdity of their posturing serves their enjoyment, and ours.

Acting is not reserved for the professionals, however; in *Nicholas Nickleby* performance is a principal manifestation of character.[30] Less innocently than the strolling players, Squeers and Ralph put up false fronts to the world for the advancement of their own selfish aims. An intention to deceive rather than to entertain motivates their behaviour, but it is role-playing nevertheless. Miss LaCreevy paints miniatures of people not as they are but as they would be; Mr Lillyvick thinks so entirely in terms of his occupation as a collector of water-rates that without his being aware of it the role becomes his sole identity. For these and other characters acting constitutes reality, and the modes of the theatre underpin their vitality. On the other hand, theatricality is also the source of the book's greatest weaknesses, the empty stereotype of hero and heroine, and the falsity of its resolution, but for large portions of the novel theatricality generates luxuriant comedy and contributes sparkling zest, as Dickens plays with the conventions he knew and loved so well. Years later, proposing a toast to Thackeray at a banquet of the Royal General Theatrical Fund, Dickens said that 'every writer of fiction, though he may not adopt the dramatic form, writes in effect for the stage' (*Speeches*, p. 262). For better and for worse, *Nicholas Nickleby* is a novel written 'for the stage'.

The perspectives outlined in the previous paragraph have been admirably illuminated by Michael Slater in his Penguin introduction. His analysis sheds considerable light on the novel, and in stressing the importance of the theatre to Dickens's methods he points to the centre of excellence in *Nicholas Nickleby*. Role-playing is, however, a concept insufficient to account for what performance actually was in the early nineteenth-century theatre, and it does not go far enough in describing the place of the actors in *Nickleby*. The stage was not restricted to impersonation of characters in plays and, a quarter of a century before Stanislavsky was born, acting certainly did not consist of the identification of the player with his part. Rather, the actor gave a performance of his role, with stylized gesture and inflated rhetoric, in a theatre which was the setting for song, dance, acrobatics and elaborate stage effects as well as for dramatic presentation. A fair indication of what was to be found on the stage of the time is provided by Mr Crummles when he recalls his

'An Outside Stage' by Phiz. Role-playing is a concept inadequate to the variety of entertainment presented on the stage as Dickens knew it.

first glimpse of the 'astonishing' woman who was to become Mrs Crummles:

> . . . she stood upon her head on the butt-end of a spear, sur-rounded with blazing fireworks. (*NN*, 25)

'Role-playing' is hardly the adequate term for a performance like this. It is spectacle, pure and simple, and Crummles is lost in admiration for the talent he beheld: '"Such grace, coupled with such dignity! I adored her from that moment."' This is nineteenth-century theatre, if not at its best, certainly at its most typical, and to understand properly what Dickens is doing with the strolling players in *Nicholas Nickleby* it is necessary to place the novel's theatricality where it belongs, in the context of popular entertainment.

IV

In the theatre as Dickens knew it, a play was virtually never presented on its own. Whether a full company was appearing in the elegance of a metropolitan Theatre Royal, or a few strollers were strutting and fretting in a humble barn, it was customary for an evening's programme to include two, or more usually three, principal attractions, and the performance of dramatic works constituted only a portion of the interest. Between the pieces, the actress who had represented the witch in *Macbeth* would step forward to sing the ballad of Rory O'More; the actor who had portrayed a murderous henchman in the melodrama would perform his celebrated jockey dance. The orchestra, in a small touring company consisting of no more than a handful of instruments, would provide music before, between and during the business on stage, and if there was a tumbler or a clown on hand he, too, would add his bit to the amusement. Within the plays, actors were liable on the least provocation – or none at all – to burst into song, brandish swords, or group for a dance. In the course of their acting they would strike the picturesque attitudes so memorably recorded in toy-theatre cutouts, and sometimes an entire play would consist of little more than a series of tableaux, with actors frozen in various statuesque poses. Costumes and settings, nearly always described as new, were invariably announced in the playbills, for the good reason that critics were known often to devote more attention to the scene-painting than to the acting. Stage machinery was called into use whenever possible, to make a ghost vanish into thin air or to effect pantomime transformations, and when all else failed there was blue fire to make a brilliant climax to the dreariest play. Nineteenth-century theatre thrived on spectacle and diversity, and the nature of an evening's provision is scarcely exaggerated by the programme arranged for Miss Snevellicci's bespeak: 'it included among other trifles, four pieces, divers songs, a few combats, and several dances' (*NN*, 24).

To be able to mount such theatrical fare, the first requirement of every actor and actress clearly had to be versatility. The range of skills expected was spelled out explicitly in Leman Thomas Rede's *The Road to the Stage*. This invaluable handbook, which was first published in 1827 and updated for a second edition in 1835, three years before *Nickleby*, contains an encyclopaedic wealth of information about the provincial theatre and detailed advice for the aspiring stroller. Besides explaining the general regulations for rehearsal, performance and benefits, and recommending the purchase of an extensive private wardrobe including stage costumes, wigs, feathers, weapons, and ornaments 'of all descriptions', Rede offers a list of 'the requisite accomplishments for an actor or actress'. Formal schooling is unnecessary, he observes, but a smattering of French is useful, and facility in dancing, fencing and singing is 'indispensable'. Knowledge of music, for example, is likely to be called upon at any time, because there is 'no line of drama in which it may not be requisite to sing. Iago, Falkland, Edgar, King Lear, and Incle, all vocalize . . .'[31] With 'vocalizing' so unexceptional a duty for a strolling player, it is no wonder that Mr Crummles is disappointed when Nicholas declines to perform 'a comic song on the pony's back' (*NN*, 30).

But even with a reluctant leading man the company as a whole is not lacking in the accomplishments deemed essential by Rede. They have a variety of dance routines on call; not only 'The Indian Savage and the Maiden', which Dickens describes in minute comic detail from beginning to end, but also a Highland Fling, a medley dance, and the 'skipping rope hornpipe' in which Mrs Crummles excelled at her latest benefit. The skipping-rope dance had been a speciality of the theatre clown Grimaldi, whose memoirs Dickens edited in February 1838, immediately before he began writing *Nickleby*.[32] For music, the Crummleses provided comic songs as well as the orchestra, and Miss Bravassa sings the love songs. As for swordplay, when the two Master Crummleses engage

> . . . a variety of fancy chops were administered on both sides; such as chops dealt with the left hand, and under the leg, and over the right shoulder, and over the left; and when the short sailor made a vigorous cut at the tall sailor's legs, which would have shaved them clean off if it had taken effect, the tall sailor

jumped over the short sailor's sword, wherefore to balance the matter, and make it all fair, the tall sailor administered the same cut, and the short sailor jumped over *his* sword.　　　(*NN*, 22)

Rede had advised that grace was more important than skill in stage fighting; it is clear that Crummles's swordsmen possess more than the 'requisite' abilities.

Nicholas observes that the Infant Phenomenon 'always sustained one, and not uncommonly two or three, characters every night' (*NN*, 24); the star billing which she received was her special privilege as the manager's daughter, but in real life such frequency of appearance was nothing out of the ordinary. Rather more ambitious was the exploit of Mr W. H. Angel, the comic man of the actual Portsmouth company, who, for his benefit night on 16 April 1834, was billed – with understandably lavish use of exclamations – as personating sixteen characters and singing six comic songs in the course of the evening.[33] This was exceptional even by nineteenth-century standards, but playbills were routinely long and crowded, and the demands on the players considerable. One old stager, looking back in 1880 to his experiences in the 1820s and 1830s with the Fishers on their circuit in Norfolk, recalled that whenever they were performing the leading players acted their parts on the stage, then 'as soon as the curtain was drawn, donned topcoats and went into the orchestra and played the *entr'acte* music'. We find a somewhat more subdued instance of doubling up in *Great Expectations* when Pip, attending Mr Wopsle's performance of Hamlet, observes that the recorder used on stage looks 'very like a little black flute that has just been played in the orchestra and handed out at the door' (*GE*, 31). David Fisher confirmed that from an early age he and his brothers were schooled in singing, dancing and fencing, and that they were equally ready to perform tragedy, comedy or melodrama. In addition, members of the company painted the stage scenery ('good enough for the approval of their patrons and supporters') and set the type and printed their own playbills.[34] Apparently just about the only job they delegated was the distribution of the playbills, and even this they might better have done themselves, lest they find, as Miss Snevellicci did with the placarding for her bespeak, that 'a part were posted sideways and the remainder upside down' (*NN*, 24).

As part of his versatility, an actor had to master his part in a very substantial number of plays. Programmes changed rapidly, with new pieces sinking almost as fast as they were produced, and except for elaborate and expensive shows such as pantomimes it was unusual for a play to have a run of more than a few nights in succession. On any given evening, besides the *divertissements* there would be one principal piece, either dramatic, operatic or spectacular – and usually a combination of all three – then a shorter play, an interlude or selected scenes from a classic; and finally a farce to conclude the bill. Sometimes two full-length dramas and a song would be performed together, or a string of variety acts were substituted for the second play; but, except when a pantomime filled an entire programme, several distinct productions were normally mounted each night. A touring company performed the same plays in each town it visited, and standard favourites such as the Crummleses have in their repertoire were revived endlessly, but an actor could be responsible for scores of roles in a single season. His task of conning lines was made somewhat easier by the stereotyping of melodrama, which meant that each actor was type-cast, portraying the similar kinds of figure which recurred in play after play. As Mr Crummles says encouragingly to Nicholas, ' "You can easily knock them off; one part helps the other so much" ' (*NN*, 23). But an actor would usually personate more than one character every night, and his appearance on the stage in several guises is further reason to qualify the notion of acting as role-playing. Because he took so many parts, and acted them in the grandiloquent style of the age, an audience would be less aware of his immersion within roles than of the virtuosity with which he moved from one to the next. His role-playing was precisely *playing*, and it made him less an impersonator than an entertainer. The multiplicity of characters in which he appeared served to distance him from any one of them, and placed the emphasis squarely upon performance.

Variety was the principle on which each programme was arranged, and it was hardly less so within the individual plays. A single example can serve to epitomize the nature of dramatic production around the time of *Nickleby*. One of the many stage adaptations of Dickens's work was a piece entitled *Pickwick; or, The Sayings and Doings of Sam Weller*, which was performed a number of times between 18 December 1837 and 27 October 1838 in theatres along the Norwich circuit. It was cobbled together by a long-forgotten member of the Norwich company, one Frederic Coleman Nantz, and although the Ipswich reviewer at the time wrote that 'Boz would have been delighted' the play, like most theatrical fare of its day, is of nugatory merit as literature, and has long since vanished from the stage. Its value for the present discussion lies not in any dramatic distinction – for it has none – but in the obviousness of the stock formulas which Nantz uses to give the play audience appeal. Like much ephemeral work, it relies on topicality to impart novelty to stereotype. The play was first performed just after the final serial part of *The Pickwick Papers* appeared, and it takes advantage of local colour by highlighting scenes which Dickens places in Ipswich and transposing others to Essex. Settings are clearly considered important, for the play contains eighteen separate scenes and prints the location of each in bold capitals on the playbills. Nantz also stresses the attractiveness of the musical accompaniment, mentioning it immediately after the title on the bills, where it is represented as 'new' music. Two scenes are singled out for particular prominence: a dance, called the 'Pickwickian Quadrilles', and described as 'the poetry of motion'; and an episode of broad farce, based on Mr Pickwick's inadvertent intrusion into a lady's bedchamber, referred to here as the 'Scene of Night Caps'. Other attractions included the sleepwalking of the Fat Boy, Mr Pickwick's ride in the wheelbarrow, a recitation of Mrs Leo Hunter's 'Ode to an Expiring Frog', and specimens of the comic patter of Sam Weller and of Alfred Jingle.[35] As drama, in short, Nantz's *Pickwick* was little more than a rapid trot through selected episodes from Dickens. As theatre, however, the play offered novelty, scenery, dancing, music, jokes and funny business. In doing so, it reflected contemporary conventions of the stage, and for us it exemplifies the extent to which essentially non-dramatic elements were integrated into nineteenth-century dramatic works. The precise mixture varied from play to play, but the basic recipe remained unchanged for many decades: popular entertainment was the staple ingredient of the theatre.

Spectacle and novelty were chief attractions. For much of the season that Stirling's *Nicholas Nickleby* was playing at the Adelphi, for example, it shared the bill with a giant, who engaged in mock battles with twelve ordinary mortals, and for the final performances of the season there were monkeys in the programme as well.[36] With his combats, scenery and animals, Crummles was in the mainstream of theatrical practice. The violent broadsword fight between the manager's two sons provides our first glimpse of the stage business undertaken by the company, and when Nicholas is hired his initial duty is to introduce a 'real pump and two washing tubs' into the playbills to advertise the company's 'new and splendid scenery' (*NN*, 22). The next day on the road to Portsmouth he learns that the pony drawing the phaeton is 'quite one of us', with credentials as illustrious as those of any other member of the troupe. 'His mother was on the stage,' Mr Crummles confides. 'She ate apple-pie at a circus for upwards of fourteen years . . . fired pistols, and went to bed in a nightcap; and, in short, took the low comedy entirely. His father was a dancer' (*NN*, 23). Sword fights (to say nothing of ghosts, witches and mad scenes) helped to make Shakespeare a staple of theatrical repertoire, and nautical plays were particularly admired in the aftermath of Nelson's famous sea-battles. Early in the century Sadler's Wells built a water-tank which covered the entire stage, the better to present elaborate marine spectacles, and even without a tank the provincial theatres frequently staged sea-sagas. Dickens introduces the two Master Crummleses dressed to the pigtail like real (stage) sailors, and in real (historical) life the most popular nautical drama of them all, Douglas Jerrold's *Black-Eyed Susan*, inevitably found its way to Portsmouth. Animals frequently drew larger audiences than mere human actors managed to do. Drury Lane, cavernously empty all too often when straight dramas were performed, was filled when Van Amburgh brought his lions and tigers to the theatre during the 1838–9 season. Dog drama, popular ever since the eighteenth century, continued to be revived well past mid-century.[37] Charley Bates offers a just assessment of the state of theatrical taste, if not of Sikes's dog Bullseye, when he remarks, '"He'd make his fortun on the stage that dog would, and rewive the drayma besides"' (*OT*, 39).

V

The theatre episode in *Nickleby* is set in Portsmouth, which was Dickens's birthplace. Forster records that Dickens visited the town while writing *Nickleby*, and presumably he passed through on his way to or from a holiday on the Isle of Wight in early September 1838, a few weeks before Crummles makes his first appearance in the novel. Scholars have speculated that, although the local theatre was closed at the time, Dickens was likely to have gone to look at it while he was there, and would have noticed old playbills pasted on the walls.[38] He could, for example, have chosen the name of Mr Folair after seeing a bill announcing an actor named Billy Floyer, who played comic roles for many years in Portsmouth. Certainly there was ample material to feed Dickens's conception of the Crummleses in the activities of the actual Portsmouth theatre in the years before he wrote *Nickleby*, and in the presence there of one visiting company in particular. Bills survive today which document that Jean Davenport, 'the most celebrated juvenile actress of the day', performed in Portsmouth in March 1837. She and her parents have long been considered models for the Crummles family.[39] Her mother was an actress, and her father, T. D. Davenport (1792–1851), who was well known in the 1830s and 1840s as an actor and manager, promoted his daughter's career up and down the British Isles, in Europe and in America. Jean Davenport (1829–1903) achieved success as a child actress and went on to become a renowned tragedienne, principally in the United States. Malcolm Morley has shown the likelihood that Dickens came across the Davenports at the Westminster Theatre in

1832 and again in 1836 at the Richmond Theatre, Surrey, but they were prominent enough in the theatre world that he could hardly have been unaware of them.[40] The puffing of a child prodigy by a fat and pompous father, as Davenport by all accounts was, offered Dickens suitable materials for his portraits of the Infant Phenomenon and Vincent Crummles.

In the novel the Crummleses produce *Romeo and Juliet* with Nicholas and Miss Snevellicci in the leads, and in fact Juliet was to become one of Jean Davenport's most celebrated roles. An anecdote connected with her performance in that play one night in Glasgow in 1846 shows the stuff the Davenports were made of, and is worth recounting at length not only for the amusement it affords, but also for the light it sheds on the nature of theatre entertainment at the time. The evening in question got off to a bad start when the energetic and eccentric Glasgow manager J. H. Alexander, who at 50 was not altogether suitable to personate the youthful lover, was greeted with derisive shouting from the gallery when he stepped on to the stage as Romeo. The uproar continued throughout the play and during the crypt scene became so great that, exasperated beyond discretion, he rose up from his supposed unconsciousness and returned abuse to the audience in good measure. It was Davenport's turn next.

> . . . Miss Davenport came forward and sang. Mr Davenport, who was on the stage, applauded his daughter very warmly, and cried out 'Beautiful! Beautiful!' The plaudits bestowed by the public on the 'phenomenon' not being by her father considered worthy of his child's efforts; inspired by the example of his Manager, Mr Davenport now thought he would have *his* words with the audience, 'I wonder', he murmured audibly to the audience, 'she could sing at all after playing tragedy in the way she has done, and "Juliet" too!' The opportunity for his addressing the Public was not long in coming. Miss Davenport sang a ballad, and then danced with somebody the polka. 'Encore!' shouted the delighted gods. Now was the time for Mr Davenport's oratorical powers to assert themselves. 'Encore!' he exclaimed, stepping forward. 'I am astonished! I am shocked! You call for a repetition of the polka! Are you aware from whom you demand that dance? Do you not recognize the fact that Miss Davenport is a tragedy actress! That tonight she has sustained one of the heaviest tragedy parts—' ('Order', cried the gods, 'Go on'.) 'Sir', exclaimed the outraged parent, pointing at one unfortunate boy in the gallery, 'if *you* had done as much as she has done – yes, YOU, sir – permit me to remark,

you would not have been able to move.' (Hisses) Mr Davenport looked round with indignant astonishment. 'These are sounds', continued the irate parent, 'which I am not accustomed to! I have travelled, allow me to inform you, and, as your journals of the universe have testified, all over Europe and America, with Miss Davenport, but have never before been treated in this way.' Mr Davenport then made an appeal to that justice which had ever, did ever, and would, he ventured to hope, continue to characterize the British public. He then bowed mechanically and retired, amid the jeering and uproar made by the scanty auditory of that eventful night.[41]

Even allowing for embellishment in the telling, the anecdote provides revealing illustration of theatrical manners and audience expectations. It gives a vivid impression of Davenport's strong personality, and of the fervour with which he sought to advance his daughter's career. If Davenport's belligerence seems remote from the genial Vincent Crummles, who never faces such overt opposition, still Dickens's character perpetually evinces a similar capacity for public self-exhibition and a disposition to orotund rhetoric in pursuit of family aggrandizement. The hostility of the Glasgow gallery to the performance of the play no doubt reflects above all the peculiar relationship between J. H. Alexander and his patrons, but the radically different response of the audience to successive portions of the programme also shows the enthusiasm with which non-dramatic entertainment was received, and it confirms the requirement of versatility in the player – even, as in this case, in one who aspired to serious dramatic representation. The incident suggests the extent to which actors played to their audiences, rather than more self-containedly entering into the personation of their roles, and it provides clear demonstration of the willingness of an audience to let its theatrical preferences be known. Patently, the performances on the stage on this particular night were an artistic shambles, and there can have been little joy among the players, but the gods undoubtedly obtained their fill of amusement.

It is distinctly possible that the Davenports sparked off Dickens's imagination when he was thinking about the theatre scenes in *Nickleby*, although to suppose that he himself acted under Davenport's direction, either at Portsmouth or at the Westminster Theatre in London several years earlier, is extremely hypothetical.[42] More important, to claim a unique source for any of Dickens's fictional characters fundamentally misrepresents Dickens's creative methods. Particular observations, such as, perhaps, Billy Floyer's name, supplied him with details, but for all their idiosyncrasy his characters represent general human types, not specific living individuals. Flamboyant theatre managers abounded; Elliston, Bunn or Buckstone – to say nothing of the prickly Macready, to whom *Nicholas Nickleby* was dedicated – could equally well as Davenport have coloured Dickens's thoughts about Crummles, and ever since the original Infant Roscius, Master Betty, had created a sensation back in 1804 the stage had been littered with juvenile actors and actresses. Dickens mentions Master Betty in his 1835 story 'The Misplaced Attachment of Mr John Dounce' (*SB*, p. 245), and in 1842 he wrote Forster a gleeful letter to say that he had seen Betty's son playing at the Margate Theatre.[43] Leigh Hunt, himself often seen as the model for Harold Skimpole in *Bleak House*, had cited the proliferation of Infant Phenomena as early as 1805 when he mounted his influential attack on the vogue for Master Betty. In 1832, Gilbert Á Beckett was complaining in *Figaro in London* about the glut of child actors, a few weeks after he had written a damning account of Mr and Mrs Davenport (but not of Jean, who was then only 3 years old) at the Westminster Theatre.[44] No regular theatregoer in the early years of the nineteenth century was likely to have missed seeing at least one Infant Phenomenon.

If the Davenports did in fact provide Dickens's inspiration for Vincent and Ninetta Crummles, then, it was because he saw in them striking instances of the kind of entertainer to be found in the theatre of the day, not because he wanted to satirize them personally. Furthermore, if it is possible for him to have seen notices for Davenport and Floyer in Portsmouth bills, he is equally likely to have noticed other details to whet his appetite for sending Nicholas among players in the forthcoming adventure. The playbills from the mid-1830s announce that the Portsmouth theatre was open Mondays, Wednesdays and Fridays during the season, with new programmes devised for every night and only a few plays ever repeated. Besides Shakespeare and such chestnuts as *Douglas, Pizarro* and *A New Way to Pay Old Debts*, the emphasis was firmly on spectacle, song and dance. *Rob Roy*, for example, which was staged on 18 December 1835, was performed as an operatic play with eleven songs; *The Tower of Nesle; or, The Black Gondola* was a historical drama with nine tableaux, presented on 8 February 1836. One of the few plays to appear more than once (on 12 February 1834 and 25 April 1836) was *The Knight and the Wood Demon; or, The Clock Has Struck*, which featured a chorus of wood-spirits, and 'Irish lilt and strathspey dance', and a giant chained to a rock. The demon himself arrived by a 'mystic appearance' and, for good measure, when he departed he vanished 'in a flame of fire'. Between the pieces, there was customarily a comic song by Mr Angel or Mr Floyer, as well as a dance by Miss Parker, the stage manager's daughter, who took her benefit performances alongside her mother, a leading actress in the company. Occasionally, imported attractions topped the bill. Barnet Burns, the New Zealand Chief, came in April 1836 to entertain with war whoops and other habits of the natives of that remote island. Like Crummles's African Knife Swallower, who 'looked and spoke remarkably like an Irishman' (*NN*, 48), his origins were of dubious authenticity, but to forestall objection the playbills reported that the New Zealander was 'born and educated in England but naturalized in that country, tattooed and appointed chief of a tribe'. A month later, 'Monseur' Javely Ravel, the 'principal dancer of Paris', visited Portsmouth and performed on the tightrope. He brought with him not one but two Infant Phenomena, his children, aged 7 and 4, who were also scheduled to dance on the rope. The billing for these wonders was well up to Crummles's standards. The Christmas pantomime, advertised for 'positively the last time' on 11 January 1836, was repeated nine days later and was still being staged in April. The evening of 10 February 1836 was billed as 'positively the last night of this season', but the theatre remained open regularly through to May.[45]

Dickens, based in London, assuredly would have been present at none of these performances, but the type of entertainment advertised was hardly unique to Portsmouth, and from his constant attendance at theatres wherever he went he would have had abundant information on which to base his portrait of the Crummleses, without knowing anything about the Portsmouth theatre in particular. Still, whether or not any of these playbills provided him with specific source materials, they offer a representative sampling of provincial theatrical fare at the time immediately before Dickens wrote *Nickleby*, and they emphasize the extent to which non-dramatic elements dominated the stage of his day.

VI

Not that entertainment of this kind was confined to the provinces or to the minor theatres in London. There was basic consonance between what appeared on the stages of the lesser theatres, of the fairground acting-booths and of the supposedly superior Patent theatres. In the novel, Mr Crummles's prize acquisition during his sojourn in Portsmouth – 'as much talent as was ever compressed into one young person's body' – is Miss Henrietta Petowker, of the Theatre Royal, Drury Lane – and of Mrs Kenwigs's sitting-room. Her celebrity at Drury Lane is not altogether exalted – she 'went on' in the pantomime there – but her *pièce de résistance*, 'The Blood Drinker's Burial', would not have been out of place there. Ostensibly committed to the preservation of England's dramatic heritage, Drury Lane and Covent Garden had by the first decades of the nineteenth century moved substantially in the direction of sensation and spectacle. Under the management of Alfred Bunn, who had control over both the premier metropolitan theatres in the mid-1830s, drama competed with opera, ballet, pantomime and extravaganza for a place on the bills; and, although *divertissement* was less common there than in the minors, lavish outlay on orchestra, scenery, costume and sheer scale of production dictated the emphasis on theatrical display. It was an age of inferior playwriting, great acting, and extraordinary staging. The notorious Licensing Act of 1737 had given Drury Lane and Covent Garden exclusive right to stage spoken drama, a privilege extended later in the eighteenth century to theatres outside London, but by the time Bulwer chaired his Select Committee on theatres in 1832 the distinction between 'legitimate' and 'illegitimate' drama had eroded beyond recognition. The law, in theory designed to ensure the purity of dramatic art, in fact forced the great majority of theatres to develop alternative forms of entertainment, which proved all too popular so far as serious drama was concerned. To compete for audiences the Patent theatres introduced programmes to rival the offerings at minor theatres; the minors responded by developing combinations of spoken drama and music. As historians of the theatre have shown, monopoly was a 'dead letter' for years before it was officially abolished in 1843, and theatricality ruled the day.[46]

Covent Garden and Drury Lane were hardly rural barns, however, and it is important not to conflate the vast differences between theatres. A few penniless strollers with motley costumes, shabby properties and a makeshift stage could not hope to muster entertainment on the same scale as the Patent houses, even if they had the talent to act well, which was not generally the case. The players in *Nickleby* are superior to this; Crummles is no idle vagabond but, as V. C. Clinton-Baddeley has shown, the manager of 'a respectable enterprise', with regular salaries, duties and rules.[47] On the other hand, he lacks altogether the resources to mount a production remotely approaching in stagecraft the costly spectacles which were routinely presented in the big metropolitan theatres. Furthermore, there was fundamental dissimilarity in the degrees of seriousness with which various managers dealt with dramatic production. Macready confided to his diary how profoundly gratified he was when Dickens inscribed *Nickleby* to him, but he would have been incredulous had it been suggested to him that there was nothing to

Sepʳ 11ᵗʰ 1844 by J. FAIRBURN Featherstone St City Rᵈ
Mʳ MACREADY as ROB ROY MACGREGOR.
Jersey. Pubᵈ by G. SKELT. 24, Clearview Sᵗ Saint Helier.

Dickens dedicated *Nicholas Nickleby* to the Eminent Tragedian, depicted here in an attitude typical of nineteenth-century acting style.

choose between Crummles and himself as artists.[48] As manager of Covent Garden between 1837 and 1839, Macready studied playtexts meticulously and attempted to bring the theatre's whole range of capabilities to bear upon each work he produced, in order to realize its dramatic potential as fully as possible; whereas, at the Adelphi, Frederick Yates, and Benjamin Webster after him, concentrated their efforts on lurid melodrama and made their theatre a byword for blood-and-thunder sensationalism. Then, again, in the fairground booth theatres the emphasis fell so completely upon fights, deaths and ghosts that plays as dramatic presentations could scarcely be said to exist at all. Theatricality was the essence of stage production at all theatres, but the sophistication of its implementation and the ends to which it was used varied enormously.

That being said, there was great mobility between theatres. Edward Stirling, for instance, was connected with the Adelphi, Surrey, Marylebone, Strand and Olympic theatres in a short space of years; David Osbaldiston managed the Surrey, Covent Garden, Sadler's Wells, the City of London and the Victoria. Such lists could be multiplied endlessly. Famous actors customarily served their apprenticeships in provincial theatres, and once they were established they were frequently tempted to return to the provinces on tour. As visiting celebrities they enjoyed the right to a clear benefit after only a few days' acting with a local company, and they could make more money in this way than by working for an entire season in London. Moreover, and this is the more important point for understanding the nature of the players in *Nickleby*, there was an extremely close affinity between theatres and other venues of popular entertainment. Michael Baker, in his important study of the emergence of acting as an accepted professional occupation in England, has rightly said that in the nineteenth century 'distinctions between the performing arts were invariably hazy', and there is abundant evidence that individual performers moved freely between theatre, circus and fair.[49] David Prince Miller, for example, who began his life as a showman in the 1820s in the same town in which Nicholas has his adventures with Crummles, was a stage-struck youth who ran away from his situation in a London barrister's office and found work bawling out enticements of a show booth to the crowds at Portsmouth fair. In common with many other performers of the era, including the great Romantic actor Edmund Kean, Miller got his start with the theatre-booth proprietor 'Muster' John Richardson. Kean, whose acting Coleridge compared to 'reading Shakespeare by flashes of lightning', became the most extravagantly admired actor in the history of the English theatre until drink and sexual scandals sent him to an early grave; Miller, after years of touring fairs throughout England and Scotland, for a while ran the Adelphi Theatre in Glasgow, went bankrupt, and became a penny showman again, conducting a magic booth at the fairgrounds. The careers of these two men could hardly contrast more sharply, but the underlying similarity emphasizes how pervasive the connections between fair and theatre were. The man who was first employer to them both was outspoken about the affinity. According to Pierce Egan, Richardson claimed to 'have seen more real talent exhibited at *Feers* than I ever saw at any of the licensed theatres', and always welcomed as 'one of us' any 'hactor' from Covent Garden or Drury Lane who came to see his show.[50] Reciprocally, Drury Lane welcomed showmen to its ranks. As we have already seen, Van Amburgh exhibited his wild beasts there in 1838–9, and Andrew Ducrow, the most famous equestrian entertainer of the century, played to full houses when he took his stud to Drury Lane. Not that showmen were always so successful when they moved into theatres. 'Lord' George Sanger once converted a hall, which had previously been a charnel house, into a theatre with the intention of putting on a pantomime, but the show closed when it was discovered that the bodies had been left behind, under the very spot where Sanger had erected his stage.[51]

The great similarity, even identity, of the kinds of entertainment to be found in theatres, streets, tents and halls enabled many performers to shift from one venue to another with frequency and ease. The manager of a giant was as likely to place him on the stage of a theatre as to exhibit him on his own in a fair booth; a tumbler might go through his routine as the sole attraction of a one-man show or serve his turn as one in a series of performers appearing in a lengthy circus or theatre programme. Strolling players, when they did not have an engagement in a theatre, would hire a room in a public house and put on a show known as 'gagging'. One actor, speaking from personal experience, described the practice as follows:

> Nothing is so common with actors who may be engaged in a large market-town at the close of a season, as, in the interregnum which generally occurs before the manager is ready to open the next theatre on the circuit, for the company to divide and start in little knots to the surrounding villages in order to enliven the rustic inhabitants with all kinds of entertainment. Dancing, spouting, posturing, magic-lanterns, dissolving views, and many other varieties of the means of amusing, are called into active requisition. A successful little tour is sometimes the result, but more frequently the affair is a miserable failure, and ends in debt and disgust.[52]

We never see Crummles actually trying to earn money outside the theatre but, much to the discomfiture of Nicholas, he is not at all averse to showing his skills offstage for practice. When Nicholas is hurrying to catch the London coach he is intercepted by the manager, who clutches him 'in a close and violent embrace', crying ' "Farewell, my noble, my lion-hearted boy!" ' Dickens laconically explains:

> In fact, Mr Crummles, who could never lose any opportunity for professional display, had turned out for the express purpose of taking a public farewell of Nicholas; and to render it the more imposing, he was now, to that young gentleman's most pro-found annoyance, inflicting upon him a rapid succession of stage embraces, which, as everybody knows, are performed by the embracer's laying his or her chin on the shoulder of the object of affection, and looking over it. This Mr Crummles did in the highest style of melodrama, pouring forth at the same time all the most dismal forms of farewell he could think of, out of the stock pieces. (*NN*, 30)

It is the unaffected heartiness with which Mr Crummles indulges in histrionic display which gives him his lovable charm. For all his vulgarity, the old ham is utterly without guile, and his evident enjoyment in his own performance contributes significantly to ours. He is taking leave of Nicholas in a professional capacity, and the presence of a knot of spectators, laughing appreciatively, under-lines the nature of the incident as a public performance. The humour of scenes such as this derives from Dickens's joke that grandiloquent stage gesture accurately conveys real emotion, a joke which is improved by our clear awareness that the posturing is not false, only extravagantly inflated. Crummles is a showman through and through, and part of the authenticity with which he is portrayed centres on the fact that he does not confine his acting to the stage. This is a function of Dickens's characterization of him, but it is also a reflection of historical fact. Popular entertainment was not compart-mentalized into wholly separate and distinct categories, but flowed easily into any location in which it was possible for an entertainer to provide amusement.

Above all, the versatile and eclectic nature of popular enter-tainment meant that people earning a living in ways which for us today would seem to have little in common were actually engaged in closely related activities. Cheap Jacks sang out lively patter and performed conjuring tricks in order to attract customers to buy their wares; travelling from fair to fair and setting up their stalls alongside the entertainment booths, they were themselves as much showmen as the exhibitors of freaks and the barkers at the fairground theatres.[53] As we shall see when we come to *Hard Times*, circus performers had to count acting among their skills, because equestrian drama was a central feature of the nineteenth-century circus. Sleary produces plays as well as exhibiting animals, clowns and acrobats; and, just as the circus in *Hard Times* partakes of the theatre, so, too, the theatre in *Nicholas Nickleby* has explicit links with the circus and fair. Sleary and Crummles have far closer affinities than most modern commentators of Dickens have appreciated.

Once again, it is important not to conflate differences. There was a strong sense of hierarchy among showmen, who were distinguishable, for a start, by the mode of transportation they adopted. The man who drove a gig was clearly superior to the owner of a wagon or cart, and all of them were socially and financially above the wretch who depended upon his own feet to get from one place of entertainment to another. This mode of differentiation serves to date the period with which we are dealing; once cheap railway travel became widespread, the old patterns of itinerant entertainment were radically altered. Crummles's status, as an aristocrat among itinerants, is indicated by the phaeton which he drives. Actors generally were considered the élite of the profession. In a retrospective article on strolling players published in *All the Year Round* two years after Dickens's death, the distinction was made between the performers in acting-booths and all other fairground showmen; the actors constituted 'almost a distinct class'.[54] At the same time, the common people in search of amusement were not concerned with any pecking order among entertainers, save when it made a difference to their own pockets. Anyone who came to town offering novelty and diversion was a showman. The stroller James Glass Bertram, who contributed articles on the circus to *All the Year Round* and, under the pseudonym of Peter Paterson, wrote a valuably circumstantial memoir which he dedicated to Dickens, is authoritative on this. '"The show-folk"', he stated, 'is the universal name given to all persons connected with exhibitions, no matter whether they are exhibitors of waxwork, shows of wild beasts, or theatrical booths.'[55]

Vincent Crummles fits into this category of entertainer. As the manager of a company of players who perform drama in a theatre, he is of course a member of the acting profession and must be considered as such. But he is also a showman, and to ignore this fact, as it has been customary for virtually every commentator on *Nicholas Nickleby* to do, is to misrepresent what Dickens is doing in the novel.[56] It conceives of Crummles's activities too narrowly, and places greater stress on dramatic personation than is consonant with their actual activity in the novel. To recognize the place of the players of *Nickleby* in a context of popular entertainment has three major consequences. First, and most straightforwardly, it enables us to understand properly what they are, and how they relate not just to other characters in Dickens who are actors, but also to the whole gallery of entertainers who appear throughout his work. Second, as we shall proceed to see, it suggests thematic connections beyond role-playing, which link the Crummles episodes with other scenes and characters within the novel. In so loosely coherent a work as *Nickleby* any threads which help to provide unity should not be overlooked. Third, and perhaps most significantly, to see the players as showfolk gives precision in locating the source of their positive vitality. This in turn can help to explain why Nicholas, and his creator as well, feel decidedly uneasy about the Crummleses, and it clarifies a useful landmark in the course of Dickens's development as an artist who was also an entertainer himself.

VII

In the plot of *Nickleby*, the players are distinctly isolated from most of the other characters. Like Squeers, Crummles gives Nicholas employment in a setting remote from London, but when Squeers comes to the metropolis he interacts with many personages in the book's cast, whereas Crummles is seen in London by Nicholas alone. Besides Smike, the only character from outside their immediate circle of companions and patrons to encounter the Crummleses is Mr Lillyvick; Miss Petowker, Mr Snittle Timberry and the African Swallower are all fellow-professionals. The actors have no contact whatever with either the book's villains or its good characters, and thus stand outside the central moral framework. In *Oliver Twist* the isolation of the criminal underworld from Brownlow and the May-lies, with only the hero moving between them, is a method of enforcing that novel's moral polarities, but in *Nickleby* the interaction between Ralph, Squeers, Hawk and Gride on the one hand and the Nicklebys and Cheerybles on the other establishes a different method of moral coding, from which the Crummleses are removed. Alternatively, in *Hard Times* Sleary's circus is a grouping alien to the Coketown dignitaries, but their isolation is presented as an appalling absence from the lives of the main characters. In *Nickleby* the hero meets the players and moves on, without significantly advancing the central action, such as it is, of the novel.

The actors are not, however, the only entertainers to appear in *Nickleby*. In the course of the novel Dickens provides glimpses of a variety of street people whose business is amusement. In Westminster, outside the office of Mr Gregsbury, MP, 'all the livelong day there is a grinding of organs and clashing and clanging of little boxes of music' (*NN*, 16) – fit accompaniment, Dickens makes clear, for the shabby legislators who reside there. Elsewhere, there are a balladsinger, whom Nicholas notices as he is returning to London from Portsmouth (*NN*, 32), and, in Clerkenwell, Punch and Judy showmen and stilt-dancers, whose fascinations detain the delivery boy charged with conveying the hat of Tim Linkinwater's sister to the house of the Cheerybles (*NN*, 37). Golden Square, home of Ralph Nickleby, is a quarter full of lodging-houses for musical foreigners. In contrast to the tight-fisted miser, who plots his secret villainies in this precinct, other residents go about their activities openly and noisily:

> . . . the notes of pianos and harps float in the evening time round the head of the mournful statue, the guardian genius of a little wilderness of shrubs, in the centre of the square. On a summer's night, windows are thrown open, and groups of swarthy mustachioed men are seen by the passer-by lounging at the casements and smoking fearfully. Sounds of gruff voices practising vocal music invade the evening's silence; and the fumes of choice tobacco scent the air. There, snuff and cigars, and German pipes and flutes, and violins and violoncellos, divide the supremacy between them. It is the region of song and smoke. Street bands are on their mettle in Golden Square; and itinerant glee-singers quaver involuntarily as they raise their voices within its boundaries.   (*NN*, 2)

Dickens makes no suggestion that the music is anything other than cacophony, and the inappropriateness of such a place for business serves as an implicit gloss on Ralph's character. The musicians are inoffensive in themselves, but no respectable gentleman would reside here.

Other entertainment is mentioned in conversation by the book's characters, and the very casualness of their references indicates that showfolk and exhibitions are entirely familiar to them. Mrs Nickleby, for example, at one point recalls that shortly before Nicholas was born she was startled by an Italian image-boy in Stratford, who gave her such a fright that '"it was quite a mercy . . . that my son didn't turn out to be a Shakespeare, and what a dreadful thing that would have been!"' (*NN*, 27). Elsewhere she mentions the Thirsty (i.e., Fasting) Woman of Tutbury, the Cock Lane Ghost, and the pig-faced lady (*NN*, 49). All of these were famous curiosities long since exposed as fraudulent: around the time Dickens was born Mrs Ann Moore of Tutbury attracted attention for her extended fasts, which were discovered to have been secretly broken to keep her alive; the Cock Lane Ghost was an eighteenth-century sensation mentioned by Boswell, in which mysterious rappings were found to emanate not from a spirit but from the 11-year-old daughter of the house's owner; the pig-faced lady was a common fairground exhibit, created by shaving a bear, tying it upright in a chair and dressing it in women's clothing.[57] By sprinkling Mrs Nickleby's speech with references to bizarre exhibitions Dickens extends the mixture of historical fact and complete invention which constitutes her sublimely inane chatter. Miss LaCreevy once compares Mrs Nickleby to a high-wire acrobat because of her 'grand and mysterious' manner (*NN*, 31); Lord Verisopht at first supposes Kate is a waxwork model, so perfect is her beauty (*NN*, 19); and Squeers, after being apprehended by the police for his part in Ralph's machinations, curses Peg Sliderskew, '"who I wish was dead and buried, and resurrected and dissected and hung upon wires in a anatomical museum, before I'd had anything to do with her"' (*NN*, 60).

Moreover, Dickens as narrator invokes entertainment on a number of occasions in comparisons to describe people and places in the novel. The house in which Noggs and the Kenwigses live is said to be so crowded that 'it would have been beyond the power of a calculating boy' to discover where a vacant room could be found (*NN*, 14); that is, the problem was too difficult for a child whose arithmetical abilities were so great that he was exhibited as a curiosity. Michael Slater suggests that Dickens may have had in mind George Parker Bidder (1806–78), a mathematically precocious child who was exhibited as 'the calculating phenomenon', but the allusion need not have been so specific; dogs, horses, pigs and humans of 'sagacious' prowess had been on show as curiosities from at least the early eighteenth century.[58] Again, the Wititterlys' establishment in Cadogan Place is compared to a freak-show exhibit; being neither quite fashionable nor altogether unfashionable, Cadogan Place is 'like the ligament which unites the Siamese twins[;] it contains something of the life and essence of two distinct bodies, and yet belongs to neither' (*NN*, 21). The joined twins Eng and Chang were exhibited at the Egyptian Hall in London in 1829.[59] When the police wield their truncheons to keep order at the meeting of the United Metropolitan Improved Hot Muffin and Crumpet Baking and Punctual Delivery Company, their procedure is compared to 'that ingenious actor Mr Punch, whose brilliant example, both in the fashion of his weapons and their use, this branch of the executive occasionally follows' (*NN*, 2). And when Squeers leaps about in ecstasy, thinking the plot to abduct Smike from Nicholas will succeed, his gyrations are spoken of as a 'war dance' (*NN*, 45) –

NOVEMBER. — St Cecilia's Day.

George Cruikshank

Dickens's early works depict London as a place teeming with street entertainment. Note the bill for an Infant Phenomenon in the upper right-hand corner of Cruikshank's engraving.

which in this novel can only refer to the behaviour of stage warriors, such as the Indian Savage depicted by Mr Folair in his balletic *pas de deux* with the Infant Phenomenon. None of these references to popular entertainment is developed beyond a passing allusion, and they do not lead to an exploration of the condition of showmen in the book's social context, as Dickens was to do in his next novel, *The Old Curiosity Shop*. They do, however, serve to keep entertainment before us as a frame of reference, and taken together they carry the strong implication that London is a place teeming with entertainers, as he had shown it to be in *Sketches by Boz*.

The one place of entertainment besides the theatre over which Dickens lingers in *Nicholas Nickleby* is the race meeting at which the growing conflict between Verisopht and Hawk reaches its climax: it is at a gaming-booth at the racecourse that a challenge is given, and in the ensuing duel the young lord loses his life. Dickens depicts the setting as a place where penny showmen congregate, which was historically accurate.[60] Before 1840 courses were not enclosed, and admittance was free; the organizers' costs were defrayed in part by ground rents charged for the numerous booths for food, drink, gambling and exhibitions, which were inextricable components of any race meeting. Newmarket was unusual in that its organizers sought to keep its clientele exclusive, but most meetings were open to anyone who cared to come. With the introduction of Arabian horses in the late seventeenth and early eighteenth centuries, racing had evolved into a highly popular and widely attended spectator sport, but with the wide variety of entertainments available in the booths many amusement-seekers came to the courses who had no interest in the horses at all.

Traditionally race meetings were seen as occasions for the encouragement of social cohesion: frequented by aristocrat and common labourer alike, the racecourse was a place where classes could mingle freely. Pierce Egan, authoritative on this as on so much sport in early nineteenth-century England, considered the turf, along with pugilism, an activity which brought out the best in the English character: to him it was a splendid manifestation of the happy, lively yet peaceable disposition of honest Englishmen. In *The Pilgrims of the Thames* (1837) Egan introduces a figure named Charles Turf, Esq., who praises King William IV for his keen interest in racing and explains that ' "from having obtained a thorough knowledge of the people – mixing with them – participating in their habits – and hearing their opinions on the laws and government, in propria persona" ', the king had gained ' "a thorough knowledge of the feelings of his people" '. His companion, Frank Flourish, responds that from such knowledge in a sovereign flow better government, truer liberty and ' "greater portion of happiness enjoyed by all ranks

of society"'.[61] Such a view was intensely conservative: it depended
on traditional notions of rank, patronage and example-setting; on
the desire to preserve old customs and old values; and on a belief that
the social function of the holiday atmosphere, rather than economic
considerations, was the heart of horse racing.

In *Nickleby* Dickens challenged central axioms of this traditionalist
ideal, and in the view of modern social historians he was correct in
his assessment. Sport, like so much else in English society at this
time, was being radically altered, to a great extent by the coming of
the railway. In the course of a few years race meetings changed from
almost wholly local occasions to truly national events. The railway
enabled owners to move their horses quickly and comfortably to
meetings far removed from their stables, and it brought spectators as
well from much greater distances. But even without this transformation there was much in the old view which was open to
disagreement. Patrons of both high and low rank were present, for
example, but, as Dickens shows, there was not much interchange
over class barriers, and certainly very little which survived beyond
the race day itself. A sign of the gap between ranks is Ralph's taunt
that Noggs, now a tippling clerk of no account, once kept horses of
his own (*NN*, 2). Race meetings were of dubious respectability: in
his study of the social history of the turf Wray Vamplew has concluded that there is 'no hard evidence' that the middle classes came in
any numbers to the races at this period, and certainly it is hard to
imagine the brothers Cheeryble in attendance here.[62] Instead, as
Dickens shows, the grounds were visited by aristocrats, country
fellows and gipsies. Hawk, patron of the ring and debaucher of the
foolishly wealthy, does not mingle with the lower ranks, and any
example-setting by him is entirely pernicious: in an earlier episode
his contemptuous behaviour leads to a thrashing by Nicholas, which
is promptly celebrated in a ballad circulated 'all over town'
(*NN*, 38), and in the present scene his defiance of Verisopht leads to
drunkenness, death and disgrace. For the humble as well, the recreation at the racecourse is far from innocent: Dickens points out the
dishonest gaming-tables and the thimble-rig man intent on gulling
the unwary. In so far as such a scene is a vestige of the old order, the
sooner it is gone the better.

On the other hand, Dickens is not entirely dismissive in his view
of Hampton. With its juggler, ventriloquist and band, it is also a
picturesque scene, full of colour and animation, and he finds 'a drop
of comfort' in the presence of children there.

> It is a pleasant thing to see that the sun has been there; to know
> that the air and light are on them every day; to feel that they *are*

children, and lead children's lives; that if their pillows be damp, it is with the dews of Heaven, and not with tears: that the limbs of their girls are free, and that they are not crippled by distortions, imposing an unnatural and horrible penance upon their sex; that their lives are spent, from day to day, at least among the waving trees, and not in the midst of dreadful engines which make young children old before they know what childhood is, and give them the exhaustion and infirmity of age, without, like age, the privilege to die. God send that old nursery tales were true, and gipsies stole such children by the score!   (*NN*, 50)

This is a view which Dickens repeats in his next novel, when the sanctimonious Monflathers accuses Nell of 'wickedness' for finding employment in the waxwork rather than assisting in the manufactures of the country (*OCS*, 31). In fact, as Dickens makes clear, Nell's position with Mrs Jarley affords her comforts greater than she is ever to enjoy again, until her grandfather's gambling mania forces her to flee once more. The gambling, dishonesty and violence of the racing episode in *Nickleby* make it emphatic that any choice to seek real pleasure here is an act of desperation. It is a scene of too much vice and corruption to provide healthy relaxation and release.

The races at Hampton stand in stark contrast to the innocent and happy entertainments in Portsmouth, and, combined with the passing references to exhibitions and showfolk which we have noted above, they establish a wider context of amusements in the novel than the Crummleses alone provide. This context is, however, too random and undeveloped to be called a unifying pattern, and it is far removed from the central organizing symbols of the fog and the prison which distinguish later novels. It also lacks the comprehensiveness of the circus imagery in *Hard Times*, which, as we shall see in Chapter 5, permeates that novel in systematic complexity. Forster praised *Nickleby* for having a 'better laid design' than its predecessors, but the plot is in fact no more than loosely episodic, and occasional recent claims to find close thematic counterpoint between adventures have been unconvincing.[63] Of all Dickens's novels *Nicholas Nickleby* is closest in structure to the works of Smollett, combining seriousness and entertainment in broadly contrasting episodes: the hero travels north to a scene of cruelty and confinement on his first journey, and after an interlude in London he takes a second journey in the opposite direction to the south, where he finds expansiveness and generosity. The isolation of the Portsmouth scenes is diminished by the presence of other instances of popular entertainment, which add colour and liveliness, and give the novel somewhat greater coherence that it would have without this wider frame of reference. But the achievement of *Nicholas Nickleby* does not reside in its unity, and the context of amusements serves principally to extend and clarify our understanding of the nature of the theatre episodes in the novel.

VIII

Dickens introduces Crummles into the novel in emphatically favourable terms. After his unhappy experiences with Squeers and Ralph, Nicholas sets off with Smike to make a new start, and the buoyancy of his hopes is explicitly signalled by a change in the weather. It was cold and foggy in London as they left, but once they are headed for Portsmouth the conditions improve:

> . . . although a dense vapour still enveloped the city they had left, as if the very breath of its busy people hung over their schemes of gain and profit and found greater attraction there than in the quiet region above, in the open country it was clear and fair . . . A broad, fine, honest sun lighted up the green pastures and dimpled water, with the semblance of summer, while it left the travellers all the invigorating freshness of that early time of year. The ground seemed elastic under their feet; the sheep-bells were music to their ears; and exhilarated by exercise, and stimulated by hope, they pushed onward with the strength of lions. (*NN*, 22)

Here, as so often in the novel, Dickens uses in all seriousness precisely the same theatrical hyperbole which appears so preposterously inflated when spoken by the actors: where Crummles's farewell of Nicholas as 'my lion-hearted boy' is presented satirically as a stage cliché, here the 'strength of lions' is offered as a genuine compliment. Critics complain that such writing is empty theatrical rhetoric which exposes Dickens's lack of control in this novel, and no doubt *Nicholas Nickleby* is less finely honed that later works. But it is also possible to argue that Dickens's serious use of such language works in just the opposite way, as a means of reinforcing the honest attitudes of the players. *Nickleby* does not achieve the stylistic excellence of Dickens's maturity, but the rhetoric of the stage has its own positive functions, both in the mouths of the book's actors and in the voice of the narrator.

After this auspicious start, Nicholas and Smike reach the inn outside Portsmouth where they meet Vincent Crummles. The manager cordially invites Nicholas to share a bowl of punch and tactfully offers him gainful employment. The entertainer's business is to provide pleasure, and Crummles's generosity to Nicholas contrasts sharply with his treatment by Squeers. It is interesting to observe that Nicholas does not actively seek out the actors; when he meets Mr Crummles he has no intention of taking to the stage, or even of going to see a play. Instead, just as Nell comes into contact with Short and Jarley, so Nicholas gravitates with seeming inevitability into the protection of the showfolk. Again like Nell, Nicholas appears to have a natural affinity with the entertainers: he quickly adapts to their lifestyle and becomes himself a principal attraction of the show. In this regard Nell and Nicholas differ from Mr Pickwick and from the narrator in *Sketches by Boz*, both of whom eagerly look for ways to indulge their curiosity; instead, Nicholas and Nell passively allow themselves to be looked after by the showfolk. Crummles recognizes Nicholas's suitability for inclusion in the ranks of the players from the first moment he sees him, and when Nicholas announces his intention of departing the manager dispassionately judges the signs of impatience as a superior display of acting.

'Dear me, dear me,' said Mr Crummles, looking wistfully towards the point at which he had just disappeared; 'if he only acted like that, what a deal of money he'd draw!' (*NN*, 30)

The notion that Nicholas belongs 'naturally' among the players takes us to the heart of their significance in *Nickleby*. Nicholas is promptly accepted by the members of the company as one of themselves, and although professional jealousy generates rivalry from Lenville and Folair the tension is released comically, and Crummles speaks truly when he says, '"We were a very happy little company . . . You and I never had a word"' (*NN*, 48). Nicholas works diligently, cons his lines readily, and when he writes the play commissioned by the manager it is a decided hit. He wins applause for his performance on the stage, and he is equally adept at dealing with his theatrical companions outside working-hours. Although he is indignant at Lenville's impertinence of offering to pull his nose, Nicholas enacts a scenario of his own when he defies the tragedian before the assembled company and knocks him down. His bow to the spectators after the confrontation shows clearly his consciousness that the action has been a performance. He is never more one of them than in this episode.

'Natural' acting was a key term in theatre criticism from long before the nineteenth century, and the players in *Nickleby* take great satisfaction in the lifelikeness of their productions. We see an example of this when Nicholas describes the principal role in the new melodrama to Mr Lenville.

> 'You are troubled with remorse till the last act, and then you make up your mind to destroy yourself. But just as you are raising the pistol to your head, a clock strikes – ten.'
> 'I see', cried Mr Lenville. 'Very good'.
> 'You pause', said Nicholas; 'you recollect to have heard a clock strike ten in your infancy. The pistol falls from your hand – you are overcome – you burst into tears, and become a virtuous and exemplary character for ever afterwards.'
> 'Capital!' said Mr Lenville: 'that's a sure card, a sure card. Get the curtain down with a touch of nature like that, and it'll be a triumphant success.'   (*NN*, 24)

The basic implausibility of the scenes which the actors consider true to life is, as Michael Slater suggests, the source of hilarity, but the joke has point as well.[64] Just as Dickens's methods of comic characterization attribute essential significance to external appearance, so, too, acting practice of the age was based on the audience's acceptance of gesture as a true expression of inner disposition. Rede's *Road to the Stage* contains a lengthy section devoted to laying down precise rules by which the passions are to be represented. For example:

> *Fear*, violent and sudden, opens the eyes and mouth very wide, draws down the eyebrows, gives the countenance an air of wildness, draws back the elbows parallel with the sides, lifts up the open hand (the fingers together) to the height of the breast, so that the palms face the dreadful object, as shields opposed to it . . . *Death* is exhibited by violent distortion, groaning, gasping for breath, stretching the body, raising it, and then letting it fall; dying in a chair, as is often practised in some characters, is very unnatural, and has little or no effect.[65]

And so on, and on. The underlying assumption of such prescriptions is that stereotyped expression creates an objective manifestation of human emotion. The acting was considered natural because it was an imitation of agreed exterior signs of feelings.[66] It is easy for us today to ridicule the large gestures and stilted poses, but Edmund Kean, who carefully preconceived each movement he made on the stage, dazzled the best dramatic critics of the age. Great acting was one of the triumphs of the nineteenth-century theatre, and it is well to remind ourselves frequently that *Nicholas Nickleby* was dedicated to the foremost player of the day. Dickens's satire is directed not merely at bad acting, but at acting which abuses the foundations upon which the performing style of the age was built. He was not to challenge these preconceptions seriously until *Great Expectations*, in which Pip learns through hard experience that he must move beyond categorizing people by their exteriors. Magwitch, Miss Havisham and Trabb's boy all enter the novel as exuberantly 'Dickensian' characters, identified by boldly conceived outward signs, but their appearances belie their true natures, and Pip must look beneath surfaces to see them properly. *Great Expectations* is a joyously theatrical book which radically undermines the theatrical conception of character.

In *Nickleby* these assumptions are still intact, and it is only their abuse which is ridiculed. The acting of the Crummleses is of a sort that Partridge in *Tom Jones* would have approved. In that novel, so beloved by Dickens, Tom, having been to see Garrick as Hamlet, asks his companion which of the players he liked best.

> To this he answered, with some appearance of indignation at the question, 'the king without doubt.' 'Indeed, Mr Partridge', says Mrs Miller, 'you are not of the same opinion with the town; for they are all agreed, that Hamlet is acted by the best player who was ever on the stage.' 'He the best player!' cried Partridge, with a contemptuous sneer. 'Why I could act as well as he myself. I am sure if I had seen a ghost, I should have looked in the very same manner, and done just as he did. And then, to be sure, in that scene, as you called it, between him and his mother, where you told me he acted so fine, why Lord help me, any man, that is any good man, that had had such a mother, would have done exactly the same. I know that you are only joking with me; but indeed, madam, though I was never at a play in London, yet I have seen acting before in the country; and the King for my money; he speaks all his words distinctly, half as loud again as the other. – Anybody may see he is an actor.' (*Tom Jones*, bk 16, ch. 5)

Through Fielding's irony, Partridge's remarks on Garrick and the king offer a radically different view of what was 'natural' on the stage, and they are worth noting here because in *Nickleby* Dickens considers this alternative conception of acting as well as the theory of performance as imitation. Because nineteenth-century acting in general was so stylized and rule-bound, there was a clear opportunity for acting which could be thought of as instinctive and untutored to find favour, and it was an opportunity which the promoters of child prodigies exploited. When Master Betty created a sensation in London in 1804–5 he was hailed as the re-embodiment of Garrick. The novelty of his youth was thought by those who were seriously impressed with him to be less important than his innate genius, which could only express itself more fully as he grew older.[67] The appeal of the Infant Roscius grew out of the attitudes towards childhood given currency by Rousseau, a point of view deeply congenial to Dickens and one which, as we have seen, coloured his approach to popular entertainment to a very considerable degree. The craze for Master Betty lasted only a single season, several years before Dickens was born, but the youth eked out a career in the provinces living off his earlier reputation, and the vogue for Infant Phenomena continued unabated for decades. Whatever the particular influence on Dickens's imagination Jean Davenport may or may not have had, it was from this wider context of the celebration of childhood that his own Phenomenon emerged. Once again, as towards the pretence of 'natural' acting by Mr Lenville, Dickens's attitude is one of amused ridicule. Vincent Crummles promoted his daughter as a genuine child prodigy, but we see enough of her behaviour offstage to recognize that she is a very ordinary child.

> The phenomenon was rather a troublesome companion, for first the right sandal came down, and then the left, and these mischances being repaired, one leg of the little white trousers was discovered to be longer than the other; besides these accidents, the green parasol was dropped down an iron grating, and only fished up again, with great difficulty and by dint of much exertion. (*NN*, 24)

Although the puffing by her father and the jealousy of Mr Folair create a smokescreen, it is clear enough that the talents of Ninetta Crummles fall well short of the phenomenal. Her childishness is innate, but her genius is the fond invention of her father.

Dickens's marvellously comic portrayals of the actors in *Nickleby*, then, not merely satirize the individual foibles of theatrical types, but also probe the excesses of two major contemporary theories of acting. From neither perspective does he accept uncritically the notion that their performances are 'natural', but the term is still pertinent to them, because beneath the posturing they are figures of instinctive warmth, generosity and kindness. Nicholas has an affinity with them not because of the way they act, but because of what they are. They represent the positive side of the old values which Dickens viewed with the most limited favour in the racecourse episode. Their company, like many of the declining circuit system, was a family enterprise, and Dickens focuses on their mutual affection and self-support, rather than upon the commercial basis of their activity. Whereas the big metropolitan theatres required large capital investment to support their hundreds of employees and to create the costly spectacle with which they attracted audiences, a small touring company was only a remove above the old-fashioned solitary showman travelling the countryside with his wife and children. Some provincial managers built and owned the theatres in which their companies performed, but Crummles's concern is more modest than this, for he merely leases the Portsmouth theatre for the duration of his visit there. Although he is dependent upon hard-won patronage, he makes a sufficient living to be able to afford passage across the Atlantic. Self-sufficient, loving, and taking great pleasure in the amusement they provide, the Crummleses are truly fit companions for the hero of a novel by Dickens. Their values of family loyalty and respect for tradition are precisely those which Nicholas affirms at the end of the novel, when he returns to the country home which had been his father's before him. His friendship with the players is consonant with his fondest hopes.

IX

Nevertheless, Nicholas is decidedly uneasy about his connection with the players. Immediately upon meeting Crummles he adopts a pseudonym, and although respectable aspirants to the stage often disguised their identity (T. D. Davenport, for example, had been plain Thomas Donald before he became an actor) the frequency of the practice in no way lessens Nicholas's individual determination to prevent his involvement with the theatre from becoming known. Once having joined the company he decides to 'postpone reflection' lest he find himself unable to square his position with his self-esteem (*NN*, 23), and writing to Noggs from Portsmouth he makes 'no mention' of his employment with the actors (*NN*, 29). When Mr Lenville and Mr Folair call upon him in his room the morning after he arrives, Nicholas considers their social visit an intrusion and congratulates himself when he has 'got rid of' them (*NN*, 24). He adopts an attitude of condescending superiority to the players' innocent pretensions, and on more than one occasion laughs outright at their notions of impressive deportment. On hearing from Noggs that he is needed in London, Nicholas chastises himself for 'fooling' in Portsmouth for so long, and he salves his conscience by telling himself that he had remained 'for the best and sorely against my will' (*NN*, 30). Even after he has been long removed from the

MARCH — Theatrical fun-dinner.

George Cruikshank

Dickens created much comedy by means of the proposition that role-playing spilled off the stage into non-professional areas of life.

players and has fleetingly rediscovered them on the eve of their emigration, Nicholas prefers 'the cool air and twilight out of doors' to the 'hot and glaring theatre' (*NN*, 48). Nicholas may be a congenial member of the company so far as Crummles is concerned, but in his own eyes his gambit on the stage is decidedly compromising.

There are several explanations why Nicholas feels ill at ease. Most simply, it is a matter of inexperience. He has no previous knowledge of the theatre and is uncertain what to expect as each new duty confronts him. His ignorance of theatrical activities means that he must be told at each point what is going on about him, and this is hard on his self-esteem, but it is a valuable narrative strategy which enables Dickens easily to introduce information as to why stage combatants must differ in size, what a bespeak is, how a play can be quickly written, and why Mr Lenville issues his challenge. Nicholas is also wary on account of his earlier adventure at Dotheboys Hall. Having misunderstood Fanny Squeers's advances and carelessly responded to Tilda Price's charms, he is on his guard afterwards, lest he compromise himself again. Like Fanny, Miss Snevellicci makes a play for Nicholas, and she has the gaiety and good looks which Fanny so conspicuously lacks. Nicholas is attracted to the actress, and with coaxing he enters into cheerful companionship with her, but he firmly rejects any serious flirtation.

A more considerable motive for Nicholas's sense of distance from the actors is his class-consciousness.[68] Requiring no recognized educational training for their activity, and providing no obviously utilitarian function in society, actors were traditionally treated as outcasts, and an actress was widely held to be little more than a prostitute. Macready's diaries are full of lamentations over the lack of social esteem which he can command, and the status of the actor at this time is tellingly signalled by the incident in *Pickwick* in which Dr Slammer refuses to duel with Jingle upon learning that his antagonist is a lowly stroller. In an age when massive economic expansion was transforming the basis of individual wealth and creating fortunes for men of lowly origins, social respectability was an acutely live issue for the Victorians, and one which their novelists pondered deeply. Class is a particularly prominent concern in *Nickleby*, moving as it does between Cadogan Place and the City, Golden Square and the East End. Throughout the novel Nicholas is concerned to maintain his dignity as the son of a gentleman, and he has more than a touch of snobbery to him. Unlike *Hard Times*, in which Sleary's moral integrity accords to him a position of superiority over the more conventionally respectable citizens of Coketown, and unlike *Great Expectations*, in which class is an issue subjected to radically searching analysis, class in *Nicholas Nickleby* is largely a matter of unconsidered prejudice against the idle aristocrat, the social climber – and the strolling player. Neither Nicholas nor Dickens gives Crummles full credit for the excellence of his personal qualities, and it is a disturbing limitation of this novel that a lack of polite airs should be held against the manager. It is a measure of the rapidity with which Dickens's vision matured during the first years of his career that such careless acceptance of class conventions was never to be repeated in his fiction again.

On the other hand, Nicholas had reason besides mere snobbery for wishing to leave Crummles behind. When he prepares to depart for London, Nicholas chides himself for having 'dallied too long' in Portsmouth (*NN*, 30), and from what we have already seen of the characteristics of nineteenth-century theatre it is clear that this charge of triviality has substance. With the playtext treated as a vehicle for stagecraft and coherent production sacrificed for stunning effects, it was commonplace for observers to speak of the decline of the drama. A variety of causes were proposed: theatre licensing was too strict, or not strict enough; playwrights were neglectful of great models, or unduly reliant upon them. All commentators were agreed, however, that the theatre had a lamentable tendency to be turned into an exhibition-hall for idle amusement.[69] Mr Curdle, the 'very profound and most original thinker' canvassed by Nicholas and Miss Snevellicci for her bespeak, expresses the opinion of the age when he simpers, ' "The drama is gone, perfectly gone" ' (*NN*, 24). Despite its currency, such a view is misleading, because, as Michael Booth rightly insists, it places too narrow an emphasis on plays as dramatic literature, and fails to register that the theatre was generating 'a visual excitement, a mechanical ingenuity, and a sense of theatrical effect not known on the English stage before or since'.[70] On the other hand, Crummles is portrayed as one of the lesser lights of the theatre, and although an evening spent in the presence of his players would have been uproarious fun it would not have inspired much conviction of the ennobling characteristics of dramatic art.

The situation of the drama was not one to foster careful playwriting. Nicholas is hired to pillage French plays and adapt them to the special circumstances of Crummles's company, and in fact authors like Fitzball, Moncrieff and Á Beckett churned out stageable hack work at a prodigious rate by this method. Playwrights of higher aspiration constructed inert imitations of classical tragedy, like Talfourd, or untheatrical closet drama, like Browning, but the hopes of contemporary critics for drama of lasting merit went unfulfilled. The frustrations for the intelligent actor were considerable, and are neatly symbolized by the antagonism between the 'eminent tragedian' Macready and the theatrical entrepreneur Bunn. Macready wished to realize on stage the full glory of English drama, whereas Bunn wanted to fill his houses with paying customers. When they worked together at Drury Lane in 1836 the tensions ran high, and one evening, humiliated at being cast in a truncated version of *Richard III*, Macready physically assaulted the manager backstage. This act of tragic desperation promptly collapsed into farce as Macready, still clad in the hump for his stage role as Richard, accused the manager of ruining him, while Bunn, crying 'Murder!', grasped the actor's little finger between his teeth until rescue arrived.[71] Even off the stage, drama gave way to extravagant gesture when actors were involved. Mr Lenville's marvellously absurd altercation with Nicholas was not without precedent in real life.

A further aspect of the 'decline of the drama' was the changing composition of audiences who attended the theatre. The concentration of population in rapidly expanding urban centres created a new pool of potential spectators, cut off from their rural, participatory amusements and eager for relief from the squalor of the cities. Although the Portsmouth theatre depended to an unusual extent on patronage from the officers of the army and navy (because of the large military presence there), the community at large more than doubled in population between 1801, when the census recorded 33,226 people living in Portsmouth and Portsea, and 1851, when the figure was 72,096.[72] At the same time, sharpening class antagonisms led to a decline in theatre patronage by the upper classes, and the grudging attitude of the respectable Mr Curdle, who short-changes Miss Snevellicci by sixpence when she is canvassing for her bespeak, is an accurate reflection of the loss of moneyed support which was putting theatres in parlous financial situations throughout the period.

There were a number of reasons in the late 1830s, then, for misgivings about the state of the theatre, and Dickens touches on them in accounting for his hero's lack of wholehearted commitment to the Crummleses. Nevertheless, these explanations are inadequate when placed beside the reality of the players as they actually appear in the novel. The drama may very well have been in decline, but Crummles emphatically is not. He successfully adapts to conditions of the day, and unlike Jingle and Codlin he makes a good living; he drives a phaeton, pays his players, and offers Nicholas financial incentives to remain with the company. Although he reserves pride of place for his own family, he exudes confidence in the abilities of all his players, and he takes frank delight in the entertainment which they create. It is a sign of his contentment and of his confidence for the future that, in our last view of the players before they sail to the

New World, we learn that Mrs Crummles is expecting another child.

But despite the positive virtues of the players and their ability to maintain themselves by working as entertainers Dickens deports Crummles out of England before the novel is ended. It is true that the search for new horizons in America was a frequent – and frequently prosperous – venture by English actors. It is also true that T. D. Davenport sailed with his wife and daughter in the steamer *Sirius* from Cork twelve months before Crummles made his final appearance in *Nicholas Nickleby*. I have not traced any notice in the theatrical press announcing Davenport's departure, and one later account of his career claims that he left suddenly, without premeditation, on learning of a berth available in the ship he took, but it is altogether possible that a puff such as the ones Crummles shows Nicholas did in fact give Dickens the idea of sending his strollers abroad, to wind up this portion of the story.[73]

Reasons do not make good excuses, however, and in the structure of the novel Crummles's departure signifies his dismissal. In so loosely organized a book as *Nicholas Nickleby* one must not make too much of this, but the fact remains that in the end the players are inappropriately rejected. They have generosity and honesty which contrast boldly with the characteristics of the book's villains, and when they are compared to the characters whom Nicholas actually does espouse the players' virtues become the more evident. Both the Cheerybles and the Crummleses work in the world without being corrupted by it; both show kindness to Nicholas and give him employment. But, as every reader of the novel knows, the Cheerybles are empty ciphers, cloyingly sentimentalized and utterly unbelievable. The Crummleses, with their petty vanities, harmless jealousies, and uncritical indulgence in histrionic excess, have a complexity and depth of characterization altogether lacking in the Cheerybles.

Moreover, in the zest, humour and imagination which are manifest not simply in their acting but in their lifestyle as entertainers, they have positive attributes which the Cheerybles – and Nicholas – sorely lack. In her brilliant analysis of *David Copperfield*, Q. D. Leavis says of Mr Micawber that he is 'witness to a pre-Victorian enjoyment of living that Dickens indignantly saw being destroyed by the Murdstones and the Littimers;' and she goes on to propose that with his 'contempt for the morrow, faith in the future and enjoyment of the present' he has essential attributes of the creative mind.[74] The same claim can, and should, be made for Mr Crummles. His vulgar creativity, although far inferior to Dickens's own, taps the same roots which nurture Dickens's imagination. Crummels has the priceless imprudence which is the healthy antidote to a vacuous heroine and a too-earnest hero.[75] Nicholas could hardly be expected to marry Miss Snevellicci and remain an actor for ever, but he could emphatically do with a bit more of the robust, outgoing good-nature and carefree indulgence in pleasure which characterize the players.

In the final analysis, the rejection of Crummles is consonant with his isolation from the rest of the book. It is likely, as many critics have suggested, that Dickens had no thought of introducing the players when he began writing this serial novel; certainly they do not appear in the wrapper illustration. *Nicholas Nickleby* gives the strong impression that Dickens has not integrated Crummles more fully into the book because he had not altogether decided what to do with him. This impression is reinforced by the fact that one of the central issues to which he turned his attention in his next novel was precisely what entertainers and entertainment had to do with the sort of novel he wanted to write. The very lack of systematic thematic function for the players allows Dickens to present them in abundant detail, with a clear eye on their limitations as well as on their virtues. It gives them a historical accuracy and a fictional complexity considerably greater than is to be found in the picture of Sleary's circus, in which thematic purpose simplifies and idealizes the raw materials on which those entertainers are based. In *Nicholas Nickleby* the actors do not contribute significantly to an overall design, but they stand out in a glorious fragment, conceived in love and portrayed in zestful vitality.

CHAPTER 4

The Old Curiosity Shop
The Assessment of
Popular Entertainment

The Saints are endeavouring to put down that ancient City
Festival, Bartholomew Fair . . . To what a state would some
morbid philosophers reduce the people of England, once merry
England . . . It affords, once a year, harmless recreation for the
people, and promotes mirth and good humour. Are the poor
and industrious classes never to smile?

Press cutting dated 28 June 1840[1]

I

In July 1840, just one year after the publication of Chapter 48 of
Nicholas Nickleby, in which Nicholas bade a final farewell to the
strolling player Vincent Crummles, Dickens once more sent the
protagonist of one of his stories among a group of showfolk.
Chapter 16 of *The Old Curiosity Shop* introduces a new series of
adventures with entertainment figures and sets the tone for the most
important presentation of popular entertainment in all of Dickens's
fiction. Little Nell, fleeing with her grandfather from their home in
London and heading she knows not whither, stumbles upon the
puppet-exhibitors Codlin and Short among the gravestones of a
country churchyard, and for the next few days she travels in company with the Punch and Judy men meeting a variety of itinerant
showfolk along the way. For Nell the entertainers constitute both a
refuge and a threat; and, unable to find lasting security either with
Codlin or subsequently with Mrs Jarley, she moves on to her
inexorable doom. Popular entertainment in *The Old Curiosity Shop* is
thus presented in a context of flight, oppression and death, as Dickens surveys the decline of traditional rural amusements which he
cherished.

As subject-matter alone, scenes and characters from the entertainment world fill the novel with curiosities and make it an invaluable document about the state of popular amusements of the day. Dickens offers visits to a country race meeting and to a metropolitan circus, and he assembles a representative sampling of kinds of entertainer who were to be found in early nineteenth-century England: vignettes of itinerant showmen, including stilt-walkers, performing dogs, conjurors, freaks, exhibitors and various hangers-on; and fuller sketches of Punch and Judy operators and of a travelling waxworks proprietor. Besides their value as social history, these characters enter Dickens's gallery of vivid personalities in their own right, and they function also on the level of plot, variously offering Nell succour, spurring her on her way, and assisting in her escape and rescue. Each of the novel's three central characters is conceived partly in relation to the entertainment world: most obviously Swiveller, whose constant quotation from song and stage and equally frequent transformation of his circumstances into the stuff of blood-and-thunder melodrama make him, a mere enthusiast rather than professional showman, the most entertaining character in the book; but also Quilp, whose folklore origins and affinities with Punch generate much of the complex significance of his character, and Nell, whom Dickens conceived from the outset in juxtaposition to the 'crowd of uncongenial and ancient things'.[2]

Dickens draws on these entertainment materials in developing the themes of *The Old Curiosity Shop*: the precariousness of the showmen's lives emphasizes Nell's plight and contributes to the general concern with the passing of old ways; the financial sharpness of some of them forms part of Dickens's indictment of commercial and economic attitudes; their practices and self-assessments are central to the novel's themes of art and artistry; and the structural deployment of these figures, particularly Swiveller, dramatizes the joyful and life-affirming potential of the creative imagination.

Begun in haste, *The Old Curiosity Shop* retains rough edges which detract from its ultimate achievement as a work of art. As Forster recorded many years later, Dickens wrote it 'with less consciousness of design on his part than I can remember in any other instance throughout his career'.[3] The awkward shift from first- to third-person narration at the end of Chapter 3 and the underemphasis of Richard Swiveller, the character who ultimately carries the weight of the book's positive resolution, are obvious instances of artistic blemish. Additionally, *The Old Curiosity Shop* is the furthest removed of all Dickens's novels from directly mimetic expression. Dickens deliberately blurs precision of time and place, idealizes his heroine, and creates a fantastic ogre for his villain. Fairy-tale motifs, non-realistic details, and a mythic conception of plot and character distance the book from verisimilitude and lift it into an imaginary realm all its own.

The Old Curiosity Shop is nevertheless a highly topical work, one in which Dickens can be seen responding with a sense of urgency to pressing issues of the moment. Topicality is manifest in Nell's glimpse at the torments of the 'Hungry Forties' in Chapter 45, when she passes through the great industrial town, but it is most pervasive in the book's treatment of popular entertainment. The year 1840 was critical in the history of the amusements of the people and was seen as such by observers at the time. *The Old Curiosity Shop*, universally loved or hated as the story of Little Nell, is also the work in which Dickens most fully assesses the condition of England's entertainment and its meaning for his own art as a popular entertainer. In the pages which follow we shall examine the importance of this subject in Dickens's novel, looking in turn at Nell, Quilp and Swiveller, as well as at the showfolk themselves. First, however, we must step back to consider an event which occurred in the summer of 1840, of great moment in the history of English popular entertainment.

II

In the heart of the City of London, in Smithfield, every September from time out of memory great crowds had gathered for a hugely popular annual festivity. Bartholomew Fair, of ancient origin, protected by royal charter, frequented by the foremost showmen of the land, and enjoyed by the humble and the noble alike, was the most notable single instance in England of the living traditions of popular entertainment. Stilt-walkers, jugglers, gingerbread-sellers and exhibitors of freaks made fortunes competing for pennies with the big menageries and theatre booths, and the noise, bustle and confusion had long been thought to epitomize the very nature of the amusements of the people. Celebrated for centuries by the fun-lover and denounced for at least as long by the moralist, Bartholomew Fair seemed an institution of eternal fixity, as secure as the months of the year and the days of the week.[4]

Then, on 7 July 1840, four days before Dickens published the chapter which introduced entertainers into *The Old Curiosity Shop*, the Court of Common Council of the Corporation of the City of London issued a proclamation which stated

That the booths for the exhibition of plays, interludes, panto-

The suppression of Bartholomew Fair was the single most important blow against popular entertainment in the whole of the nineteenth century. It happened in 1840, the year in which Dickens was writing *The Old Curiosity Shop*.

mimes, and all other theatrical representations be henceforth excluded from the fair.[5]

Technically this was no more than one clause in a routine updating of regulations concerning ordinary activities which came under the jurisdiction of the City. The legal status of the fair was unaltered. The civic authorities were fully aware, however, that their action was tantamount to utter suppression, and they acted with that express purpose. There is no evidence to indicate how quickly or in what detail Dickens became aware of this enactment, but it is inconceivable that he was long ignorant of the result, which effectively brought to an inglorious end the most famous of all English fairs.

Bartholomew Fair had been founded in the twelfth century by the monk Rahere, and granted a royal charter by Henry I in 1133. From its very inception, entertainment was a principal attraction of the fair, and its commercial function had virtually ceased by at least 1671, when the City first considered suppression. The fair's reputation as a scene of debauchery and vulgar amusement was already well established by the time Jonson wrote his play about it in 1614, but in the eighteenth century the foremost actors of the land performed in its theatre booths. Gentry, even royalty, frequented Bartholomew Fair in its heyday, between the Restoration and the middle of the eighteenth century. Throughout these years loud calls were made for its suppression, but it took half a century of official action, of riots and deaths to restrict its duration from a fortnight to three days. By the end of the eighteenth century respectable visitors had abandoned the fair to the lower classes, but it remained a lucrative field for showmen. George Daniel offers the following list of receipts for 1828:

> Wombwell's menagerie, £1700; Atkin's ditto, £1000; Richardson's theatre £1200; the price of admission to each being sixpence. Morgan's menagerie £150; admission 3d. Balls £80; Ballard £89; Keyes £20; Frazer £26; Pike £40; Pig-faced Lady £150; Corder's head £100; Chinese Jugglers £50; Fat boy and girl £140; Salamander £30; diorama Navarin £60; Scotch giant £21. The admission to the last twelve shows varied from 2d to ½d.[6]

With earnings of this magnitude available, it is no wonder that showmen flocked to Smithfield each September. Daniel's list indicates something of the variety of attractions of the fair, and makes clear just how large the crowds must have been for exhibitors to collect so much money for such low admittance fees. Bartholomew Fair was truly popular, both in its wide appeal and in the type of audience which came.

Despite its size and longevity, however, the fair was in serious decline by the 1830s. In 1831 the theatrical showman John Richardson lost £50 and Wombwell's menagerie only made expenses; in 1838 the number of shows plunged from eighteen to ten. One cause of decline was the great social upheaval in the nation at large, and the City Solicitor, concluding his report on the fair to the Market Committee in 1840, took a high moral view of the situation, pointing complacently to the March of Progress:

> . . . and when we consider the improved condition and con-duct of the working classes in the Metropolis, and reflect upon the irrefragable proofs continually before us, that the humbler orders are fast changing their habits, and substituting country excursions by rail roads and steam boats, and other innocent recreations, for the vicious amusements of the description which prevailed in Bartholomew Fair, it is perhaps not too much to conclude that it is unnecessary for the Corporation to apply to Parliament to abate the nuisance.[7]

No doubt the country's burgeoning wealth and increasing social mobility were improving the manners of some sections of the com-munity, but this was hardly the whole story. The simple fact is that the Corporation systematically raised tolls and ground-fees throughout the preceding decade, until it was financially impossible for the showmen to make a profit at Bartholomew Fair. In 1831 the City charged Wombwell £120 to set up his wild-beast show at the fair, and there were reports that year of the authorities refusing to let grounds for shows. In 1832 no booths or shows were allowed in any outlying avenues, and in 1838 the dues for standings at the fair were doubled; although City collectors were unable to make the showmen pay the new rates that year, at the next fair the doubled charges were enforced. The exhibitors' difficulties were plaintively summarized in May of 1840 in a memorial from Nelson Lee and John Johnson, who had purchased Richardson's theatre after the great showman died in 1837. They observed:

> That from a regulation at the first Bartholomew Fair they became proprietors an advance was made from £25 to £35, each year following it had been raised to the enormous sum of £70.
> That your memorialists thereby find their interest so materi-ally injured that they feel bound in justice to themselves and

families to approach you gentlemen with their humble memorial.

That your memorialists relying upon custom from time immemorial and having obeyed the law to its very letter having ventured to risk such an outlay as must by the present arrangement prove a heavy and ruinous loss . . .[8]

This plea, although based on appeals to human decency, family obligation, financial responsibility and the sanction of longstanding precedent, fell upon deaf ears, and by the time it was presented their cause was already lost. In 1830 the City had purchased toll rights for the fair from Lord Kensington, thus removing legal obstacles to suppression. On 18 October 1839, in response to a petition from the London City Mission urging suppression of Bartholomew Fair, the Market Committee ordered Charles Pearson, the City Solicitor, to look into the powers of the Corporation regarding the fair. His report, submitted on 19 June 1840, noted the difficulty in applying to Parliament to revoke an ancient royal charter, but proposed the simple expedient of circumscribing the fair to its original object – trade – and banning the use of the fairgrounds for show-booths. Since all trading purposes of the fair had long since vanished, this proposal was, as the Solicitor noted, 'equivalent to its entire suppression'. The Market Committee gratefully acknowledged Mr Pearson's services, and forwarded his report to Common Council for approval, pausing long enough in the process to dismiss Johnson and Lee's memorial. On 7 July, Common Council accepted the report, and published new orders for the fair, containing the fatal clause excluding theatrical representations. Swings, roundabouts and other machinery were also banned, and the result was immediate and conclusive. That year only three wild-beast shows were exhibited at the fair, along with the toy- and gingerbread-stalls, and in 1842 even the menageries were excluded. Although it limped on until 1855, from 1840 Bartholomew Fair was effectively dead.

After fair-time that year, on 16 October the Common Council noted a communication from the Commissioner of the City Police, reporting with 'the greatest satisfaction' the 'tranquil character which pervaded St Bartholomew's Fair from the proclamation to its close'; like the City Solicitor, he attributed the peacefulness to 'the cheering influence of moral improvement in the sentiments and character of the people'.[9] Newspaper reports concerning the fair were more mundane in what they pointed to as the source of tranquillity.

. . . The fact is, the fair is virtually defunct, leaving thousands of mourners inconsolable for its premature and untimely end; the *Law* has overtaken Old Bartlemy, and, though as robust and wickedly inclined as ever, the veteran vagabond has been duly strangled by the 'Civic Functionary' and (ah! ingrate body!) by the order of the Corporation.[10]

Other reports echoed the conviction that Bartholomew Fair was dead, killed by civic action, and they questioned the wisdom of its suppression.

Bartholomew Fair having fallen into a bad odour during the last few years . . . it has been voted a public nuisance . . . the general opinion is it will never be held again . . . It is a question of sound policy, however, whether, when the inhabitants of the metropolis are deprived of their amusements in one quarter, they ought not to be provided with something of an amusing and instructive kind in a more convenient locality.[11]

Expressions of regret, although certainly not unanimous, were widespread.

We wish the Corporation had made arrangements to hold the fair on some other spot. 'Tis a pity the amusements of the people should be altogether crushed.[12]

What these press reports make clear is that there was considerable public awareness at the time of an irrevocable end to Bartholomew Fair. The newspaper accounts are obituaries, and they are emphatic in attributing the cause of death to the policies of the civic authorities.

The suppression of Bartholomew Fair was the single most devastating blow to popular entertainment in the whole of the nineteenth century. Other fairs died, and some grew healthier; old sports and recreations declined, and new ones took their places; but Bartholomew Fair had symbolic value far beyond its role as a famous annual festival. As the press reports just quoted suggest, Old Bartlemy was seen to be representative of the traditional right of the English people to leisure amusements, and its suppression thus struck at something fundamental, not only for the showmen whose occupations were threatened, but also for the common people who enjoyed the shows. If there was any one moment in Dickens's lifetime when the state of popular entertainment called for immediate concern, it was the summer of 1840, the very months during which he was composing the scenes with travelling showmen in *The Old Curiosity Shop*.

Dickens's novel is not about Bartholomew Fair, but it is concerned centrally with the collapsing state of popular entertainment symbolized by the termination of this great event. The showfolk with whom Nell comes into contact are precisely the sort who would include Bartholomew Fair as the prime venue on their tours about the country, and the precarious fortunes of Dickens's fictional figures accurately reflect the lot of the itinerant entertainer in England at this critical time.

'"Many's the hard day's walking in rain and mud, and with never a penny earned,"' Short tells the Single Gentleman (*OCS*, 37), and all of the entertainers whom Nell meets are hard pressed to make a living. Their legal position was no better: the Punch show is run out of town on one occasion, when it is deemed 'a libel on the beadle' (*OCS*, 17). Mrs Jarley, with a more extensive exhibition and a more comfortable lifestyle, considers herself far superior to mere puppet-operators, but the combined blandishments of Slum the poet, Little Nell and Mrs Jarley herself are incapable of securing paying customers for the waxworks, and the hollowness of Mrs Jarley's social pretensions is exposed when the self-righteous schoolmistress, Miss Monflathers, threatens to have her put in the stocks (*OCS*, 31). Beset by figures of authority, financially insecure, and turning against one another in their struggle for survival, Dickens's entertainers eke out an existence on the fringes of society.

None of Dickens's characters visits Smithfield at fair-time; indeed, it is never mentioned in the novel. Dickens wrote the chapter which sent Nell out of London more than two months before the date of the fair, and by September he had reached the point in the book's composition at which Nell's association with Mrs Jarley – the last of the entertainers she meets – is rapidly nearing its end. It would have required radical restructuring of the plot for Dickens to have brought Nell to Smithfield instead of to the rural race meeting and, of the characters who remain in London, Quilp and Swiveller have other occupations and Kit goes to the circus, not to the fair. Furthermore, none of Dickens's letters written during these months in 1840 refers to Bartholomew Fair, and when the time came he was far away in Broadstairs on holiday with his family.

Bartholomew Fair is thus neither an overt topic in *The Old Curiosity Shop* nor a demonstrable influence upon Dickens's novel. Nevertheless, the suppression of this famous ancient festival is deeply symptomatic of the situation of popular entertainment at the time he was writing. The demise of the foremost gathering-place in England for itinerant performers and the greatest annual festivity for the common people in London adds poignant dimension to the nostalgic tone of the novel and gives the utmost timeliness to its themes.

Popular entertainment in *The Old Curiosity Shop* was a matter of urgent significance.

III

Dickens's fourth novel was conceived as the story of Nell, a young girl who lives with her grandfather in a shop filled with antiques, and he designed it for publication in the periodical which he had just begun, *Master Humphrey's Clock*. Early in the composition of *Clock* materials and before a word had been published, Dickens wrote to Forster to express his conviction that he had hit upon a striking idea. 'I think of lengthening Humphrey, finishing the description of the society and closing with the little child-story, which is SURE to be effective, especially after the old man's quiet way.'[13] Most commentators have assumed this to be a reference to the opening sketch of Nell, but Malcolm Andrews has persuasively argued that 'the little child-story' is rather 'A Confession Found in a Prison in the Time of Charles the Second', a brief tale which Dickens placed immediately prior to Chapter 1 of *The Old Curiosity Shop* in *Master Humphrey's Clock*.[14] Recounting the murder of a 4-year-old boy, the 'Confession' contrasts boldly in tone with the *Clock* society and thus fulfils Dickens's desire for material 'effective . . . after the old man's quiet way'. But, whether or not the child in the letter is Nell, there can be no question but that her story took strong hold on Dickens's imagination and quickly subsumed his plans for the *Clock* as a miscellany.

From the very outset, Dickens thought of Nell in relation to curiosities, animate and inanimate, which surround her. His conception depended primarily on contrast, the juxtaposition of starkly opposed images. The opening episode is constructed, as Robert Patten has demonstrated, on a series of oppositions, between beauty and ugliness, innocence and evil, female and male, youth and age, health and decrepitude, day and night, warmth and cold.[15] Master Humphrey, an observer of life, who, as he informs us in the story's opening sentences, wanders the streets by night 'speculating on the characters and occupations of those who fill the streets' in a manner typical of Dickens's curiosity-seeking narrators, meets a lost child and leads her home. Nell's purity and loveliness are highlighted by the gloomy setting to which Master Humphrey restores her, and he reacts to what he sees with considerable disquiet. But both Nell and her grandfather are surprised at this; both staunchly deny that Nell is in an alien environment, and they assure their visitor of the deep love they share for one another. Both of them have implicit faith that Nell belongs in the shop with the old man, who insists to Master Humphrey that '"she is the one object of my care"'. Nell is presented, in short, in a complex image of connectedness and separation; the shop setting is integral to her presence, and yet she is sharply differentiated from it.

The final paragraph of the chapter recounts Master Humphrey's troubled recollection of Nell alone in the shop.

> But, all that night, waking or in my sleep, the same thoughts recurred, and the same images retained possession of my brain. I had, ever before me, the old dark murky rooms – the gaunt suits of mail with their ghostly silent air – the faces all awry, grinning from wood and stone – the dust, and rust, and worm that lives in wood – and alone in the midst of all this lumber and decay and ugly age, the beautiful child in her gentle slumber, smiling through her light and sunny dreams.   (*OCS*, 1)

What Dickens emphasizes here, and what the accompanying illustrations portray, is that Nell is to be seen not in isolation, but in intimate connection with the grotesque objects about her. The vividness of Dickens's image of Nell in this scene goes some way to suggest why her story so attracted him, and when he came to excise *Clock* materials from the text in preparation for the publication of *The Old Curiosity Shop* in volume form he found room near the end of Chapter 1 to interpolate a paragraph which meditates on the source of impact.[16]

> We are so much in the habit of allowing impressions to be made upon us by external objects, which should be produced by reflection alone, but which, without such visible aids, often escape us, that I am not sure I should have been so thoroughly possessed by this one subject, but for the heaps of fantastic things I had seen huddled together in the curiosity-dealer's warehouse. These, crowding on my mind, in connection with the child, and gathering round her, as it were, brought her condition palpably before me. I had her image, without any effort of imagination surrounded and beset by everything that was foreign to its nature, and farthest removed from the sympathies of her sex and age. If these helps to my fancy had all been wanting, and I had been forced to imagine her in a common chamber, with nothing unusual or uncouth in its appearance, it is very probable that I should have been less impressed with her strange and solitary state. As it was, she seemed to exist in a kind of allegory; and, having these shapes about her, claimed my

interest so strongly that (as I have already remarked) I could not dismiss her from my recollection, do what I would.   (*OCS*, 1)

Dickens directs his focus in this paragraph, as throughout the chapter, principally upon Nell, and he subordinates the curiosities as 'visual aids' to his interest in her. But he is equally clear that without these aids his narrator, Master Humphrey, would have been 'less impressed' with her. Although 'foreign to her nature', the grotesque objects around Nell arouse his interest in 'her strange and solitary state' and provide an essential component in the total image. Nell is in, but not of, the curiosities.

Dickens's correspondence concerning the two illustrations which accompany number 4 of *Master Humphrey's Clock*, in which Nell's story first appeared, further clarifies his idea. Both engravings depict Nell in the shop, and Dickens took his customary scrupulous care to ensure that his illustrators would realize his intentions. The initial design of neither drawing satisfied him, and he returned both to the artists for retouching. To Ebeneezer Landells, who engraved the frontispiece, he wrote, 'I was more than doubtful of the child's face, and the subject is one of the last importance to the work'.[17] And to Samuel Williams, illustrator of 'The Child in her Gentle Slumber', he explained more fully:

> The object being to show the child in the midst of a crowd of uncongenial and ancient things, Mr Dickens scarcely *feels* the very pretty drawing inclosed, as carrying out his idea: the room being to all appearances an exceedingly comfortable one pair, and the sleeper being in a very enviable condition. If the composition would admit of a few grim, ugly articles seen through a doorway beyond, for instance, and giving a notion of great gloom outside the little room and surrounding the chamber, it would be much better. The figure in the bed is not sufficiently *childish*, and would perhaps look better without a cap, and with the hair floating over the pillow. The last paragraph of the paper (which perhaps Mr Williams has) expresses Mr Dickens's idea better than he can convey it in any other words.[18]

Dickens's instructions to his illustrators insist that the contrast between Nell and her setting is his overriding concern. The child's face must be youthful and innocent, an effect which Landells achieves in the finished illustration by placing Nell upright in the full glow of candlelight, while the two old men are stooping beside her, Master Humphrey obscured in shadow and the grandfather's back to us. Nell's face is the clear and bright centre of the drawing, surrounded by a clutter of ungainly objects and thrown into relief by the darkened door behind the figures. Similarly, Williams's reworked engraving of Nell asleep casts a strong light upon her face and pillow, and fills her room with grotesque and darkened objects. In both engravings the juxtaposition of the young girl and the gloomy surroundings provides the central impact of each scene just as the introductory chapter places its major emphasis on this contrast.

The inextricable link between Nell and the shop provides the keynote for the popular entertainments theme of *The Old Curiosity Shop*. We are not yet in the world of the showfolk, but from the outset we are very definitely in the realm of early nineteenth-century amusements. Dickens describes the shop as

> . . . one of those receptacles for old and curious things which seem to crouch in odd corners of this town, and to hide their musty treasures from the public eye in jealousy and distrust. There were suits of mail standing like ghosts in armour, here and there; fantastic carvings brought from monkish cloisters; rusty weapons of various kinds; distorted figures in china, and wood, and iron, and ivory; tapestry, and strange furniture that might have been designed in dreams.   (*OCS*, 1)

What this description makes evident is that Nell's home is hardly distinguishable from a museum. There is no suggestion that any more customers ever come to browse through Nell's grandfather's collection than visit Sol Gills's nautical instruments shop in *Dombey and Son*, and financial ruin would have been all too probable even without his gambling losses, but the shop is nevertheless a picturesque example of a kind of popular entertainment which was widespread in its day. It is the repository of a shabby collection of miscellaneous antiques, incoherently arranged and haphazardly exhibited, and indefinite as to whether its objects are available for sale or solely for display. We are made aware from the very outset that Nell lives in an exhibition-room.

From the early eighteenth century, exhibitions of every sort, including collections of random paraphernalia such as Nell's grandfather's, attracted wide interest in England and played a not unimportant role in amusing and educating the public. Newspapers were regularly full of advertisements celebrating the latest wonders on show, and several major collections of exhibition-bills from the period have survived to suggest the extent and variety of this form of amusement. Curiosity, as Dickens proposes in the book's title, was a key source of attraction to exhibitions in an age which saw massive expansion and discovery but which lacked photography to disseminate visual evidence of new and old wonders. The exhibitions offered an incredible variety of objects for display, ranging from antiquities to modern inventions, from shells and stuffed animals to waxworks, paintings, stained glass and paper statuary. They were large or small, itinerant or permanently settled, exclusive or open to all, and there were many of them. In eighteenth-century London, Don Saltero opened his coffee-house with a huge and various collection of miscellaneous curiosities on display; in early nineteenth-century Portsea, an enterprising showman advertised his exhibition consisting exclusively of a plank covered with barnacles, which had been washed ashore in a recent storm.[19] The shop of Mr Venus, the bone-articulator in *Our Mutual Friend*, is a later, specialized example of the same continuing phenomenon.

Although extravagant puffing was invariable in advertisements for the shows, the actual contents were frequently exceedingly modest both in quality and in quantity. As Richard Altick has suggested, the old curiosity shop is a seedy descendant of the elegant cabinets which were the hobby of a number of eighteenth-century gentlemen.[20] Altick has lavishly documented the genealogy of London exhibitions and shown how fine – and not so fine – collections all too frequently degenerated into dusty junk shops. Exhibitions were ubiquitous in London, but all save a few were financially precarious, disappearing nearly as rapidly as they appeared. Quilp's first action, on taking possession of the shop, is to have all its lumber hauled away, and such brutal dispersal was the common fate of exhibitions far more pretentious than that of Nell's grandfather.

As a place of amusement, even though it 'hides its musty treasures from the public eye', the shop is a wholly appropriate setting for several of the people we meet there. Nell's grandfather is described as 'wonderfully suited to the place . . . nothing . . . looked older or more worn than he' (*OCS*, 1). For Nell, of course, the old man is her chief companion and care in the world, but for Master Humphrey and for us as readers he appears initially as the shop's foremost curiosity. Master Humphrey invites us to view Nell's grandfather as not so much a human personality as an old, dilapidated and mysterious object, at one with the shop he inhabits.[21] As the story proceeds, he develops into a more substantial character, but to the very end he remains a bizarre contrast to Nell, a constant reminder of the shop which they have left behind, and throughout their travels the old man's constant fear is that he may literally be turned into an object on exhibition, by being incarcerated in a madhouse. In fact, Bedlam had closed its doors to the idly curious as far previously as 1770, but physical restraint, which so terrifies the old man, was still customary procedure at the time Dickens was writing in 1840.[22]

Other characters who appear in the shop in the book's opening pages participate even more conspicuously in the entertainment world. Kit, the shop's only constant visitor, is introduced in the opening scene in the immediately recognizable role of clown. Master Humphrey describes him as 'a shock-headed shambling awkward lad with an uncommonly wide mouth, very red cheeks, a turned-up nose, and certainly the most comical expression of face I ever saw' (*OCS*, 1). And he concludes his description by reporting that Kit was 'the comedy of the child's life'. Dickens evidently changed his mind almost at once about the boy's function in the story, for Kit soon sheds his near-idiocy and becomes Nell's faithful but largely ineffectual champion. In later chapters he is noteworthy not for Grimaldi-like antics but for cheerful, honest and earnest devotion to duty. At the same time, however, the book's illustrations retain the image of Kit as clown to the very end, and not only he but also the entire Nubbles family are invariably pictured as the grotesque figures of the opening presentation.

The next two chapters introduce Swiveller, devotee of song and stage, and Quilp, freak-show creature let loose. Swiveller reveals himself from the moment of his first appearance as a raffish swell, wholly immersed in the low-life culture of the metropolis, with his catalogue of curious observations, his whistles and snatches from song, his stage whispers and melodramatically inflated rhetoric. Dickens clearly projected much of his own fascination with humble amusements into Swiveller and he expressed great satisfaction with Forster's immediate approval. 'I *mean* to make much of him,' Dickens confided.[23] Quilp's presence is striking even before he says or does anything, on account of his wildly grotesque appearance. Kit later calls him '"a uglier dwarf than can be seen anywhere for a penny"' (*OCS*, 6), and Quilp's affinity with monstrosities offered for exhibition is clear from Dickens's first words describing him, 'so low in stature as to be quite a dwarf, though his head and face were large enough for the body of a giant' (*OCS*, 3). By the time Master Humphrey excuses himself from the duties of narration at the end of Chapter 3, a clear and varied context of popular entertainment has been established. No actual showmen appear until Chapter 16, after Nell has fled to the countryside, and the shop is not an arena for professional performance; but the setting and the characters in it have firm roots in traditional amusements of the people. Nell is conceived in this context, and it is a natural transition from the shop and its visitors to her later meetings with showfolk and to her employment in the waxwork.

When she flees from London, a considerable portion of her journey places her in direct contact with professional entertainers. Her position among them parallels that in the shop: she is simultaneously part of the scene and apart from it. Nell helps the puppet men to repair their damaged properties and readily accepts their invitation to travel together. At the races, despite the bustle and the distinct lack of gentility of the crowds, she 'felt it an escape from the town and drew her breath more freely' (*OCS*, 19). This welcome relief from her troubles is short-lived, however, and, discouraged by her inability to beg successfully, frightened by the bold pledges of friendship from Codlin and Short, and urgently warned away by the handsome 'lady' in the carriage, Nell flees again. With Mrs Jarley, Nell feels 'joy of hearing that they were to go forward in the caravan' (*OCS*, 26), and she soon becomes herself the principal attraction at the waxwork. Even under the kindly wing of Mrs Jarley, however, Nell has nightmares which mingle waxen effigies with Quilp; she is ostracized from society – not merely scorned by the absurdly snobbish Monflathers, but able to witness the true affection of the Edwards sisters only 'at a little distance' – and she is forced once again to flee because her new income only serves to subsidize her grandfather's manic gambling. In these ways the complexity of Nell's relation to the entertainment world persists after she has left the shop.

Three key aspects of Dickens's presentation of Nell's adventures among the showfolk require detailed attention. First, we must consider the relationship of these episodes to historical time and place. As she is leaving London, Nell compares herself to Christian in *The Pilgrim's Progress* (*OCS*, 15), an explicit indication that Dickens thinks of her flight as a spiritual journey. He refrains from assigning an explicit date or location to her travels, and there is a distinct aura of dream landscape when Nell passes through fire and over water. Details abound, however, to suggest that as he wrote Dickens had a clear route in mind for Nell, and the topical urgency of his entertainment themes is just one of several factors which prevent the story from rising to a level of abstraction outside temporal and spatial considerations. Recognizing the nature of the show-figures Dickens presents can help to clarify the dynamics of this tension. Second, we must discuss the authenticity of these characters as historical types. All of the entertainers in *The Old Curiosity Shop* represent figures familiar in village squares, city streets, and fairgrounds up and down England in the early nineteenth century. By considering them in relation to their prototypes we can simultaneously clarify the value of Dickens's sketches as social history and appreciate more fully their significance within the structure of the novel. Third, we must examine the thematic function of these entertainers. Because Dickens conceived of Nell in conjunction with curiosities, the showfolk play an integral part in his development of the book's main interests, just as her plight adds dimension to our understanding of them.

IV

Dickens purposely leaves nameless the locations of Nell's adventures with the showfolk, but there is strong evidence that he had the Midlands between London and Wolverhampton in mind while he was writing this section of the novel. In a letter to Forster he commented on the terrifying industrial town which appears in Chapter 45, after Nell has left Mrs Jarley: 'You will recognise a description of the road we travelled between Birmingham and Wolverhampton: but I had conceived it so well in my mind that the execution doesn't please me quite as well as I expected.'[24] In itself, this remark would not require Nell to have crossed the intervening territory between London and Birmingham, since the unspecified nature of her route freed Dickens to invent a wholly fictional landscape drawn from diverse settings, but the consensus among Dickensian topographers favours this part of England for Nell's route. Dickens and Hablôt Browne visited the Midlands on a holiday tour a year and a half before the writing began, taking in both the industrial Black Country and the rural countryside around the Welsh border, including the village of Tong, which is generally thought to be Nell's final resting-place.

In a 1924 article in the *Dickensian*, Walter Dexter assembled the conclusions of all previous proponents of an itinerary for Little Nell, and he offered a detailed table incorporating his own views. A year later, in *The England of Dickens*, the indefatigable Dexter wrote in considerably more detail defending a precise route for Nell through the Midlands: from London through Uxbridge, to Aylesbury (where she meets Codlin and Short), Buckingham (site of the Jolly Sandboys), Banbury (the racetrack), Warmington (the school), Warwick (where Mrs Jarley sets up her waxwork), then on to Birmingham, Wolverhampton and Tong.[25] To tie Dickens's fictional geography so rigidly to actual locations involves highly suspect critical assumptions, and because Dickens so consistently avoids giving place-names during Nell's journey one must demur from the specificity of Dexter's route. Nevertheless, there is considerable plausibility in the more limited contention that Dickens had in mind a Midlands setting as a *source* for the symbolic landscape which he pictured in the novel, and it is worth looking to the area for evidence of early nineteenth-century popular local entertainments which may have suggested characters and events to him.

That fact-finding could have been the motive for Dickens's expedition to the Midlands in 1838 is altogether possible, because, as we saw in Chapter 3, in January of the same year he had gone with Browne to Yorkshire to investigate the schools there for background to *Nicholas Nickleby*. His second bachelor holiday with Browne occurred nine months later, in late October and early November. Dickens's diary entries for the trip are cryptic, primarily recording expenses, and his letter to his wife written during the trip offers only brief reactions to Kenilworth and Warwick castles, to the squalor of the Black Country, and to a night at the theatre.[26] But the impressions were characteristically lasting, and they found direct expression eight years later in *Dombey and Son*, in the episodes containing Mr Dombey's trips to Kenilworth and Warwick while courting Edith Granger. That Dickens was familiar with the Midlands by the time he wrote *The Old Curiosity Shop* is indisputable: he had been to Birmingham on reporting duties for the *Morning Chronicle* in 1834; he had sent Mr Pickwick from Bristol to Birmingham, and he had visited there again in April of 1840 when the first number of *Master Humphrey's Clock* appeared, observing his habit of being absent from London on the dates of first publication of his works.[27]

Dickens's direct knowledge of the area thus predates the composition of *The Old Curiosity Shop* by several years, and the story's action is set back in time. The internal dating of the book is clear and consistent, and, as in *Pickwick*, the fictional seasons correspond closely to the time when the various episodes first appeared serially. Thus Nell leaves London in June, and number 13, in which this action occurs, was published on 27 June 1840; it is autumn when she arrives at her final destination, and 31 October when number 31 appeared; and 30 January 1841 for number 44, in which she dies, in mid-winter. But the historical year in which these seasons occur is nowhere nearly so specific. Dickens is as indefinite about date as he is about place in this novel, and, as Angus Easson has shown, he seems even as he was writing to have pushed back the chronology of the book's events from near-contemporaneity to about a decade earlier. Noting a reference to *Her* Majesty's attorneys in Chapter 13, Easson observes:

This dates the story at this point after the accession of Queen Victoria in 1837. However, Dickens progressively pushed back the supposed date of events; by [Chapter 33] he is stressing Bevis Marks as '*once* the residence of Mr Sampson Brass' and says 'in the days of its occupation by Sampson Brass'. In Chapter 63, reference is made to *His* Majesty, either George IV or William IV since Lord Byron is dead (Chapter 29), which gives us a date after 1824. By the end of the tale Kit has children six and seven years old, so that events are placed at least that time back after 1841 (i.e. 1835–6).[28]

Such vagueness about dating within a work is not unusual for Dickens at any time in his career, but scattered references such as those noted by Easson make it certain that a period between the 1820s and the mid-1830s was in Dickens's mind when he imagined the action of *The Old Curiosity Shop*.

Records survive for these years which document an extensive and diverse array of circuses, waxworks, dwarfs, giants, stilt-walkers and other entertainers who performed along Nell's proposed route. In Birmingham, the largest town in the region, visiting showmen included: Monsieur L. Jacques, a seven-foot-four-inch giant from France, in 1823; a French-speaking doll in 1824; the Industrious Fleas of Signor Bertolletto in 1837; and the Gnome-Fly Hervio Nano in 1838. Stilt-dancers appeared regularly on circus bills. During a slow theatrical season in 1817, R. W. Elliston, then manager of the Theatre Royal, Birmingham, advertised a Bohemian Giant and attracted a huge house, then stepped on to the stage himself to lament that the giant had deceived him and never appeared, but that the rock he was billed to lift was there on the stage for all to see.[29] Vuffin, the proprietor of freaks in *The Old Curiosity Shop*, clearly was not alone in his discontent with giants for ruining the trade (*OCS*, 19).

In Aylesbury on 17 April 1826 a man named Courtney spent a day walking backwards over a quarter-mile patch of ground until he had completed forty miles; on 19 June 1832 there was donkey racing, a bonfire and other 'nonsense' to celebrate the passing of the Reform Bill.[30] Aylesbury churchyard, which Walter Dexter proposes as Nell's meeting-place with Codlin and Short, was notorious as a ground for rough sports and thus a plausible site for Punch to be found. Clement Shorter, supported by other local historians, writes of it:

> Tradition tells of a time when Aylesbury churchyard, now so carefully railed off from the footpaths, was the scene of cock-fighting, card-playing, and other Hogarthian exploits, and when soldiers were flogged there on occasion. Even up to the beginning of the nineteenth century the elections were held there, and the rival candidates addressed their constituents from the tombstones.[31]

Aylesbury was known as a gathering-place for gipsies and, although racing was never very popular there, in the nearby village of Marlow a two-day race meeting was revived in 1837, and run annually until 1847. Also in Great Marlow, the famous 'Muster' Richardson was buried in 1837 next to his beloved spotted boy, whom he had exhibited twenty-five years previously.[32]

In Buckingham there was a room above a coach house which was used as an occasional theatre by strolling players, and darts, dominoes and the ancient pastime of shove-ha'penny were popular tavern games there.[33] Banbury was a prosperous market-town, with as many as nine fairs and two great markets annually from 1797 to 1836; after the latter date, the newly reformed corporation abolished tolls and changed the days of fairs. The Holy Thursday Fair, which was the great holiday fair, held on Ascension Thursday, achieved local notoriety in 1827 when a smallpox epidemic, in which seventy-three people died between June and September, broke out at a sideshow, and by 1837 for the first time there were no amusements of any kind at this fair. B. S. Trinder, writing about Banbury Fair in the nineteenth century, describes its popularity as follows:

> In 1832 it was reported that there had never been a greater number of people in the town than there were for the fair, and throughout the 1840s and 1850s Banbury was so crowded on fair days that it was difficult to move in the streets, and many shopkeepers had to board up their windows to avoid having them broken by the crush of humanity on the pavements . . . Many 'cheap Johns' came to sell their wares at Banbury fair. The chief trade was in novelties of various kinds, toys, pictures, and printed songs . . . Another popular trade was in patent medicines . . . Other traders offered to measure the force of punches with a machine or to take heights for a penny . . . The most impressive feature of the fair was the vast array of amusements erected throughout the town centre.

Racing was also held in Banbury; the first recorded races took place in 1729, and there was a one-day racing programme held in July in the early 1840s.[34] (Number 17 of *Master Humphrey's Clock*, in which Nell goes to the races, was published on 25 July 1840.)

Warwickshire is George Eliot country, and nineteenth-century historians of local folklore and recreations invariably cite 'Mrs Cross' as a prime authority. Arthur Donnithorne's birthday games in *Adam Bede*, as we noted in Chapter 2, provide a vivid account of a village festival at the turn of the century. *The Mill on the Floss, Felix Holt* and *Middlemarch* are all set in Warwickshire in the era of the first Reform Bill (1832), and contain abundant glimpses of leisure pursuits, superstitions and popular activities. Hiring fairs at

Michaelmas, or 'mops', were annual scenes of festivity, at which farm servants of both sexes festooned their clothes with some ornament indicating the type of service they wished to undertake, and from 1610 until 1853 an 'Olympick Games' was held at Dover's Hill, with wrestling, leaping, pitching the bar and hammer, handling the pike, walking on hands, leapfrog, dancing, horse-racing, handball and hare-hunting. These games were finally suppressed in 1853 because of 'disorderly behaviour'. There was a tradition of giants in the area (the town of Bromsgrove was named for the resting-place of the giant Breme – 'Breme's Grave' – and other warlike giants lived, according to legend, at Birmingham, Kinver, Dudley, Halestown and elsewhere). Warwick was famous for its racing: three-day race meetings in both spring and autumn were well established by 1834. Undoubtedly the most memorable single event in Warwick entertainment annals was the lion-baiting staged by Wombwell, England's foremost wild-beast proprietor of the day, on Tuesday, 26 July 1825. William Hone, with considerable expression of disgust, gives a lengthy, circumstantial report of the baiting in his *Every Day Book*, recording how three dogs, followed by another three, attacked an extremely docile lion named Nero, and how a second bout was held within the week, in which a more ferocious lion, Wallace, was likewise beset by six dogs.[35] The lion-baiting was the most spectacular instance of violent sports such as cock-fighting, bull-running, bull-baiting, badger-baiting and the like, all of which flourished during the eighteenth century in the area we are considering, but which were slowly dying out in the 1820s, and occurred only in isolated instances thereafter.

What is clear from this brief survey, which is no more than a representative sampling of surviving evidence, is that, however prominently a Midlands setting may have figured in Dickens's mind when he wrote about the showfolk in *The Old Curiosity Shop*, no particular events there for which records have survived can be identified as likely sources. It is possible that he was aware of certain appropriate facts, such as the notoriety of the Aylesbury churchyard or the early-summer date of the Banbury races (although this was only a one-day meeting, whereas the spring and autumn races at Warwick extended over three days, as in *The Old Curiosity Shop*). But no legitimate claim can be sustained for the exclusive derivation of his fictional events from specifically local activities. Race meetings and churchyard romps were common all over England, and none of the details of Dickens's descriptions localizes his meetings to the extent that only one distinct source is possible. With the single exception of the lion-baiting, which does not gain notice in the novel, all of the activities traced are simply local instances of extremely widespread

English customs. Blood sports, fairs, tavern games, and races can be documented from medieval times up to the period we are dealing with anywhere in England that records of public pastimes exist. These kinds of popular entertainment (with regional variations, to be sure) were general phenomena, and Dickens could perfectly easily have observed a show in one place and translated it to a quite different setting without in the least stretching the plausibility of his fiction.

Furthermore, as Short remarks to the Single Gentleman, penny showmen earned their livings by moving from one public gathering to the next, often covering a large part of England in a single season.

> 'It's our reg'lar summer circuit is the West, master,' said Short; 'that's where it is. We takes the East of London in the spring and winter, and the West of England in the summertime.'
>
> (*OCS*, 37)

Short's claim can be verified by consulting the memoirs of actual entertainers of the day. 'Lord' George Sanger, who became one of the foremost celebrities in his profession, and whose career conveniently overlaps with Dickens's, boasted late in life that

> There is not, I believe, a town or village of over one hundred inhabitants in this United Kingdom I have not at some time or other visited. So, too, abroad. With the exception of Russia, I have carried my tents into every European country.[36]

Sanger was exceptional, both in the length of his life and in the size of show which his later prosperity enabled him to present, but the experience of tramping from one fair to the next, from market to racecourse, never hesitating to perform wherever a group of people was to be found, often singing for supper, is a mode of life circumstantially recorded not only by Sanger but also by other itinerants as various as David Prince Miller (penny showman and later strolling player and theatre manager), Billy Purvis (clown), William Green (cheap Jack) and Joe Smith (waxwork proprietor). Because the showmen were itinerant, it follows that the same performances and performers would be found in entirely different settings; not only were the types of entertainment similar throughout the country, but also the individual entertainers themselves were the same. Like the Single Gentleman, Dickens would have been able to meet showmen in London who had travelled widely in the countryside.

It is thus possible – indeed, it seems extremely likely – that

Traditional types of entertainment were taken up and down the country by individual itinerant showmen, most of whom had only a single attraction to offer.

Dickens based his notion of the countryside in *The Old Curiosity Shop* on a Midlands route such as that proposed by Dexter, and at the same time, without the least impropriety, he sketched the originals of some, or all, of his showmen without himself taking one step outside the environs of London. There was ample opportunity for anyone interested in common forms of entertainment to indulge his enthusiasm in London, and an act he saw one day in Hyde Park or at Bartholomew Fair could be seen at other times in towns and villages up and down the country. In the era we are considering, the 1820s and 1830s, most entertainments were, and had been for centuries, itinerant, and concentrated together in any given place at fair or festival times. The showmen of *The Old Curiosity Shop* reflect this state of affairs, and are representative not of local characters, found only in a single, particular setting, but of the humble entertainers who travelled throughout the country,

Because they roamed up and down the country putting on their shows, and because the shows themselves were traditional, dating back for decades, centuries, even millennia, entertainers in this mould were singularly appropriate for Dickens's purposes in *The Old Curiosity Shop*. Their mobility enabled him to range far beyond the Midlands in selecting images suitable for the novel. The changelessness of their acts and exhibits allowed him to draw without inconsistency on memories from his own childhood (he was 8 years old in 1820) at the same time as he responded to events which were occurring even while he wrote, notably the suppression of Bartholomew Fair. Oxymoron was inherent in the nature of these entertainers: colourful figures as individuals, they were also embodiments of age-old types. Of high profile as lone, distinctive characters, they merged into the generality of the traditional patterns they perpetuated. Timely and timeless, specific and universal, the itinerant showfolk were precisely the kind of figures to further Dickens's aims in his topical novel about eternal concerns.

V

The types of entertainer Dickens chose to include in *The Old Curiosity Shop* have firm grounding in historical reality. All of them were engaged in amusements which were traditional and well known throughout England, and as such they provide a vivid picture. The accuracy of detail with which they are presented gives these figures considerable value as social document, and thus, even as they contribute to the immediate concerns of Dickens's fiction, they also demonstrate his journalistic skills at their best. These skills led

Walter Bagehot to praise Dickens as a 'special correspondent for posterity', and in the description of the itinerant showfolk in *The Old Curiosity Shop* he has left a record of great interest.[37]

Specific sources have been proposed for some of these characters, such as a Punch and Judy show watched by an old man with a little girl, which Dickens is supposed to have encountered in Windsor Park, and the waxwork-exhibitor Madame Tussaud, who toured England for more than a quarter of a century before setting up a permanent show at the Bazaar, Baker Street, Portman Square, a short walk from Dickens's home, after 1839, at Devonshire Terrace.[38] But, while it is possible that such persons influenced his conception of the entertainers in the novel and provided him with memorable details, the types of figure he drew were too familiar to require particular sources, and in any case, as we saw with the allegation of Jean Davenport's role in *Nicholas Nickleby*, Dickens's fictional methods rarely depended slavishly on single individual sources. The showfolk in *The Old Curiosity Shop* represent individualized types of character, not specific originals.

Dickens first introduces the Punch and Judy showmen, Codlin and Short. A team of two was customary for Punch shows; one man handled the puppets from inside the booth while the outside man held the audience's attention – which Codlin does by playing panpipes – and collected the money. Whereas modern Punch booths generally sport red and white striped cloth, Dickens's puppeteers decorate their booth with checked drapery, which early nineteenth-century illustrations invariably corroborate. Dickens itemizes the puppets in the show, including a live dog for Toby, who has graduated from playing opposite Punch to dancing for Jerry. Although all the cast were puppets in most shows, historians have traced the use of actual dogs in a few instances, and, as we saw in Chapter 3, movement between different kinds of show was a frequent occurrence in this era.[39] Codlin is reported also to have tried his hand elsewhere, appearing formerly in fairground theatre booths in the role of a ghost (*OCS*, 16).

Next to appear are Grinder's lot.

Mr Grinder's company, familiarly termed a lot, consisted of a young gentleman and a young lady on stilts, and Mr Grinder himself, who used his natural legs for pedestrian purposes and carried at his back a drum. The public costumes of the young people was of the Highland kind, but the night being damp and cold, the young gentleman wore over his kilt a man's pea jacket reaching to his ankles, and a glazed hat; the young lady too was muffled in an old cloth pelisse and had a handkerchief tied about

her head. Their Scotch bonnets, ornamented with plumes of jet
black feathers Mr Grinder carried on his instrument. (*OCS*, 17)

Contemporary illustrations, notably those dated 1831, 1833 and
1841 in George Scharf's sketchbook, depict young stilt dancers in a
variety of colourful costumes, with a musical accompanist, in open
streets. Circus bills confirm that stilts often appeared in the ring;
Mayhew interviewed the manager of one stilt-dancing team who
worked in fairs and pleasure gardens. Like Grinder, the man himself
was not a performer, but trained his wife and daughters and arranged
their bookings – as many as eighteen performances in a single day.
An indication of the height of the stilts, which make the performers
look like 'gaunt giants' to Nell, comes from the artist Henrietta
Ward, who recalled that 'Men on stilts, wearing Pierrot's and Harlequin's costumes, came and peeped into windows of the drawing
room in Fitzroy Square'.[40]

Also sporting elegant costumes are another of the groups Nell
meets, the dancing dogs belonging to the showman named Jerry.
Eighteenth- and nineteenth-century illustrations confirm that dogs
performed in elaborate dress: an illustration dated 1753, for example,
shows a troupe of dogs attired for a formal ball, while another from
1824 depicts a dog dressed as an admiral, dancing in a village street
while another dog jumps through a hoop. They performed a variety
of tricks. Bob, purported author of his own autobiography, *The Dog
of Knowledge* (1801), which was exceedingly popular all through the
nineteenth century, being reprinted in 1805, 1815, 1848, 1885 and
1891, claimed that he danced in a Harlequin's jacket, fenced with a
stick and did gymnastics.[41] *Aficionados* of canine acts were disparag-
ing of 'those straggling dancing dogs still occasionally seen in the
streets', and Dickens observes that one new member of Jerry's
company was 'not quite certain of his duty' (*OCS*, 18). Jerry's way
of dealing with such a dog is to withhold food and, although
nineteenth-century animal-trainers generally claimed to use kindness and encouragement rather than whips and deprivation, Philip
Astley is reputed to have claimed that his equine performers acted
better than humans 'because mine know if they don't indeed work
like horses, I give them *no corn* – whereas, if your performers do, or
do not, walk over the course, they have their *prog* just the same'.[42]

The other principal entertainer to be described in *The Old Curiosity
Shop* is Mrs Jarley, the waxwork proprietor. Dickens satirizes her as
'the delight of the Nobility and Gentry and the peculiar pet of the
Royal Family' (*OCS*, 27), undoubtedly glancing in this remark at
Madame Tussaud, the most famous of all waxwork-exhibitors,
whose memoirs, published in 1838, revealed that she had lived as a

young woman at Versailles in the French court before the Revolution. Madame Tussaud's advertising routinely boasted of Royal Patronage after 1834 when Princess Augusta, sister of George IV, visited the waxwork at Brighton Town Hall. Like many entertainers of the day, including Madame Tussaud, Mrs Jarley sought to stimulate trade by announcing imminent closure of her show and then extending her stay 'by popular demand'.[43] She also employed the services of the poet Slum to sing the wonders of her exhibition. The sort of competition Slum faced can be illustrated by the following verse from an advertisement for Simmons's waxwork in Holborn around 1832.

> To Holborn we trotted away,
> And got for our pains well requited,
> 'Twere crowded as much as a play,
> And yet ev'ry one seem'd delighted!
> Six rooms filled with figures you'll see,
> All crowded in groups, such a many,
> But it seems such a wonder to see
> That they show the whole lot for a penny.
>
> Rumpti, etc.[44]

On the day Nell joins Mrs Jarley she catches a glimpse of Quilp, and at night when she sleeps in the caravan she has nightmares of being 'hemmed in by a legion of Quilps' (*OCS*, 27). This detail is consonant with her terror of the dwarf, and of considerable thematic importance to the novel. It is thus fascinating to discover that such a response to living among wax effigies was not merely an invention of Dickens's imagination. One exhibitor, Joe Smith, who began his career with waxworks at Barnet Fair in 1840, the very year of *The Old Curiosity Shop*, left circumstantial memoirs of his life as a showman, in which he recalled:

I look back even now with a shudder to think of my first night in the show, and of many following nights. I knew perfectly well that the figures were all made up, but when I saw their faces gleam in the moonlight which came through the tent, just sufficient for me to see them, they all looked to be living and staring directly at me. I felt sure they were living ghosts. The distant howling of the dogs about the fair made me think they were groaning. I shut my eyes while I undressed, because I dared not look towards them. When I got into bed the first night, I trembled dreadfully, and groaned quite unintentionally. My aunt thought I was ill. She came out to me and saw by my trembling that it was only fright. She made me get up and go round and touch all the faces of the figures, to assure me that they were only wax.[45]

These examples illustrate the authenticity of detail with which Dickens portrayed his showfolk in *The Old Curiosity Shop*. In addition, Codlin, Jerry, Vuffin and the rest share a number of characteristics which make them representative not only of specific types but also of a class. All of them are independent itinerant entertainers, operating on a small scale and offering amusements long tested by time. Each is proprietor of a single, unelaborate attraction, which provides employment for himself alone or at most for himself in partnership with one or two others. Codlin and Short work in tandem; Grinder's 'lot' consists of two young stilt-walkers accompanied by himself on the drum; Vuffin exhibits two freaks; Jerry has a team of dogs; and Sweet William performs conjuring tricks on his own. All of them thus operate on a scale smaller than even the smallest company of strolling actors or the tiniest circus. The shows are no bigger than what they can carry on their backs or, in the case of Grinder's stilt-walkers, no bigger than can carry them on their way. Practical considerations kept their establishments small. As one showman observed:

You cannot have more in your show than you can carry in your van; or maybe you have two or more vans, but the same holds good. In our case, we had a van and a cart which carried the tent and other fixtures.

This same entertainer commented wryly upon an Act of Parliament which forbade the use of dog-carts; in consequence the wives now had to pull the vans instead.[46] Lacking vans, Dickens's entertainers depend on their own feet for transportation, and without fixed exhibition-centres of their own they travel from place to place performing wherever customers can be attracted. Although they routinely congregated at fairs and race meetings, where they could take advantage of the crowds assembled at such places, each of them travelled and exhibited independently. Rivalry, as evidenced in Short's early start from the Jolly Sandboys, was inevitable in such circumstances, and countless instances are recorded in showmen's memoirs of deception, chicanery, puffing and violence to gain precedence. One famous instance can serve to epitomize the rest. On this occasion the menagerie-owner Wombwell, racing his counterpart Atkins to Bartholomew Fair, undertook a forced march from Newcastle, and during the journey his elephant died. Atkins accordingly advertised his show as the one with 'the only live elephant in the fair'; the enterprising Wombwell promptly set out a banner proclaiming 'the only dead elephant in the fair', which proved the greater attraction.[47]

Among Dickens's itinerant showfolk Mrs Jarley, with her elegant wagon and more extensive exhibition, is in some ways a case apart. Certainly she considers herself superior to the other entertainers, as she indicates by her horrified reaction to Nell's innocent question whether she knows Codlin and Short.

> 'Know 'em child!' cried the lady of the caravan in a sort of shriek. 'Know *them*! But you're young and inexperienced, and that's your excuse for asking sich a question. Do I look as if I know'd 'em, does the caravan look as if *it* know'd 'em?' (*OCS*, 26)

She admits that she has gone to the races, but strictly in a private capacity as a spectator, and not as an exhibitor herself; whereas the others trudged on foot to the racetrack in order to earn their livelihood, she rode in a gig, on an 'expedition of pleasure', with no thought of 'any matters of business or profit'.

'"There is none of your open-air wagrancy at Jarley's,"' she insists (*OCS*, 27), and Dickens uses the book's plot to separate Mrs Jarley from the other showfolk. She has a legitimate claim to higher status. Her exhibition includes some hundred life-sized human figures, which require several vans for transportation, in addition to her own travelling caravan. Besides her companion, George, she has two regular assistants to help with the unloading of vans and the decorating of the hall, and she is in a financial position to hire both Nell and her grandfather, and to pay for the services of an advertising agent, the poet Slum. Her exhibition bills boast that she is patronized by Royalty, Nobility and Gentry, and, however improbable clientele of such rank may be, it is certain that she has a show which far surpasses in size and expense anything the other itinerant showmen have to offer. Alone among them she can claim to present 'rational amusement', a show which meets the customary nineteenth-century requirement for entertainment which not only pleases but also instructs. The educational component is versatile, to say the least, since a single effigy can serve as Mary Queen of Scots or Lord Byron, as Grimaldi the clown or Mr Lindley Murray composing his English grammar, but the appeals to realism, morality and history give Mrs Jarley's exhibition a substance far beyond the knockabout fun of Punch and Judy.

Yet Mrs Jarley has much in common with the other entertainers. Although she exhibits in halls or assembly-rooms, she, too, lacks a permanent base and travels about the country in search of customers. Her exhibition is larger, but it is no more diverse in kind: a single type of attraction is all she boasts. Even with her assistants, her show remains simple in comparison to the more elaborate organization required for a theatrical company or a circus. At 6d admittance price the waxwork is more expensive to see than the street-shows at which a hat is passed for pennies but still far less than entertainment catering to more exclusive clientele. Jarley's waxwork, like the open-air shows, is essentially popular entertainment.

All of the shows on offer in *The Old Curiosity Shop* have their roots in the distant past. Conjury, performing animals, and curiosity about human freaks all date from antiquity. Wax effigies and portraits were associated with funeral ceremonies in Egypt, Greece and Rome, and during the Middle Ages they were used in necromancy and in adoration of saints. For centuries wax models of English monarchs were included in royal funeral processions and then put on display in Westminster Abbey, where their dilapidated condition and the greed of the vergers who touted them like vulgar showmen were a national scandal. Waxwork exhibits at Bartholomew Fair are recorded from the seventeenth century, and during the eighteenth century wax models were shown for anatomical instruction, as artistic portraiture, and in miscellaneous exhibits.[48]

Still dancing has been traced back to the Middle Ages. Joseph Strutt relates it to ladder dancing and cites a source from the reign of Henry III; William Hone cites a 1440 manuscript from Norwich, which describes Shrovetide mummers, including some who 'walked on high stilts, with wings at their backs, as cranes'; one of Henry Mayhew's informants recalled family teams who danced on stilts to the accompaniment of a barrel organ in streets, fairs and pleasure gardens early in the nineteenth century.[49]

Canine acts, which still appear in circuses today, are recorded in early seventeenth-century England, and their heyday was the eighteenth century. Dogs undertook a variety of roles, ranging from the mere savagery of the beasts used in baiting bears, bulls and tigers, to the exhibitions of so-called learned dogs, who performed with numbers, letters of the alphabet, and playing-cards, enacting feats of purported intelligence at fairs and in drawing-rooms. Canine drama filled theatres well into the nineteenth century. There were two distinct classes of performing dog, those highly trained for the theatre and circus where they earned fortunes, and the less polished performers of the streets and fairgrounds capable of earning only pennies.[50] Jerry's dancing dogs in *The Old Curiosity Shop* clearly belong to the latter category.

Scholars disagree whether the Punch show is primarily Italian or

Dancing Dogs.

London, Published Sept.ʳ 1 1804 by Harriett Knights Sweetings Alley Cornhill.

Highly trained dogs earned fortunes in the circus and theatre for their owners, but straggling street performances were far from lucrative.

English in origin. In sixteenth-century Naples a *commedia dell'arte* character named Pulcinella flourished both as played by a living actor with a mask and as a puppet. He first appeared in England as a marionette called Punch during the Restoration, and glove puppets blossomed in the first decades of the nineteenth century.[51] Swiveller does not exactly clarify the problem of origin with his remark (cancelled in manuscript) that ' "Punch is about the best thing, in the way of a national stage – after the ballet at the Italian Opera House" ', but Dickens treats Punch as a native phenomenon, naming his puppet-men Harris (known as Short, or Trotters) and Codlin, and including such wholly English characters as Judy and Toby.[52] As a marionette Punch had been confined largely to halls and fairgrounds, owing to the bulk and complexity of this kind of puppetry, but as a glove puppet, with both the entire cast and the booth readily portable, he took to the streets, setting up anywhere a crowd could be assembled. Codlin and Short perform in an empty barn, on the streets, at the races, and in front of the Single Gentleman's window, and their practice reflects the habit of all Punch and Judy men of the day, who are pictured in contemporary illustrations performing indoors and out, daytime or night.

Large, even fabulous sums were available to the most fortunate of popular entertainers. Frederick Reynolds, writing in 1826, recollected a dog troupe at Sadler's Wells in the 1780s which cleared £7,000 for Wroughton, the manager. There were fourteen dogs in all, and they performed a military drama, led by their star canine, Moustache, 'in his little uniform, military boots, with smart musket and helmet, cheering and inspiring his fellow soldiers, to follow him up scaling ladders, and storm the fort'.[53] Madame Tussaud was in a financial position to pay £300 in 1840 for the coronation robes of George IV (to which Dudley Costello, writing in *Household Words* in 1854, took particular aversion); in a six-week visit to the Lowther Arcade, Strand, in 1834, she paid £7 10s per week for her space and took a total of £202 in receipts.[54] And the great 'Muster' Richardson was reported to have left £20,000 at his death in 1837, a fortune earned entirely from his fairground theatre booth.[55]

Less exceptionally, comfortable earnings were possible for street and fair performers. John Payne Collier, compiler in 1828 of the first published text of a Punch and Judy drama, estimated that a pair of exhibitors at that time could earn around thirty shillings a day between them, by giving ten performances and collecting two to four shillings for each. This figure is corroborated by the puppeteer Henry Mayhew interviewed, who claimed to have earned around five pounds a week all through the year when he started in 1825.[56] Two other of Mayhew's informants said that even better income was usual for the early 1830s. One reported that at that time stilt-vaulters (performers on exceptionally tall stilts) could earn three to four pounds in a single afternoon; another referred to race meetings as particularly lucrative, normally bringing in three pounds a day at Epsom and once seven pounds from a single carriage there, although his usual earnings at this time were fifty shillings a week.[57]

These figures disguise the fact that, far from performing all the time, itinerant showfolk spent long hours travelling from one site to another. And when the country suffered a severe economic depression between the late 1830s and the early 1840s income fell accordingly. Dickens presents an altogether less sanguine picture, and his showman Vuffin, the proprietor of a giant and a little lady without arms and legs, is loquacious about the problems. He attributes their causes to an oversupply of curiosities.

> 'Once make a giant common and giants will never draw again. Look at wooden legs. If there was only one man with a wooden leg what a property *he*'d be!'
>
> 'So he would!' observed the landlord and Short both together. 'That's very true.'
>
> 'Instead of which', pursued Mr Vuffin, 'if you was to advertise Shakespeare played entirely by wooden legs, it's my belief you wouldn't draw a sixpence.' (*OCS*, 19)

Vuffin's gloomy outlook, if not his reasoning, is confirmed by historical evidence. We have already considered the financial decline of Bartholomew Fair in the 1830s; by the 1850s Mayhew recorded that Punch was attracting only five shillings a day, stilts twenty-five shillings a week, and the Italian dog-trainer he interviewed was a lonely and pathetic figure, earning 'de tree shilling – sometime de couple – sometime not nothing' for twenty, thirty, even forty performances in a day. Sick, hungry and dirty, this old man, who started work around 1840 with ten dogs, had now only three, was often unable to work, and then liable to stoning by street urchins.[58]

Even Astley's, the prosperous metropolitan circus, which Kit and Barbara visit in Chapter 39, was going through hard times. Despite the fillip of a visit by Queen Victoria and Prince Albert on 20 May 1840, Andrew Ducrow, the proprietor and star, was ill with asthma; his wife was pregnant; and 'La Petite Ducrow', his 11-year-old niece, was killed in a household accident. These woes depleted the ranks of performers, and attendances fell off. Worst of all, a few months after Dickens completed *The Old Curiosity Shop*, for the third time in its history Astley's suffered a disastrous fire.[59] On 8 June 1841 the entire amphitheatre burned to the ground, a fate all too common for every venue of entertainment in that era: the Theatres Royal both at Covent Garden and at Drury Lane had burned down earlier in the century, and in 1845 the booth theatre of Johnson and Nelson Lee, late Richardson's, was destroyed by fire. Whatever the pretension or prosperity of an amusement enterprise, such a fate was in more senses than one a great leveller.

Nell does not visit Astley's, the only stationary show in *The Old Curiosity Shop*, and in stark contrast to the presentation of all the other showfolk in the novel, who appear principally when they are not performing, the actors at Astley's are seen only in the ring, their private lives being entirely withheld. Because of this, the visit to Astley's is the sole detachable entertainment episode in the novel, and its separateness from the lives of the chief characters increases the feeling of holiday in the chapter.

VI

The novel does not give us more than a few glimpses of these entertainments in action, but takes us instead behind the scenes and portrays the showmen off duty, talking about their trade, preparing for exhibition, and coping with their daily tasks of eating, drinking, sleeping and moving on. Dickens's picture is affectionate, lingering with warm humour over their speech and mannerisms, not blinking their very real failings, but finding in them the genuine dignity of imperfect human beings coping with the business of being alive, and according to them the ultimate compliment of artistic seriousness, presenting them in vivid, historically accurate detail. He finds them on the lower fringes of society, poor, ignorant and shabby, but he recognizes the humanity of their cheerful conviviality; even the misanthropic Codlin, tempered for us as he is by Short's easy sociability, seems to have more relish than bitterness in his taciturnity, and the scene at the Jolly Sandboys, in particular, invites us to respond positively to these figures.

Dickens's assessment of them, which radiates into the larger concerns of the book and accords with the historical evidence, is that these showmen are the remnants of a dwindling breed. Dickens is fascinated, and he is charitable, but the overwhelming impression of his depiction is of impending collapse. All of these figures live on the edge of poverty, with no real prospect of improvement. Our first view of the puppet-men is – as significantly for them as for Nell – in a graveyard, where Punch 'seemed to be pointing with the tip of his cap to a most flourishing epitaph, and to be chuckling over it with all his heart' (*OCS*, 16). Dickens is at pains to tie Codlin and Short to the character of their puppet. Short 'seemed to have unconsciously imbibed something of his hero's character', and Codlin had a look 'perhaps inseparable from his occupation as well'. Talking to Short after a performance, the spectators are 'unable to separate him from the master-mind of Punch', and Codlin is seen a little later inside the booth looking out, 'presenting his head and face in the proscenium of the stage, and exhibiting an expression of countenance not often seen there'. We are never granted a look at a performance in progress, but we next find Punch 'utterly devoid of spine, all slack and drooping in a dark box, with his legs doubled up round his neck, and not one of his social qualities remaining' (*OCS*, 17). This association of Punch and his exhibitors with graveyards and coffins sets the tone for the entire episode with the showmen, and contributes to the book's overall mood of poverty and decay, which is summed up in the final sentence: 'Such are the changes which a few years bring about, and so do things pass away, like a tale that is told' (*OCS*, 73).

Closely linked to this sense of passing is the nostalgia which pervades *The Old Curiosity Shop*. Nell flees from the mouldering shop in the hope of finding 'a return of the simple pleasures they had once enjoyed' (*OCS*, 12), and throughout the book she is repeatedly associated with old men, old buildings and old values. It is significant in this regard that her brother, who is devoid of any sense of veneration, is described as 'young' Trent, whereas Christopher Nubbles, several years Fred's junior, is generally referred to as 'old' Kit. Among the showmen, traditional forms of entertainment command their allegiance, and sitting by the fireside of the Jolly Sandboys after supper Vuffin regales the assembled travellers with reminiscence of his mentor, old Maunders.

> 'Why I remember the time when old Maunders as had three-and-twenty wans – I remember the time when old Maunders had in his cottage in Spa Fields in the winter-time, when the season was over, eight male and female dwarfs setting down to dinner every day, who was waited on by eight old giants in green coats, red smalls, blue cotton stockings, and high-lows . . .' (*OCS*, 19)

Such leisurely recollection 'beguiled' the time for the showmen, and reminds us, as well as them, of the days gone by.

The showmen respond to their difficulties with keen awareness of economic necessity. As James Kincaid has pointed out, they are ruled by a 'cash nexus' which debases them and their calling.[60] Codlin and Short are eager to betray Nell and her grandfather in the hope of financial reward, and their tactic of attempting to reassure her with pledges of undying – but false – friendship is a sorry perversion of the moral value which the novel places in highest regard. Jerry withholds food from the old leader of his troupe of dogs because the unfortunate creature 'lost a halfpenny today'. Most ominously, Vuffin hints darkly about the fate of a giant who was bad for business.

> 'There was one giant – a black 'un – as left his caravan some years ago and took to carrying coach-bills about London, making himself as cheap as crossing-sweepers. He died. I make no insinuation against anybody in particular,' said Mr Vuffin, looking solemnly round, 'but he was ruining the trade; – and he died.'   (*OCS*, 19)

Such an overriding concern with monetary gain links the showmen thematically with the book's villains, Quilp, Brass and Fred, each of whom is motivated largely by greed. The ultimate social consequence of the money ethic is made emphatic immediately after Nell leaves the last of the showfolk behind for ever, in the lurid vision of industrial debasement as a living hell (*OCS*, 44–5).

Mrs Jarley is different. There is more than a hint of magic about her: Nell finds it 'an unfathomable mystery' to discover 'by what kind of gymnastic exercise the lady of the caravan ever contrived to get into' her sleeping-berth, and the very caravan blunders on 'as if it too had been drinking strong beer and was drowsy' (*OCS*, 27). Despite the emphasis on her weaknesses of the flesh, Mrs Jarley is seen invariably in a humorous light, a perspective which J. B. Priestley has admirably defined as 'tender mockery, as found in a loving family'.[61] Jarley's limitations (such as her insistence that she has been unable to sleep a wink on a night when her snoring has kept Nell awake) are treated throughout not as vices but as engaging vanities and foibles, and her kindness, generosity and tolerance give her a moral stature of a wholly different order from that of the other show people. Her first action is to feed Nell, and she next offers her a job, allows her to keep the gratuities she receives, and is genuinely grieved when Nell and her grandfather disappear. In a book which places the highest premium on faithful loyalty to others, her true friendship for Nell is a very positive virtue. Mrs Jarley is of a superior status to the other itinerants whom Nell meets, but her respectability is nevertheless anything but secure. There are more urchins than royalty in evidence among those her show attracts, and like Codlin and Short she is liable to legal harassment under the vagrancy laws. Although the threat to have her put in the stocks is mere bluster from the ridiculous Monflathers (who also calls Nell 'wicked' for being a waxwork child instead of assisting in her country's manufactures), there is sufficient basis in the schoolmistress's prejudice to move the amiable Jarley to tears, and all Slum's poetry and even a personal visit from Nell to the school are unable to turn more than a portion of the pupils into paying customers. Mrs Jarley is philosophical about her tribulations, however, and she is quickly able to laugh at Miss Monflathers's threats. Perhaps the most emphatic indication that Dickens intends affirmation in his portrait of Jarley is our final glimpse of her, on her wedding day. In a novel in which the principal characters are frantically driving each other to destruction, and in marked contrast to the graveyard setting for Punch, Mrs Jarley is last seen celebrating her marriage to the faithful George, refusing money from the Single Gentleman for her kindness to Nell, and happily jolting away in the caravan to spend her honeymoon 'in a country excursion' (*OCS*, 47).

In her adventures with Mrs Jarley, Nell is rapidly established as the 'chief attraction' of the waxwork show, and her position there epitomizes her relation in general to the other entertainment elements of *The Old Curiosity Shop*. When she meets Mrs Jarley, Nell and her grandfather are wandering aimlessly, tired and fearful in an environment wholly new to them. As Mrs Jarley observes, Nell looks 'out of her element' at the racecourse, and she is hardly any less bewildered by the caravan and its contents; in her innocence, Nell has at first no idea what waxworks are (*OCS*, 27). Once befriended by Jarley, however, Nell fits comfortably into her new surroundings, learning the lore and patter of the entertainer and becoming herself 'an important item of the curiosities', indeed, 'quite a sensation' when she rides in the waxworks parade (*OCS*, 28). But, however extraordinary she seems to others in such a setting, Nell herself is soon quite at home; she feels 'no cause of anxiety in connection with the wax-work' (*OCS*, 29). All of her terrors arise from external threats: the menace of Quilp and the criminal irresponsibility of her grandfather. When she discovers the old man's plot to rob Mrs Jarley, Nell's security in the waxwork is shattered, and she is forced once more to take flight, an action which is simultaneously a sacred mission – Dickens describes her at this moment as an 'angel messenger' – and a source of unmitigated woe – once away from the caravan she is seen 'bursting into tears' (*OCS*, 42).

Nell's situation in the company of Mrs Jarley is thus both special and typical. The caravan offers her a unique haven, and she feels more inner comfort at the waxworks than anywhere else we see her, save the shop and the village where she dies. It is by far the most congenial encounter Nell experiences with the entertainment world, but it is a typical adventure in that she is at once part of the environment and apart from it. Just as Master Humphrey reacts to the incongruous juxtaposition of a lovely young girl and the musty lumber of the shop, so, too, Dickens emphasizes the bizarre contrasts between her and her surroundings. Nell is an alien creature in the world of show business, but her presence in it both complements and contrasts with Dickens's vision of the fading vitality of early nineteenth-century entertainment.

It is through Nell's travels that we make acquaintance with all of the itinerant showfolk, and through her perspective that we view their activities. Dickens's presentation of Nell is thus firmly tied to his sketches of these characters, and an understanding of his aims in the novel depends, in significant measure, on our response to the popular entertainment in it. *The Old Curiosity Shop* is about the inability of an innocent young girl to survive in a cruel world. We saw in Chapter 2 the premium Dickens places on childhood, and the integral association he makes between the qualities of childhood and the values of entertainment. The poignancy of Nell's fate depends crucially on her tender years. Throughout the book she is 'Little' Nell, 'the child' – 'fine girl of her age, but small', remarks Swiveller (*OCS*, 7) – and her youth is a constant reminder of her need for love, help and support, a need which goes largely unfulfilled. Dickens places a child in a context of entertainment and demonstrates that she does not find adequate refuge there. It is a story of betrayal – a betrayal by the very force which should be the mainstay of one who is, in the words of the epitaph Dickens had carved on the gravestone of his beloved sister-in-law Mary Hogarth, 'young, beautiful, and good'.[62] Dickens's indictment of popular entertainment in this novel is its failure to provide the healing graces which ought by right to be among her chief supports.

VII

Nell is betrayed by the entertainers to whom she turns for help in her flight from the villainous Quilp. Codlin and Short, like Quilp, pledge disinterested affection for her but act from motives of mercenary greed. Mrs Jarley, sincere in her concern for Nell, tries to succour her, but the waxwork is incapable of protecting Nell first from horrible visions of Quilp, then from the Quilpine figure of her grandfather sneaking into her bedroom by night. In the shop Nell has nightmares of 'ugly faces that were frowning over her and trying to peer into her room' and of her grandfather's blood 'creeping,

creeping, on the ground to her own bedroom door' (*OCS*, 9). These terrors are realized when she sees not his blood but the old man himself 'creeping along the floor' to rob her of the money she has earned from Mrs Jarley. Quilp is the threat which drives Nell to her premature death, and Quilp, she finds, resides in the world of popular entertainment.

He is the most extraordinary curiosity in *The Old Curiosity Shop*. Dickens introduces him as a freak worthy of exhibition and routinely refers to him as 'the dwarf'. Quilp is associated with a veritable menagerie of exotic animals: in the course of the story he is called 'shrimp', 'rat', 'hawk', 'monkey', 'lion', 'snake', 'ferret', 'salamander', 'mole', 'fly', 'weazle', 'lynx', 'hedgehog', 'bull', and 'toad'; he himself adds to this list by abusing others variously as 'crocodile', 'minx', 'parrot', 'worm', 'jade', 'rhinoceros', 'tortoise', 'rat', 'bird', 'pigeon', 'monkey' and, most frequently, 'dog'. Dogs are the animal with which he is systematically linked, usually of the ferocious rather than dancing variety, but his gleeful taunting of the chained dog in Chapter 21 is a scene straight from Mr Punch's fight with Toby. Additionally, his one affectionate impulse, the 'strange and mutual liking' he shares with Tom Scott, is for a boy who spends most of the time standing on his head, a skill which ultimately gives Tom 'extraordinary success' before 'overflowing audiences' as a professional tumbler (*OCS*, 73), but which also serves succinctly to indicate the unnatural and inverted basis of their friendship.

Much critical attention has been devoted to Quilp in recent years, and a number of sources in popular culture have been proposed for his character: an actual dwarf named Prior who lived in Bath, the evil dwarf and devil of folklore and the comic devil of the English stage, a fairy tale called 'The Yellow Dwarf', the father of Joseph Grimaldi, and Punch.[63] Of these possible sources, Punch is by far the most rewarding to consider, not only because numerous parallels can be drawn between transcriptions of nineteenth-century Punch and Judy shows and the character and activities of Quilp, but also because parallels within the book itself between Quilp and the Punch-exhibitors in the story can be shown to generate purposeful resonance.[64] Like Punch, Quilp is little, ugly, violent and frenetically mirthful; like Punch, he delights in surprise, pops up unexpectedly, feigns death, torments his wife, fights with a dog, and hurls verbal and physical abuse at everyone in sight. These and other similarities have been discussed by Rachel Bennett, who amply demonstrates that 'although Quilp does not hold the stage as much as Punch he affects the lives of most of the characters by his machinations. His spirit of Punch-like activity also reaches far.' This is admirable, but when she argues that Quilp provides 'Dickens's main opposition to

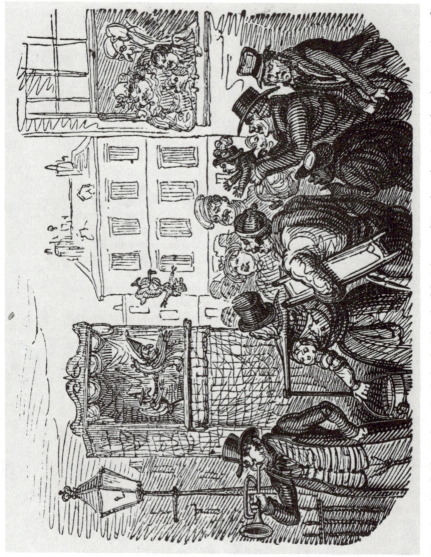

'Punch and Judy' by Robert Cruikshank. The gleeful violence of Punch underpins Dickens's conception of Quilp and generates resonance well beyond the scenes including entertainers in *The Old Curiosity Shop*.

the death-directed world' and 'confers invulnerability' to life's calamities and afflictions one must disagree entirely.[65] Dickens uses the image of Punch not as he finds him, but for his own artistic purposes in *The Old Curiosity Shop*, and in his hands Punch is transformed from the immortal hero of the street performers into an agent of evil and death.

In the puppet play of Punch and Judy, Punch represents the extravagant wish-fulfilment of total humour, in which no obstacle can overcome the self-sufficiency of the hero. He demands unbridled personal freedom and cheerfully dismisses one subordinate figure after another, including the devil.[66] To achieve this stature, Punch alone is permitted sympathetic identification from the audience; only he appears all through the episodic performance, and no moral stricture offered by the other characters can stand up to his carefree cynicism. Structurally, then, Punch is the wholly dominant emotional core of the play, and the audience can indulge in the anarchic holiday which his activities represent, secure in the knowledge that all of the puppets will pop up again for the next performance.

Imbibing many of the qualities of Punch, Quilp assuredly provides readers of *The Old Curiosity Shop* with the entertainment of a great comic character. He is less the figure of mechanical rigidity which Bergson saw in puppet-like activity than a potent emblem of the aggressive self-gratification which Freud diagnosed as the root of jokes.[67] For all the emphasis on his physicality, in descriptive detail, animal imagery and overt sexuality, Quilp is amazingly free from normal physical limitations which beset ordinary mortals and every other character in *The Old Curiosity Shop*. He stays up all night without getting tired, smokes and drinks without getting light-headed, eats indigestible foods without getting sick, and seems capable of popping up at any time and any place. His special status is wish-fulfilment of the most extravagant kind. He torments his wife and mother-in-law, humiliates his enemies, goes off to live by himself and sleep in a hammock, watches his own funeral preparations, bites his fingernails – which are dirty – scratches his head, sticks out his tongue, makes faces, shouts, sings, makes love to whomever he pleases, and hits whomever he hates.

Additionally, the association of his character with the traditional puppet hero (who in his turn has historical kinship with the Vice figure of medieval morality plays, with Harlequin, with the Fool and with Falstaff) colours our attitude to him and prepares us to find his actions comically entertaining.[68] The demotion of a human figure to the level of a puppet makes him an object of ridicule and simultaneously creates an interplay of fantasy with reality in which the need for motivation and responsibility are qualified by a puppet's obsessive action and a puppet's harmless violence: Punch hits people because it is his nature to do so, and Judy is back on stage exchanging blows with him the next time the curtain rises. Quilp's delight in himself and in his jokes, surprises and schemes is infectious, so that ridicule is tempered with enjoyment. He is not only comic object but also comedian, an entertainer with a wharf full of tricks on display. Dickens invites us to participate in Quilp's enjoyment by describing him frequently in ironically decorous language. Thus Quilp is a 'gentleman' who torments his wife for her 'comfort', an 'agreeable figure' who sneaks up on Nell out of 'delicacy'. His habitual cheating at cards is a 'humorous habit', and he brandishes his poker 'amiably'.

But, for all these vital qualities and for all the narrative invitations for us to take delight in him, Quilp, unlike Punch, exists in a narrative structure which insistently condemns him. Instead of fighting the devil, Quilp becomes himself diabolical, in a pervasive imagery pattern which links him with Satan. He strives to seduce Nell, rob her grandfather, imprison Kit and humiliate nearly everyone else in the book; but, unlike the hero of the puppet show, Quilp is not the sole focus of interest, and the reader is made to feel the threat which Quilp's destructiveness poses to the vitality of the other characters, who, however far removed from literary realism, have only single lives within the story. Furthermore, as James Kincaid points out, Quilp's independence gradually proves to be 'self-imposed isolation', retreat and regression; as he cuts himself off from all human contact, his cheerful pranks turn into maniacal assaults on a wooden figurehead, and by locking the gate and extinguishing the light in his final moments he effectively prevents his own rescue.[69] The inquest verdict of suicide fittingly concludes his career.

By transforming Punch into a villain, Dickens establishes a context in *The Old Curiosity Shop* for exploring the underside of the popular amusement of the day. Quilp is a compelling image of entertainment as utter licence. He is Dickens's fantasy on the holiday spirit of pleasure-seeking propelled to frenzied extremes of freedom and aggression. Merriment causes him not merely to laugh, sing and dance, but to howl, stamp his feet, roll about, and chop the ground with his knife 'in an ecstasy' (*OCS*, 13). Dickens is explicit that Quilp's antics are not simply odd characteristics but performances with spectators in mind. For those spectators within the book, however, Quilp offers not amusement but cause for dismay. The only audience he seeks to please is himself alone. Far from promoting fellow-feeling, amusement for Quilp is entirely self-serving. He takes advantage of his ugliness by making faces at everyone from his mother-in-law to the chained dog; his mere threat to grimace at

Jacob Nubbles freezes that young gentleman 'into a silent horror' (*OCS*, 21). He takes malevolent delight in startling people and has a savage streak of ridicule, which frequently turns to violence. His idea of a joke is to cause discomfort to others, whether by denying Mrs Jiniwin access to the case-bottle while they are playing cards, pouring boiling rum down the throat of Sampson Brass, or beating Tom Scott with a poker. For him holiday release is a defiance of all restraint. Quilp rejects law, custom, decency, propriety, responsibility and even physical necessity in his raging demand to do whatever he wants, whenever he wants. The anarchic nature of Quilp's sort of freedom is contrasted with Nell's flight to peace, Swiveller's creative fancy and Kit's release from prison.

Freedom for Quilp means oppression for others, and his licence is ultimately destructive to himself as well as to Nell. And because Punch appears in *The Old Curiosity Shop* not only in his adapted image as Quilp, but also in his own right as the puppet of Codlin and Short, a parallel is created through which the implications of the one extend over to the other. Punch's character informs basic components of Dickens's conception of Quilp, as we have just seen; reciprocally, Quilp pervades the scenes with Codlin and Short.

In her terror of Quilp, Nell flees from the curiosity shop with her grandfather, only to find herself soon in the presence of Quilp's other self, Punch. She does not recognize Punch as Quilp at once, cheerfully volunteering to sew Judy's dress for the puppeteers, but it is only a matter of hours before Punch becomes as threatening to her as Quilp, and she flees at her first opportunity. Her action gains coherence of meaning when we recognize the interrelation of Quilp and Punch.

Punch, as we would expect, appears fully in character, ugly, cheerful and mocking – just like Quilp. We have noted already that from the outset he is associated with death, sitting gaily on a tombstone when Nell first sees him. In addition, he is as domineering as Quilp, subjecting his companions, the puppeteers Codlin and Short, to his own comfort. Dickens makes explicit that Codlin's monetary profit from the puppet show makes him as fully Punch's slave as Brass, for similar motives, is Quilp's creature.

And here Mr Codlin's false position in society and the effect it wrought upon his wounded spirit, were strongly illustrated; for whereas he had been last night accosted by Mr Punch as 'master' and had by inference left the audience to understand that he maintained that individual for his own luxurious entertainment and delight, here he was, now, painfully walking beneath the burden of that same Punch's temple, and bearing it boldly upon his shoulders on a sultry day and along a dusty road. (*OCS*, 17)

Punch displays his power not only on the stage, where he beats all his relations and acquaintance and at last kills the devil; he maintains his supremacy even when he is crumpled in a dark box, forcing the puppet-man to carry him on his back.

For Nell, however, there is little to choose between Punch, Codlin and Short. Because Dickens gives the puppeteers characteristics of the puppet, their words and actions towards her combine to form a single, identifiable threat. Codlin and Short view the company of Nell and her grandfather as an opportunity for their own profit and resolve to hold them hostage until searchers appear. To keep Nell unsuspicious, they each make profuse offers of eternal – and false – friendship. Codlin and Short thus become a threat to Nell in their desire to limit her liberty for their personal gain, and the child becomes frightened and flees from them. Nell suspects but does not know the exact nature of their scheme, and the lack of precision to her fears ties her entire encounter with the puppet-men into one frightening experience, in which Punch's jaunty derision of the graveyard, his domination of Codlin and Short, and their offers of friendship loom together as motivation for her flight. Punch and his men are not Quilp, but to Nell their threat is certainly Quilpine: the mockery, power, and professions of personal admiration which instil fears in her make the puppet show a second manifestation of the very things from which Nell is fleeing in Quilp. In this sense, Quilp is as much present to Nell in the puppet form of Punch as he is in his dwarfish form back in London. Mrs Jarley is emphatic that her entertainment is far removed from Punch, but Nell soon finds the terror of Quilp in the waxwork as well. The waxen effigies take on the aspect of Quilp to her, and her grandfather's gambling endows him, too, with Quilpine threat.[70] For Nell within the world of the showfolk the dwarf is palpable nightmare, and the horrifying discovery of this evil in her only friend and helpmate, her grandfather, proves fatal to her now solitary flight. From this moment (*OCS*, 30) Nell's strength fails until she collapses and dies.

Conceived in popular entertainment and manifest to Nell among the entertainers, Quilp's nature is nevertheless antithetical to the values of entertainment. At a time when the amusements of the people were under great pressure, Dickens chose not only to compose a threnody for a dying culture but also, through the indirection of a fantasy figure, to expose qualities of that culture which ought not to survive. When Quilp drowns Dickens offers a final glimpse of the 'blazing ruin' of his body, his hair and clothes which 'fluttered idly in the night wind'. Emphatically, this is an image of the mocker mocked, presented in stark contrast not only to Nell's peaceful passing but also to Quilp's own earlier supposed death. When he was alive Quilp took perverse delight in watching his own funeral preparations; as a corpse, he has lost that pleasure for ever and is himself subjected to the ultimate 'mockery of death' (*OCS*, 67).

This death is the deserved fate of a malign individual personage. It is the opposite of vitality. It is also Dickens's exorcism of poisons which he diagnosed in popular entertainment. In the hardness of their lot, the entertainers in *The Old Curiosity Shop* take greater interest in their own comforts than in the pleasure for others on which their very existence is predicated. Their financial straits incite them to place undue emphasis on gain, and to promote companionship on only a limited and superficial level, since rivalry determines their actions with regard to one another. These negations of the proper spirit of entertainment, which make it impossible for Nell to remain for long among the showfolk, are embodied in extreme form as the greed, selfishness and malice of Quilp. By projecting these vices on to a villain Dickens made it possible to touch them only lightly as characteristics of the entertainers themselves, who are portrayed instead with affection, charity and sorrow.

VIII

Having explored the unpropitious state of entertainment and having condensed its worst excesses into an extraordinary comic villain, Dickens offers in contrast and counterpoint a joyous image of the next stage beyond entertainment, in the career of Richard Swiveller. Through this character he shows the creative and humanly beneficial power of a willingness to respond positively to the essential core of entertainment, its capacity to stimulate fancy.[71] Swiveller is the thematic alternative to the destructiveness elsewhere in *The Old Curiosity Shop*, and a transition figure in the development of Dickens's fiction. After this novel entertainers were to figure far less than they had done previously, while the necessity for fancy and the strength of character it is capable of bestowing became increasingly important.

Dick Swiveller enters the novel as a drunken wastrel, fond of melodramatic gesture and endlessly adapting snatches of Tom Moore and other songwriters popular at the time.[72] He never gives over his love of melodrama and song, but in the course of the story his moral stature grows considerably; he rescues a hungry waif from harsh servitude, helps to secure Kit's release from prison, and instigates the exposure of Quilp and Brass. Unlike Nell, Swiveller is

DURING BARTON FAIR.

MOST

Extraordinary Novelty!

THE WONDER OF THE PRESENT AGE!

Under the Patronage of the ROYAL FAMILY, and the First of Nobility,

TOBY!

THE

SAPIENT PIG,

From the Royal Promenade Rooms, Spring Gardens, London.

He is in colour the most beautiful of his race; in symmetry the most perfect, and in temper the most docile.—He far exceeds any thing ever yet seen, for his intelligent Performances It is impossible to form an adequate idea of the surprising sagacity of this Animal; in him the power of Instinct is so extremely striking, that it seems superior to reason in many instances, and to some Persons it may have the appearance of romance; but the curious may form some just idea of his extraordinary capacity from the following particulars:—

THIS MOST SURPRISING CREATURE WILL

SPELL AND READ,

CAST ACCOUNTS,

Tell the Points of the Sun's Rising and Setting.

Any Lady or Gentleman may put Figures in a Box, and make what numbers they please, and then shut up the Box, and this wonderful Pig absolutely will tell what number is made before the Box is opened. *He will tell any Person what o'Clock it is to a Minute, by their Watch;*

TELL THE AGE OF ANY ONE IN COMPANY;

AND WHAT IS MORE ASTONISHING,

HE WILL DISCOVER A PERSON'S THOUGHTS!!

And when asked a Question, will give an immediate Answer. In fact, he is beyond every conception, and must be seen to be believed. He is the only Scholar of his Race ever known or heard of in the world.

Those Ladies and Gentlemen who please to honour MR. HOARE with their presence may depend on witnessing the greatest prodigy in existence.

An Elegant Place is prepared for the Scene of his Exploits, adjoining the Turnpike Gate, Barton-Street, Gloucester;—To commence each Day during the Fair at the following Hours:—viz, One, Two, Three, Four, Five and Six.—*Admittance One Shilling.*

[W. Price, Printer, Gloucester.]

Dick Swiveller, whose every observation serves to stimulate his fancy, attempts to encourage 'bliss and concord' between Fred and his grandfather by telling them about a pig he saw 'with a straw in his mouth' (*OCS*, 2).

unafraid of Quilp or the Brasses – indeed, he is fascinated by all three. He is able to stand up to Quilp in a direct fight and to find positive enjoyment in entertainment too boisterous for Nell. His early adventures with Sophy and Nell are conceived, produced and acted single-handedly by him as elaborate stage romances, and the entirely theatrical nature of his attentions to Nell prevents us from ever thinking of him as a serious danger to her. Under the tutelage of Sampson and Sally Brass, Swiveller learns the pitfalls of carelessness, even as his idle search for amusement in their office leads him to befriend their persecuted servant. Since she lacks a name, he gives her a title, and because she responds to this extravagant re-creation of herself the Marchioness changes in fact from a passive victim into an active heroine capable of saving Swiveller's life and of setting the forces of justice in motion. Their romance is a low-life version of Keats's description of Adam's dream: by dint of imagination, reality is transformed to match the idea. Swiveller wakes to find it true, and he and the Marchioness live happily ever after, as is only right. Their transformation affirms more emphatically than any other moment in Dickens's work the potency of healthy imaginative life in however humble a condition.

Swiveller's entrance into *The Old Curiosity Shop* (*OCS*, 2) seems hardly suitable for the ultimate hero of the story. The 'profligate' accomplice of young Trent in an errand of extortion, Dick looks so shabby and speaks so affectedly that he bores and irritates his listeners, and his effort to charm Fred's grandfather is a total failure. He is at first a minor character whose affectations expose him to ridicule, and in some ways he remains a subsidiary and satirized figure throughout the story. His poetical quotations and fanciful observations never disappear; his carelessness leads to foolish complicity in Fred's plot against Nell and Quilp's against Kit; his susceptibility to 'sunshine' makes him a tool in Quilp's hands. Swiveller appears in the book far less often than either Nell or Quilp, and he wholly lacks either her moral purity or the dwarf's active villainy. For these reasons he appears an unlikely candidate for prominence in the novel's resolution. But Swiveller's flights of fancy provide an alternative to Nell's search for pastoral calm and Quilp's isolation; he alone is able to survive in an evil world.

The primary use to which he puts his fancy is the entertainment of himself and others. In his eagerness to share the pleasures to which he responds so abundantly, he differs fundamentally from other entertainers in the book. He tries to inject merriment into his conference with Fred after their failure to get money at the shop; he sits beside the dour Sally Brass when Punch plays outside the office, and he sends Kit a daily mug of beer in prison.

The decisive moment in his career occurs in Chapter 57, in which he discovers Sally's tiny housemaid spying on him and confronts her with a series of questions. When her answers kindle his curiosity and imagination, he offers her a glass of beer and entertains her with conversation and card-games. The situation is humble enough – a ne'er-do-well clerk drinking beer with a hungry servant-girl in the cellar of a disreputable law-office – but Dickens and Dick conduct the scene with such delicacy and fancy that it transcends its dull circumstances, and for a few fairy-tale moments the little girl becomes the Marchioness and Dick her romantic hero, until the time arrives when they must lock up for the night and send Dick home to bed. Although extravagant scenes and characters fill *The Old Curiosity Shop*, and Dick himself is full of wild fantasies, this encounter is, in Dick's own words, 'a most inscrutable and unmitigated staggerer' (*OCS*, 58).

The scene arises from Dick's search for entertainment. And so often in his hours at the office, Swiveller is alone and bored, and 'for the better preservation of his cheerfulness' and 'to prevent his faculties from rusting' he tries to amuse himself with cards, playing cribbage with a dummy, 'for twenty, thirty, or sometimes even fifty thousand pounds a side, besides many hazardous bets to a considerable amount' (*OCS*, 57). When he distinguishes an eye at the keyhole, he changes his method of passing the time by welcoming the eye's diminutive owner, asking her questions, eating and drinking with her, and playing cards with her instead of by himself. For further amusement he assumes the manner of a theatrical bandit, 'handing the tankard to himself with great humility, receiving it haughtily, drinking from it thirstily, and smacking his lips fiercely' (*OCS*, 58). When such demonstrations alarm the little girl, Dick 'discharges his brigand manner', converses cheerfully and recites poetry. The whole episode begins as no more than an effort to find enjoyment on a dull evening, yet it is magical from the start.

There is much need for all the distraction Dick's enterprise can provide, for the circumstances are humble and depressing. Swiveller we know to be an impoverished clerk, and the Marchioness has been introduced as a timid slavey mercilessly harassed by Sally. Dickens offers plentiful detail to ensure our recognition of the lowliness of the scene, particularly emphasizing the privations of the Marchioness: her remarkable thinness, her ignorance, her terror and her loneliness – her only 'company' comes from spying through the keyhole. She has a 'very little' fire, and the cellar floor is 'damp' and 'sloppy'; the food they eat is no more than bread, beef and beer, and the stakes of their gambling are a couple of sixpences. There is nothing in the facts of their situation to arouse enthusiastic delight.

Such humble circumstances are customary fare for Swiveller, whose imagination has found frequent employment in efforts to infuse dullness with colour and interest, and whose fancies have ranged from silliness to the transformation of harsh reality: the entertainment of self-dramatization, as romantic lover to Sophy, as epic hero chiding his Fate, or as managing partner in the House of Brass; the pleasure of grandiose description, of his single room as 'apartments' or of his social acquaintance as 'Glorious Apollers'; the poetry of exotic comparison, seeing Sally as a 'dragon' and a 'mermaid'; the accommodation to practical necessity, by rooming above a tobacco-shop for want of a snuff-box, by philosophizing on the glories of potatoes with the skins left on, and by pretending that his bedstead disappears during the daytime. In every instance, either the object before him or he himself appears in a new light, brightening ordinary existence and turning it into something novel and vivid.

In the scene before us, something more happens. Dick not only imparts imaginative colour but actually alters reality, turning the underfed servant into a marchioness and himself into an actual romantic hero.

Swiveller rescues a friendless orphan, ignorant not simply of the world outside the office but even of her name, age and parentage, and transforms her into a heroine capable of saving his life. In the days that follow his friendly entertainment, Dick falls into a dire fever, and the Marchioness runs away from Sally to nurse him back to health. As a direct result of Dick's encounter with the Marchioness, his life is saved, her oppression is ended, Kit is released from prison, the villainy of Brass and Quilp is overthrown, and Swiveller finds that 'there had been a young lady saving up for him after all' (*OCS*, 73).

In contrast to Quilp's malice, which destroys life, and to Nell's flight, which transcends it, Swiveller's determination to welcome every experience, to dramatize every incident and to regard all his activities with comic detachment leads to creativity, growth and love. Dick Swiveller emerges in a world full of fear and destruction as a positive force for life, and the comic poet inherits the earth. It is but a short step from this to see Swiveller as Dickens's affirmation of a central pillar of his own artistry. Critics have pointed out similarities in personality and in name between Dick and his creator, but the vital resemblance is between them as artists. Swiveller's imagination, like Dickens's, is rooted in observation, in recognition of surprising connections, and in love of language. Above all, it is rooted in love of popular entertainment. Swiveller's positive orientation towards entertainment, his disposition to seek stimulus for his fancy in all things, and his consequent awareness of distinctions and interrelations between fact and fantasy make his romance with the Marchioness credible and help the reader to find the way through the dynamic concoction of reality and invention that is *The Old Curiosity Shop*. By implication, he stands for a perspective on life which offers genuine possibility of survival and happiness in our own world. With the Marchioness, Dick brings to the tragic world of Little Nell an affirmation of hope and joy, as Dickens through the novel itself brings to a society which was crushing ways of life which he cherished an art which showed that, in his hands at least, popular entertainment still had great vitality.

CHAPTER 5

Hard Times

The Necessity of
Popular Entertainment

I entertain a weak idea that the English people are as hard-worked as any people upon whom the sun shines. I acknowledge to this ridiculous idiosyncrasy, as a reason why I would give them a little more play.

(*HT*, I, 10)

I

The Old Curiosity Shop was the culmination of one major phase of Dickens's art. With this novel he paid homage to a passing generation of entertainers and celebrated the joy to be found by the individual who opens himself to the capacity for wonder; in terms of his own artistic development he reached a bolder conception of the creative possibilities of the imagination and its capability of breathing life-sustaining value into the most humble ingredients. Having faced as well the darker recesses of the entertainment world, his affirmations carried the more conviction and gave him the confidence to move, in his subsequent novels, to more ambitious explorations of man and society. The thoroughness of Dickens's analysis in *The Old Curiosity Shop* of the nature and condition of entertainment in the England of his day freed him to move on from that subject as a major focus of his art, and for the next thirteen years showfolk receded to the periphery of his novels. We catch glimpses of the occasional entertainer in his later work – the street juggler who passes with poignant incongruity outside Mr Dombey's house when its windows are shrouded in mourning for the death of Paul (*DS*, 18); the tavern singing of Little Swills, who serves with shrill hilarity as chorus to the inquest on Nemo in *Bleak House* (*BH*, 11) – but not until 1854 and *Hard Times* did Dickens again place entertainers at the centre of one of his novels. At the same time, the avowed purpose of writing fiction which would offer laughter and diversion to his readers was never abandoned, however much other aims entered into his later work. Similarly, the entertainment-seeking perspective evident from the outset of his career – the disposition to respond actively to the most trivial detail which came under his notice, the open-eyed curiosity eager to find amusement wherever he looked – remained with Dickens throughout his life, and gained a new kind of importance as the synthesizing power of his vision matured. Entertainment continued to be fundamental to Dickens's art, even when it was not his overt subject.

Dickens's novels up to *Dombey and Son* are emphatically pre-industrial in their settings. They depict a society in which traditional forms of gregarious, participatory recreation still constitute the principal outlet for people seeking entertainment. One portion of *The Old Curiosity Shop*, it is true, takes Nell into the factory towns of the Black Country, but this episode is a nightmare vision of a world gone berserk, and the 'real' world in which she lives and dies is pastoral. The London portions of the book are dominated by Quilp, who is an old-fashioned miser, not a modern capitalist. Dickens's early fiction shows traditional forms of entertainment declining, hedged in on every side by uncongenial circumstances. The dying clown in *Pickwick* is ruined by his own habitual drunkenness, but Dismal Jemmy, who tells his tale, points out that pantomime actors generally die early or else 'by unnaturally taxing their bodily energies, lose, prematurely, those physical powers on which alone they can depend for subsistence' (*PP*, 3). The cheerful puppet-man, Short, chats convivially with his fellow-entertainers at the Jolly Sandboys in the evening, but he is up betimes the next morning to sneak out ahead of the dancing dogs and the conjuror, to glean pennies before the others have a chance to do so (*OCS*, 19). The self-abasement which the charming Miss Snevellicci is constrained to undergo in order to raise an audience for her bespeak is representative of the financial straits which were closing provincial theatres up and down the country, and her manager is not long afterwards sent packing to the New World.

But if entertainers are seen in retreat in Dickens's early fiction, from the time of *Dombey and Son* (1846–8) they are presented as being ostracized from society altogether. Although historically they had always existed on the fringes, legally denominated 'rogues and vagabonds' from the days of Elizabeth, Dickens initially treated them as welcome guests, exuberantly interacting with other characters in the books and finding eager audiences among some, at least, of the fictive population.[1] His own delight in their endeavours to amuse led him to deal generously with them, and to present their impudence, venality or lack of ability as part of the fun.

Dickens's middle and late fiction, however, betrays a growing pessimism about the possibilities of finding a place for entertainment in the new social fabric. *Hard Times* is the single novel of Dickens's given an industrial setting, but other novels of his maturity, notably *Bleak House, Little Dorrit* and *Our Mutual Friend,* also envisage a contemporary urban environment fundamentally antagonistic to the very notion of carefree amusement for its inhabitants, and even those later novels which are set back in time find no congenial outlet for leisure activities.

In *Dombey and Son* we hear of a giant, a dwarf and a conjuror, objects of dread to Paul's schoolmate Tozer, whose uncle takes him to see them with a 'pretence of kindness', not for any amusement they might provide but as raw materials for a test in classical allusions (*DS*, 14). In *Little Dorrit* Arthur Clennam visits Tite Barnacle in a 'hideous little street' where 'Punch's shows used to lean against the dead wall in Mews Street while their proprietors were dining elsewhere' (*LD*, I, 10). In *Our Mutual Friend* the little fair in the village to which Lizzie Hexam flees is a 'vicious spectacle', consisting of a Fat Lady, Learned Pig, some 'despairing gingerbread that had been vainly trying to dispose of itself all over the country', and a peep-show 'which had originally started with the Battle of Waterloo, and had since made it every other battle of later date by altering the Duke of Wellington's nose' (*OMF*, IV, 6). And in Dickens's last, unfinished novel, *The Mystery of Edwin Drood,* the Christmas entertainments in Cloisterham are no better: there is a waxwork 'on the premises of the bankrupt livery-stable keeper up the lane' and a 'new grand comic Christmas pantomime' advertised by a portrait of the clown, 'quite as large as life and almost as miserable' (*MED*, 14). In each of these instances the entertainment is leaden, associated with decay, death, and traditions which have been drained of vitality. It offers scant means of livelihood to its purveyors and even less possibility of amusement to its patrons. Forms which had once sustained gaiety and wonder have become so degraded that no light of fancy can now find nourishment from them. Perhaps the most distressing example of the brutalization of popular entertainment to be found in Dickens's fiction occurs as metaphor in *Great Expectations.* Pip's horror at discovering that his benefactor is Magwitch (whose formal education was imparted to him by a travelling giant) is increased by the convict's disposition to survey Pip's gentlemanly accomplishments complacently, 'with the air of an Exhibitor' (*GE*, 40, 42). Entertainment has come to be associated with exploitation, not amusement.

Pip's hopes suffer a catastrophic blow with the arrival of his

'Exhibitor', and his progress is mirrored by the career of Mr Wopsle, who finds his own great expectations greeted with derision. Mr Wopsle's venture in the title role of *Hamlet* is the most gloriously comic episode in all of Dickens, but our delight is largely at the aspiring actor's expense, and the derisory nature of the production which seals his doom indicates Dickens's sense of the general level of far too much of the entertainment available at the time he was writing. But if the lot of the entertainer struggling to secure respect (and a living) was precarious the situation for those looking to find relief and amusement was equally unpromising. Symptomatic of Dickens's sense, late in his career, of the possibilities for the innocent entertainment of the common man is his picture of the Six Jolly Fellowship Porters in *Our Mutual Friend*. The boisterous high jinks at the inns of *Pickwick* have given way here to more sedate pleasures, scrupulously supervised by the Porters' mistress, Abbey Potterson. The attractions of the Porters are genuine, with its 'polite beer-pulls that made low bows when customers were served with beer', its 'comfortable fireside', 'delectable drinks' and 'cloth everlastingly laid'. But to keep these comforts secure the strictest regimentation must be imposed. Customers are allowed only as much drink as Abbey sees fit, and they are firmly instructed when it is time for them to leave. Closing-time is a 'ceremony of review and dismissal', and the cost of maintaining the good name of the house is indicated by the banishment of Gaffer, on account of his association with Riderhood, despite Lizzie's plea that it is the only place she knows he is safe. Dickens humorously hints at the quasi-religious authority of the proprietress by noting that some waterside types suppose her related to the Abbey at Westminster, and he links her with the novel's education themes by referring to her as a 'school-mistress' – far more benign in her instruction than the murderous Bradley, but no more permissive than he with her 'pupils' (*OMF*, I, 6).

Throughout the nineteenth century the public house, both in town and in country, was for many the sole available place of amusement, a social centre offering warmth, companionship, and often music and theatrical entertainment; but, as its critics were quick to point out, it was also an exclusively male preserve, which kept a man from his family, encroached on his already limited time and money, and invited drunkenness. Abbey Potterson rigorously strives to eliminate these known evils from the establishment, and the appealing vitality of the Six Jolly Fellowship Porters is suggested from the outset by its crazy appearance; bizarre architecture is invariably a source of delight to Dickens, and the Porters is one of the most eccentric buildings he ever described. Its function as a sanctuary is clear from the pastoral associations it evokes:

> Not without reason was it often asserted by the regular frequen-
> ters of the Porters, that when the light shone full upon the grain
> of certain panels, and particularly upon an old corner cupboard
> of walnut-wood in the bar, you might trace little forests there,
> and tiny trees like the parent tree, in full umbrageous leaf.
>
> (*OMF*, I, 6)

As a verdant retreat from the dust-heaps and riverside violence, the
Porters is a 'haven . . . divided from the rough world'. It is an
isolated refuge rather than a palace of delight, and its limited but
invaluable pleasures are sanctified by links with the past. In its 'old
age fraught with confused memories of its youth', it is in a 'state of
second childhood', hearkening back to less parlous times when
leisure hours could be more carefree and less painstakingly guarded.

The scope for amusement at the Six Jolly Fellowship Porters is
severely constrained: its place is cramped; it boasts no entertainers;
its activities are kept under the strictest control. Nevertheless, it
provides a venue for social conviviality and for the sustaining graces
of life – literally, in the case of Riderhood. Altogether less prepos-
sessing are the private sanctuaries which Dickens envisions for characters denied even the modest relief of a public house. Mrs Plornish's
sitting-room in *Little Dorrit*, for example, has more than a touch of
the absurd to it.

> Mrs Plornish's shop-parlour had been decorated under her own
> eye, and presented, on the side towards the shop, a little fiction
> in which Mrs Plornish unspeakably rejoiced. This poetical
> heightening of the parlour consisted in the wall being painted to
> represent the exterior of a thatched cottage; the artist having
> introduced (in as effective a manner as he found compatible
> with their highly disproportionate dimensions) the real door
> and window . . . No Poetry and no Art ever charmed the
> imagination more than the union of the two in this counterfeit
> cottage charmed Mrs Plornish. It was nothing to her that Plor-
> nish had a habit of leaning against it as he smoked his pipe after
> work, when his hat blotted out the pigeon-house and all the
> pigeons, when his back swallowed up the dwelling, when his
> hands in his pockets uprooted the blooming garden and laid
> waste the adjacent country. To Mrs Plornish it was still a most
> beautiful cottage, a most wonderful deception.   (*LD*, II, 13)

As the final noun indicates, Dickens is alert to the ridiculous nature
of this expression of freedom, but at the same time he is warmly

sympathetic to Mrs Plornish and the extraordinary expedients to which she resorts in her attempt to compensate for lack of leisure-time and minimal recreational opportunities. By looking back to former days Dickens makes explicit the needs which she seeks to fill:

> In London itself, though in the old rustic road towards a suburb of note in the days of William Shakespeare, author and stage-player, there were Royal hunting seats, howbeit no sport is left there now but for hunters of men, Bleeding Heart Yard was to be found. A place much changed in feature and in fortune, yet with some relish of ancient greatness about it.   (*LD*, I, 12)

In the great days of the English theatre, Dickens is saying, the site which is now Bleeding Heart Yard was a place where royalty took its recreation; now, in a gruesome parody of sport, the huntsmen give way to predators upon the impoverished. How fine a touch it is for Dickens to stress the necessity of identifying Shakespeare in this benighted age; the ennobling delights which the Elizabethan stage so abundantly imparted are almost wholly forgotten in the present day, and it is left to poor Mrs Plornish to keep alive the remaining vestiges of value which imagination creates.

Wemmick's gothic castle in *Great Expectations* and Jenny Wren's roof garden in *Our Mutual Friend* are other notable examples of desperately constricted outlets for expansive spirits. Walworth is overtly an escape from the sordid business of criminal law, and in his determination to achieve absolute separation of work and home Wemmick is an archetypal image of a peculiarly modern form of schizophrenia. His calculated self-interest at Little Britain generates its antithesis in his efforts towards wholly spontaneous behaviour in private life, and he seeks the most leisurely of recreations to counter-balance the ruthless efficiency of Jaggers's office. The fishing-pole he shoulders on his walk to the church where he marries Miss Skiffins neatly symbolizes the unconcern of his Walworth sentiments for time and profit. Jenny's garden, high above the offices of Pubsey and Col, where she can 'come up and be dead', consists of 'no more romantic object than a blackened chimney stack over which some humble creeper had been trained' (*OMF*, II, 5). Like Mrs Plornish's parlour and Wemmick's castle, it is a city-dweller's pastoral retreat, depen-dent principally upon imagination to transform ugly reality into spiritual vision. Jenny's only entertainment is the book she shares with Lizzie, and Dickens invites not only our admiration for the valour with which she salvages this morsel of pleasure, but also dismay that so little is possible for her. Small, crippled and prema-turely adult, Jenny is an extreme instance of the person for whom relief is essential, and the constraints she faces give her aspirations the greatest value.

I do not wish to overschematize the shift in Dickens's attitudes: the same late novel which contains Jenny's roof garden also offers one of the most joyful outings Dickens ever described, Bella Wilfer's 'innocent elopement' to Greenwich with her father (*OMF*, II, 8), and interpolated amid the festive delights of Dickens's first novel is the stroller's grisly tale of degradation and death (*PP,* 3). Nevertheless, the clear tendency, which contributes substantially to the growing pessimism which readers have always recognized in Dickens, is a diminution of scope for spontaneous enjoyment; fewer entertainers figure in the later fiction, and amusements are less readily available. The increasing urgency of Dickens's defence of imagination is correlative with his conviction that carefree entertainment is decreasingly possible.

II

Entertainers, peripheral elsewhere in Dickens's novels after 1840, re-emerge as the central repository of human value in *Hard Times*. This novel begins by dramatically juxtaposing the circus people with the proponents of the philosophy of fact; it ends with the exposure of the hypocrisies and inadequacies of that philosophy and the rescue of its survivors by the showfolk. The ringmaster, Sleary, is spokesman for the novel's avowed message; the clown's daughter, Sissy, although not a performer herself, acts as a moral beacon throughout the book, drawing on her circus-inculcated values to dismiss the intending seducer Harthouse and to guide the fallen Louisa and Gradgrind out of disaster. Dickens presents the circus in polar opposition to the perversities of the schoolroom and the factory; motifs of circus and fairy-tale pervade the novel, functioning both as indicators of positive value and as satiric counters with which to ridicule false and misguided attitudes. Additionally, narrative perspective combines with plot and symbol to reinforce themes; as the reader proceeds it becomes apparent that the book's meaning is closed off to an approach by way of Gradgrindian fact, and that only by admitting circus values, and giving reign to imagination, will *Hard Times* yield up its fullest implications.

The novel was begun in haste early in 1854 after a conference between Dickens and his publishers, Bradbury and Evans, to discuss ways of reversing a decline in sales of his periodical, *Household Words*.[2] Dickens wrote to Madame de la Rue shortly before serial publication of the novel commenced: 'It was considered, when I came home [from Italy, where he had spent the latter months of

1853], such a great thing that I should write a story for *Household Words*, that I am at present up to my eyes in one.'[3] But, despite the slightly persecuted tone he adopts here, Dickens was greatly taken with his new task, and after the book was completed he gave a somewhat different account of its inception. 'I intended to do nothing that way for a year when the idea laid hold of me by the throat in a very violent manner,' he wrote in November to Mrs Richard Watson, and his letters during the months of composition show him 'stunned with work' and complaining of the 'crushing' difficulties of adapting to a format of weekly instalments.[4]

His 'idea' for the new book was not, in the first instance, concerned with popular entertainment, but rather with what he saw as the baleful attitudes of utilitarianism. His preliminary list of fourteen possible titles for the novel all focused on either the kill-joy calculations of his philosopher of fact (*Stubborn Things, Two and Two are Four*) or their consequences (*Rust and Dust, Hard Times*).[5] The topics in his mind from the outset were education and industrialism; in January he consulted the Educational Board's methods of examining teachers, and he travelled to Preston that same month specifically to view for himself the conditions resulting from the prolonged strike and lockout there.[6] Later, when the novel neared completion, he was emphatic about the polemical intention behind it. Writing to Carlyle for permission to dedicate *Hard Times* to him, Dickens explained: 'It contains what I do devoutly hope will shake some people in a terrible mistake of these days, when so presented.'[7]

But Dickens's determination to mount a vigorous attack on contemporary attitudes which he deplored led him inevitably to want a counterweight of positive value to relieve the oppression of those negations. In the words from the novel which appear as epigraph to the present chapter, Dickens declared that the very nature of life in industrialized, fact-ridden society was irrefutable justification of people's need for recreation. The existence of this world's Bounderbys calls forth Sleary for the succour of the factory hands; the philosophy of Gradgrind is incomplete because it omits all authentic cognizance of Sissy. Dickens's negative subject, in short, requires his positive one, which echoes Lear's cry, 'Reason not the need'.

In the circus Dickens had an appropriate alternative to Gradgrind and Bounderby immediately at his disposal. Within three weeks of his trip to Preston we find him writing to his friend Mark Lemon, editor of *Punch*, asking for 'any slang terms among the tumblers and circus-people that you can call to mind – I have noted down some – I want them in my new story'.[8] But long before the appeal to Lemon the circus was a subject with which Dickens was intimately familiar. The joys of the circus were fused in his mind with his happiest memories of childhood; as he wrote in his first published piece on the circus, the article on Astley's in *Sketches by Boz*, 'there is no place which recalls so strongly our recollections of childhood as Astley's' (*SB*, p. 104). In this sketch Dickens claims to have attended the circus before the days of Ducrow, who arrived at Astley's (after starting his career there before Dickens was born) in 1824, when Dickens was 12 years old. Like Wordsworth in the 'Intimations' ode, Dickens laments his inability to recapture the fullness of joy which he experienced in youth, but this sense of loss is largely an affectation for the purposes of the sketch, rather than an actual event in his life, since he responded with a child's enthusiasm to circuses and menageries to the end of his life.

On holiday in Broadstairs in 1847, for example, he was caught up in a 'whirl of dissipation' upon discovering a female lion-tamer (Ellen Chapman, soon to become the wife of 'Lord' George Sanger), and he dashed off two characteristically exuberant letters. To Thomas Beard he wrote:

> That you should have been and gone and missed last Saturday! Wild beasts, too, at Ramsgate, and a young lady in armour, as goes into the dens, while a rustic keeper who speaks through his nose exclaims, 'Beold the abazid power of woobbud!'

And describing the same marvel to Marguerite Power he concluded: 'Seriously, she beats Van Amburgh. And I think the Duke of Wellington must have her painted by Landseer.'[9] From Paris in 1855 he wrote to his sister-in-law Georgina Hogarth, describing the thunderous reception accorded by the audience at Cirque Franconi to a clown from Astley's: 'His name is Boswell and the whole cirque rang last night with cries for Boz Zwilllll! Boz Zweellll! Boz Zwuallll!. etc. etc. etc. etc.'[10] In 1865 he joked to Forster about the celebrated Adah Isaacs Menken, 'who is to be seen bound on the horse in Mazeppa "ascending the fearful precipices not as hitherto done by a dummy"'.[11]

The extent of his familiarity with the circus can be seen even more clearly in the way he casually refers to it in the course of letters concerned with matters quite different. From France in 1844 he wrote to Forster describing the proposal of a toast by the French Consul-General, who 'turns up his fishy eyes, stretches out his arm like the living statue defying the lightning at Astley's and delivers four impromptu verses in my honour, at which everybody is enchanted'. Again, to express exasperation with Macready's American rival, the 'raving madman' Forrest, Dickens wrote that 'I would shave his head, blister his legs, and apprentice him for seven years at

Astley's to ride dray-horses'. Or, declining an invitation from Sir Edwin Landseer, who had painted the famous picture of the American lion-tamer Van Amburgh at work with his big cats in the cage, Dickens signed himself 'Charles Dickens, otherwise Wan Amburg'; years later, with the same picture in mind, Dickens referred to Landseer as 'that Van Amburgh of Trafalgar Square', alluding to the stone lions there which the painter-sculptor 'subdued by his genius'.[12] The ebullient good-humour of remarks such as these reflects Dickens's partiality for the circus and makes abundantly clear how ready at hand it was when he reached for a striking allusion.

Among his earliest published work, collected as *Sketches by Boz*, there appeared in the *Evening Chronicle* for 9 May 1835 a sketch of Astley's circus; in *The Old Curiosity Shop* Kit and Barbara take their families on a holiday outing there (*OCS*, 34), and in *Bleak House* Trooper George goes to Astley's to seek temporary relief from his troubles (*BH*, 21). *Pictures from Italy* describes Dickens's meeting with a circus in Medona; *The Uncommercial Traveller* records a visit to Cirque Franconi in Paris; in *Bentley's Miscellany*, *Household Words* and *All the Year Round* Dickens published a variety of articles on aspects of the circus, among them W. J. Thoms's piece on equestrian clowns and Peter Paterson's circumstantial account of a travelling circus.[13] Publicly as well as privately, then, Dickens made his interest manifest.

Dickens loved the variety, the spectacle, the skill and the comedy of the circus, and as with his taste for other forms of popular entertainment he was not overly rigorous in the level of artistic perfection he demanded. In his *Sketches by Boz* essay, the clown's jokes are stale and his gymnastics evince 'the most hopeless extreme of human agony'; the riding master looks like 'a fowl trussed for roasting', but there is no suggestion that Dickens appreciated them any the less for these things. Delight in the shabbiest exhibitions of histrionic art recurs throughout his writing – the amateurs in 'Private Theatres', the strolling players of Crummles's company, and Wopsle as Hamlet are conspicuous examples – and one must conclude from the evidence that Dickens greatly enjoyed unpolished art. He responded enthusiastically to the energy and good will with which performers took themselves seriously and, as in his accounts both in *Sketches by Boz* and in *The Old Curiosity Shop* of hippodramas at Astley's, he was fascinated with the patent absurdity of the conventions by which reality was represented. Peter Paterson, who wrote on the circus for Dickens in *All the Year Round*, suggested that for him part of the fun was the clumsiness of the actors and the accidents which befell the props, and it seems clear that Dickens agreed entirely with this view.[14] He was perfectly aware of the aesthetic limitations of such performances, as the hilarious comic touches in his descriptions demonstrate, but the gusto of humble players appealed favourably to him, and like Duke Theseus in *A Midsummer Night's Dream* Dickens found in their very awkwardness a sign of the authenticity of their intentions. Dickens's own art marvellously transcends the limitations of the ephemeral entertainment out of which it grew, but one major reason for the perennial popularity of his work is that throughout his life he nurtured its roots in the unsophisticated amusements of the people.

The holiday atmosphere of the circus was an important part of the fun. In the *Sketches by Boz* piece he describes the enjoyment of the spectators whom he singles out for comment, and he concludes the sketch by turning his attention to the performers as they leave by the stage-door after the show. He admits to 'a feeling of mysterious curiosity' at seeing the actors in street-clothes, but flatly denies that the equestrians could have any existence outside the ring. They are

> . . . mysterious beings, never seen out of the ring, never beheld but in the costumes of gods and sylphs. With the exception of Ducrow, who can scarcely be classed among them, who ever knew a rider at Astley's, or saw him but on horseback? Can our friend in the military uniform, ever appear in threadbare attire, or descend to the comparatively up-wadded costume of every-day life? Impossible! We cannot – we will not – believe it. (*SB*, p. 110)

Dickens's tone here is humorously hyberbolic, but his point is the important one that the magic of the circus exists only within the amphitheatre. A necessary condition of such entertainment is its distance from everyday life, its creation of a special world of its own. Here Dickens defines it in relation to the unique existence of the performers, who, if their mysterious aura is real, can have no contact with the outside world and its humdrum activities. In *The Old Curiosity Shop* chapter on Astley's Dickens makes the same fundamental point from a different perspective, when he stresses the holiday ambience which makes their visit so happy for Kit and Barbara. He spends the greater part of his account there chronicling the business of collecting wages, taking leave of their employer, reuniting with their families, and after the performance going off for a gala meal in a private box in an oyster-shop. The essential character of the occasion depends on the fact that it is not an ordinary part of Kit and Barbara's everyday activities, but a very special escape from their usual routine.

Part of the excitement of that atmosphere arises from the energy of the circus, which offers them such variety and such extravagance. Dickens is most emphatic about this aspect of the circus in his account in *Pictures from Italy* of a travelling French equestrian company he met at Modena, 'tearing round the corner, flouting griffins, lions, and tigers and other stone monsters in the town's exterior' (*PI*, pp. 320–1). The bustling noise and activity of these equestrians on parade seems all the more intense in contrast to the stagnant torpor of the town where Dickens encountered them, but in all of his descriptions of circuses he responds enthusiastically to their energy. Indeed, it was a quality in entertainment generally which he considered particularly valuable. Writing to Macready in 1857 about an art exhibition in Manchester, he was full of praise for its provisions for the common people; but, he added,

> . . . they want more amusement, and particularly (as it strikes me) *something in motion*, though it were only a twisting fountain. The thing is too still after their lives of machinery and art flies over their heads in consequence.[15]

For working men and women, in short, Dickens felt active amusements had more appeal than sedate ones, and the circus was a particularly attractive form of entertainment for them.

On the other hand, he disliked acts which involved great danger. He was once 'beguiled' into witnessing a performance by Leotard on the flying trapeze, which he found 'at once the most fearful and most graceful thing I have ever seen done', but he was decidedly cool about Blondin, the 'hero of Niagara', who was appearing at Crystal Palace in 1861 and whose most famous exploit, repeated several times, was to walk over Niagara Falls on a rope.[16] One of the stories Dickens published in *All the Year Round* recounts a terrible accident to a young trapeze artiste who fell while performing in a travelling circus in Scotland and was paralysed in his lower limbs. The narrator, who is the doctor caring for the injured man, feels personally guilty for tempting him to encounter such danger by having paid money to see him do it.[17] Dickens took a similar attitude towards the encouragement of such acts 'by those who should know better' in a letter of 1862, after a performer had fallen at Cremorne Gardens, but he was prepared to exonerate the working classes for being attracted to death-defying spectacles.

> It always appears to me that the common people have an excuse in their patronage of such exhibitions which people above them in condition have not. Their lives are full of physical difficulties, and they like to see such difficulties overcome. They go to see

them overcome. If I am in danger of falling off a scaffold or a ladder any day, the man who claims he can't fall from anything is a very wonderful and agreeable person to me.[18]

Dickens's dislike of dangerous acts was consonant with his delight in the capacity of the circus to bombard the spectator's capacity for wonder and to encourage a special feeling of shared enjoyment. For Dickens, the circus was an active benefit to society.

III

What he valued in it were the qualities to which he had first responded as a child, qualities which it shared with other entertainments from his past. He saw the circus not in contrast with theatrical performance and the declining traditions of street and village amusements, but as a particularly notable and vigorous instance of their survival. There were solid grounds for this view. As we saw in Chapter 3, lines of demarcation between various forms of entertainment were fluid in the nineteenth century. Showmen moved as readily in and out of the ring as they did between stage and fairground and street. A particularly amusing incident in 1856 illustrates how interchangeable these entertainments were in Dickens's mind. At that time he was mounting an amateur theatrical production of Wilkie Collins's play *The Frozen Deep*, and with his customary energy he was overseeing every detail of the arrangements. Requiring certain structures for the stage he was having built in his house, Dickens turned to William Cooke, then lessee and manager of Astley's, whose visit Dickens described to Forster in the following terms:

One of the finest things I have ever seen in my life of that kind was the arrival of my friend Mr Cooke one morning this week, in an open phaeton drawn by two white ponies with black spots all over them (evidently stencilled) who came in at the gate with a little jolt, and a rattle, exactly as they come into the Ring when they draw anything, and went round and round the centre bed of the front court, apparently looking for the clown. A multitude of boys who felt them to be no common ponies rushed up in a breathless state – twined themselves like ivy about the railings – and were only deterred from storming the enclosure by the glare of the Inimitable's eye. Some of these boys had evidently followed from Astley's. I grieve to add that my friend, being taken to the point of difficulty, had no sort of suggestion in him; no gleam of an idea; and might just as well have been the popular minister from the Tabernacle in Tottenham Court Road. All he could say was – answering me, posed in the garden, precisely as if I were the clown asking him a riddle at night – that two of their stable tents would be home in November, and that they were 'twenty foot square' and I was heartily welcome to 'em. Also he said, 'You might have half a dozen trapezes, or my middle-distance tables, but they're all six foot and all too low sir'. Since then, I have arranged to do it in my own way, and with my own carpenter.[19]

The zestful humour with which he describes this incident, recounting a private meeting between individuals as if it were a public exhibition in the circus ring, is yet one more instance of his customary perspective of viewing an everyday event as if it were a performance devised specifically for entertainment. And although he was frustrated in his particular needs on this occasion – a trapeze not being called for in the script of *The Frozen Deep* – in the very act of turning to the proprietor of Astley's for assistance Dickens showed how closely linked in his mind were the theatre and the circus.

Although it was after he wrote *Hard Times* that daredevil acts swept the public, other types of performance, such as tumbling, juggling, clowning, rope dancing and animal acts, dated from antiquity. But it was not until the latter half of the eighteenth century that these different acts were combined to form the medley which came to be known as the circus. What distinguished it from other forms of entertainment, its historians are agreed, was that it brought together into a single show a variety of acts, and always included performing animals as well as humans, and comic business as well as exhibitions of physical skill.[20] From its beginnings when the enterprising army officer Philip Astley began putting on shows which soon outdistanced his early rivals, the circus was based on exhibitions of equestrian skills, trick riding, comic skits, and tumbling. Soon Astley built a stage in his amphitheatre at Westminster Bridge and introduced equestrian drama as a staple ingredient of his shows. With developments and variations this combination became the basic routine for all circuses through the time Dickens wrote *Hard Times*. Astley's Royal Amphitheatre was the largest and most famous English circus; it was the one Dickens knew most intimately and, as Sleary attests, it was also the best; the highest pinnacle of achievement Sleary can envisage for the 3-year-old son of Mr E. W. B. Childers is star billing at Astley's (*HT*, III, 7).

Small travelling shows continued throughout the century to rely

on the tested formulas. In the mid-1860s James Lloyd started up a circus with only seven horses and a pony, and the programme for his first benefit night consisted of trick riding and posturing, tumbling, clowning, a comic sketch on horseback, and, as the main feature, an equestrian production of *Richard III*. In 1881, Charles Montague, a retired equestrian manager, reported that at that date, in addition to five permanently sited circuses in England, there were eight established tenting shows, plus smaller companies which tended to last only a few months. The big shows, however, evolved considerably. After Van Amburgh's success at Astley's in 1838 wild-beast shows became a frequent attraction. Greater changes came with the development of trapeze and daredevil acts by Leotard and Blondin in the 1850s and with the presentation of increasingly lavish spectacle, which culminated in Sanger's zoological extravaganzas during the final years at Astley's, up to 1893. By 1861, Peter Paterson could claim in *All the Year Round* that 'the circus is so entirely changed from what it was some thirty or forty years ago, as to be almost a new institution.[21]

The historical importance of these developments made the circus representative of the wider changes which were taking place in the organization of popular entertainment from before the start of the nineteenth century. We noted in Chapter 1 that the circus was the foremost instance of the emerging trend towards commercialization, which was displacing older patterns of leisure activity. From its inception the circus offered larger and more varied entertainment than could be found in separate fair booths and from wandering street performers; it assembled more artistes and bigger audiences; it effected a significant change in the economic basis of the performers' lives, and it constituted an emphatic move away from the more modest attractions of the individual busker who had amused the common people for centuries.

It was the obvious image for a writer to select who wished to consider the nature of entertainment in the urban, industrial society of mid-century England. What is striking about the circus in *Hard Times*, therefore, is not that Dickens included it, but that he virtually ignored its relevance to the increasingly dominant tendencies of popular entertainment. It is deeply revealing of his attitudes that, instead of including demonstrable evidence of the circus as an enterprise consonant with modern society, he chose to focus on the desire for shared enjoyments of small groups of spectators and the desire to please which motivated the performers. This perspective holds true for all his writing about the circus, but its significance is greatest in *Hard Times*, where it is presented as the novel's central symbol of positive value.

Dickens minimizes the commercial side of Sleary's circus, pointing instead to moral qualities of the performers and the opposition they face from the establishment figures. The company consists of a handful of showfolk, closely interrelated and personally devoted to one another; willing to train for long years in furtherance of their art, and dedicated to the unpretentious aim of providing innocent recreation for their spectators. Sleary's troupe seems altogether more otherworldly than the hard-pressed showfolk of *The Old Curiosity Shop*, whose precarious existence necessitates constant attention to every possibility of turning an extra penny, or than the harassed players of Crummles's company, canvassing each town with personal visits in the attempt to enlist patrons, and ultimately emigrating in hope of finding greener pastures abroad. The ringmaster admits that Gradgrind is ' "one of the thort, thquire, that keepth a prethiouth thight of money out of the houthe" ' (*HT*, I, 6), but there is no indication that the circus lacks for customers; people – even Gradgrind's children – are attracted to Sleary's horse-riding despite anything Gradgrind can say against it. By withholding information about the economic basis of Sleary's circus, Dickens blurs its distinctiveness as an example of the growing commercialism of entertainment. As a result, the circus is distanced from the industrial strife which is a major subject of the novel. Much of *Hard Times* is concerned to show how hard-pressed the hands are and to expose the falsity of Mr Bounderby's claim to be a self-made man. The disparity in the quality of life possible for the men and their masters arises, Dickens proposes, from misguided attitudes, but it is also crucially an economic issue. By offering circus values as a solution to these problems, while omitting the circus's commercial side, Dickens implies in his industrial novel that financial matters are finally unimportant.

Dickens further removes the circus from any immediate, practical concerns about the place of entertainment in English society in the 1850s by locating it emphatically outside the novel's social fabric. The distance is indicated by the location of Sleary's pitch, in 'the neutral ground upon the outskirts of town, which was neither town nor country' (*HT*, I, 3). As an institution, the circus has no place in the lives of the Coketown personages. We catch only the most fleeting glimpse of the company in performance, late in the book when Gradgrind, Louisa and Sissy wait impatiently to meet Sleary (*HT*, III, 7), and although Tom is rescued by a dancing pony and a learned dog whose professional tricks keep Bitzer at bay we see the company largely as private individuals, not as performers. Sissy, the chief representative of the circus in the novel, is not herself a performer at all, and it is while she is living as a member of Gradgrind's household that she takes steps important to the novel's plot. It is her values, not her professional capabilities, which matter. This is wholly in keeping with Dickens's themes, but again the lack of integration into the non-leisure activities of the characters serves to lift the circus above specific social concerns.

Nor is the presentation of the circus in *Hard Times* topical. As we shall see in a moment, much of the detail in his depiction of Sleary's show can be documented in performances actually given in the years immediately prior to 1854. On the other hand, most of this detail had been equally available to Dickens in the circus as he experienced it as a boy. He introduced no elements in his fictional circus which smack of novelty; all of the acts and actors had been standard for decades. The 1850s were prosperous years for the circus, but, unlike the troubled days for itinerant showmen in 1840 which gave his treatment of them in *The Old Curiosity Shop* considerable urgency, no circumstances which I can identify make his choice of the circus an especially timely subject for 1854. He may have been reminded of Astley's at this date by the presentation of acts depicting characters he had invented – during the week of 12 December 1853 characters from *Oliver Twist* were impersonated on horseback, and for two weeks in February roles from *Pickwick* were enacted – but theatrical and equestrian adaptations of his novels were commonplace all through his career and no special significance can be attached to these revivals. There had been a change of management at Astley's in March of 1853 when Cooke took over from Batty, but the shows remained much the same. Nor did any circus events in Preston, Dickens's source for the industrial issues of the novel, exert any influence on the novel. Travelling circuses periodically visited Preston on their rounds, but none was advertised during the three days of Dickens's flying visits to observe the strike there, and his only recorded pleasure-seeking while in Preston was a visit to the local theatre to see a performance of *Hamlet*, of which he observed that he 'should have done better to "sit at home and mope" like the idle workmen'. Topical issues, in short, were not on his mind so far as the circus was concerned, despite the urgency he felt about the matters relating to industry and education in the novel.[22]

Instead, he thought of the circus as being outside time altogether. In his *Sketches by Boz* piece he had remarked on its changelessness. Referring back to his earliest visits, he wrote:

It was not a 'Royal Amphitheatre' in those days, nor had Ducrow arisen to shed the light of classic taste and portable gas over the sawdust of the circus; but the whole character of the place was the same, the pieces were the same, the clown's jokes were the same, the riding-masters were equally grand, the comic performers equally witty, the tragedians equally hoarse, and the 'highly trained chargers' equally spirited. Astley's has altered for the better, – we have changed for the worse. (*SB*, p. 104)

The concluding sentence suggests that the circus has moved towards fuller realization of its essential nature, while the spectator, by growing out of childhood, has a diminished capacity for enjoyment. But 'the whole character' of the circus was fixed in his mind when he wrote this sketch, and there is nothing in *Hard Times*, nearly twenty years later, to suggest that he thought differently then. For Dickens the circus was essentially timeless.

Indeed, Sleary's circus is not even distinctive as a travelling troupe. Circus acts were interchangeable between permanent and temporary rings, but touring companies had a number of notable features all their own. Moving into town, setting up, finding lodgings, putting on a show and then packing up to depart were essential activities in touring circus life, and for spectators the parade through their town of all the performers, wagons and animals was not only the chief advertisement for the show but also one of the highlights of its appearance. Virtually all accounts of travelling circuses deal prominently with the parade and with the elaborate bustle involved in moving from town to town, but these things receive no mention in *Hard Times*. Partly this can be explained as a matter of plot in Dickens's shortest novel, where no obvious place for such details occurs, but the strong implication, supported by the evidence for generalization given above, is that Dickens was not thinking specifically of a travelling circus at all. Astley's, in its permanent amphitheatre in London, was the circus he knew best and, although much larger than Sleary's affair, it offered entertainment which was always similar and often identical to that described in *Hard Times*.

All of the factors we have been considering – the avoidance of economic issues, the distancing from social and topical concerns, the non-specificity of type of show – give Dickens's treatment of Sleary's circus a strong tendency towards idealization. Dickens lifts it out of the contexts which would make the circus a distinctive representative of the emerging patterns of entertainment, in synchronization with the emerging patterns of society. Instead, he presents a circus attuned to idealized characteristics of older forms of entertainment, in which humble showmen, imperfect but generous and affectionate, earned an honest living by providing simple amusement to people who wanted and needed it. Dickens's solution to the industrial and educational problems which he confronted in *Hard Times*, then, is one outside of time and place, in a realm of eternal human verities. Although the members of Sleary's company are presented in some detail, their function in the novel is overtly symbolic: the circus in *Hard Times* matters far more for what it means than for what it is.

To some extent this is no more than the kind of general signification which Dickens always practised. However idiosyncratic the characters in his earlier work might have been, they invariably had a degree of representativeness; rarely did he tie a figure exclusively to an individual prototype. However much the themes of his novels centred on pressing issues at the time of composition, and however specific the date he assigned for the action of a work, in his fiction he was always prepared to draw upon his memory of details from his childhood and youth.

But to a greater extent the idealization of Sleary marks a distinct development in his artistry. This development involved both gain and loss. *Hard Times* is incomparably more sophisticated in style and structure than any of Dickens's early fiction. The idealized image of the circus is orchestrated into the texture of the novel to create a high degree of artistic coherence and thematic significance. On the other hand, its functional purposes substantially decrease the contingency of Dickens's presentation – what George Orwell admired as 'unnecessary detail' in Dickens's style – and the circus figures have far less individual distinctiveness as characters than Crummles or Jarley.[23]

In the remainder of the present chapter we shall explore these gains and losses. Three key aspects of Dickens's handling of the circus in *Hard Times* require attention. First, we must examine the relationship between Dickens's fiction and the circus as it existed in nineteenth-century England. To do so will particularize the nature of the image he used and demonstrate its authenticity. Although he moulded evidence to suit his purposes, he did not misrepresent, but offered a plausible, if incomplete, interpretation of this important kind of popular entertainment. Second, we must consider how Dickens used the details he selected within the structure of *Hard Times*. Sleary himself appears only briefly in the novel, but imagery of the circus permeates the rest of the book in artistically meaningful ways. Finally, we must discuss the values which Dickens assigns to the circus, to see how they inform *Hard Times*. By this stage in his career the subject of entertainment has developed substantially into the theme of fancy, which Dickens integrates into the living core of the novel.

IV

The central feature of the circus from its outset and through Dickens's day was equestrianism, as spectacle or in dramatic setting, with solo and group performances, in acts of daring and of farce, but always with the emphasis firmly on the horses. And since circuses were generally named after their proprietors 'Sleary's horseriding' was a wholly appropriate designation for Dickens's fictional circus in *Hard Times*. Particularly well-trained horses would be proclaimed by name on the bills: Beda, Harlequin, Firefly, Taglioni, Snowdrop were but a few, and there was a 'celebrated spotted barb' called 'The Flying Childers' performing at Astley's during the 1853 and 1854 seasons, a name too pointedly coincidental with that of Sleary's principal equestrian not to have been the source for the name Dickens gives to Mr E. W. B. Childers – except that the horse at Astley's had in turn been named for the most famous eighteenth-century thoroughbred, also 'The Flying Childers'.[24] Here is a typical instance of contemporary detail with clear traditional roots. Even more renowned than the horses were the riders, among the most famous of whom were John Astley, Philip's son; Andrew Ducrow, the greatest equestrian of his, and perhaps of any, age; Louisa Woolford, Ducrow's second wife, a particular favourite of both Dickens and Thackeray; Kate Cooke, daughter of the manager at Astley's in the 1850s, William Cooke.[25] Frequent intermarriage among circus performers and the grooming of their children to the ring meant that the star billing given to Sleary's daughter was nothing out of the ordinary.

The principal item on show at the large circuses was a grand equestrian spectacle, with forty to a hundred riders going through their paces simultaneously. In Philip Astley's first shows, with a smaller company, this act consisted of military exercises, but after the turn of the century elaborate mock battles became favourite attractions, the most famous of which was the presentation at Astley's of the battle of Waterloo, first performed in 1824 and repeated frequently in subsequent years. This spectacle was in three acts and included scenery, machinery, costumes, decorations and music, and it required large, closely printed playbills to list the various wonders of such an exhibition. Sleary's circus, with only fifteen or twenty performers, was too small to put on anything on so grand a scale, but Dickens demonstrably recalled other events in Astley's programme when he itemized the acts of his troupe. Thus, in the late 1820s clear up to the 1840s, Miss Woolford, billed as 'the sylph of the circle' and 'the first female equestrian', appeared regularly in a solo performance called 'The Italian Flower-Girl', and floral motifs were often associated with other equestriennes as well. Miss Woolford also starred in a duet with Ducrow entitled 'The Swiss Maid and the Tyrolean Lover', in which they performed an 'equestrian ballet on two horses, at the same time, while delineating in pantomime action, whilst the horses are at their swiftest speed, a rustic scene of the Mountain Shepherd and the Swiss Milk Maid'. This act was revived at Astley's during the 1853 season, with Mr Bridges and Miss Barrand and later with Miss Avery and Mr Barlow in the title roles.[26] Whether Dickens was recalling childhood memories of Miss Woolford, or was thinking of the more recent revivals of 'The Tyrolean Shepherd', it seems likely that the act itself was his source for the pastoral ballet he places at the top of Sleary's bill, the 'graceful equestrian Tyrolean flower-act' performed by Miss Josephine Sleary.

One of Ducrow's most frequently enacted roles in the mid-1820s was 'Le Chasseur Indien' or 'The Indian Hunter on his Two Wild Horses', in which he went through a routine atop a pair of galloping, bareback horses. As an exhibition of riding skill, he later developed this act into the more daring and famous performance of 'The Courier of St Petersburgh', in which he controlled four, five and eventually nine galloping horses while standing on their backs. The Indian motif survived as well, recurring often in a variety of forms in different circuses over the years, and Mr Barlow performed 'The Indian of the Far West or the Wild Horse of the Prairie' at Astley's during the weeks of 18 July and 5 December 1853. A particularly full description of one such act appeared on bills in 1828, first at Astley's, later at Clarke's, when an unnamed equestrian performed the following sketch.

First appearance of the
Indian Horseman

Just arrived and will perform on a single horse, his astonishing act of horsemanship, representing a

War Chief Going To Battle.

The singular action and peculiarities of this artist are as follows – the chief appears in his full costume of battle array, with his native warlike weapons, prepares to meet his enemy, but before he marches he takes a most tender and affectionate leave of his beloved wife and children, – Their embraces are disturbed by a sudden alarm which proves false – the noble chief's courage being roused, he advances towards the field, where he hears the second alarm, which proves to be the real one, – puts himself in a posture of defence – the enemy meets him – the fight commences – and after a most dreadful contest, succeeds in placing a tremendous blow on the head of his antagonist, which brings him lifeless to the ground – this adds greatly to his mortification for it proves to be his friend, – in this discovery, the chief displays a nobleness of nature beyond comparison, which comprises all the beauties of a tender parent to his friend, uses every possible means to recover him, administers reviving berries – and at length to his unspeakable joy succeeds in restoring him, after which a rude reconciliation takes place and the act finishes with

His grand attitudes.[27]

The finale of 'grand attitudes' with which this act concludes is described on a subsequent bill as representing 'The Flying Mercury', a leap from the Wild West into classical mythology which gives a precedent for Master Kidderminster's outrageous transformation in *Hard Times* from Indian child to Cupid.

Whether Dickens saw this specific performance or not is unknown, but the playbill description has a genuinely Dickensian flavour to it and provides some indication of the sort of performance which inspired him to invent Mr E. W. B. Childers

. . . so justly celebrated for his daring vaulting act as the Wild Huntsman of the North American Prairies; in which popular performance, a diminutive boy with an old face, who now accompanied him, assisted as his infant son: being carried upside down over his father's shoulder, by one foot, and held by the crown of his head, heels upwards, in the palm of his father's hand, according to the violent paternal manner in which wild huntsmen may be observed to fondle their offspring. (*HT*, I, 6)

E. W. B. Childers's act differs in detail from the performance noted above, but the essential character is identical, and Dickens evokes the humour implicit in such an exhibition by exploiting the pretence that the balletic scene reflects faithfully the actual behaviour of such types as are impersonated in the ring. In this context, it is not inappropriate to recall that in *Nicholas Nickleby* another ageing youngster, the Infant Phenomenon, performs a ballet called 'The Indian Savage and the Maiden'. Once again the links between Crummles and Sleary are very close.

A comic equestrian act presented by Sleary's troupe is the routine of 'the highly novel and laughable hippo-comedietta of the Tailor's Journey to Brentford', in which Signor Jupe appeared in 'his favourite character of Mr William Button, of Tooley Street' (*HT*, I,

Master Kidderminster, 'made up with curls, wreaths, wings, white bismuth and carmine . . . soared into so pleasing a Cupid as to constitute the chief delight of the maternal part of the spectators' (*HT*, I, 6).

3). Laughable it certainly was, but 'highly novel' it emphatically was not. Billy Button's ride to Brentford was the single most frequently enacted comic entertainment in the circus, devised by Philip Astley in his first season in 1768 and revived year after year for a century by one company after another. As described in a chapbook dating around 1830, the Tailor's Ride involved a novice horseman mounting backwards, losing his book and measures when the horse is startled by geese, threatening to cut off the horse's ears with his scissors, flying off the horse when it bucks, remounting and being terrified when the horse sets off at full gallop, tumbling off again and being chased into his house by the horse.[28] This exhibition of supposed bad riding involved a good deal of knockabout fun, and it is no wonder that Jupe would be in need of nine-oils afterwards. The basic story was lavishly developed by Nelson Lee into Astley's Christmas pantomime for 1853, *Billy Button's Journey to Brentford; or, Harlequin and the Ladies' Favourite*, with more than thirty named roles, magical transformations and elaborate spectacles.[29] This production, coming as it did when Dickens was first working on *Hard Times*, may have reminded him of Billy Button, but Sleary's troupe performs the traditional riding act, not the pantomime, which was far beyond the resources of his company.

Every circus had its dancing horses. In *Hard Times* Bitzer's attempt to catch the thief is frustrated by one such horse, which dances a polka on the spot, allowing Tom to make his escape in a gig pulled by a racing pony. Equestrian acts in exotic costume were also staple features, with Cossacks, Saracens, eastern and western Indians, Italian lovers, Spanish grandees and Chinese cavalry among the cast – to say nothing of spectacles such as the Burmese War, Timour the Tartar, the Cataract of the Ganges, and the Scenes of Kaffir Warfare. Sleary's Emperor of Japan would have been nothing out of the ordinary in such company, and may have been directly inspired by an act entitled 'The Emperor of Japan' performed by Mr Bridges at Astley's during the week of 24 January 1853.[30] Even if twirling five wash-hand basins at once on horseback was not a royal activity, as Dickens asserts with ironic credulity (*HT*, III, 7), gymnastics and juggling were nevertheless routine acts, sometimes associated with oriental performances, as when Ching Lau Lauro balanced acrobatically on the backs of two chairs and danced a hornpipe on his head.[31] Among the excursions into remote times and places were evocations of classical antiquity, most obviously in the names 'olympic' and 'circus' itself, and also in equestrian acts which drew on themes from Greece and Rome. Ducrow was famous for his 'classical exercises of the Roman Gladiator on his rapid courser'; in 1838, Cooke offered a series of sculptural poses on horseback – the dying gladiator, Apollo,

Atlas, Romulus, Ajax – of which he claimed 'but little was required to lead the beholder to suppose he was looking at the genuine and celebrated statues'; in 1851, Batty staged Roman chariot races in the ring; in 1853 there was a whole series of scenes in the circle at Astley's based on classical motifs: 'the Spartan Olympians', 'the Greek Maid' and 'the Dance of the Dryades and Sylvan Youths' were a few of these, and an extravaganza entitled 'Jupiter's Decree' was presented sixty-seven times that season.[32] The Greek chariot drawn by six in hand at Sleary's circus was thus another typical act, for which Dickens had ample historical precedent.

Of all the kinds of equestrian act which flourished in the circus as Dickens knew it, the most distinctive was the entertainment known as hippodrama. This curious hybrid, part circus, part theatre, was enormously popular throughout the first half of the nineteenth century and achieved its most spectacular success in the endlessly represented saga of *Mazeppa*, based on Byron's poem and featuring a wild ride with the hero (normally replaced by a dummy, until the arrival of Adah Isaacs Menken in 1861) strapped to the back of a charging steed. Performances of hippodrama required a special playing-area, with both ring and stage, and Astley's third amphi-theatre, built by Batty after the 1841 fire, boasted a stage 75 feet by 101 feet, the largest in London. The plays themselves were simply 'equestrianized melodramas' (in the words of their historian), and Sleary gives a glowing description of a typical example.[33]

> 'If you wath to thee our Children in the Wood, with their father and mother both a dyin' on a horthe – their uncle a retheiving of 'em ath hith wardth, upon a horthe – themthelveth both a goin' a black-berryin' on a horthe – and the Robinth a-coming in to cover 'em with leavth, upon a horthe – you'd thay it wath the completetht thing ath ever you thet your eyeth on!' (*HT*, III, 7)

Except for the horses, the action here recounted follows precisely the events of the popular ballad of 'The Children in the Wood', which was adapted for the stage many times, from before the beginning of the nineteenth century until after its close. I have not traced an actual performance of it on horseback, but it was so well loved as a poem and so frequently staged as a play that it is hard to think of its not being adapted for hippodrama.[34] The other two productions which are mentioned in *Hard Times* both have precedent at Astley's during Dickens's childhood and young adulthood. *Jack the Giant Killer* was performed on horseback by Ducrow with the Infant Ginnett in 1833 as a comic interlude during intervals between scenes in the circle, and two plays with roles not unlike that in which young Tom Gradgrind finds himself were written by Barrymore for Astley's a few years earlier. *Agamemnon; or, The Faithful Negro*, a 'new and interesting melo-drama, with new and appropriate scenery, dresses, and decorations, duets, chorus, and dances', was presented on several occasions in 1824, and a melodramatic tale called *The Negro's Hate* appeared fleetingly in 1829.[35]

Except for the very smallest of circus companies, hippodrama was a customary attraction in the first half of the nineteenth century. Performing menageries did without it, as did the tiny travelling circuses seen at fairgrounds, sometimes with no more than three or four horses, an acrobat, a clown, a handful of riders, who would put on a show consisting of two or three riding acts, a tightrope exhibition and a display of tumbling.[36] Sleary, in contrast, is substantial enough to set up his pavilion without the attraction of further entertainments nearby, but rudimentary plays were possible for all but the smallest of troupes, because the line between skits in costume with one or two equestrians and full-scale dramas was fairly flexible and, in any case, in even the most ambitious of Astley's hippodramas the emphasis was firmly on the riding rather than on complexities of plot and character. Any circus could follow Ducrow's proverbial maxim, 'Cut the dialogue and come to the 'osses!' As in Richardson's Theatre Booth, where more than a dozen Shakespearean productions could be completed in a day by turning the plot into a rapid sequence of ghosts, fights and deaths, so, too, in the circus action, spectacle and novelty, along with riding skills, were the essential ingredients.

Animals other than horses were frequent, if not invariable, attractions of the circus from its earliest days. Elephants appeared periodically throughout the nineteenth century in menageries and circuses up and down the country; Ducrow rode one at Astley's in 1827, and in 1846 an elephant balanced on a tightrope in the same arena. The most celebrated novelty of the 1853–4 circus season, just before Dickens began writing *Hard Times*, was the routine performed by William Cooke's 'wise elephants of the east', two trained elephants which could stand on their heads, balance on their hind legs, and perform other prodigies, to the delight of audiences at Astley's, at Cirque Franconi in Paris, and at a command performance given for Queen Victoria, Prince Albert and their children.[37] A company as small as Sleary's would have been unlikely to have been able to afford an elephant, although Dickens's ringmaster tells Sissy that Emma Gordon's husband lost his life falling off one; but, as I have been suggesting, Dickens drew his knowledge of the circus less from provincial touring circuses than from the big, permanent Royal Amphitheatre at Westminster Bridge, where elephants did indeed sometimes appear.

Dogs were by far the most commonly seen animals in the circus after the horses. They starred in melodramas written especially for them, such as *The Dog of Montargis* (1814), *The Dog of the Château* (1845) and *The Dog of the Pyrenees* (1845), but more frequently they appeared as 'learned' dogs, performing counting and spelling tricks, usually in company of the circus clown. The 'sagacious' dog Rolla joined in the action of the Tailor's Ride in Clarke's circus in 1825. A dog named Hector was billed along with the clown Stonette at Astley's throughout the 1853 season; when Stonette left in February of 1854 the new clown, Egan, appeared regularly with two dogs.[38] And since the circus clown was generically known as 'Merryman' the name of Jupe's dog, Merrylegs, is thoroughly appropriate. Sissy describes to Louisa one of Merrylegs's tricks, which was 'to jump up on the backs of two chairs and stand across them' (*HT*, I, 9); there is an engraving of this routine in a late nineteenth-century book on the circus, depicting a dog perched on three legs atop the backs of two chairs, with its tail in its mouth.[39] Like Jerry's dogs in *The Old Curiosity Shop*, circus dogs would also appear in costume, standing on their hind legs, pushing wheelbarrows, jumping through hoops, bouncing balls, and so on. Van Hare trained Newfoundland dogs to perform a steeplechase routine, with baboons dressed up as jockeys to ride them; his 'wizard' dog Napoleon contested jumping skills against human rivals, leaped over horses from a springboard, and danced to music. John Sanger's grandson performed a clown act in which a dog's antics repeatedly thwarted the work of an old coster with a donkey cart.[40]

After the horses and riders, the most important figure in the circus was the clown. He was not merely a funny man, taking pratfalls and exchanging quips with the ringmaster while the next scene in the circle was getting ready, but a highly skilled and versatile performer in his own right, undertaking feats of tumbling and riding, as well as animal-training and utility work, and making more appearances in each show than any other member of the company. Sleary's playbill, eleborating the acts which Signor Jupe is called upon to perform, gives a fair indication of the clown's role in the circus.

Among the other pleasing but always strictly moral wonders which must be seen to be believed, Signor Jupe was that afternoon to 'elucidate the diverting accomplishments of his highly trained performing dog Merrylegs'. He was also to exhibit 'his astounding feat of throwing seventy-five hundred-weight in rapid succession back-handed over his head, thus forming a fountain of solid iron in mid-air, a feat never before attempted in this or any other country, and which having elicited such

CIRCUS CLOWN AT FAIR.

The demanding business of circus clowning left the performer much in need of 'nine-oils' after the show.

rapturous plaudits from enthusiastic throngs, it cannot be withdrawn'. The same Signor Jupe was to 'enliven the varied performances at frequent intervals with his chaste Shakespearean quips and retorts'. Lastly, he has to wind them up by appearing in his favourite character of Mr William Button, of Tooley Street, in 'the highly novel and laughable hippo-comedietta of The Tailor's Journey to Brentford'. (*HT*, I, 3)

All of these acts were well-established clowning routines long before the days of Signor Jupe. Strong men, acrobats and jugglers had been performing since antiquity, and their acts were adopted by circus clowns from the first. One of Astley's early clowns, Baptiste Dubois, was billed as the English Hercules and danced on the rope with two boys tied to his feet; in 1820 the clown Bradbury supported six men on his body while lying between two chairs; in 1842 the clown Dewhurst leaped over a garter fourteen feet high; examples could be multiplied endlessly.[41] We have already seen that the Tailor's Ride dated from Astley's first season, and that dog acts predate the circus by centuries; besides dogs, donkeys, pigs, geese, cats and other animals were frequent companions for circus clowns. What needs stressing in this context is that several of these diverse acts would appear on a single programme, all performed by a single artiste; Dickens is not exaggerating the versatility required of a clown in the skills he attributes to Signor Jupe.

According to circus historians, the clown of the ring developed out of comic equestrian acts which were staple ingredients of Astley's first shows. He was a country bumpkin, or Pierrot, a stupid lout whose antics cast ridicule on himself. His skills were more acrobatic than verbal, and he was comic as much for what he was as for what he did. In this guise he was quite distinct from the stage clown created by Grimaldi for the pantomime, who was a clever trickster, stupid only in pretence, a 'personification of deliberate and calculated satire'.[42] Circus clowns were often known as 'Joeys', but Grimaldi himself never appeared in the ring, and the principal action of the harlequinade, the clown's pursuit of the lovers, was never a major facet of circus clowning. In the words of M. Willson Disher:

> Although theatre clowns have frequently found employment in the ring and circus clowns on the stage, the types have remained distinct. Their training has been of two entirely different schools. While the theatre clown was reared as a dancer, actor, and dumb-show performer, the apprenticeship of the circus clown is served to an acrobat, juggler, musician, rider or animal trainer if not to all four.[43]

Ducrow's brother, John, was the 'Mr Merryman' at Astley's from whom Dickens gained his early acquaintance with clowns. With white face, red cheeks and enormous mouth, dressed in baggy red and white costume, John Ducrow exchanged banter with the ringmaster, offered burlesque assistance to the riders, and repeated the jokes which, according to an article which Dickens published when editor of *Bentley's Miscellany*, were invented by pupils at Westminster School for the clowns at Astley's.[44] His routine was far from being his exclusive property, and Dickens was not alone in remarking the repetitive nature of the jokes and gags of circus clowns; as late as 1875, Thomas Frost published a mock 'Act of Parliament' to forbid further performance of the same routines which Dickens recalled with affection in *Sketches by Boz*.[45] Clowns are almost invariably described in their private lives as the most taciturn and sober of all performers, and John Ducrow, like Jupe, had two wholly distinct characters: the frolicsome zany of the ring was racked with consumption and died prematurely in 1834.

As the nineteenth century proceeded, clown acts became more specialized, and it was not uncommon for several to appear in a single performance. Around the year of *Hard Times*, Astley's on occasion billed an act with six clowns, and routines by two to four separate clowns were normal by this date. One clowning development of direct relevance to Jupe was the arrival of the Shakespearean clown, or jester. Wallett, with characteristic immodesty, claimed to have introduced the type in the 1830s, but he had a number of rivals by the 1850s: Boswell, billed as 'the Shakespearean jester'; Stonette, 'the Touchstone of the Circle'; Egan, 'the Modern Yorick, or court jester'. This type of clown relied less on tumbling skills than on patter, 'long recitations, sometimes in prose, sometimes in verse, studded with political and moral sentiments'.[46] Wallett achieved considerable acclaim in this role, but he comes over as a pompous ass in his memoirs, and was not without his critics in his own day. The liability of boring an audience was high with mock-Shakespearean harangues, which were not enough on their own for successful clowning; that, at least, is the considered view of Mr E. W. B. Childers, who sums up Jupe's failure by saying 'He has his points as a Cackler still, but he can't get a living out of *them*' (*HT*, I, 6).

Other feats of skill which Dickens includes in the repertoire of Sleary's artistes – tumbling, leaping, juggling, dancing on bottles, balancing a pole, forming human pyramids, lifting great weights, dancing on tight and slack ropes – were all routine accomplishments for circus performers in the nineteenth century. Two performances a day were normal for travelling circuses, one in the afternoon, the other in the evening. Although there is precedent for morning performances at Astley's in the 1850s, the 'morning' show in progress when Sissy and Louisa arrive near the novel's end is the regular daytime performance; since Dickens mentions that the show began at one o'clock it is clear that he is using 'morning' in its now archaic sense of 'before dinner' (*HT*, III, 7). Similarly authentic are the details which Dickens provides of the physical characteristics of the circus building. Like Sleary's establishment, travelling shows in Britain in the first half of the century generally set up temporary wooden booths rather than the tents which became common after mid-century. Contemporary illustrations reveal that a Gothic structure in front of the building served as an entrance for customers, and that flags were customary ornament; the building would be placed in fields on the outskirts of towns.

In the light of so much authentic detail in *Hard Times*, it comes as something of a surprise to find the best nineteenth-century historian of the English circus, Thomas Frost, dismissing Dickens's presentation of the circus as 'rot'. Frost notes several slang words used by Childers and Kidderminster which he never heard circus people utter, but primarily he objects to the versatility which Dickens attributes to Sleary's artistes, and to the domestic arrangements they are shown to adopt. 'Sleary's people must certainly have been exceptionally clever,' he states, and urges that few clowns and acrobats can ride, few equestriennes can perform rapid bareback acts, and the majority of wives married to performers never appear in the ring themselves. As for their private circumstances, Frost declares that married circus men generally occupy private apartments rather than lodging in an obscure inn, and that Sleary's company was 'gregarious in a very remarkable degree', even supposing an inn like the Pegasus's Arms could accommodate an entire company.[47]

One must take Frost's objections seriously, since he was exceptionally well informed about many aspects of nineteenth-century popular entertainment and based his books on interviews with performers as well as on documentary evidence and personal recollection. Nevertheless, his charges against *Hard Times* suffer from a misapprehension of Dickens's novelistic purposes. Dialogue in fiction is never simple transcription of conversation as it is actually spoken, but depends on rigorous selection of key words and rhythms to evoke the flavour of the language which a particular personage might be expected to use. As in other aspects of fiction, selection, adaptation and invention are the novelist's tools for representing the essential quality of human experience, and Dickens's requirement for the speech of Sleary's artistes was that it sounds exotic and specialized to readers for whom the private lives of circus performers would be wholly unknown. As we have seen, Dickens consulted Lemon about circus vocabulary, and a portion at least of the terms he attributed to his showfolk was, Frost acknowledges, in customary usage. If other of the slang words were invention, still they contribute to the air of authenticity by fitting readily into the context, and in this of all novels truthfulness depends not on inert recording of fact but on accurate feeling for a subject. Sleary's equestrians talk like men using a specialized jargon familiar to them but alien to outsiders, and for this reason their dialogue is appropriate.

Frost's other complaints can be met in two ways. In the first place, instances may be cited to show that performers and their wives did have diverse talents and that inns were used for accommodation. Much of the historical data presented already confirms the case: Ducrow was talented on the tightrope as well as on horseback, and his wife was a celebrated equestrienne; comic riding was closely associated with clowning; circus families such as the Clarkes and the Cookes exhibited talents alike of fathers and mothers, uncles and aunts, brothers and sisters. But the very fame of such individuals may serve to confirm Frost's point that such closely knit versatility was the exception rather than the rule. A better defence can be made on the grounds of artistic unity. Condensation of raw materials taken from life is a principle of most art, and one which Dickens has followed in *Hard Times*. As we have seen, all of the acts in Sleary's circus have historical precedent, and for Dickens to distribute them among a limited number of performers gives a vivid and coherent impression that introducing a separate character for each skill could never have done. In a like manner, situating the entire troupe in a single inn facilitates the assembly of them all in Sissy's room for the initial confrontation with Gradgrind and Bounderby; were they scattered about the town in separate lodgings Dickens would have had to resort to improbable expedients to achieve the desired result of bringing them all together quickly and naturally. In order to achieve his artistic aims with regard to economical disposition of character, setting and action, Dickens has gathered historically accurate detail into a more limited scope than would have been likely to have occurred outside a work of fiction. This is not wilful distortion of fact, but finely judged arrangement of factual materials in order to heighten the effectiveness of his story. To object that Dickens's procedure invalidates the presentation of the circus betrays entirely too limited a sense of how fiction can be truthful, and a failure to understand what Dickens is saying in this novel about fact and fancy.

V

The central theme of *Hard Times* is the inadequacy of fact as exclusive explanation for all human enterprise, and it is announced in the book's opening sentence:

'Now, what I want is, Facts.'

So begins *Hard Times*, with a proclamation of the central tenet of the Gradgrind philosophy, before time, place or characters have been mentioned. With the focus directed squarely upon the outlook he intends to demolish, Dickens moves quickly to sketch in the speaker and setting, and to dramatize interaction between characters. The first exchange of the book comes almost at once, as Mr Gradgrind calls on girl Number Twenty and proceeds to alarm and humiliate her, by refusing to acknowledge her name, her father's occupation or her understanding of that which she knows most intimately. It is a confrontation between a dogmatic theorist and a bewildered child, and, within the schoolroom, a wholly unequal contest. Mr Gradgrind rejects everything which is genuine about Sissy in his determination to categorize and catechize her according to the dimensions of his Procrustean bed, and complacently prefers the conformity evidenced by the bloodless Bitzer.

In the next paragraphs Dickens fills in the elements of Gradgrind's character and educational system, and proceeds to the book's second dramatic moment, which again juxtaposes school and circus. Meditating upon the excellence of the regimen he had devised for his children's upbringing, Mr Gradgrind is startled to discover these very children eagerly striving to catch but a glimpse of the diversions of the circus. The father is 'dumb with amazement', but Dickens has no doubt in assigning the reason for this act of disobedience by Louisa and Tom.

> There was an air of jaded sullenness in them both, and particularly in the girl: yet, struggling through the dissatisfaction of her face, there was a light with nothing to rest upon, a fire with nothing to burn, a starved imagination keeping life in itself somehow, which brightened its expression. Not with the brightness natural to cheerful youth, but with uncertain, eager, doubtful flashes, which had something painful in them, analogous to the changes on a blind face groping its way. (*HT*, I, 3)

Gradgrind's system, Dickens insists, has starved the children of an ingredient essential for their well-being, and, hardly knowing by

Mr Gradgrind is horrified to discover his own children 'in a number of stealthy attitudes, striving to peep in at the hidden glories' of Sleary's circus (*HT*, I, 3).

themselves what it is they lack, Louisa and Tom turn instinctively to the nourishment of the circus.

Confronted with this 'loophole' in his system, Mr Gradgrind turns to his friend Bounderby for advice, and together they seek out the entertainers in order to eliminate the problem for once and for all. Their meeting with the members of Sleary's troupe is the set piece which concludes the novel's introductory movement, and in it Dickens elaborates the alternatives of hard fact and fancy. By including Bounderby, the factory-owner and 'bully of humility' in this scene, Dickens expands the scope of his inquiry to wider issues of class and industrial relations, and he distinguishes between the basically decent and thoughtful application of principle which we find in Gradgrind, and the brutal hypocrisy with which Bounderby turns principles into slogans for his own selfish ends.

As this brief summary of the action of the first six chapters indicates, the structure of the novel's opening moments is built upon a juxtaposition of two opposing attitudes to life. Mr Gradgrind's two initial skirmishes with the children reveal their longing for more than his system allows, and reflect Dickens's belief that wonder and curiosity are not learned activities, as Gradgrind would have it, which proper education can dispense with, but rather instinctive attributes, which are inalienable parts of human existence. With the confrontation at the inn which follows, Dickens develops this opposition, laying bare the irreconcilability of Gradgrind's views with those of the circus. In this scene, Mr E. W. B. Childers, the principal equestrian in Sleary's company, explains Sissy's situation – her father's decline and flight, and her reason for being in the school at all – while Bounderby scoffs loudly at everything he hears about Sissy, her father and the circus. Bounderby's response is unequivocal; like Mr Podsnap in a later novel, he deals with everything which falls outside his blinkered vision by sweeping it behind him. He urges Gradgrind to reject Sissy immediately – a mode of behaviour which he himself adopts when dealing with uncomfortable situations later in the book. Mr Gradgrind, however, with a high-minded desire to do what is right, hesitates – an indication of seeds for his future reformation – and decides to offer sanctuary to Sissy, on the condition that she will sever all ties with her present companions. He explains carefully the option which he proposes to the girl, to which Mr Sleary responds with an equally clear (if more hoarsely expressed) statement of Sissy's alternative. The scene develops, in short, to a climax akin to that of a morality play, in which mutually exclusive options are systematically set forth and a character is faced with the necessity of absolute choice. Dickens's deployment of the circus in *Hard Times* is not merely a splash of colour in a bleak setting – although it is that – but a thematic opposition of two value systems, of which the circus symbolizes the positive alternative of right feeling and humane response to life. Sissy makes her decision, choosing to follow Mr Gradgrind, not in rejection of the circus, as he intends, but in order to obey one of its highest dictates and show her loyalty to the person she loves most dearly. Her father wanted an education for her, and that is reason enough for Sissy to choose to go with Gradgrind.

Neither Mr Gradgrind nor Mr Bounderby understands or sympathizes with the motives which underlie Sissy's decision. Indeed, the value system represented by the circus is treated by its opponents, when they think of it at all, with supercilious contempt. In the opening encounter, Mr Gradgrind refuses to accept Sissy for what she is, and Mrs Gradgrind, on learning of her children's venture to see the circus, declares it irrelevant to reasonable pursuits.

> You know, as well as I do, no young people have circus masters, or keep circuses in cabinets, or attend lectures about circuses. What can you possibly want to know of circuses then? (*HT*, I, 4)

Dickens says of the schoolmaster, Mr M'Choakumchild: 'If he had only learnt a little less, how infinitely better he might have taught much more!' (*HT*, I, 2). The pillars of Coketown society consider the discontent of the hands with incredulity: the people *won't* come to church, and they *would* get drunk, and resort to low haunts, and indulge in low singing and low dancing, but, the members of the church and the Teetotal Society and the Members of Parliament are quite convinced, these people 'never knew what they wanted' (*HT*, I, 5). This sentiment echoes a familiar refrain in Dickens, from *Sunday under Three Heads* to 'Dullborough Town', from Little Bethel in *The Old Curiosity Shop* to the maddening church bells in *Little Dorrit*, that religious and moral reformers are benighted in their efforts to deny the need of recreation to the oppressed masses. As is his wont, Dickens is explicit in *Hard Times*:

> That exactly in the ratio as they worked long and monotonously, the craving grew within them for some physical relief – some relaxation, encouraging good humour and good spirits, and giving them a vent – some recognized holiday, though it were but for an honest dance to a stirring band of music – some occasional light pie in which even M'Choakumchild had no finger – which craving must and would be satisfied aright, or must and would inevitably go wrong, until the laws of the Creation were repealed.   (*HT*, I, 5)

Dickens charges the opponents of amusement, who set themselves up as arbiters of human nature, not only with false assumptions of superiority, but also with real ignorance. As Gradgrind and Bounderby go to deal with the circus, both of them are bound to confess that they do not know the direction to Pod's End, where the equestrians lodge; and when Sissy leads them there they are unable to see the sign of the Pegasus's Arms.[48] The symbolic import of these details is underlined by the final words of the decision chapter, which point to Gradgrind and Bounderby, with Sissy in tow, taking leave of Sleary and 'soon lost . . . in the darkness of the street' (*HT*, I, 6). It is a wilful lack of enlightenment for which they are to pay dearly.

In these opening chapters Dickens indicates that Gradgrind and Bounderby need the circus far more than it needs them. At the same time, the performers do have acknowledged limitations – not as a seedy mirror image of a debased Coketown, but as the result of their struggle for existence in uncongenial circumstances.

> They all assumed to be rakish and knowing, they were not very tidy in their private dresses, they were not at all orderly in their domestic arrangements, and the combined literature of the whole company would have produced but a poor letter on any subject.   (*HT*, I, 6)

Lack of education was certainly a peril of the profession. Many, perhaps most, circus performers of the time were illiterate – Ducrow's meagre command of language, to take one conspicuous example, was notorious – and the early and arduous apprenticeship most of them served did little to encourage formal education. Not that they were exactly welcome when they did seek schooling: just as, in the novel, Sissy's presence in the classroom is viewed with suspicion, so in real life their itinerant existence made settling into any one school difficult, and James Lloyd, the circus proprietor, was certainly not exceptional when, as a child, he did apply, and was refused admission on the grounds that a circus boy would 'contaminate' the school.[49]

In any case, Sleary's company are sceptical of the importance of classroom education. Mr E. W. B. Childers is frankly puzzled by Jupe's eagerness to send Sissy to school: '"Her father always had it in his head . . . that she was to be taught the deuce-and-all of education. How it got into his head, I can't say, I can only say that it never got out"' (*HT*, I, 6). And, as the novel proceeds, it is clear that Sissy's virtues are quite independent of any scholastic prowess. After years under the Gradgrind curriculum, her accomplishments in the school are indifferent. Gradgrind deplores her 'wretched ignorance' (*HT*, I,

174

9), and considers her quite ineducable, but even he has to admit 'that there was something in this girl which could hardly be set forth in a tabular form' (*HT*, I, 14). When his world collapses at his feet, Sissy is there to guide him and Louisa out of exclusive belief in the wisdom of the head into that of the heart. As Dickens writes of Sissy's devotion to Louisa: 'In the innocence of her brave affection, and the brimming up of her old devoted spirit, the once deserted girl shone like a beautiful light upon the darkness of the other' (*HT*, III, 1).

If Sissy has a lustre quite independent of all that Gradgrind has to offer, Dickens's presentation of the world of fact treats it as a grotesque perversion of the circus. This is most apparent in the case of Mr Bounderby, the novel's most outspoken critic of the circus. It is Bounderby himself who suggests the parallels, although they apply in a manner quite different from what he intends. Learning of Sissy's purchase of nine-oils for her father's bruises, Bounderby blusters, 'Serve 'em right . . . for being idle', and he compares his own activities with those of the showmen.

> 'By George!' said Mr Bounderby, 'when I was four or five years younger than you, I had worse bruises upon me than ten oils, twenty oils, forty oils, would have rubbed off. I didn't get 'em by posture-making, but by being banged about. There was no rope-dancing for me; I danced on the bare ground and was larruped with the rope.'   (*HT*, I, 5)

There is considerable irony in this statement, because, while we never see Bounderby doing anything but eating and talking, it is clear that the entertainers are far from idle; they train from infancy, and expend great effort in their daily performances, which require physical stamina and involve serious risk of injury. We know from showmen's accounts about the long hours of toil required of every member of the circus, and not just in the performance of his own acts.

> It is no joke to rehearse with bodily hard work all day, and then work at night. I have had to change my dress thirteen times in the course of a night, because, when not otherwise engaged, I had to dress in a smart uniform and stand at the entrance way, to be ready to hold balloons, garters, poles, whatever else was required. All who enter a Circus are engaged for 'general utility'.[50]

In addition to hard work, there was also the danger of injury, or even of death. Circus history is littered with casualties, from the very nature of the performances, which consist, as a matter of routine, of leaping, tumbling, balancing, and otherwise acting in ways which test the human frame to its limits. Circus people accept the accidents as an inevitable part of their lives. In the words of one:

> I got so callous and indifferent to all that happened – accidents with carriages and horses through drunken men. It's strange how I forgot the past. I got so that I smiled at calamity. To be a circus proprietor you ought to know how to splice ropes, sew canvas, to box a wheel, shoe a horse, make your seating and be a letterer, and not afraid of work, and an early riser, and be a performer, know the country, and the best seasons for each part and be a Jack of all Trades.[51]

Bounderby's accusation of idleness is belied by the evidence, and the opprobrium of his remark reflects back upon himself instead.

He continues, nevertheless, to draw parallels between himself and the entertainers. When he hears of Jupe's disappearance, Bounderby laughs away any notion of disinterestedness in the action, and boasts that his mother ran away from him. He cites this 'fact' as evidence of his own meritorious rise to success, by dint of his own efforts and unsupported by the least parental assistance. But this claim is doubly false: first, because, as Childers explains, the clown had fled not to rid himself of Sissy, but out of shame, in order to spare her the pain of witnessing his failures in the ring; and, second, because, as Mrs Pegler reveals near the novel's close, the only self-made thing about Bounderby is his public posturing, for it was by her maternal love and sacrifice that he got the start which ensured his later position. Yet again, Bounderby compares himself favourably to the circus performers when he refers to them as vagabonds. 'When I was a vagabond myself, nobody looked with any interest at *me*; I know that' (*HT*, I, 4). But this comparison is also false, and for similar reasons; growing up under his parents' roof, he never was a vagabond; and despite the Elizabethan statute which labelled all itinerant entertainers rogues and vagabonds the circus performers in *Hard Times* are skilled and hard-working in their gainful employment, and have a definite social function to fill. Whatever Bounderby's opinion of them, people do in fact look with considerable interest at them.

Besides Bounderby's own unwittingly ironic comparisons of himself to the showfolk, Dickens elaborates on the parallel by associating images of entertainments with the braggart. Thus, in his introductory description of Bounderby, he calls him 'a man with a pervading appearance on him of being inflated like a balloon, and ready to start' (*HT*, I, 4). Hot-air balloon risings were among the most popular of amusements during the century, and people flocked in large numbers to fairgrounds and pleasure gardens to witness the latest ascent; Philip Astley had offered a balloon ascent – possibly the first in England – as an attraction in the early days of his circus, at which 'a greater number of spectators than were, perhaps, ever assembled together on any occasion' gathered to witness the event.[52] Later, Dickens likens Bounderby's hat to a tambourine, from the way in which he beat upon the crown to punctuate his speech, at the conclusion of which 'like an oriental dancer [he] put his tambourine on his head' (*HT*, II, 8). Circus bills abound with notices of dancing routines in foreign attire, and oriental costumes were not among the least frequent; contemporary engravings show that tambourines were often in requisition for such acts, and a tambourine dance on horseback was advertised during the year before Dickens wrote *Hard Times*.[53] In this context, it is not perhaps too fanciful – a forgivable sin when thinking of this novel, in any event – to regard Bounderby's boasting about his 'climb up the ladder' of success (*HT*, I, 4) as another circus image, referring to the balancing acts which acrobats performed on ladders. (Compare Harthouse's description of his 'Great Pyramid' of failure (*HT*, III, 2), a metaphor which refers directly back to one of the stunts performed by Sleary's acrobats.)

Dickens's purposes in linking these circus motifs with Bounderby are complex, and of considerable importance as a means of integrating the symbol of the circus more fully into the texture of *Hard Times*. At the simplest level, these images serve as agents of comic ridicule, incongruously coupling the pompous man with diverting entertainments. In a like manner, Bounderby's own references to the circus function as ironic self-deflation. More significantly, Dickens presents the circus as an appropriate context from which to view Bounderby correctly. Elsewhere in the novel Dickens insists that the human needs, which the circus is one means of fulfilling, must be acknowledged and nurtured, or they will burst out in distorted shape. Bounderby's every word and action are denials of everything the circus symbolizes for Dickens and, as a result, Bounderby exists as a grotesquely perverted mutant of the healthy circus image. One of Dickens's primary intentions as an artist, throughout his career and nowhere more emphatically than in *Hard Times*, is to affirm the necessity of recognizing and responding to man's innate needs for what he generally called 'fancy'. He held its value as an axiom of his writing and saw it as an essential component of individual and social well-being.

It does not seem to me to be enough to say of any description that it is the exact truth. The exact truth must be there; but the merit or art in the narrator, is the manner of stating the truth. As to which thing in literature, it always seems to me that there is a world to be done. And in these times, when the tendency is to be frightfully literal and catalogue-like – to make the thing, in short, a sort of sum in reduction that any miserable creature can do in that way – I have an idea (really founded on the love of what I profess) that the very holding of popular literature through a kind of popular dark age, may depend on such fanciful treatment.[54]

In the light of this profession, his coupling of Bounderby with the circus takes on its fullest implications. For a central characteristic of that braggart is his hypocritical repudiation of anything to do with fancy – hypocritical, because the public image he thrusts upon the world is wholly the invention of his own self-important imaginings. In this he violates the necessary condition of any fanciful creation, that 'the exact truth must be there'. Moreover, Bounderby's invention is born solely for self-aggrandizement, and – fatal flaw, in Dickens's eyes – not in the least to nurture his own humanity or to expand his range of human sympathy. Fancy is a healing balm which enables men and women to surmount their privations and help their fellow-creatures; any redirection away from these ends is a misuse of a sacred human faculty. In *Hard Times* the circus (along with fairy-tale allusions and Louisa's fire-gazing) is Dickens's objective correlative for fancy, and thus to link it incongruously with Bounderby is the best possible means for Dickens to take the measure of fancy's enemy.[55] The distorted image of the circus is Dickens's moral judgement upon Bounderby's imperfections.

In a like manner, Dickens associates circus images with other characters in the book, for satiric purposes. Thus the school inspector in the opening scene is compared, at some length, to a pugilist.

> He had a genius for coming up to scratch, wherever and what-ever it was, and proving himself an ugly customer. He would go in and damage any subject whatever with his right, follow up with his left, stop, exchange, counter, bore his opponent (he always fought All England) to the ropes, and fall upon him neatly. He was certain to knock the wind out of common sense. . .   (*HT*, I, 2)

Boxing was an enormously popular sport in its own right during the nineteenth century, receiving royal patronage and attracting huge crowds even when matches were strictly illegal, and Pierce Egan made his first reputation, before the success of *Life in London* (1821), as the author of *Boxiana* (1812), a compendium of the lives and battles of famous pugilists, which went through many editions. But boxing was also added, on occasion, to the attractions of the circus, giving the reference more immediate relevance in *Hard Times*. At the Royal Amphitheatre in 1823, for example, for four weeks the bills were topped with proclamations of the appearance of Cribb, the retired champion, and Spring, his pupil, the present champion, in a 'scientific display of the modern art of attack and defence', although, the bills hastened to add, 'the trial of skill between the champions exhibits nothing offensive to delicacy'. This sparring was incorporated, fittingly enough, into a dramatization of Tom and Jerry (i.e., Egan's *Life in London*), in a scene at Jackson's sparring-room, adapted from the novel. Between the customary activities on horseback, the pugilists offered their attraction by way of an interlude. Such alternation of different kinds of display in consecutive scenes of a single hippodrama was wholly conventional, although it was more usual to employ the clown than the actual pugilists for the sparring scene in *Tom and Jerry*.[56] It is just possible that Dickens saw this exhibition by Spring and Cribb but, whether he had ever seen this or any other boxing exhibition in one of his visits to the circus, he was certainly familiar both with pugilism and with *Tom and Jerry*, and in any case his use of the pugilism conceit in *Hard Times* fits generally into the novel's context of popular amusements, used here, as in the presentation of Bounderby, with comic incongruity for ironic purposes.

Perhaps, given the extent of circus imagery integrated elsewhere in the novel, Dickens intends a hint of pantomime transformation in the initial description of Mr Gradgrind, with his 'plantation of firs' for hair and 'crust of a plum pie' for pate; unquestionably, these are images of fancy rather than of fact. But the single most striking instance of circus motifs for satiric ends appears in the 'keynote' chapter, introducing the setting of Coketown.

> It was a town of red brick, or of brick that would have been red
> if the smoke and ashes had allowed it; but as matters stood it was
> a town of unnatural red and black like the painted face of a
> savage. It was a town of machinery and tall chimneys, out of
> which interminable serpents of smoke trailed themselves for-
> ever and ever, and never got uncoiled. It had a black canal in it,
> and a river that ran purple with ill-smelling dye, and vast piles of
> building full of windows where there was a rattling and a
> trembling all day long, and where the piston of the steam-

engine worked monotonously up and down, like the head of an elephant in a state of melancholy madness.   (*HT*, I, 5)

This lurid description is a nightmare vision of a circus gone berserk. Painted savages, smoke serpents and live elephants were all features of the circus as Dickens knew it, and he deploys them here to characterize a town in which repressed fancy has erupted in obscene perversions of innocent amusements. As we have seen, elephants appeared periodically in the circus, and acts by American Indians, or by European artistes dressed up as Indians, were frequent attractions. The smoke serpent was a kind of pyrotechnic exhibition, such as the 'stupendous serpent, or boa constrictor, pursuing a butterfly, and a most magnificent change' billed at Astley's in 1821 as the finale to a fireworks display.[57]

Dickens evokes circus performances such as these in his description of Coketown in order to suggest the presence there of longings for amusement, in however deformed shapes, despite the most strenuous efforts of the civic authorities to eliminate them altogether. The ugliness and melancholy of these shapes is a reminder that, forbidden healthy outlet, people's need for entertainment will surface in wildly distorted form. In the midst of this discord and wretchedness Dickens shows us poor, rejected Mrs Pegler, whose one annual holiday is an arduous but joyful expedition to look upon the wonders her son Bounderby controls.

> The bell was ringing, and the Serpent was a Serpent of many coils, and the Elephant was getting ready. The strange old woman was delighted with the very bell. It was the beautifullest bell she had ever heard, she said, and sounded grand!
>   (*HT*, I, 12)

Dickens insists that for her to find harmony in such a scene is entirely natural and touching, but for the hands suffering under Bounderby's tyranny the setting is far from one of joy, and Dickens finds no cause for surprise in the rebellion that breaks out, however much he deplores the form that outburst takes. Along with the allusion to the factories as 'fairy palaces', the monstrous serpent and the melancholy-mad elephant are invoked repeatedly throughout the novel, in a refrain to keep ever present our awareness that one of the chief indictments Dickens levels at the industrial and educational authorities is their endeavour to suppress the life-enhancing recreations of the sort that Sleary's circus represents.

VI

These positive qualities, as Dickens dramatizes them in *Hard Times*, are his perennial themes of decency, kindness, good-humour and fellow-feeling. In our first view of Sleary's equestrians, he is explicit about their virtues. For all their limitations, he writes,

> Yet there was a remarkable gentleness and childishness about these people, a special inaptitude for any kind of sharp practice, and an untiring readiness to help and pity one another, deserving often as much respect, and always of as much generous construction, as the every-day virtues of any class of people in the world.   (*HT*, I, 6)

Dickens is clear that their virtues are not specially confined to them as members of a particular élite, but rather qualities which flow naturally from any person who cherishes imagination. Proper cultivation of fancy means, for Dickens, to be more fully human. The commitment of the circus people to providing entertainment thus makes it singularly appropriate for Dickens's thematic purposes that they should be generous and kind, and he takes clear steps to avoid sentimentalizing them. The first two performers to appear, Childers and Kidderminster, fall to quarrelling almost at once, and continue until Childers ejects Kidderminster bodily from the room. Dickens also gives us comic details such as Kidderminster's marital fate – blighted in love by Sissy's departure, he marries a fat widow "old enough to be hith mother" (*HT*, III, 7) – and not so funny details about the toil and danger the circus people routinely face. Such information detracts in no way from the esteem they command, and it accords with the kind of lives showmen actually lived, in which rivalry and clashes of temperament were inevitable, but bonds of fellowship were strong. As David Prince Miller puts the case:

> Although showmen do wage war against each other in their professional capacity, there are few who will not assist either one of their fraternity or any other individual in distress.[58]

Circus history is full of incidents which corroborate this view – both of the vigorous competition, and of the fraternal support.

As part of this basic human decency which Dickens attributes to his entertainers, they have a solid integrity of character. Sleary, in explaining their function in society to Gradgrind, makes evident that he has a confident and accurate self-knowledge far superior to that of any of the more respectable personages in the story. Childers and Kidderminster bridle instantly when challenged about their way of life by Gradgrind and Bounderby, and such reaction is not mere defensiveness in the face of overt hostility, but open-eyed commitment to the value of what they do. This wholeness, or lack of inner division, is most apparent in Sissy, who is able to deal with troubles – both her own and those of others – precisely because of the inner strength, or 'beautiful light', in Dickens's metaphor, which her circus values give her.

One of the most astute modern commentators on the circus, Antony Hippisley Coxe, distinguishes performances in the ring from those on the stage in a way which is suggestive for Dickens's purposes in this regard. Theatre, Coxe proposes, is based on illusion, with actors pretending to be personages they are not; circus, on the other hand, is 'spectacle of actuality'.

> It can be seen from all sides. There can be no illusion. There are eyes all round to prove there is no deception. The performers actually do exactly what they appear to do. Their feats of dexterity and balance and strength must never be confused with the make believe world of the actor. In the ring, nothing should be done to destroy the sense of actuality.[59]

Without subscribing entirely to this view (are clowns exactly as they seem? Do not costumes and mime suggest make-believe?), I think it does point to a fundamental quality in the circus, and one which is of the utmost usefulness to Dickens in *Hard Times*. For if authenticity – being and doing what one appears to be and to do – is basic to the circus it provides Dickens with an emphatic contrast to the delusions of Gradgrind, the hypocrisy of Bounderby, the calculation of Slackbridge and the cynicism of Harthouse. Dickens obviously could not have known this theory, proposed a century after *Hard Times*, but he could very well be attracted to the same quality in the circus which Coxe identifies. Dickens says of the circus people that their skills in the ring are genuine, and their motives for being performers pure; this professional honesty makes it appropriate for him to attribute integrity to their private lives as well, for his symbolic purposes in *Hard Times*.

The central function of the circus is to provide entertainment. In the most-quoted words of the novel:

> 'People must be amuthed, Thquire, thomehow,' continued Sleary, rendered more pursy than ever, by so much talking; 'they can't be alwayth a working, nor yet they can't be alwayth a learning. Make the betht of uth; not the wurtht. I've got my living out of the horthe-riding all my life, I know; but I con-

thider that I lay down the philothophy of the thubject when I thay
to you, Thquire, make the betht of uth: not the wurtht!' (*HT*, I, 6)

This is the most direct and explicit statement of the circus 'philothophy' which underpins *Hard Times*. In it, Dickens puts into Sleary's
mouth a proclamation of the non-utilitarian, non-educational value
of his entertainment as the fulfilment of an essential human need.
Circus proprietors occasionally made gestures in the direction of the
'uplifting' qualities of their shows: Cooke in 1838 boasted that his
'classic' entertainments were 'well worthy of the most cultivated
minds'; and Batty inserted in an 1841 playbill a long peroration on
the 'moral import' of his circus as 'an effective spur to the youthful
mind'; but circus advertisements were usually content to vaunt their
offerings as exhibitions of drama, skill and spectacle, and there can
be no doubt but that these were the attractions for their customers.[60]
A degree of curiosity about the costumes of foreign lands and about
animals from the wild increased the motivation of circus-goers, and
Thackeray's Colonel Newcome found gratification in recognizing
the likeness of the principal actor in a production of 'The Battle of
Waterloo' to the actual features of the Emperor Napoleon (whom he
had never seen), but at root the circus provided a source of carefree
recreation, a few hours' escape from the dreary routine of life into a
magic world of colour and daring, a happy indulgence of the
capacity for wonder and imagination.[61] The circus was a truly
popular form of entertainment; Astley's third amphitheatre alone
could hold between 2,000 and 2,500 spectators at a single performance, and frequently played to capacity audiences.[62] The performers
offered a social function – whatever Gradgrind and Bounderby
might think – which Dickens considered vital to the stability and
happiness of the people, and Sleary's circus was thus a wholly
appropriate symbol to set against the exclusively calculating and
practical attitudes of its opponents.

In *Hard Times* the circus is beset by vocal opposition. Its performers, who ask no more than toleration from the civic authorities,
are looked down upon as idle and useless vagabonds at best, and at
worst as evil seducers of the ignorant and unwary. The precariousness of their position, on the edge of society and with powerful
enemies, accounts for the vigour with which Dickens champions
their cause; he holds up Sleary's circus as a small spark of light in a
world of darkness, an oasis in a bleak desert of fact, much as, in *Little
Dorrit*, his next novel, he cherishes the small but vital victory of Amy
and Arthur, who walk together while all about them 'the noisy and
the eager, and the arrogant and the froward and the vain, fretted, and
chafed, and made their usual uproar' (*LD*, II, 34).

But, however precarious the utility of any form of entertainment in the eyes of Gradgrind and Bounderby, Sleary's circus appears to be flourishing. Sleary's circus attracts paying customers – as well as peeping Toms and Louisas – in sufficient numbers to keep the troupe together for a period longer than the several years' duration of Dickens's story; it maintains recurrent appeal, which makes viable a fixed annual itinerary (this is how Sissy is able to locate the circus in the book's final pages); it generates enough surplus income to finance newspaper advertising and to allow Sleary to decline Gradgrind's offer of financial remuneration for his services on behalf of Tom. As we discussed earlier, Dickens distances the circus from economic considerations and social issues. It is not part of the mainstream of Coketown society; rather, its periodic visits offer to the hands a rare holiday treat, much as the visit to Astley's by Kit and Barbara in *The Old Curiosity Shop* is a special event. Its prosperity, then, is part of the idealizing tendency of Dickens's portrayal, not something authenticated within the text. It is a fact that circus attracted enormous capital in the nineteenth century, but 'fact' was not Dickens's purpose in *Hard Times*. The circus exists in the novel not as a portent of developments in popular entertainment, but as an emblem of moral value. And that value is 'fancy'.

VII

Because his concern is more with the stultifying results of denial than with the positive benefits of a life imbued with fancy, the circus itself appears only briefly in the novel, at its start and conclusion. Nevertheless, its symbolic presence is felt throughout the book, through the use of circus motifs, through constant reminders of the inadequacy of Gradgrind's view of things, and through the character of the clown's daughter, Sissy. It is she who moves into the Gradgrind household early in the story, and Dickens pointedly calls attention to her at moments of crisis. When Louisa agrees to marry Bounderby, the implications of this decision are spelled out in a silent exchange between Lousia and Sissy.

When Mr Gradgrind had presented Mrs Bounderby, Sissy had suddenly turned her head, and looked, in wonder, in pity, in sorrow, in doubt, in a multitude of emotions, towards Louisa. Louisa had known it, and seen it, without looking at her. From that moment she was impassive, proud and cold – held Sissy at a distance – changed to her altogether.   (*HT*, I, 15)

Phil wishes he was married.

The glamour of the circus offered a powerful stimulus to the fancy.

This moment is emphatically more than an interchange between two characters, but stands as a highly charged confrontation of opposing values. In acquiescing to Bounderby's proposal, Louisa is irrevocably estranging herself from the gentle and caring ways she craves, and the resulting distance between her and Sissy is the measure of her loss.

Similar thematic importance can be seen in later appearances of Sissy in the novel. When Louisa flees from Harthouse and Bounderby, it is Sissy who comes to her bedside, offering comfort and renewal to her and her father. When Rachael seeks Stephen, once again it is Sissy whose presence underlines the faith and affection vindicated by the discovery of the dying man at the bottom of Old Hell Shaft. Dickens's use of plot to signify theme is at its most explicit in the book's closing pages, when Sissy directs Tom to Sleary, and the circus literally rescues the whelp from the consequences of his misguided selfishness.

Sissy's intrinsic virtues give her alone the strength to deal with the collapse of Gradgrind's world, and make her the appropriate agent to cast out the most pernicious villain in the book, the seductive Harthouse. Espousing the philosophy of fact without conviction, languidly drifting into the vacuum left in the wakes of Gradgrind and Bounderby, Harthouse plays 'the very devil' with Louisa, because her stunted goodness has no defence against the 'honesty in dishonesty' with which he confesses disbelief in her father's system, and his weary cynicism strikes a responsive chord in her. But Harthouse is no match for Sissy, who goes to him unbidden and confronts him with no more than 'plain faith in the truth and right of what she said' (*HT*, III, 2). Their confrontation further clarifies the symbolic weight which Dickens attributes to the circus in the novel, by distinguishing sharply between the mere idleness of Harthouse and the positive dedication to values other than work and fact, which Sissy and the circus represent. In so far as he cares about anything, Harthouse is devoted to his own languid pleasure, and his humiliation by Sissy underlines the active nature of Dickens's conception of the circus; far from being moral lassitude, the defence of recreation and amusement is intense commitment to qualities of life essential to emotional well-being.

The most eloquent and moving expression of this theme occurs independently of Sissy and the circus, in the scene which Dr Leavis singles out as an instance of Dickens's 'consummate' artistry, the interview between Gradgrind and Louisa concerning Bounderby's proposal of marriage.[63] In this scene Louisa listens to her father's recitation of the facts relating to Bounderby's offer, with a demeanour of dispassionate stoicism disconcerting even to Gradgrind. Her exterior hides the emotions seething within her, however, and, frustrated in her longing to 'throw herself upon his breast and give him the pent-up confidences of her heart', Louisa gazes out of the window at the chimneys of the Coketown factories. In answer to her father's puzzled question as to what she finds to consult there, Louisa responds:

> 'There seems to be nothing there but languid and monotonous smoke. Yet when the night comes, Fire bursts out, father!'   (*HT*, I, 15)

This remark brings into focus the motif of fire-gazing which is associated with Louisa throughout the novel (and with other inhibited dreamers in Dickens, most notably Lizzie Hexam), as an image of the imaginative life. The warmth, light and creativity symbolized by the fire are all stifled in Louisa, who smoulders sullenly, until, ignited by Harthouse, her emotions are controllable no longer, and for her, as for the chimneys, fire bursts out.

What makes this exchange between the book's central personages so effective thematically is that apprehension of its significance depends fundamentally on the very values which Dickens is defending. Only someone prepared to respond imaginatively to Louisa's image will understand its significance, for her utterance is meaningless from a factual perspective, as Gradgrind's baffled response indicates. '"I do not see the application of that remark,"' he confesses, and Dickens emphasizes his incomprehension by adding, 'to do him justice, he did not, at all'. Dickens's method in this dialogue enacts his content, imaginatively dramatizing the book's theme of man's need for unrepressed imaginative life. The consequences of Louisa's acquiescence to Bounderby are encapsulated in the image, and the parallel scene late in the book shows both Louisa and her father irrevocably scarred by the flames which inevitably erupt. The later interview between father and daughter is equally important to Dickens's scheme, but it lacks the power of this scene because there Dickens relies on abstract explanation about heart and head rather than allowing his symbols to work for themselves. At its best, form and content are one in *Hard Times*, with circus themes inextricable from Dickens's methods.

The tragedy of Louisa and Gradgrind is one of Dickens's triumphs, and stands as the crowning achievement of *Hard Times*. As a whole, however, the novel does not rank among Dickens's greatest. Self-imposed constrictions of length and format limited the space Dickens generally took to develop his novels, and left the skeleton of his polemical purpose less substantially fleshed than was usual for him. His relative unfamiliarity with provincial industrial towns – the more evident in comparison with the novel which followed *Hard Times* in *Household Words*, Elizabeth Gaskell's *North and South* – led to stilted dialect for his workers and a damaging duality of function for Stephen, at once representative of the hands and ostracized from them. In short, the novel lacks the scope and density of Dickens's best work.

These reservations extend in some degree to Dickens's presentation of the circus as well. By idealizing it as an image rooted in the past he sacrificed its potential as a representation not only of modern entertainment but of modern society as well. Its large-scale, commercially organized structure gave Dickens an opportunity to use the circus as an image of popular entertainment within the anonymous, bureaucratic, urban environment which he was to explore with such extraordinary insight in his next novel, *Little Dorrit*. Perhaps had he thought of the circus this way he might have viewed society less despairingly in his later years; then, again, from this perspective he might instead simply have enjoyed the circus less. Dickens thought of it not as a part of society, but as an alternative, for the very good reason that that alternative embodied cherished values which he felt society either passively ignored or actively crushed. We have seen repeatedly that Dickens considered imaginative release, for which entertainment was a potent catalyst, essential to human well-being, because it was a means to selflessness, affection, interest in and awareness of the outside world. It trivializes his conception of the importance of popular entertainment to claim, as John Holloway did in challenging Dr Leavis's celebration of the novel, that Sleary's circus betrays a 'shallow' and 'Philistine' mind because in the end all it represents is the creed 'All work and no play makes Jack a dull boy'.[64] It is Bounderby, not Dickens, who thinks of entertainment as idleness.

The circus is not offered as a practical solution to industrial strife, any more than Oliver's cry for More provided detailed guidelines for the Poor Law administrators in Somerset House. Dickens was concerned with prior causes, with the fundamental attitudes which dispose men and women to seek means to implement generous policies. The idealizing of the circus is an aspect of the generalizing tendency of all great art, which does not limit itself to the particular and the specific. Nevertheless, by removing Sleary so completely from the complexities of everyday life, Dickens does not provide us with nearly so thorough an acquaintance of the circus as he did with Crummles's strollers. The ambiguities of motive and behaviour which gave such vitality to the showfolk in *Nickleby* and *The Old Curiosity Shop* are missing among the circus personages in *Hard Times*, who are, as Sally Vernon accurately judges, 'less striking

because more explicit'.[65] Finally, however, Sleary's horse-riding is
an affectionately drawn expression of Dickens's lifelong delight in
sawdust and tinsel, and a vigorous restatement of his commitment to
people's right to recreation and entertainment. The circus in *Hard
Times* is inextricably linked with his defence of imagination in the
novel; its symbolic function underpins the book's themes, and by
extension reaffirms the centrality of popular entertainment to Dickens's artistic vision.

CHAPTER 6

Popular Entertainment in Dickens's Journalism

Although the subject of popular entertainment was maintained in generally low profile in the fiction of Dickens's middle and late years, the periodical which he founded in 1850 gave him a major alternative outlet for its continued expression. In *Household Words* and its successor, *All the Year Round*, Dickens devoted a substantial proportion of space to a wide variety of public amusements. A number of essays on the subject he wrote himself, and some of them, in their wit, vigour and incisiveness, are among his outstanding pieces of journalism. A great many more were composed by hands other than his own but, as Harry Stone has demonstrated, Dickens kept strict control over the contents and the perspectives of *Household Words*.[1] Every pair of facing pages bore the imprimatur 'Conducted by Charles Dickens', and it was axiomatic that the entertainments of the people were to be fostered and defended. His policy was emphatically not undiscriminating – amusements judged to be dangerous, degrading or morally corrosive were firmly disapproved of – but the hallmark of the journals' treatment of popular entertainment was broad toleration and warm support.

A periodical of his own was a congenial medium for presenting his views on a subject close to his heart. Appearing weekly it was far more capable of responding quickly to topical developments of interest than an extended work of fiction – even serially published fiction. As a miscellany, it made possible a highly eclectic selection of materials, written by a number of contributors. Not that there was anything unique in journalism dealing with entertainment: a positive deluge of such publications poured out in the nineteenth century. Many of these journals dealt exclusively with the theatre or sporting events, and most of them folded after a very few issues. What distinguished *Household Words* and its successor, and ensured the survival of *All the Year Round* long after Dickens's death, was that they were themselves genuinely popular and genuinely entertaining.

Nor was journalism a new departure for Dickens. He had been a highly capable newspaper reporter in the days when he made his first ventures in the publication of creative writing. When *The Pickwick Papers* was barely under way he had an outspoken pamphlet printed, *Sunday under Three Heads*, which defended the people's right to Sunday pleasures in the face of proposed Sabbatarian legislation. Before *Pickwick* was half-written, he accepted the position of editor of a new miscellaneous journal published by Richard Bentley; and in 1840 he launched a weekly periodical of his own, *Master Humphrey's Clock*. Articles on entertainment appeared in *Bentley's Miscellany*, and the *Clock* was intended to be a compendium of popular tales, reports and amusements. But Dickens soon quarrelled with the owner of *Bentley's Miscellany*, and in any case his chief interest in that journal was the novel of his which first appeared in its pages, *Oliver Twist*. *Master Humphrey's Clock* was a disappointment to readers from the start, and it was soon overtaken by *The Old Curiosity Shop* and *Barnaby Rudge*, continuous tales which engulfed the miscellaneous structure of the *Clock*, in which they were published. *Household Words* was thus a fulfilment of earlier aborted hopes to edit a popular journal.

As regards the presentation of popular entertainment in *Household Words* and *All the Year Round*, the periodicals had three main functions. First, they included a wealth of observation on the subject, surveying the contemporary scene, comparing it with earlier activities and with foreign practices, responding to topical events, both to promising new developments in the state of entertainment and to new manifestations of hostility by influential opponents of the people's amusements. Second, they provided a forum for explicit statements of principle. Often such statements were no more than brief reiteration of basic premises as part of a case made against a particular instance of opposition, but on occasion they offered full and significant expression of Dickens's thinking on the subject. Third, there were essays which offered proposals for the improvement of leisure opportunities for the people. Taking seriously the responsibility which he felt his own stature as a public entertainer involved, he used his periodicals to suggest directions in which enlightened advances in the provision of entertainment might proceed, and means by which they might be accomplished. In the present chapter we shall consider these three aspects of Dickens's treatment of popular entertainment in his journalism. The evidence presented must necessarily be highly selective, but by isolating main themes and perspectives we can clarify the nature of Dickens's convictions.

I

First of all, then, Dickens used his journals to observe and assess the state of entertainment available. This was an extension of the appeal to curiosity which had been a primary motive in *Sketches by Boz*, and it was in keeping with the professed intention of *Household Words*, as stated in the 'Preliminary Word' with which the first number opened. 'In all familiar things', Dickens declared, 'there is Romance enough, if we will find it out.' *Household Words* and *All the Year Round* were dedicated to the proposition of revealing the Romance of things both familiar and unfamiliar. 'Finding it out' meant circumstantially exploring materials which would serve to stimulate the imagination, awaken kindly affections and provide relief from 'moody, brutal fact'.[2] Entertaining objects and events were precisely suitable for this purpose, and in his journals Dickens published lively accounts of opportunities for amusement which his roving correspondents noted abroad, and of wonders both native and imported which were to be found at home.

There were articles about exhibitions, large and small, commonplace and exotic, educational and absurd; it was typical of Dickens's broadly tolerant tastes that he found a collection of stuffed humming birds on display at the Zoological Gardens 'as worthy' as the more celebrated inventions which were to be witnessed a mile away in the Crystal Palace during the Great Exhibition.[3] There were articles about the theatre, describing productions and audiences in Paris, Bucharest, Pera, Penang, and in the Adelphi off the Strand. There were articles about fairs, giving accounts of a great city fair in Munich and an unpretentious little fair in an Irish market-town; of a bazaar in Colombo, a carnival in Greece, and a May festival in Starnberg. There were articles about sport: prizefighting, fox-hunting, elephant-catching in Ceylon, sheep-shearing in Cumberland ('a sort of rural Olympics'), shooting in Albania and Austria and Scotland, fishing under the ice in Canada and in what Dickens declared the best place of all for the sport, the Billingsgate fish-market. His contributors reported on a singing match in Russia, a bullfight in Malaga, and an English village band competition which generated as much noise as Bartholomew Fair 'in its palmiest days'.[4] In these, as in numerous other articles, the emphasis was on the plenitude of sights and sounds and activities capable of affording entertainment for those who would spend the time – or, more important, for those who had the time and money to spend.

Dickens found much to applaud in the variety of opportunity for amusement. He recorded the survival of old forms of entertainment as evidence of the resiliency of truly popular amusements. The pantomime, for example, showed 'amazing stamina' in its annual return to the stage, just as the continuing appearance of strolling players in country villages affirmed 'a principle of life in them stronger than a whole family of Shallows'.[5] The decline of brutal sports, of magic and superstition, gave grounds for belief that the tastes of the people were improving, while the spectacular success of excursion trains, as reported in several articles, showed how innovation which catered to the popular demand for amusement could be commercially profitable.[6] With R. H. Horne, Dickens composed an article in 1851 praising the work of Samuel Phelps in turning Sadler's Wells Theatre from a sink of depravity to a scene of artistic and moral excellence; it was an example, he wrote, of 'what an intelligent and resolute man may do, to establish a good Theatre in the most unpromising soil'.[7] Just under a decade later, in one of his *Uncommercial Traveller* essays, 'Two Views of a Cheap Theatre', Dickens described with enthusiasm his observations of the Britannia Theatre, Hoxton. Clean, bright, spacious, and designed in all aspects for the convenience of its patrons, the theatre was a model of achievement in its appealing provision of entertainment for a largely working-class audience, who responded with cheerful, attentive and orderly deportment. Dickens came away convinced of the 'unquestionably humanising influence in all the social arrangements of the place'.[8] It gave striking proof that popular entertainment could endure, thrive, and confer positive benefit in the changing conditions of nineteenth-century England.

Articles such as these show Dickens's alertness to the wide range of possibilities for enjoyable diversion near at hand and far away. They demonstrate emphatically that, even as the vision of his novels assumed greater seriousness – a development which owed quite as much to the extraordinary advance in the technical complexity of his artistry as to any increase in gloom about the condition of England – he still retained the eager curiosity and disposition to enjoyment which had distinguished his character from the first. The steady stream of circumstantial reports attest to his abiding interest in entertainment and to his firm conviction that people could and would seek out amusement wherever it was to be found. The lively, cheerful tone of these articles supported his aspiration to fill his periodical with bright reflections of 'the stirring world around us' and with appealing encouragement to hope, contentment and tolerance.[9] And, not least, the large proportion of material dealing with the subject of entertainment contributed in a major way to ensuring that *Household Words* was itself entertaining.

Nevertheless, Dickens saw considerable deficiencies in the availability of entertainment for the people, and he expressed grave

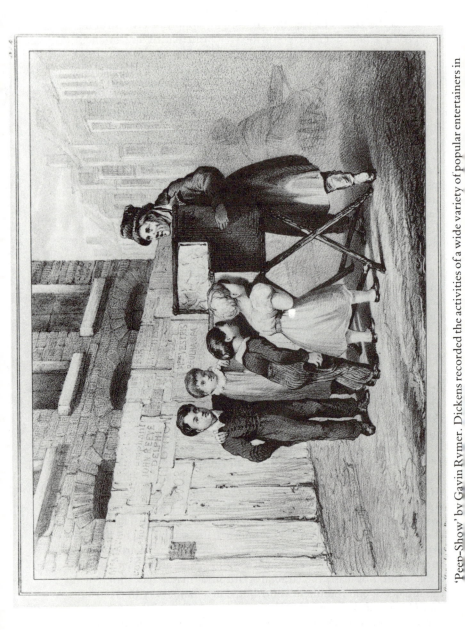

'Peep-Show' by Gavin Rymer. Dickens recorded the activities of a wide variety of popular entertainers in

concern over contemporary attitudes to leisure. There was no contradiction here; what was sufficient for him, as a prosperous, exceptionally perceptive observer, with a professional commitment to searching out avenues of entertainment, was in many cases wholly inadequate for the labouring masses. In consequence, he used his periodicals not only to inform his readers of opportunities for amusement which did exist, but also to urge fundamental improvements in the provision of entertainment for the people.

A recurring refrain in *Household Words* is the inadequacy of inexpensive amusements in Britain. 'We are lamentably deficient in Cheap Pleasures', an article of 1851 stated, 'and this deficiency influences materially our national character.' In their reports on holiday customs and public amusements in other countries, Dickens's correspondents concluded more often than not that foreign people were better off for cheap pleasures than the English. Describing some 'very exquisite' *tableaux vivants* in a Berlin pleasure garden, for example, one staff writer applauded the ways in which, unlike the English, 'the commonest of the Prussian people are civilized and enlightened by the influences of art, which meets him at every turn'. In France, another of Dickens's writers witnessed a 'real holiday' one Ascension Sunday and was left wondering 'whether many towns in England with the same population . . . could produce the same variety of amateur ability'. In England, by contrast, commercial speculation and blinkered moral attitudes were seen to hedge in innocent amusements on every side.

> Fairs, as holidays, are nothing now to the inhabitants of the cities. In the country, their amusements mostly commence with horse-chaunting and pig-jobbing, to terminate in much that is still less to be boasted of. There is little to cheer, and nothing to elevate, but quite as much cause for melancholy as for mirth . . . After all, I think, it may be safely asserted that we have no real holidays in England.[10]

If the state of popular entertainment compared unfavourably with many established customs abroad, *Household Words* reported the overall situation at home to be deteriorating. 'Whole hosts of street arts and street artists are among things departed,' one essay declared, a lament which finds echo in the memoirs of showmen and in the interviews which Henry Mayhew conducted with street people in the 1850s.[11] Dickens was not disposed, in general, to think very highly of the accomplishments of the past when compared to the present. The set of dummy books entitled 'The Wisdom of Our Ancestors', which he had installed in the door of his library in Gad's

Hill Place, sums up his attitude. The volumes in the set were: Volume 1, Ignorance; Volume 2, Superstition; Volume 3, The Block; Volume 4, The Stake; Volume 5, The Rack; and Volume 6, Dirt.[12] But the course of popular entertainment was an altogether different matter. On nearly all sides he saw traditional pastimes in retreat. The Tower of London was in a state of dilapidated disrepair, 'exactly like a show at a fair, the morning *after* the fair'. The theatre was in no better condition: 'Heavily taxed, wholly unassisted by the State, deserted by the gentry, and quite unrecognised as a means of public instruction, the higher English drama has declined.' Sport, improved by the virtual disappearance of cock-fighting, bear-baiting and other brutal pastimes, was still notorious for dissipation and shoddy practices: 'We are not quite spotless in our sports, yet.' In villages, there was a lack of opportunity for the labourer to find amusement except at the public house, whereas in the past public commons, church-ales, quarterly festivals, Plough Monday, harvest homes and Christmas mummings made life less barren: 'No poor man in the world has fewer holidays than the English labourer of our times.' Puppet shows had been declining since the eighteenth century; Sunday promenades in Sydenham had been invented 'because less objectionable places of amusement were closed by enactment'. In short, Queen Mab, patroness of the fancy which amusements nurtured, was 'sadly reduced' by reason of red tape and utilitarian attitudes; she was 'a case of real distress'.[13]

In the first volume of *Household Words*, in 1850, Dickens contributed one of his best-known and most significant essays, the two-part 'Amusements of the People'. In the company of 'Joe Whelks, of New Cut, Lambeth', he takes his readers to the Victoria Theatre, notorious for its raucous crowds and sensational melodrama, and to the Britannia Saloon, 'perhaps the most notable instance' of the junction between old-time taverns and variety theatres which was to produce the music-hall. Both of these theatres were immensely popular gathering-places, bywords in their day for vulgar amusement. Dickens found the audiences happily enjoying themselves (although sometimes bemused by the moral confusion of the dramatic fare, and derisive of the supernatural effects, which were 'not half infernal enough'). But the entertainment itself was another matter. The drama consisted of lurid plots and extravagant sentiments, patent unreality and shoddy performance. After attentively witnessing several plays, Dickens judged them 'an incongruous heap of nonsense'.[14] Sixteen years later a series of five articles in *All the Year Round* revived the character of Whelks for a survey of popular amusements, and found scant cause for congratulation. With the single exception of the music-hall, the writer, Andrew

Halliday, saw no improvement over these years in the quality of entertainment on offer. Instead, places of amusement were badly overcrowded; nominally improving entertainment was boring; unimproving shows were at best 'wearisome nonsense', and at worst indecent, filthy and disgusting. 'Mr Whelks', the series concluded, 'deserves better things of those who, in catering for his amusement, thrive upon him remarkably well.'[15]

This last comment sums up a factor which Dickens and his writers identified as a major cause of the decline in popular amusements: the exploitation by cynical operators of the people's natural inclination to seek pleasure. Instead of providing entertainment in a spirit of moral idealism, showmen entered the field as the merest of financial speculators, calculating on their profits in obliviousness to the great educative potential of leisure pursuits. Again and again Dickens insisted that 'a really first-rate entertainment will always draw the people'; Joe Whelks should be 'played up' to a higher level 'by good sense, good purpose, and good art'. Instead, he complained repeatedly, amusements were excessively costly, and all too often devoid of rational content. The best seats in theatres which drew predominantly from the working classes were too often priced beyond the means of the very clientele who made such theatres prosperous; the costliness of food and drink compared unfavourably with the inexpensive culinary pleasures available abroad; historic monuments, which attracted visitors on account of romantic and legendary associations which were free to all, were fenced off by 'speculating showmen' who charged admission fees to 'their' property.[16]

Foremost among the aspects of popular entertainment to be discussed in *Household Words* and *All the Year Round* was the Sunday question. No other related issue received so much attention in Dickens's journals, and with good reason. As one of his most frequent contributors, G. A. Sala, put it, 'Sunday in England must perforce be taken as a holiday, as we have scarcely any other holidays during the long year'. During the one day in the week when it was possible to find 'peaceable, honest, industrious humanity in peaceful, honest, happy recreation', its preservation as a day of recreation was central to the cause of popular amusements. Dickens and his writers repeatedly surveyed the Sunday situation in England, and contrasted the constricted opportunities for pleasure at home with the countless festive activities to be found abroad.[17]

In Vienna, Sunday was 'a kind of fair', in Hamburg, 'stalls, booths, and baskets lined the way'; in Paris, thousands spent Sunday visiting cemeteries, and 'the scene taken as a whole is a very gay one'; in Constantinople, 'you might fancy the town was being stormed, instead of holding high festival – so violent is the noise and uproar . . . Everywhere there is the same eager, noisy, picturesque crowd.' The gaiety of such scenes was contrasted sharply with the 'air of death' which oppressed the English Sunday.

> We have hardly a real holiday in England; executions and races make the nearest approach to one, but they are both too much in the way of business. A Sunday's holiday is looked upon as a heinous sin by so many worthy and respectable people, that it cannot be indulged with impunity.

Such a dismal picture was seen as a 'national misfortune', and, ominously, the example of a condition infinitely worse was to be found just across the border. In Scotland, nothing profane was tolerated on a Sunday; even whistling and fishing were denounced as 'great crimes'; every window-shade in Edinburgh was pulled down on Sundays, turning it into a 'city of Whited Sepulchres'. With nothing to do outside of church, for many Sunday became an 'intolerable burden', a 'mockery of our high state of civilisation'. It was to such a condition, Dickens felt, that the Sabbatarians were attempting to reduce Sunday in England; the legislative proposals of Sir Andrew Agnew, himself a devout member of the Church of Scotland, were, as a *Times* leader put it, 'torment' inflicted upon Englishmen by a 'Scotch fanatic'.[18]

Sir Andrew's Sabbath Observances Bills incited Dickens to write *Sunday under Three Heads*, and many other pieces which he published on popular entertainment were likewise in direct response to specific proposals for new restrictions on Sunday activities. Legislation to stop military band concerts in public parks, for example, occasioned a defence of music as 'a rational, cheerful, innocent amusement for the tens of thousands of overworked humanity', and Dickens personally contributed £10 to a fund to support private band concerts in replacement of the forbidden military ones.[19] When, in parliamentary discussion of a bill to restrict the availability of drink on Sundays, the argument was put forward that the working classes were 'very much in the condition of children' and therefore required assistance from the law in their struggles with temptation, Dickens wrote an essay entitled 'The Great Baby', in which he fulminated about the offending attitude as a 'national scandal'.[20] Again, Sabbatarian legislation to close the Post Office on Sundays aroused his wrath; such closure, he insisted, was not a laudable endeavour to ensure the rest of postal workers, but part of a general campaign to spread gloom on the Lord's Day, and he used the issue as a vehicle to launch yet another impassioned defence of the people and their right to amusements.[21]

As with Sabbatarianism, Dickens was outspoken about temperance reforms. For all their differences and internecine rivalries, the two movements were at one, Dickens felt, in their determination to put down popular amusements, even as they both paid lip-service to the welfare of the poor. In his *Drink and the Victorians* Brian Harrison has ably demonstrated just how central drink was to virtually every aspect of life in early nineteenth-century England, and how integral it was to leisure activities in particular. But the abuse of drink, Dickens was convinced, was the result rather than the cause of evil.

> Drunkenness, as a national horror, is the effect of many causes. Foul smells, disgusting habitations, bad workshops and workshop customs, want of light, air, and water, the absence of all easy means of decency and health, are commonest among its common, everyday, physical causes. The mental weariness and languor so induced, the want of wholesome relaxation, the craving for *some* stimulus and excitement, which is as much a part of such lives as the sun is; and, last and most inclusive of all the rest, ignorance, and the need there is amongst the English people of reasonable, rational training, in lieu of mere parrot-education, or none at all; are its most obvious moral causes.[22]

These, he argued, were the remediable evils which the moralist should confront first. Dr Harrison, writing from a modern perspective, offers abundant evidence in support of this position, and adds the following astute observation:

> There was much to be gained from stressing the need for moral reform at a time of political and ecclesiastical danger, and for attributing popular discontent to conspirators and drink rather than to any genuine social injustice.[23]

Instead of seeking the root causes for the distress of the poor, the temperance reformer infringed upon the already limited sources of pleasure available to them. This was the substance of Dickens's indictment of the temperance movement, which he found condescending to the people it sought to reform, and ignorant of their real wants and needs. The attractions it offered as alternatives to drink were, he thought, dreary in the extreme; above all, it would penalize all of the people for the sins of a few.

Writing a notice, for example, of Cruikshank's series of engravings 'The Drunkard's Children', Dickens praised the artistry of his sometime collaborator, but issued a stern warning that

Cruikshank misjudged the nature of the problem. By showing a happy family suddenly devastated by the casual purchase of a bottle of gin, Cruikshank avoids the 'teeming and reproachful history anterior to that stage', and as a result will 'defeat the end these pictures are designed to bring about'.[24] Later, composing a vignette for *All the Year Round*, 'The Poor Man and His Beer', Dickens surveyed the inducements invented by 'my friend Philosewers' to entice the worker away from drink, and after inspecting the allotment club, the pig club and the orchestral society he came away bored and depressed by the foolish inadequacy of such remedies.[25] Again, responding to a pronouncement by the Head of the Court of Aldermen of the City of London that 'recreation was a special cause of crime', he assisted his son Charley to write a heavily satirical essay for *All the Year Round* entitled 'The Great Drunkery Discovery', in which they derided the 'close observation and accurate knowledge on which this dictum is founded', noting the 'wicked and cruel game of cricket', the 'constant inbibation of ardent spirits' required to train for rowing, and the 'orgies that take place at the rifle butts'.[26]

Here, as often, Dickens's satire against the enemies of leisure activities is bracing in its hyperbolically expressed ridicule of what he saw as hypocrisy, wilful ignorance, or just plain numskull wrong-headedness. He cheerfully reduced the case against particular amusements to absurdity by invoking the alleged position of such figures as the Monomaniacal Patriarch, the Member for Whitened Sepulchres, and the Whole Hogs from America.[27] Even in his counterattacks, that is, Dickens generated high comedy by treating antagonists as figures of fun. In doing so he in no way blunted the edge of his purpose. His message was serious and it was constant: most people behave decently in their enjoyment of leisure; they have a right to their pleasures; and it is irresponsible to advocate wholesale suppression of amusements by invoking Sloggins's Principle (since some abuse, none shall enjoy).[28] Instead of being restricted, popular entertainment should be made less expensive, and more readily available. 'Please Sir can I have some More!' was the cry he put forward for expanded leisure opportunities: more free time, more holidays, more playgrounds, more excursion trains, more concerts – simply, as for Oliver, More.

II

A wide-ranging examination of the state of popular entertainment, then, figured prominently in *Household Words* and *All the Year Round*. This survey included assessments of its excellences and deficiencies, its friends and enemies. The recurrent move from observation to judgement made the treatment of the subject in Dickens's journals decidedly polemical. He showed a crusading resolve to promote the best opportunities for entertainment and to decry all factors which interfered with its vitality. Despite the diversity of subjects presented and the large number of contributors who wrote about them, in his journals the general outlook on popular amusements was remarkably clear and coherent. Such consistency was the result not only of Dickens's close personal supervision of *Household Words* but also of his strong sense of the importance of entertainment. The principles which underpinned his thinking about it were intense, and they remained constant throughout his lifetime.

Central to his thought was the unassailable conviction that love of amusement was an essential human characteristic. We saw in the previous chapter that this was a major theme of *Hard Times*; it was set forth as an irrefutable truth in 'A Preliminary Word', the introductory announcement with which the first number of *Household Words* began; he repeated it in letters and speeches, and he stressed it prominently in his *Household Words* essay 'The Amusements of the People'.[29] This last is a particularly important statement of principle, published during the first weeks in existence of his new periodical. We have already noted that this essay contains a valuable eyewitness account, both sympathetic and thorough, of an audience and its entertainment in two of the more successful London theatres. It is significant also as a ringing declaration of his beliefs about popular entertainment. Here as elsewhere the words he uses to describe man's inclination towards entertainment are 'innate' and 'inherent'. 'It is probable that nothing will ever root out from among the common people an innate love they have for dramatic entertainment,' he declared; 'we believe a love of dramatic representation to be an inherent principle in human nature.' Focused specifically on the attraction to theatrical entertainment which is his immediate topic, in its wider implications the essay reaffirms the fundamental axiom of Dickens's approach to the subject: the imagination to which amusement appeals is 'inherent in the human breast'.[30]

> There is a range of imagination in most of us, which no amount of steam-engines will satisfy; and which The-great-exhibition-of-the-works-of-industry-of-all-nations, itself, will probably leave unappeased . . . The Polytechnic Institution in Regent Street, where an infinite variety of ingenious models are exhibited and explained . . . is a great public benefit and a wonderful place, but we think a people formed *entirely* in their hours of leisure by Polytechnic Institutions would be an uncomfortable community.[31]

Dickens is making three distinct claims here: that utilitarian science alone is not enough to satisfy human curiosity, that the achieving of such satisfaction is important to man as an individual, and that it is also important to society at large. The first is an affirmation of the 'more than one thing needful' which it was to be his purpose in *Hard Times* to demonstrate. Dickens is convinced that it is an improper restriction on the rich variety of experience latent in the world to attribute worth only to what is functional or verifiable. Simple pleasures and imaginings have their own sometimes considerable value as well. Second, amusement contributes significantly to the emotional well-being of the individual. Relaxation, freedom and expansiveness are all benefits which entertainment can promote. By providing stimulus to the imagination and relief from mundane existence, it is also capable of broadening the basis of man's awareness. Third, it is an invaluable aid to social harmony, by breeding contentment with one's own lot and affectionate feelings towards others. In Dickens's conception entertainment is thus a socializing force as well as an individual need. The natural instinct for amusement not only confers a right upon all men; it also creates a potent agency for social progress. The widest possible provision of the best possible entertainment is thus a matter of considerable moment.

The substance of his complaint about the theatres visited in 'The Amusements of the People' was their failure to tap this resource effectively. He had no quarrel with the audiences, for he was the last person to begrudge the noisy, unwashed crowds of people the indulgence of carefree idleness. Nor did he blame the actors, overworked and underpaid, struggling to follow their vocation without despising it. What he found deplorable was not even the absurdity of the plays being performed, but rather the valuable opportunity being missed. For the principal point of his investigation was that Mr Whelks was 'susceptible of improvement through the agency of his theatrical tastes'. The educational potential of the theatre was being squandered by the inattention of those in a position to do something about it, and the country was the poorer as a result. Dickens's message was plain:

> The people who now resort here, *will be* amused somewhere. It is no use to blink that fact, or to make pretences to the contrary. We had far better apply ourselves to improving the character of their amusement. It would not be exacting much, or exacting anything very difficult, to require that the pieces in these Theatres should have, at least, a good, plain, healthy purpose in them.[32]

BOXING-NIGHT – A picture in the National Gallery.

Dickens was convinced that Joe Whelks was 'susceptible of improvement through the agency of his theatrical tastes' but that the educational potential of the theatre was being squandered by the poor quality of entertainment being offered.

His tone here is stern, because the derisory quality of the plays in the theatres he has visited could do nothing to improve the lives of the audience who see them. But there is an underlying optimism in his belief that entertainment is capable of conferring great good. Man's innate love of entertainment means that audiences are predisposed to be receptive: their interest is present even before the show begins. Reciprocally, it is in the very nature of entertainment to draw men out of themselves: by stimulating their imaginations through colour, novelty and excitement, it extends their perception both of themselves and of the world about them. And when this stimulus is direct and purposeful it can clarify understanding, teach discrimination and improve taste. For all his exasperation with the opponents of entertainment who failed to admit these truths, and for all his dismay that so little entertainment was really good, he was nevertheless fundamentally hopeful in his conviction that a natural human inclination was indomitable.

What was required to take advantage of this opportunity was, as one essay in *Household Words* whimsically put it, a little 'grease'.

> This human machine, which goes on the whole with so much regularity, and turns out so large a quantity of work, material and intellectual, with such satisfaction to society, requires a little grease, too, sometimes. That cunning engineer, Nature, has of herself provided a natural spontaneous oil for the lubrication of the joints of the body, else would the muscles grow rigid and the sinews crack. But the joints of the mind: do not *they* require to be greased occasionally?[33]

The writer here was G. A. Sala, who contributed a large number of essays on popular entertainment to Dickens's periodicals, many in a vein similar to that expressed above. Dickens was not always in full accord with Sala's views, but he published some 145 articles by him in *Household Words* alone, and he had no reservations about the basic desirability of amusements.[34] He stated the case with particular force in a letter written while he was at work on *Hard Times*. Echoing the sentiments of that novel, he wrote to Charles Knight, himself a sometime contributor to *Household Words*:

> The English are, so far as I know, the hardest-worked people on whom the sun shines. Be content, if, in their wretched intervals of pleasure, they read for amusement and do no worse. They are born at the oar, and they live and die at it. Good God, what would we have of them![35]

204

Not only did Dickens consider the English people particularly unfortunate in their limited opportunity for amusements, he also thought of instinctive, gregarious enjoyment as a peculiarly English characteristic. The English people, he wrote, are

> . . . universally respected by intelligent foreigners who visit this country, for their unobtrusive politeness, their good humour, and their cheerful recognition of all restraints that really originate in consideration for the general good . . . They are moderate, and easily pleased, and very sensible to all affectionate influences.[36]

In contrast to the French, 'There is, in the English character a rich vein of dry, quietly chuckling humour and merriment'. This opinion, of a sympathetic openness to the pleasurable variety of experience as a national characteristic, finds precedent in the writings of Addison and Hazlitt, and later expression in J. B. Priestley's analysis of English humour, but Dickens felt that all too often the Englishman's natural readiness to be pleased was dampened by the spirit of Mrs Grundy, obtruding on people a fear of being laughed at for indulging in simple pleasures: 'In no country but England have the only means and scenes of relaxation within the reach of some million or two people been systematically lampooned and derided.' He deplored the tendency to associate recreation with idleness and dissipation, with the result that 'Pleasures of any kind, be they ever so harmless, are nowhere so unpopular as in Great Britain'.[37]

Ignorance about the actual attitudes and behaviour of the English people and attempts to deprive them of their sources of enjoyment were matters which he constantly opposed in his periodicals. A corollary of his belief in love of entertainment as an instinctive attribute was his conviction, supported by abundant evidence, of the disposition of most men and women to enjoy their free time responsibly. Again and again in accounts of festivities and recreations which Dickens and his staff writers witnessed in person, the decency and contentment with which the people pursued their amusements was insisted upon. 'Experience has proved' that mischief and misconduct seldom occur; 'it is a fact' that people seek entertainment in a spirit of good-humour. To claim that the great body of the people 'spoil things' in the public places of amusement which they visit is a 'vulgar calumny'. In pleasure gardens, art galleries and museums, even in taverns, behaviour is respectful and free from excess. As for the dissipation and vice which undoubtedly do occur:

> This is the natural depravity of the common people, of course! It

is not at all because real education is wanted, or because the common folk must get their open-air entertainments by stealth and while the law is winking, or because anybody, – saint or sinner, pot or kettle – proceeds on the prodigious assumption that the question lies between the worst amusements and none; between the declarations of a pet prisoner gnashing his teeth at sour grapes, and the striving fancy that there is in most of us, which even a lecture or a steam-engine will not always satisfy! No doubt.[38]

Convinced of the responsibility of the people seeking amusement, Dickens was also outspoken in his certitude that most entertainers, as well, were hard-working, dedicated artistes. The portrayal of Sleary's showmen in *Hard Times* serves as emphatic contradiction of Bounderby's accusation that 'idleness' was their only occupation (*HT*, I, 6), and a visit behind the scenes of any circus or theatre quickly revealed that these places were 'not temples of idleness, but mines of industry in which the miners work hard at extremely modest wages to produce their glittering results'. The preparation of a pantomime consisted of 'work, work, work, everywhere', by a theatre corps who were 'hard-working, industrious and persevering'; and the desire of people to be entertained provided honest labour for those who did the entertaining. 'A very large class of people in all ranks depends for its bread and meat on the world's willingness to take some wholesome recreation in the intervals of toil.' The energy which Dickens himself devoted to the cause of amusing others was testimony to his belief in the value of entertainment and in the usefulness of the service which entertainers fulfilled. He was philosophical about the prejudices which prevailed against entertainers; in one *Household Words* essay he wrote, 'I wish, myself, that we were not so pleased to think ill of those who minister to our amusement'. And another article which he published speculated whimsically that the animosity directed towards entertainers was misplaced, directing attention away from the real suffering and evil to be found in the world. 'I am very much amused to think what a good world this must be, as it is now to most of us, when Londoners can find no worse tyranny to complain of than being ground under the barrels of the foreign organ-boys.'[39]

Dickens proclaimed these beliefs from the outset of his career. We saw in the opening pages of this book that he used the occasion of Queen Victoria's coronation to defend the people's right to entertainment and their decency in seeking it. Two years earlier even than that, when *Pickwick* was only just under way in the spring of 1836, he composed *Sunday under Three Heads*, a vigorously polemical pamphlet in which he spelled out the convictions which were to last him a lifetime. Reacting to proposed Sabbatarian legislation as 'a piece of deliberate cruelty and crafty injustice', Dickens recorded as demonstrable fact the responsible way in which ordinary people behaved in their pursuit of pleasure.

> The great majority of the people who make holiday on Sunday now, are industrious, orderly, and well-behaved persons. It is not unreasonable to suppose that they would be no more inclined to an abuse of pleasures provided for them, than they are to an abuse of the pleasures they provide for themselves; and if any people, for want of something better to do, resort to criminal practices on the Sabbath as at present observed, no better remedy for the evil can be imagined, than giving them the opportunity of doing something that will amuse them, and hurt nobody else.[40]

Concurring with the arguments of radical Members of Parliament who opposed Sir Andrew Agnew's Bill, Dickens charged then and later that Sabbatarian attitudes were discriminatory at root, since they would explicitly safeguard the privileges of the wealthy even as they would deny temporary leisure to the poor. Such practices, he claimed, brought authority into disrepute, whereas the encouragement of sports, entertainments and amusements would create a Lord's Day associated with happiness and rest rather than with gloom and oppression; religion seen by the people to soften their lot would earn their respect and thus alleviate frustration and prevent social unrest.[41]

Here as elsewhere Dickens immeasurably strengthens his case by grounding it in circumstantial observation. The journalist in Dickens accumulates detailed evidence of the behaviour of crowds on a Sunday, and he chronicles the activities which they actually engage in. He finds Sunday for most people to be a day of conviviality, in which individuals gather together with family and friends in a spirit of cheerful gregariousness. Food, drink, recreation and diversion are the principal attractions and, although he frankly admits cases of drunkenness and debauchery, his observations convinces him that most people seek enjoyment, not excess. This approach lends an air of discovery to the essay and imparts liveliness and interest to his writing, as he portrays large areas of experience of which his readers are likely to be ignorant. He was soon to exploit this method brilliantly in *Oliver Twist* (as Elizabeth Gaskell was to do a decade later in *Mary Barton*): once hitherto unknown facts are revealed, he posits, all right-thinking men will accept his conclusion because 'IT

IS TRUE'.[42] It is a tactic which also enables him to accuse his opponents of arguing either from wilful ignorance or from deliberate malice, on the basis that openly available evidence demonstrates the falsity of their position. In dedicating *Sunday under Three Heads* to the Bishop of London, Dickens sarcastically declares:

> That your Lordship would ever have contemplated Sunday recreations with so much horror, if you had been at all acquainted with the wants and necessities of the people who indulged in them, I cannot imagine possible.[43]

The basis in observation, in short, gives authority to the principles which Dickens espouses, just as deep conviction provides a coherent framework for the welter of diverse evidence which he accumulates. Observant reporting and outspoken declaration of principle mutually reinforce each other and give Dickens's journalism enduring vigour.

III

Within this firm context of principle and observation Dickens sought to encourage improvements in the provision of entertainment available to the people. He used his periodicals to suggest directions which progress should – and should not – take if the opportunity which pastimes provided to cultivate the tastes of all classes of society were to be developed. Once again 'The Amusements of the People' is a key document. In it he offered an explicit proposal of means by which the quality of theatrical entertainment could be raised. That means, he stated, was government surveillance. The office of the Lord Chamberlain, on the authority of the 1737 Licensing Act, strengthened in 1843 by the Theatre Regulations Bill, already had legal jurisdiction over all dramatic pieces intended for performance anywhere throughout Great Britain, but Dickens proposed to transform this power from a mere 'conventionality' to a 'real, responsible educational trust'. In fact, the Lord Chamberlain's Examiner of Plays exercised considerable control over the content of plays, and official censorship of the theatre did not cease until 1968. But the control was largely negative, guarding against political, moral and religious offence, rather than positive, intervening to infuse value into theatrical offerings, and the state of the drama in the first half of the nineteenth century was decidedly subliterary. Dickens did not impugn theatre managers who catered to the taste of the masses for the absence of improving content in the works they staged, because, he observed, 'Those who would live to please Mr Whelks, must please Mr Whelks to live'. Nor did he suggest more rigorous control over cheap theatres than over those which served more respectable clientele. But he did wish to 'interpose to turn to some wholesome account the means of instruction which it has at command'.[44]

Given the outspoken distrust expressed elsewhere by the creator of Lords Boodle and Coodle, and of the Circumlocution Office, it is surprising to find Dickens endorsing government intervention in the case of theatres. Certainly he was not always so confident about the advisability of legislative control of entertainment; indeed, he was sometimes as unequivocal in his objections to government interference as he was in its favour in 'The Amusements of the People'. No consistent policy is to be found in *Household Words* and *All the Year Round* as to the appropriate role for Parliament in dealing with the people's pleasures; some essays advocate the extension of government supervision, while others demand its withdrawal. Symptomatic of this inconsistency is Dickens's treatment of an article by J. A. Heraud, proposing legislation to establish a National Theatre. Dickens published the essay in *Household Words* in 1850, but appended to it an editorial note firmly rejecting Heraud's idea: 'This is the individual Play-goer's "Crotchet". We doubt its efficacy, and do not adopt it.'[45] On the specific matter of the Lord Chancellor's authority over the theatre, a similar divergence occurs: the series in *All the Year Round* reviving the character of Joe Whelks, sixteen years after Dickens first introduced him in *Household Words*, extends the proposal of the 1850 essay by suggesting that the Lord Chancellor should, 'in the interests of public decency and public morality', examine not only the texts of the plays for the theatre, but also the content of songs performed in music-halls; whereas, in between the two appearances of Whelks, Dickens published other essays on the subject, deriding the office of the Examiner of Plays as 'one of the most feeble, the most ineffectual, the most unnecessary, and the most ridiculous of all the many absurd offices that custom and an indolent country have placed at the disposal of a British minister', and demanding that the department be closed: 'music and drama should not be regarded as prey, to be hunted and driven about as something unworthy'.[46] One of the later Whelks essays, too, follows in this vein, comparing minor pieces of amusement in the East End with those 'under the shadow of the august towers of Parliament' in the New Cut, and concluding that proximity to the seat of government is a dubious blessing: 'The nearer to the Queen, Lords, and Commons, the Archbishop of Canterbury, and the Dean and Chapter – the further from all that is elevated, refined, well-ordered, and Christian-like'.[47] Citing evidence from abroad, one piece in *Household Words* reported on the tyranny of state censorship in Naples, while another described the benefits to be gained from licensing street entertainers in Paris. Sala contributed an article which noted the ease with which legal restrictions on drink could be evaded; while Hollingshead decried the absurdity of maintaining inequitable and unenforceable restrictions on street merchants.[48]

Each of these contributions to Dickens's journals addresses itself to the issue of government regulation of popular amusements, and, as can be seen from the sampling given, conclusions vary considerably. But the inconsistency is more apparent than real. Dickens sees a crucial distinction between the creative use of legislation by an enlightened government and the repressive control imposed by an unsympathetic one. A government with a record of mishandling an issue ought not, he argued, to be called upon to enact restrictive legislation, because it is more likely to produce a bludgeon of oppression than an avenue to development, and will thus reflect opprobrium back upon itself. Alternatively, a legislature which is well informed about the needs and wishes of the people it governs, and responsive to their legitimate higher aspirations, is capable of performing prodigies towards their advancement and contentment. Dickens is differentiating between the creative possibilities of an ideal government and the all-too-likely bungling of an actual one.

These matters are clarified in another essay which Dickens himself contributed to *Household Words*, entitled 'Betting Shops'. In this article he examines the temptations presented to young men by flagrantly dishonest touts, and he finds the situation in need of immediate remedy. But, despite the 'very serious social considerations' involved, government action is not, he decides, the answer to the problem, because

> . . . we do not think it wise to exhibit a legislature which has always cared so little for the amusements of the people, in repressive action only. If it had been an educational legislature, considerate of the popular enjoyments, and sincerely desirous to advance and extend them during as long a period as has been exactly the reverse, the question might assume a different shape; though, even then, we should greatly doubt whether the same notion were not a shifting of the real responsibility.[49]

Several points of importance emerge here. First, Dickens argues that the known lack of sympathy of the government of the day towards popular amusements disqualifies it from being called upon to deal wisely with the problem. For it to act upon the matter would serve to expose its incapacity and arouse deserved contempt, without effecting any benefit for the victims of the touts. Second, he contrasts the attitudes of the present government with those which it could espouse, for the betterment of all the people governed. The potential for promoting a more enriching environment, in which betting shops would hold less attraction for the unwary, is a real possibility, but one which requires a government of greater enlightenment and less self-interest than is evident in the one currently in office. Indeed, Dickens accuses the honourable Members of themselves playing the part of betting touts, cynically exploiting the fragile political coalitions of the day out of mere opportunism. Finally, Dickens argues that, even with the best of governments in office, to demand legislation would be to deflect responsibility away from its proper place: 'Parents and employers must do more for themselves.'

This last point is a key to his thought, here as elsewhere: the great Victorian virtue of doing one's duty. Leisure pursuits are but one area of concern: a major purpose in all his writing is to inform his middle-class readership of the urgent social matters requiring their attention. No contemporary reader of Dickens could plead ignorance of the problems he exposed, nor could any reader be in doubt but that it was his personal obligation to seek remedy, and to act. One of the most laudable characteristics of the Victorians – and of Dickens in particular – was that, in their general reluctance to call upon government to deal with domestic issues, they demanded of all citizens alertness to the needs of their society, and positive activity to improve the quality of life for the entire nation. At their best, the Victorians took very seriously the second Commandment, and espoused love of their neighbour as a personal commitment. Passing the buck did not amuse.

Whether or not legislation was the appropriate way forward, Dickens was clear that the issue of leisure for the people was a matter for the more privileged classes to recognize and act upon. In this he agreed with Carlyle that 'Surely, of all "rights of man", this right of the ignorant man to be guided by the wiser, to be, gently or forcibly, held in the true course by him, is the indisputablest'.[50] Dickens held this view with less condescension than Carlyle, and his model for social cohesion was not hero-worship but family love. His most frequently used image of the relations within the state was the family, with the loving guidance of the father held up as a paradigm of the proper exercise of authority. This image is most notably developed in *Bleak House*, in which the parlous state of society is mirrored by the almost total absence of normal family relationships. Early in the novel Esther says of the Lord High Chancellor that at his best he 'appeared so poor a substitute for the love and pride of parents' (*BH*, 3), and the plight of fatherless orphans is epitomized by the fate of poor Jo, the crossing-sweeper.

In his sympathy for the underprivileged, Dickens was acutely conscious that there was much they could not do for themselves to improve their condition. As we have seen, he had strong faith in their fundamental decency – their collective disposition to behave without resorting to excess or destructiveness – and he defended passionately their right to enjoy such harmless pleasures as they might choose. But he knew that many possibilities were closed to them, and could only be made available by the interposition of men and women better off than they. Museums and galleries, Dickens complained frequently, were shut on Sundays, regardless of the wishes of the public which would visit them; drink and music in places of public resort were subject to restrictions which required legal action to remove; plays, spectacles and shows depended for their quality not upon the audiences which frequented them but upon the managers who put them on. These were problems beyond the power of the lower classes to correct, Dickens believed; improvement depended on the vision and altruism of their betters.

And there was ample room for improvement. Instead of the mindless, demeaning amusements which he found at the Vic and the Britannia, Dickens envisaged a quality of entertainment which would be educative and morally uplifting. 'There are not many things of which the English as a people stand in greater need than sound rational amusement,'[51] he stated elsewhere, and in this view he was at one with his age; even some antagonists of popular culture endorsed the notion of 'rational' amusement. The temperance movement, as a notable example, was dedicated not simply to weaning the drunkard from his bad old ways, but to encouraging him to alternatives which would make him responsible and respectable; and that most Victorian of virtues, self-help, was intimately related to the concept of rational amusement: the pursuit, in leisure-time, of activities which would increase a man's intellectual and economic powers took him straight to working men's clubs, scientific exhibitions, galleries, museums – places which could indulge his curiosity even as they uplifted his character. As Peter Bailey has shown, middle-class interest in rational recreation derived from a combination of 'sympathy with the plight of the urban masses' and 'practical considerations of social stability'.[52] Faced with the problems of the Condition of England, men of humanitarian ideals promulgated the doctrine that the lot of the poor could be substantially ameliorated by assisting them to better recreational opportunities. Bulwer put the case succinctly when he declared: 'Whatever amuses men innocently is a great civiliser.'[53] Even more emphatically, the journalist William Cooke Taylor stated

'Dancing in a Public House' by Robert Cruikshank. Dickens took a broad view of 'rational' entertainment.

. . . the great but neglected truth, that moral education, in spite of all the labours of direct instructors, is really acquired in hours of recreation. Sports and amusements are, and must be, means by which the mind is insensibly trained; the lectures of the schoolroom will be utterly ineffective when they are counteracted by the practical lessons of the playground.[54]

For Dickens, theatre was just one of countless possibilities for rational recreation. He spoke frequently at societies and institutions, where he invariably had praise for the 'moral and social elevation' which he found combined there with 'harmless relaxation'.[55] He wrote one essay for *Household Words* in which he described the 'extraordinary traveller', Mr Booley, able to circumnavigate the world without ever leaving London; his secret was the gigantic moving panorama, a new and cheap means, Mr Booley explained, 'for conveying the results of experience, to those who are unable to obtain such experiences for themselves; and to bring them within the reach of the people'. Another essay in *Household Words* which Dickens particularly liked was 'The Hippopotamus', by R. H. Horne, which lamented the strange taste of the English in their preference for Tom Thumb, Jim Crow and the hippopotamus above poets and philosophers, but held out hope for 'more discrimination in the objects of our devotion'. A number of entries in the journal extolled the improving pleasures to be found in the Zoological Society's gardens, a 'favourite retreat . . . for relaxation and recreation'; a horticultural show, with a band of music in attendance, was a 'wholesome' rural event; even the window-boxes to be found in slum dwellings were evidence of 'higher faculties of enjoyment and of taste'. The founding of musical clubs cultivated the sensibilities of large numbers of people and fostered salutary habits; the invention of new children's toys gave unrestrained enjoyment by which 'a child's mind is most usefully developed'; and the development of adult minds was assisted by the popularization of science and industry at the Royal Polytechnic Institution, where knowledge was made 'beguiling' rather than boring.[56]

As this sampling indicates, Dickens took a broad view of the 'rational' component of entertainment: both in variety and in quality a great many amusements satisfied his generous criteria. For him, it was not necessary for a diversion to be narrowly educational in order to be morally improving; indeed, one of his major complaints about the activities which moral reformers proposed as alternatives to popular culture was that all the fun was drained away. In the hands of reformers short on fancy and unsympathetic to the natural inclinations of the people they sought to improve, entertainment became mere didacticism, and defeated its very purpose. In failing to entertain, such instruction bored and unsettled potentially receptive audiences, and drove them back upon their own inadequate resources. All of the Whelks essays, both those by Dickens and those by Halliday, make it a central point to protest against the content of the entertainment available to the man in search of rational amusement. In one essay in the series, Joe Whelks is described on his way to an evening at the Polytechnic Institution; even in anticipation, the combination of instruction with amusement appears unattractive:

> It did not appear to us that Mr Whelks was going joyfully or hopefully to his evening's amusement. He looked subdued and depressed, as if he were labouring under a saddening sense of the grave respect due to amusement when combined with instruction.

And in the event, the performance is 'as dull and depressing as possible . . . not quite worthy of a Royal Institution founded for the diffusion of useful knowledge with pleasant entertainment'.[57]

Dickens had a name for the purveyor of such a deadeningly utilitarian approach to moral and mental improvement: he called him 'Mr Barlow', after the tutor in Thomas Day's novel *Sandford and Merton* (*UT*, pp. 338–44). A man who never made or took a joke, who was 'adamantine' in his inadaptability to fancies and amusements, Mr Barlow was to be found not only in the classroom, but also in moving panoramas, in minstrel shows, in burlesque entertainment and in the theatre. Not only did Mr Barlow destroy the pleasure of diversions, Dickens complained, he made inquisitiveness after knowledge 'detestable' by showing its results in the priggish pupil Sandford. Rational entertainment with so palpable a design upon its victims is devoid of the spontaneity essential to true delight; it hacks away all the delicate implications which grace the inventions of fancy; and it substitutes bullying for gentle persuasion. This is the substance of Dickens's charge against George Cruikshank, for rewriting fairy-tales as temperance tracts, and against Miss Twinkleton, the schoolmistress in *Edwin Drood*, for turning high-flown romance into domestic platitudes. Exposing the bowdlerisms of the harmless Miss Twinkleton – 'She cut the love-scenes, interpolated passages in praise of female celibacy, and was guilty of other glaring pious frauds' – Dickens defuses any possible bitterness in the satire by indulging in a comic juxtaposition of delightful silliness (*MED*, 22). But in condemning the 'Whole Hog' intrusion of Cruikshank into a 'fairy flower garden' Dickens is stern:

In an utilitarian age, of all other times, it is a matter of grave importance that Fairy tales should be respected . . . To preserve them in their usefulness, they must be as much preserved in their simplicity, and purity, and innocent extravagance, as if they were actual fact. Whosoever alters them to suit his own opinions, whatever they are, is guilty, to our thinking, of an act of presumption, and appropriates to himself what does not belong to him.[58]

Dickens's conception of rational entertainment, it is clear, had no place for the merely utilitarian; he dismissed overtly didactic forms of amusement as boring and therefore unlikely to attract the people most in need of diversion as well as of instruction. The imperative component of rational entertainment, he knew, was its capacity to amuse. As we have just seen, he approved of the aims of the Polytechnic Institution but doubted that its entertainment value was wholly satisfactory; he had similar misgivings about the Great Exhibition. During the summer of the Exhibition and again when the Crystal Palace was moved to Sydenham, Dickens published a number of essays praising its attractions: in *Household Words* Knight called Paxton's edifice a palace more wonderful than Aladdin's; Wills and Sala celebrated it as 'a grand spectacle of artistic contrivance, which has left the mark of the modern magician's wand'. Publicly Dickens endorsed this view, describing the Crystal Palace as that 'wonderful building' in a speech to the Gardeners' Benevolent Institution; but privately he was more sceptical, and expressed misgivings in letters which he wrote at the time. The sheer size of the Exhibition, it seems, offended him, and his ambivalence about what he allowed his writers to call a 'magical' mixture of the familiar and the sublime helps to clarify his position on rational entertainment.[59] For all his conviction about the educational potential of entertainment, he was less than wholehearted about directly instructional amusements, and his personal preference was decidedly for activities such as the circus and the theatre, in which didacticism was conspicuously absent.

His relish for the *lack* of edifying content in these entertainments can be demonstrated by applying that litmus test of his seriousness about any subject, his readiness to laugh about it. One of his most frequently repeated jokes about theatrical productions was the pretence that costume or gesture accorded with reality. In *Nicholas Nickleby*, for example, the balletic duet of 'The Indian Savage and the Maiden' performed by the Infant Phenomenon and Mr Folair is described by Dickens as a psychologically accurate rendition of the customary mating rituals of American Indians (*NN*, 23); in *The*

Uncommercial Traveller he describes at length the attire of a blackface troupe, dressed in black coats, with white waistcoats, ties and wristbands, 'which constitute', he remarks, 'the dress of the mass of the African race, and which has been observed by travellers to prevail over a vast number of degrees of latitude' (*UT*, p. 341). The performance of *Hamlet* in *Great Expectations* commences with Dickens's observation that

> The whole of the Danish nobility were in attendance; consisting of a noble boy in the wash-leather boots of a gigantic ancestor, a venerable Peer with a dirty face who seemed to have risen from the people late in life, and the Danish chivalry with a comb in its hair and a pair of white silk legs, and presenting on the whole a feminine appearance.
>
> (*GE*, 31)

In each case the comicality of Dickens's presentation depends on his affectation that the spectator should expect to learn authentic information about foreign customs and dress by observing their representation on the English stage. The very absence of educational content provides much of the pleasure, and the credulity of anyone who thinks he is discovering useful knowledge in these displays is an object of uproarious mirth. Dickens described one such character in his *Household Words* account of Mr Booley's visit to Astley's Circus.

> Mr Booley said, he had acquired a knowledge of Tartar Tribes, and also of Wild Indians, and Chinese, which had greatly enlightened him as to the habits of those singular races of men, in whom he observed, as peculiarities common to the whole, that they were always hoarse; that they took equestrian exercise in a most irrational manner, riding up staircases and precipices without the least necessity; that it was impossible for them to dance, on any joyful occasion, without keeping time with their forefingers, erect in the neighbourhood of their ears; and that whenever their castles were on fire (a calamity to which they were particularly subject) numbers of them immediately tumbled down dead, without receiving any wound or blow, while others, previously distinguished in war, fell an easy prey to the comic coward of the opposite faction, who was usually armed with a strange instrument resembling an enormous, supple cigar.[60]

Dickens's enjoyment of entertainment without any immediately obvious educational value did not conflict with his endorsement of rational amusement; rather, it was a matter of identifying in what the

217

rationality consisted. A late essay in *All the Year Round* invoked
Scott's warning not to dismiss frivolous fun too lightly:

> Who recollects not Sir Walter Scott's admonition to his
> daughter, not to despise vulgar things merely on that account,
> for probably they had become such because they had been
> proved to be good?[61]

Dickens was far from uncritical about the inheritance from the past,
but he was alert to the benefits to be derived from the traditions of
lowly entertainment. 'There are many things from which I might
have derived good, by which I have not profited, I dare say',
declared Scrooge's nephew, with Dickens in full accord (*CC*,
stave 1). He could not, in all honesty, accord unqualified praise to
amusements in which utilitarian function loomed large, but he happily approved the unalloyed delights of purely escapist entertainment. Analysing the pleasure of pantomime, he singled out its
creation of a 'jocund world' as its principal source of appeal. By
creating a magical place full of disasters but devoid of pain, pantomime offered joyful consolation to people for whom affliction was
all too real. It was a world

> . . . where there is no affliction or calamity that leaves the least
> impression; where a man may tumble into the broken ice, or
> dive into the kitchen fire, and only be the droller for the acci-
> dent; where babies may be knocked about and sat upon, or
> choked with gravy spoons, in the process of feeding, and yet no
> Coroner be wanted, nor anybody made uncomfortable; where
> workmen may fall from the top of a house to the bottom, or
> even from the bottom of a house to the top, and sustain no
> injury to the brain, need no hospital, leave no young children;
> where every one, in short, is so superior to all the accidents of
> life, though encountering them at every turn, that I suspect this
> to be the secret (though many persons may not present it to
> themselves) of the general enjoyment which an audience of
> vulnerable spectators, liable to pain and sorrow, find in this
> class of entertainment.[62]

Such entertainment was patently without didacticism, or any
specifically useful application; rather, pantomime was the kind of
amusement which nurtured the 'sympathies and graces' Dickens
espoused in 'A Preliminary Word'. The 'rational' element consisted
not of bald instruction but of the undefinable feelings of affection
and contentment which such entertainment could engender. As Sala

put it in another essay published in *Household Words* around the same time, the attractiveness of pantomime derived from the festive season, from the associations of childhood, and from the kindly memories it evoked; 'There can't be anything aesthetic in a pantomime,' he declared.[63]

Rational amusement, then, was not for Dickens the 'relentlessly didactic' provision favoured by campaigners for moral reform.[64] Instead, it was entertainment which would lift a man temporarily out of his cares and duties into a state of untroubled delight; which would soften his sensibility through the beneficent agency of his fancy; which would nurture fellow-feeling through the sharing of enjoyments and the awakening of childhood recollections. Its rationality consisted in the contentment which it fostered, the curiosity it indulged, the expansiveness it promoted. Clearly, this is an inclusive definition, which ranges well beyond mere training of intellect. But Dickens was far from undiscriminating in his judgement of entertainment. He was quick to sniff out the least absurdity, and disposed to pounce when a pastime was offensive. Often there is a positive pleasure to be had from the ridiculousness he identifies – for us as readers, if not always for the participants described – but this pleasure is inevitably tempered by a sense, often explicit, that a better quality of entertainment would be preferable. The extravagance of his response to absurdity often lifts his condemnation into sheer enjoyment, as on the occasion described by Forster, when they attended a dramatization of *Oliver Twist*: '. . . in the middle of the first scene he laid himself down upon the floor in a corner of the box and never rose from it until the drop-scene fell'.[65] In describing ludicrous entertainments Dickens would sometimes express mock horror, as when he wrote of the 'slow torture' of an Orrery; at other times he would respond with humorously solemn understatement, as when he declared, 'I cannot rate high' the thespian talents of an ineptly trained stage dog.[66]

'We are certainly strange people, we English,' remarked the author of one *Household Words* essay, shaking his head at the credulity of spectators who would patronize such attractions, and Dickens dismissed the notion that lack of discrimination was a fault only of the uneducated. Playing the ventriloquist to a raven contemptuous of humanity, he declared:

Don't flatter yourselves that I am referring to the 'vulgar curiosity' as you choose to call it, when you mean some curiosity in which you don't participate yourselves. The polite curiosity in this country, is as vulgar as any curiosity in the world.

219

As these pages abundantly testify, Dickens was more than tolerant in his fascination with sources of amusement, and unashamedly willing to enjoy the least sophisticated of entertainments. But he did urge his readers not to leave their judgement at the door, along with their umbrella, when they entered a place of diversion; rather, they should exercise their own wits, and be prepared to recognize the absurdity of much of the entertainment available to them.[67]

His novels, letters and journals are full of comical reportage of preposterous attractions, and his satire is directed at the entertainments, the entertainers and the audiences. *Sketches by Boz* alone is full of tales of misadventure befalling seekers after pleasure, through their snobbery, lack of skill, or simply bad luck: the mistaken milliner's abortive attempt at public singing, the calamitous private theatricals of Mrs Joseph Porter, the unfortunate steam excursion of Mr Percy Noakes, the trouble-ridden holiday of the Tuggses at Ramsgate. Each of these characters makes a misguided attempt to use amusements as a means of appearing more important than he really is, but since they harm no one but themselves Dickens's satire is affectionate. He gently pokes fun at their social pretensions and circumstantially exposes the lugubrious fate of their ventures at amusement. Such absurd people are laughable, not culpable.

Similarly cheerful satire occurs frequently in *Household Words*, directed at such silliness as the exhibition of freaks, the balloon ascent of a horse, fish swimming in wine, the gilding of rats' tails to construct a halo for a museum Madonna; or facetiously lamenting the nuisance occasioned to lovers of peace and quiet by the cacophony of street entertainers.[68] Rather sharper ridicule is reserved for pompous display, which for Dickens was a sure sign of hypocrisy. 'The Mudfog Papers', contemporaneous with *Oliver Twist*, contains a laboured exposure of the empty self-importance of Mr Tulrumble, as evidenced in his mayorality show; later, Chops the Dwarf finds, on 'Going into Society', that society is disappointingly like a sideshow, complete with fat ladies and make-believe. A visit from the queen to English towns, Dickens objects, occasions 'unpardonable' municipal displays, in which each town tries clumsily 'at considerable expense, to make itself look as like a bad travelling circus as possible'; and meditating on possible sources of amusement for Posterity he concludes bitterly that public honours and hereditary titles will provide the best of entertainment.[69]

But the form of empty ceremony which most exasperated Dickens was the 'hideous, elaborate, and splendid' pomp of Victorian funerals. Solemn expression of sincere grief over the death of loved ones was replaced, he felt, by mere public performance, and generally second-rate entertainment, at that. The chief mourner at

Anthony Chuzzlewit's funeral is an obese professional, 'who from his great experience in the performance of funerals, would have made an excellent pantomime actor' (*MC*, 19); the hired attendants at the funeral of Mrs Gargery are 'dismally absurd persons, ostentatiously exhibiting' their ludicrous symbols of mourning (*GE*, 35). And fiction was imitation of reality: at the funeral of the publisher William Hone, the clergyman appeared to Dickens more concerned with the figure he cut than with any consolation he might offer to the bereaved family; above all, at the state funeral for the Duke of Wellington, Dickens was appalled by the 'gigantic mockery' of the 'Public Fair and Great Undertakers' Jubilee', which he saw as a 'palpably got up theatrical trick'. In these ceremonies he was offended by the replacement of 'respect and affection' by 'expense and show': 'As if', he protested, 'any two-and-sixpenny masquerade, tumbled into a vat of blacking, wouldn't be quite as solemn, and immeasurably cheaper!' He was outraged by the grotesque extravagance of such display, and explicit that the pomp was a travesty of real grief; at Anthony Chuzzlewit's funeral the undertaker, Mr Mould, is 'greatly scandalised' at the real tears of Anthony's old servant, Chuffey; and in *Great Expectations* it is only when the funeral party has disbanded that Joe, having removed his mourning costume, 'looked natural, and like the Man he was'.[70]

The pretentiousness of funerals was an instance of public display in which absurdity went beyond the merely ridiculous and became matter for objection. When entertainment involved danger, deceit or depravity, it met with emphatic disapproval from Dickens. He recognized the appeal of death-defying stunts: it was not ghoulish delight in calamity that attracted an audience; rather,

> Their pleasure is in the difficulty overcome. They are a public of great faith, and are quite confident that the gentleman will not fall off the horse, or the lady off the bull or out of the parachute, and that the tumbler has a firm hold with his toes. They do not go to see the adventurer vanquished, but triumphant.

In identifying the surmounting of peril as the source of delight, he saw a parallel with the fun of pantomime which we noted above:

> It always appears to me that the secret of this enjoyment lies in the temporary superiority to the common hazards and mischances of life; in seeing casualties, attended when they really occur with bodily and mental suffering, tears, and poverty, happen through a very rough sort of poetry without the least harm being done to any one – the pretence of distress in a

pantomime being so broadly humorous as to be no pretence at all. Much as in the comic fiction I can understand the mother with a very vulnerable baby at home, greatly relishing the invulnerable baby on the stage, so in the Cremorne reality I can understand the mason who is always liable to fall off a scaffold in his working jacket and to be carried to the hospital, having an infinite admiration of the radiant personage in spangles who goes into the clouds upon a bull, or upside down, and who, he takes it for granted – not reflecting upon the thing – has, by uncommon skill and dexterity, conquered such mischances as those to which he and his acquaintance are continually exposed.

At the same time, because stunts from balloons, the flying trapeze and the high wire all involve serious risk of life to the performers, such exhibitions were 'very wrong indeed, and decidedly to be stopped'.[71]

He was equally firm in his stand against amusements which involved dishonesty. Of the many low people Nell meets on her travels in *The Old Curiosity Shop*, none is more wicked than the three gamblers who incite her grandfather to turn against her and to steal the last of her money (*OCS*, 30); the blackmail practised in *Our Mutual Friend* by that craven rascal Wegg, hired by the genial Mr Boffin in his good fortune, to provide him with amusement and instruction, ends in the deserved ignominy of the ballad-seller being tossed into a passing scavenger's cart (*OMF*, IV, 14). The insidiousness of deceitful entertainers is, as Sala put it in one *Household Words* essay, that they give all amusements a bad name: 'The worst of it is that, knowing how many of the curiosities and rarities in these seeming shops are cunning deceits, a man is apt to get sceptical as regards them all.' The result, Dickens knew, was ammunition for the enemies of popular entertainment, who sought to suppress all amusements according to the principle that because Sloggins abuses, none shall use.[72]

Of all bad entertainments, the worst were those which were actively depraving in tendency. Dickens published attacks on brutal sport, vile exhibitions, and debauchery, and in 1849 attracted 'a roaring sea of correspondence' in response to two letters he wrote to *The Times*, protesting the 'inconceivably awful' scene at the execution of the murderers Frederick and Maria Manning. He was appalled that a solemn act of state justice was turned into an obscene festival by the tens of thousands of spectators who gathered to witness the excitement of the show.

As the night went on, screeching, and laughing, and yelling in

strong chorus of parodies on Negro melodies, with substi-
tutions of 'Mrs Manning' for 'Susannah', and the like, were
added to [the cries and howls]. When the day dawned, thieves,
low prostitutes, ruffians and vagabonds of every kind, flocked
on to the ground, with every variety of offensive and foul
behaviour. Fightings, faintings, whistlings, imitations of
Punch, brutal jokes, tumultuous demonstrations of indecent
delight when swooning women were dragged out of the crowd
by the police with their dresses disordered, gave a new zest to
the general entertainment.[73]

His complaint was twofold: that public executions 'chiefly attract the
lowest, the most depraved, the most abandoned of mankind'; and
that 'the public infliction of a violent death is not a salutary spectacle
for any class of people'. He was clear, in short, that the public
infliction of capital punishment, far from being a sober warning to all
of the wages of crime, was in fact the most degrading of entertainments, occasioning 'brutal mirth' instead of awe. The audience,
Dickens observed, consisted not of the 'respectable poor' – that is, of
men and women eager to improve their condition in life by
employing their leisure-time to cultivate their moral and intellectual
abilities, but rather of people so benighted that no stimulus, however
worthy, possibly could enlighten them. This distinction is an indication of the limits of Dickens's conception of the 'popular' element
in popular entertainment; not merely utterly depraved villains, such
as Sikes and Blandois, but the brutalized humanity at the very
bottom of society, such as the brickmakers in *Bleak House*, fell
outside his fondest hopes for the beneficent influence of rational
amusements. For all his impassioned idealism, and his practical
efforts on behalf of the less fortunate members of society, Dickens
was no Utopian; he envisaged no realistic likelihood that any kind of
leisure opportunity would benefit some classes of people. An attraction which catered to their depraved taste could only be harmful, and
not only to them; even for the sensitive and susceptible there were
kinds of spectacle which in their very nature were degrading. Dickens deplored the 'ruffian blackguardism' which blighted the 'man-
liness' of English sport; the 'fighting, screeching, yelling,
blaspheming' at a 'mangy' fairground; the 'truly diabolical clamour'
of a low theatre, 'resounding with foul language, oaths, catcalls,
shrieks, yells, blasphemy, obscenity'.[74] Like the 'inexpressibly
odious' behaviour he witnessed at the execution of the Mannings,
these were scenes of iniquity, the very reverse of 'innocent'
amusement.

In his defence of the right of common people to leisure pursuits,

THE TRIAL-FOR-MURDER MANIA.

Dickens deplored public executions and funerals as degrading forms of popular entertainment.

Dickens was concerned not only to provide them with entertainment where there was none, but also to replace bad sorts of
entertainment which were available to them. Not to do so was an
indictment of government and of all right-thinking citizens. As he
put it in 'The Amusements of the People':

> If, on looking round us, we find that the only things plainly and
> personally addressed to them, from quack medicines upwards,
> be bad or very defective things, – so much the worse for them
> and for all of us, and so much the more unjust and absurd the
> system which has haughtily abandoned a strong ground to such
> occupation.[75]

It was the moral duty of the privileged classes to ensure the improvement of popular entertainment, for the sake of the poor, and of
society as a whole.

In the event, things did not work out quite this way. It is an irony
of social history that the idealism of concerned Victorians, earnestly
seeking ways to uplift the 'rational' component of the entertainment
of the people, had far less effect, in the long run, than simple
commercial pressure: managers interested in making money grew
increasingly sophisticated in responding to the interests of their
clientele, and the nature of entertainment developed not because of
enlightened attitudes imposed from above, but because of the willingness and increasing ability of those from below to pay money for
amusements they liked. By the time of Dickens's death, the uneasy
relationship which so exercised early Victorians, between entertainment and education, diverged as never before, and managers of
that most popular of all Victorian forms of entertainment, the
music-hall, found that it paid to upgrade the respectability of their
premises and their shows, while more purely instructional forms of
culture devolved upon government.[76] The progress of popular
entertainment, as we have already seen in Chapter 1, owed more to
commercial interests than to idealism. It is uncharitable, however, to
chide Dickens for incomplete power of prophecy; what was of
incomparable value in his journalism was the acute observation
presented in a spirit of high moral principle.

CHAPTER 7

Dickens's Public Readings
The Abiding Commitment

[Public reading] necessitates no departure whatever from the
chosen pursuits of my life . . . I proceed to read this little book,
quite as composedly as I might proceed to write it, or to publish
it in any other way.

> Charles Dickens, speech at the first
> reading for his own profit, 29 April
> 1858 (*Speeches*, p. 264)

I

Dickens took the most significant step in his career as a popular
entertainer in December 1853 when, at the Birmingham Town Hall,
he performed the first of his public readings from his works. On
behalf of the Birmingham and Midland Institute he read *A Christmas
Carol* on 27 December aloud to 1,700 persons; this was followed on
the 29th by a reading of *The Cricket on the Hearth*, and on the 30th he
read the *Carol* again, this time, in accordance with his express wish,
to a predominantly working-class audience of 2,000. He prefaced the
last of these three readings with a brief statement in support of the
Institute and with an even briefer declaration of his motive in
offering the reading. He was animated, he said, 'by the wish to have
the great pleasure of meeting you face to face at this Christmas time
and accompany you myself through one of my little Christmas
books' (*Speeches*, p. 166). This was a sentiment which he became
accustomed to repeat in slightly expanded form whenever subsequently he gave readings for charity. As recorded at a reading in
Bristol on 19 January 1858, what he said to audiences before he
commenced with his performance was that

> . . . if, as they proceeded, any of his audience should feel
> disposed to give vent to any feeling of emotion, he would

226

request them to do so in the most natural manner, without the slightest apprehension of disturbing him. Nothing could be more agreeable to him than the assurance of their being interested, and nothing would be more in accordance with his wishes than that they should all, for the next two hours, make themselves as much as possible like a group of friends, listening to a tale told by a winter fire, and forget all ceremony in the manner of their coming together.

> (*Speeches*, p. 246; see also pp. 169 and 259)

He 'always' prefaced his charity readings with these remarks, and although he normally dispensed with introductions once he began his paid readings – for them merely walking on to the stage, pausing briefly, and commencing the performance – by then the rapport between himself and his audiences had become so much the spirit of the readings that direct statement was superfluous.[1]

What this address indicates is that Dickens's readings were self-professedly intended to fill his highest aspirations for popular entertainment. They offered to his audience a release from the conventional constraints of everyday life. They invited active imaginative participation in a free expression of emotional sympathy. The direct appeal to 'natural' response suggested that his readings were to be 'rational' entertainment, in the sense of being morally beneficial in ways which we considered in Chapter 6; as he said twelve years later in his farewell address, he used his readings to present his 'most cherished ideas' to his audiences (*Speeches*, p. 413). Above all, a reading by Dickens was to be an occasion of human fellowship, in which feelings of friendship, shared emotion and unaffected behaviour would draw the members of the audience together with him in a common bond of cheerful concord.

Dickens's public readings were the culmination of his lifetime's dedication to the cause of popular entertainment. Faced with a declining tradition of the age-old participatory amusements and with unceasingly clamorous opposition to all forms of leisure enjoyments for the poor, Dickens heroically threw himself into the breach. This momentous decision consumed the greater portion of his energy in the later years of his life; indeed, the readings so drained his strength and affected his health that he can quite literally be said to have killed himself in the effort. They brought fame (Forster judged that it was the readings 'by which, as much as by his books, the world knew him in his later life'), wealth (his manager George Dolby estimated that altogether he earned about £45,000 from the readings) and intense personal gratification to him, and joy to legions of listeners.[2] The public readings mark the apogee of

Dickens's career as a public entertainer, and they constitute his most direct response to the complex state of popular entertainment which it has been one purpose of this book to explore. Dominating his later career and representing the most thorough synthesis of his ideas on entertainment, they provide the most appropriate note on which to conclude a study of Dickens and popular entertainment.

In the remaining pages we shall examine Dickens's public readings to consider how they represent an extension of his commitment to popular entertainment, in a highly personal accommodation of the old traditions with the new. The readings raise two issues of major importance to the themes of the present book. First, there is the question of how he reconciled his engagement in this commercially lucrative and highly professional enterprise with his predisposition towards the more informal and convivial pleasures of family and friends. We must ask, that is, how Dickens's type of performance accorded with the favoured entertainments of his childhood. To answer this question reveals more clearly than anything else can do how Dickens ultimately responded to the changing patterns of entertainment with which the present study began. That he was able to forge an activity which satisfied his own deepest instincts even as it succeeded triumphantly in an age which he considered in many ways uncongenial to public entertainment is token of Dickens's integrity, as well as of his achievement, as a popular artist. Second, we must ask whether he compromised his genius by devoting so much of his energy, at the height of his powers, to the public readings. He himself thought not, but his closest adviser, John Forster, never approved, and recent commentators have agreed with Forster that the readings involved the sacrifice of his incomparable gifts as a novelist to the transitory thrill of a circle of stage fire. Since Dickens considered the readings wholly consonant with his responsibilities as an artist – in his words which I have quoted as epigraph to this chapter, public readings represented 'no departure whatever' from his other artistic purposes – to judge them adversely is to raise the most fundamental of issues: it is to ask whether Dickens would have been a greater artist had he been less determined to be a popular one.

II

In his fiction and his journalism Dickens never abandoned his intention of providing entertainment. However sophisticated the achievement of his artistry was to become, and however polemical the purpose of his journalism, he always considered both activities to be suitable outlets for his profession as an entertainer. On the other hand, particularly in the latter half of his career, he used his novels and essays to serve too many other purposes for their value as entertainment to be exclusive. We have seen in the previous chapter that the presentation of popular entertainment in his periodicals routinely included large components of social comment; even at their most light-hearted, individual pieces of amusement appeared in conjunction with insistent expression of concern that the state of popular leisure was not all that it should or could be. In his fiction as well Dickens gave repeated warning that there were forces at large in society bent on infringing the pleasures of the people, and as his career progressed the novels evinced a sense of diminishing opportunity for the enjoyment of innocent entertainment. Dickens was passionate in defending the cause of popular amusements, but the very intensity of his concern made its expression less than carefree, and contemporary readers of his later works longed for the exuberant delights they had savoured in *Pickwick*.

This was precisely what he gave them in his public readings. In selecting materials for performance he turned initially to his Christmas books, especially the *Carol*, the most obviously festive of all his works. When he later extracted passages from his longer fiction for reading-texts, his choices were made exclusively from novels written no later than *David Copperfield*; again the subjects predominantly emphasized the ebullience of his early work. He prepared readings from two later novels, *A Tale of Two Cities* and *Great Expectations*, but neither was ever performed publicly, and the shorter works selected which he had written at later dates – *Boots at the Holly-Tree Inn* (1855), *Doctor Marigold* (1865) – were emphatically in the vein of his earlier fiction. He excised passages of social criticism, highlighted old jokes, interpolated new passages of drollery as he went along, and developed otherwise insignificant minor characters such as Mrs Raddle's housemaid (in *Mr Bob Sawyer's Party*) into memorably comic figures. By far the most frequently given of his readings was the enormously popular trial scene from *Pickwick*, and among his more extended readings the *Carol* was performed half as many times again as any other. Philip Collins assesses this repertoire as 'the essential "popular" Dickens', and it is hard to disagree.[3]

Comedy and sentiment were the keys which Dickens most frequently struck, and when he evoked the pathetic in *Little Dombey* or the horrific in *Sikes and Nancy* these, too, were readings taken from the works of tested popularity. As death scenes the latter were among Dickens's closest approximations to tragedy, but they constituted no real change of purpose from the other readings. They were designed to impress rather than to challenge his auditors; they were entertainment in another register, not art as exploration. In them Dickens exhibited heightened emotional states in highly theatrical ways, with the emphasis on intensity of expression rather than on complexity of pyschology. In common with the other readings, that is, these were the virtuoso performances of an entertainer, and lest they leave audiences in too sombre or terrified a condition Dickens never ended a programme with either of these items, but always chose a comic piece with which to conclude an evening's performance.[4]

To be attractive and beneficial, Dickens considered it imperative for entertainment to appeal directly to its audience. Effective address meant avoidance of falsity and confusion; it depended, he believed, not upon narrow realism, but upon the clear presentation of recognizable characters and situations, of truthfulness to life as the audience knew it, of moral content which met the needs, fears and aspirations of the audience.[5] These were qualities which he sought to achieve in all his art, but nowhere more prominently than in his readings. Both in his choice of texts for performance and in his focus within those texts we can see him striving for clarity of emotional content and vividness of character and incident. Thus he chose to feature several of the most memorable characters from his fiction, including Sam Weller, Mr Micawber and Sairey Gamp. To heighten the effectiveness of these characters for the readings, he ranged throughout the novels for characteristic sayings of theirs to interpolate, even as he restricted their appearances to single scenes. Similarly he brought some readings to a climax with particularly striking incidents, such as the hanging of Sikes and the thrashing of Squeers; in others he concentrated on poignant emotion – the sentiment surrounding the child lovers in *Boots at the Holly-Tree Inn*, the hilarity of the courtroom scene in *Bardell vs. Pickwick*, the festive happiness of the Cratchits' Christmas fireside (this last scene, significantly, the only portion of the *Carol* left largely unrevised for performance). His most successful readings developed several characters in a single incident or in a single narrative thread; variety and much of the comedy arose from sharp juxtaposition of contrasting characters, and climactic moments such as the much-praised storm scene in the *Copperfield* reading achieved intensity by means of carefully modulated crescendo. Commentators familiar with the works from which the readings were taken complained sometimes about the omission of favourite passages, but Dickens's cuts shortened his original texts for more immediately coherent impact, even at the expense of felicities in the episodes as written. Direct appeal was of the essence in his public readings.

This directness was achieved not only through the shaping of the

content of the readings, but much more through the personal media-
tion of Dickens the performer. The dynamism of the man is legend –
what Forster described as Dickens's 'restless and resistless energy'
and Sala as his 'almost aggressive' confidence was manifest in the
vibrancy of his presence, the expressiveness of his countenance, the
penetrating keenness of his eyes. Kate Field said that no photograph
revealed the real Dickens because none could capture his electric
vitality; of all visual records left to us after his lifetime, perhaps only
the Maclise portrait of 1839 comes close to conveying the warmth,
humour, sensitivity and ardent intensity universally acknowledged
by his contemporaries.[6] On the stage these characteristics were
concentrated into a commanding presence. Dickens himself was
confident from an early age of his abilities as an actor; applying for an
audition at Covent Garden in 1832, he wrote that 'I believed I had a
strong perception of character and oddity, and a natural power of
reproducing in my own person what I observed in others'. Those
who saw him act corroborated his self-estimate. Macready confided
to his diary that he considered Dickens the only amateur actor 'with
any pretensions to theatrical talent'; the *Morning Post*, reviewing his
performance as Bobadil in an amateur production of Jonson's *Every
Man in His Humour* in 1845, declared Dickens had the ability to be
'not less successful' as an actor than as a writer; Leigh Hunt, the
foremost dramatic critic of the age, found Dickens's acting 'beyond
anything the existing stage has shown'.[7] Translating these skills as an
actor into his readings, Dickens was able to increase the immediacy
of his presence even further. He practised diligently; in preparation
for a private trial reading of *Doctor Marigold*, he confided to Charles
Kent, he went through the piece two hundred times. Facing his
public, he stood on the stage with a plain dark curtain behind him
and with only an open desk and a book as props, thus creating a
setting which allowed nothing to distract the attention of his audience from the delivery of his spoken words.[8]

With a format and content conducive to that clarity of purpose
which he considered essential for good entertainment, and with his
own unaided delivery shaping each nuance of his performance to
produce the effects he desired, the readings were the most
immediately entertaining of Dickens's various modes of contact
with his public. They were also conscientiously popular in intention.
He used the readings specifically as an opportunity to establish a
closer relationship between himself and those who knew him only
through his writings and his reputation. There were of course other
factors behind his decision to read; he was candid with Forster that he
was attracted by the chance of quickly earning enough money to pay
for Gad's Hill Place, and that he was desperate for an all-consuming

activity to distract him from his domestic discontents (his marriage broke up within days after his first paid reading series began in April of 1858).[9] But he was outspoken that a primary motive for giving the readings was a wish to bring himself into contact with the people who admired his work. On the occasion of his first paid reading he declared:

> I have long held the opinion, and have long acted on the opinion, that in these times whatever brings a public man and his public face to face, on terms of mutual confidence and respect, is a good thing.   (*Speeches*, p. 264)

There was nothing disingenuous in this; Dickens thrived on his popularity as a public figure and, as John Butt and Kathleen Tillotson have said, Dickens's 'lifelong love-affair' with his public is 'by far the most interesting love-affair of his life'. His letters are full of expressions of pleasure at the 'overwhelming' personal affection shown him on the reading tours, not only in the rapturous enthusiasm of his audiences, but also in the chance encounters with people who stopped him in the street, like the man in Dublin who came up to him and asked:

> Do me the honour to shake hands Misther Dickens and God bless you sir; not only for the light you've been to me this night, but for the light you've been in mee house sir (and God love your face!) this many a year!

Dickens was not imagining the extent of his popularity; the long queues of people waiting to buy tickets to hear him read and the crowds following him about in the streets testify to a degree of adulation comparable to that given to pop stars in our own day.[10]

His readings were popular not only in the sense that they attracted clamorous applause, but also in that the audiences for them were not exclusive. We noted at the outset of the present chapter that Dickens requested as his 'particular wish' that ticket prices for one of his initial readings should be low enough for ordinary working men and their families to be able to afford to come and hear him (*Speeches*, p. 166). On that night and for subsequent readings over the next four years, proceeds went to charity; specifically, he read often on behalf of Mechanics' and Literary Institutes, which were a cause close to his heart. Conceived as self-help organizations to assist working-class individuals to better themselves, the Mechanics' Institutes were a burgeoning movement in the 1840s, but already by the 1850s the patronizing tone of middle-class promoters of the scheme and their leaden insistence on restricting activities for the provision of useful knowledge (which, as we saw in Chapter 2, Dickens parodied in 'Dullborough Town') impaired the attractiveness of the Institutes to the men they were designed to assist, and Dickens was in the vanguard of interested parties who sought to make them more appealing. His readings were witness to his belief that the first priority of Mechanics' Institutes was to win audiences, not only on the grounds that the common people had want and need of entertainment, but also because he thought practical instruction useless if the people who could benefit stayed away.[11] His commitment to attracting a working-class element in his audiences continued after he began reading for his own profit. Despite the financial incentive to increase the price of admission when potential customers were being turned away from full houses, Dickens remained determined not to restrict his clientele, even though this involved personal financial sacrifice to himself and even though, particularly in America, it left ticket sales prey to speculators, who made fortunes by scalping tickets at prices far above what Dickens charged. Although fêted by civic and national leaders, including Queen Victoria and President Andrew Johnson, Dickens insisted on keeping a portion of seats at modest prices, to enable working men and their families to enjoy entertainment within their means.[12] It was a matter of firm principle with him to make available to the common people the best entertainment of which he, the greatest entertainer of the century, was capable.

III

Dickens's career as a public reader was of long gestation. When in the spring of 1858 at the age of 46 he turned professional and embarked for the first time on an extended series of readings, it was more than four years after his initial public performance of the *Carol* in Birmingham and nearly twelve years after he had first mentioned to Forster that he was considering the attractions of reading in public. He read on many occasions in private, to gatherings of family and friends, most notably in December 1844, when he travelled to London from Genoa for the express purpose of reading *The Chimes*, which he had then just written, to select audiences in Forster's chambers in Lincoln's Inn Fields.[13] And his interest in the stage predated the public readings by much longer time. His sketches of his childhood, particularly 'Dullborough Town' and 'Our School', reveal a fascination with all things theatrical from an early age; at the outset of his writing career he composed several plays; and at various times he produced, directed, stage-managed and acted in ambitious amateur theatricals.

He very nearly became an actor. In 1832, barely 20 years old, he applied to Covent Garden for an audition and was given an appointment, but being ill on the day was unable to present himself and, making a success of his newspaper reporting soon afterwards, he did not renew the application. The hope of making a career of acting went for nought, but the audition piece which he prepared for the occasion was of the utmost significance for things to come. He had proposed to perform one of Charles Mathews's entertainments, which he knew intimately from having gone to the theatre nearly every night for three years and 'always to see Mathews whenever he played'.[14] Charles Mathews (1776–1835) was the most famous comedian of his day, whose reputation was based principally on solo performances known as 'At Homes', consisting of a mixture of narrative, impersonation and song. Mathews's influence on Dickens's stylistic methods of comic characterization has long been recognized, and Philip Collins described Dickens's predilection for Mathews as 'a bridge' between his 'early ambition to become a professional actor and his eventually becoming a great soloist'.[15] A bridge it certainly was, and much more. Dickens's admiration for Mathews provides the single most important influence on Dickens's career as a public reader. Although differing formally, in their essentials Dickens's readings bear a striking similarity to Mathews's 'At Homes'. Typically of Dickens, a youthful impression came to fruition in his maturity. Once again the prime inspiration for his approach to popular entertainment is to be found in his own past.

'At Home' was the title Mathews first used in 1817 for a season of performances which he put on at the Haymarket Theatre in London.[16] The show consisted of a comic entertainment performed entirely by Mathews and was a form which had evolved out of one- and two-person acts which he had given in the provinces in previous seasons. In the first years of the nineteenth century he had been a successful comic actor, with a notable gift for mimicry, But frustration with the limited scope of roles offered by regular stage comedy, a desire to exploit the distinctiveness of his individual talents, and an accident which left him partially lame led him to develop the solo performances on which his later fame depended. He made a successful American tour in 1822, and from 1824 to 1834, with the exception of a single season, he performed a regular London engagement as well as touring the provinces. In 1834, in poor health and financial embarrassment, he made a second trip to America which had to be cut short, and he died in June 1835. His heyday, in other words, began when Dickens was 5 years old and was over by the time Dickens was 22.

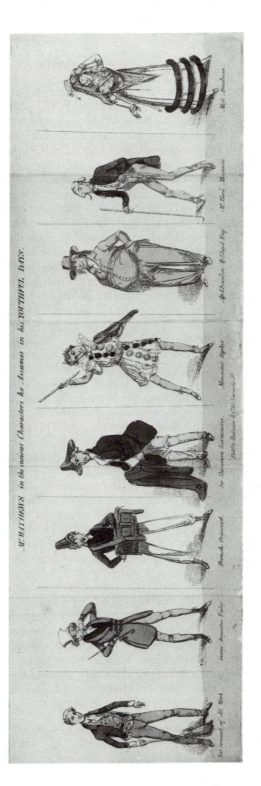

Charles Mathews's impersonation of several roles in a one-man entertainment was the chief inspiration of Dickens's public readings.

Mathews created several distinct programmes of 'At Home' entertainments but, although the contents and their arrangements varied from season to season, the basic form, once established, remained consistent. The stage was appointed simply, as a drawing-room, and Mathews walked on in his own clothes, as himself. He proceeded with the narration of a journey he had taken – his 'Trip to Paris', a 'Trip to America', travels in a balloon through 'Earth, Air, and Water', or 'Mail Coach Adventures' – and, interspersing his story with songs and recitations, he regaled his audience with descriptions of people and adventures he met along the way. He assumed the parts of the characters he described and rapidly developed his monologue into dialogue. This portion of the programme, generally in two acts, was followed by what he called 'monopolylogue', a stage farce in which, by means of quick changes of costume, ventriloquism and sharp differentiation of character, Mathews played all the roles.

The broad similarity of the 'At Homes' to Dickens's readings is immediately apparent. In both, the starting-point was the appearance of the solo performer in his own person. Both used narration as the primary structure of the entertainment, and both displayed the actor's versatility as he rapidly moved through a multiplicity of character roles within a single sketch. Mathews's shows were invariably comic as Dickens's predominantly were; and, although Mathews generally relied on elaborate costuming and scenery, he often performed with only a table and a screen to hide his changes of costume, while Dickens performed with only his desk and his book. But the parallels between Dickens's and Mathews's entertainments are to be found in the very nature of the performances as well as in the accidentals. The important areas of consonance are three.

First, both performers relied centrally for the effectiveness of their shows on the rapport they were able to establish with their audiences. We have seen already that Dickens frequently announced his desire to strengthen the bonds of friendship between himself and his audiences, and his admirers responded accordingly. In part this was because his reputation as a writer preceded him; but, as Philip Collins has shown, audiences thought of Dickens not only as a great writer and actor, but also as a good man and a personal friend. Dickens wrote often to Forster of the 'personal affection' which audiences accorded to him, and he did his best to promote this, not only through the sentiments of the readings chosen, but also by the lack of ostentation with which he took the stage, the unaffected and (for its day) restrained manner of his delivery, and the quiet aplomb with which he dealt with disturbances.[17] Charles Kent compared Dickens's power over his audiences to that of the Ancient Mariner over the Wedding Guest:

The narrator had his will with one and all. However large and however miscellaneous the audience, from the front of the stalls to the back of the gallery, every one listened to the familiar words that fell from his lips, from the beginning to the end, with unflagging attention.[18]

Mathews also worked to win the favour of his audiences. As Dickens was to do, he commenced each performance by appearing in his own guise and quickly taking the audience into his confidence by addressing his narration directly to them. Also like Dickens, he sometimes made short statements of intention and of gratitude before or after a performance. He sustained interest in the diverse nature of his act by keeping his own personality as a unifying feature. Critics commented favourably on Mathews's ability to put his audiences at ease and make them 'merry and happy'; compared with other solo actors, Mathews was superior because he generated 'the great charm, that of sympathy', by which he captivated his audience.[19] Both he and Dickens, that is, projected images of themselves as genial men wishing unaffectedly to offer amusement to their audiences, and their appearance, not only in roles but as themselves, was a vital factor in creating the popularity of both of their shows.

At the same time, the aspect of their entertainments for which both were most highly praised was the skill with which they stepped out of their own persons and assumed a variety of roles in each sketch. This is the second key area of similarity: the distinctive combination of a solo performance in which a whole cast of characters was presented. *Blackwood's Edinburgh Magazine* in 1820 proclaimed Mathews 'the very best actor on the English stage at this day'; he could 'embody an infinitely greater variety of characters' than other actors were capable of, because his physical powers were 'more plastic' and his intellectual resources 'more various'.[20] Similarly, Kate Field, the most perspicacious of contemporary observers to write about Dickens's readings, allowed that it was possible to imagine a different actor surpassing Dickens's portrayal of a single role, but 'no one actor living can embody the twelve characters of this reading [*David Copperfield*] with the individuality given them by Dickens, unaided, too, as he is, by theatrical illusion'.[21]

But Mathews and Dickens were admired as actors not merely for their virtuosity; what was seen to be of peculiar merit was the truth to life of their role-playing. Both were credited with exceptional powers of expression. A critic of Mathews's first season of 'At Homes' observed that

Mathews had, by some expeditious changes, dressed himself

for the external resemblance; but with the face he seemed also to put on the mind. This appeared to us the most complete adoption of a character, the most perfect identification of one being with another, we had ever seen.[22]

Dickens, who relied on no changes of costume or props to assist in the depiction of character, was likewise skilful at imitation. In the words of the *Scotsman* critic of Dickens's farewell tour, 'His powers of vocal and facial expression are very great . . . There has been nothing so perfect, in their way, as these readings ever offered to an English audience.'[23]

Mathews was concerned to defend what he did on the stage as serious art, which was not to be degraded as mere mimicry. In his introductory address before the very first of his 'At Homes' he insisted that: 'The best authorities have characterized the drama by the title of the mimic art; and I humbly conceive that, without mimicry, there can be no acting. It is the very essence of personation.'[24] Mimicry was not caricature, he claimed at another time, because it was his purpose to show human characteristics 'by general delineations'; as one of his sympathetic critics remarked: 'There are two kinds of mimicry: the one simply imitates what it observes; the other observes and combines.' Mathews, the critic went on, was the latter kind of mimic. Another observer went further and praised Mathews for an ability which 'individualizes classes of character, and is so far Shakesperian. His capacity exhibits an extent of observance far beyond that of the common mimic, who can seldom compound, but must have all his originals in positive existence.' If Mathews's impersonations were not caricatures, neither were they stock type-figures: again and again he was praised for the particularity of his portraits. This was seen as an achievement of considerable merit; as one contemporary observer remarked: 'The ability to individualise a general conception is one of the rarest properties of the mind.'[25] And a century later the theatre historian E. B. Watson accurately assessed the innovative quality of Mathews's performance: 'He departed entirely from the set types of comedy and therefore introduced what later would have been called "character acting".'[26]

Mathews's ability to generalize and individualize simultaneously is also, of course, a hallmark of Dickens's superlative skills of characterization. We have seen numerous instances of this process in previous chapters, when we looked at his use of source materials in creating his fiction. In his readings, observers felt, this ability to give individual vitality and general significance to character was taken a step further. The term which was used repeatedly to describe Dickens's methods of presenting character during the readings was 'impersonation'. As Charles Kent put it: 'The different original characters introduced in his stories, when he read them, he did not simply describe, he impersonated; otherwise to put it, for whomsoever he spoke, he spoke in character.' For Kent, what Dickens sought always to achieve was 'the human element in his imaginings when they were to be impersonated'.[27] The *Saturday Review* critic, likewise, noted that 'his impersonation – for such it was – of Mr Peggoty [sic] and Micawber in *David Copperfield . . .* well repaid the trouble of a visit' to hear Dickens read. 'Mr Dickens', this critic declared, 'is endowed with histrionic talent of no common order', which distinguishes him 'palpably' from 'those literary gentlemen who, without oratorical gifts, seem merely to make an exhibition of their own faces'.[28] Kate Field, too, stressed repeatedly Dickens's powers of impersonation: he was the 'incarnation' of Scrooge; there was 'not a trace of Dickens' in his portrayal of John Browdie; and in presenting Justice Stareleigh 'Dickens steps out of his own skin'.[29]

Impersonation of character, then, was the essence of performance by both Mathews and Dickens. The result, in both cases, was that observers marvelled at the sense of reality and of naturalness in the characters enacted. Again and again Mathews was praised for his 'accurate descriptions of nature'; his comic portraits which were 'ludicrously natural'. The *Blackwood's* critic, already cited, described Mathews's talent as 'nothing less than genius': 'In some of Mr Matthews's [sic] performances it would be actually impossible to detect *him*, unless one knew beforehand that it *was* him – for it is the thing itself.'[30] Dickens too was credited with 'natural' characterization; as Kate Field said, 'It is in the genius of Dickens to hold the mirror up to nature on the stage.' The *Scotsman* critic admired the 'natural feeling' of Doctor Marigold and praised Dickens's stage presence because 'he acts so little.'[31]

The 'natural' quality of their impersonation of character takes us to the third important area of resemblance between the performances of Mathews and Dickens. Because the roles they enacted struck audiences as vividly lifelike, the entertainments were not merely frivolous diversions, but offered contents of significance. Mathews's modern biographer, Richard Klepac, argues that the 'At Homes' are purposeful because of the large element of social satire in them.[32] Certainly ridicule is prominent in Mathews's routines, as it is also in some of Dickens's pieces, such as *Bardell and Pickwick* and *Nicholas Nickleby at the Yorkshire School*. But far more valuable than the exposure of folly and the moral uplift with which *Little Dombey* and *Doctor Marigold* conclude is the truth to life to which audiences responded so positively. By convincing the people who came to be amused that the thoughts, emotions, and situations which were portrayed accurately represented life as they knew it, Dickens and Mathews were able to increase the stock of human sympathy and to lead their audiences on to a fuller and more generous conception of the world they lived in. Such, at any rate, was the goal which these artists set themselves. In one of his preliminary addresses Mathews elaborated on his notion of mimicry, then tried to suggest its value.

A more than ordinary accuracy of observation is necessary to hit off successfully those nice distinctions of character and manner which form the wide difference between a correct portrait and a vulgar caricature; and if I have succeeded, or can succeed (by holding the mirror up to Nature, and showing Folly her own image, and Vice its own deformity) in correcting any one of a foolish habit, or an offensive peculiarity; and, above all, in affording the public a few hours of harmless mirth, I think my labours amply rewarded, and that my life had not been altogether passed, or my humble talents exerted, without some degree of usefulness.[33]

This accords admirably with Dickens's conception of rational amusement, as we considered it in the previous chapter. Amusement could be educationally beneficial, Dickens believed, not because of any bald instruction offered, but because of the 'sympathies and graces of imagination' which it nurtured.[34] The unalloyed delight which he received from the entertainment of Mathews was precisely the response Dickens wished to evoke through his own public readings. In their essential qualities, the 'At Homes' gave him a model of excellence on which to base his own performances.

There were large differences, of course. Dickens's act was a reading, not a play; although he assumed the voices and gestures of his characters, he adopted no costumes and used no sets. That he brought his various personages and descriptions vividly to life is testimony to the power of fancy he was able to inspire, for he did it entirely by voice, expression and gesture. He read in halls rather than in theatres; there were no songs, ventriloquism, or imitations of other actors. Dickens's mode of entertainment was, in short, an invention of his own, as unique in its own way as Mathews's was in its. But the points of contact with the 'At Homes' are real, and they are of seminal importance.

It is also true that Mathews was not the sole example on Dickens's horizon. Solo entertainments by actors had been seen on the English stage well back into the eighteenth century, and a number of imitators followed in Mathews's footsteps. Furthermore, as Philip Collins has shown, there was a diverse range of related entertainments, which were increasing in number and popularity in the years before and during Dickens's own readings. In his initial remark to Forster about the possibility of his taking to the platform on his own, he wrote of 'these days of lecturings and readings', and there were numerous instances to which he could point: the instructive entertainments, of which Albert Smith's *Ascent of Mont Blanc* was most conspicuous; the readings from playtexts by professional actors and actresses, most notably Fanny Kemble; literary lectures such as Thackeray's; professional recitals, amateur readings, and institutional entertainments up and down the country.[35] All of these were important in establishing a favourable climate for Dickens's readings, and for encouraging him to embark on his career as a solo entertainer, but none had the depth of influence on the nature of his form of entertainment which Mathews's 'At Homes' had.

Charles Mathews mattered to Dickens because he epitomized the kind of actor Dickens himself had once aspired to be, before his own success as a writer, first of news and later of fiction, turned his primary energies elsewhere. The comedian's entertainments offered a kind of enterprise which, adapted to Dickens's own talents, was well within his capabilities and suitable to his purposes. At a time of personal crisis, the example of Mathews offered a chance for Dickens to return to his roots even as he faced the future: it was a cherished memory from the past, susceptible of adaptation to the circumstances of the present. And this consonance of past and present was not exclusively personal. It united Dickens's own youthful hopes with the needs of his adulthood, but it also forged a workable accord between the declining and emerging traditions which co-existed in Dickens's lifetime. As a solo entertainment, depending greatly on the impact of Dickens's personal presence and fostering harmonious intimacy with his audiences, a reading by him incorporated key values of the gregarious amusements from the past. As a commercial venture, undertaken for financial reward, administered by professional agents, and performed before large audiences, it represented a highly successful accommodation to the trends of the present. Public reading enabled Dickens, as nothing else at this stage of his career could have done, to renew his commitment to popular entertainment, not only as its defender, but also as its provider.

IV

That Dickens's readings were popular is beyond dispute. What was debatable, however, from the very outset, was whether they compromised his position as a serious artist. Dickens was entirely aware that public reading was open to this charge. Years before he first stepped on to the stage in Birmingham, he mooted the question with Forster. In 1846, while writing *Dombey* in Lausanne, he read his work in progress aloud to a circle of friends and speculated about reading in public. To Forster he wrote:

> I was thinking the other day that in these days of lecturings and readings, a great deal of money might possibly be made (if it were not infra dig) by one's having Readings of one's own books. It would be an *odd* thing. I think it would take immensely. What do you say?[36]

Forster's response, then and always, was categorical: readings were entirely 'infra dig', and Dickens would demean himself by giving them. He summarized the grounds of his opposition succinctly in his *Life of Dickens*.

> It was a substitution of lower for higher aims: a change to commonplace from more elevated pursuits; and it had so much of the character of a public exhibition for money as to raise, in the question of respect for his calling as a writer, a question also of respect for himself as a gentleman.[37]

Dickens obviously was not persuaded, and he went his own way. But Forster continued to advise him against the readings and nearly drove Dickens's manager, George Dolby, to distraction by his adamantine refusal to countenance the American tour of 1868.[38]

And Forster's has not been a lone voice. A century later Emlyn Williams, himself an accomplished reader of Dickens's works, expressed reservations about Dickens's selection and editing of texts for his repertoire. 'Dickens the actor did not do full justice to Dickens the author, in the material he chose to perform,' he stated, a view which finds the reading texts inferior in aesthetic quality to the fiction.[39] Philip Collins, too, the foremost modern authority on Dickens's readings, judges that Dickens cannot be wholly absolved from the accusation of 'a betrayal of his duty to the more enduring art of the written word'. Despite his very considerable fascination with the readings, Collins thinks that there were large elements of vanity and vulgarity in Dickens's career as a public reader. He agrees with Forster, and with R. H. Hutton, whose 1874 remark he quotes on several occasions, that 'There is something a little ignoble in this extravagant relish of a man of genius for the evidence of the popularity of his own writings'.[40]

Certainly there are aspects of the readings which lend themselves to the imputation that they were 'low'. The spectacle of a public man barn-storming up and down the countryside, crossing the Atlantic to exploit the known lucrative potential of America, and often leaving to the last moment the decision where to venture next was not altogether removed from the 'wandering speculation' of a Vincent Crummles. His practice of improvising within his texts as he warmed to audiences was his own form of 'gagging' – the extempore patter of the cheap Jack and the strolling actor.[41] His type of show brought inevitable comparison with that of his most famous immediate predecessor as a solo entertainer, Albert Smith (1816–60), the self-advertising raconteur whose *Ascent of Mont Blanc* ran for some two thousand performances and became as much a London institution as Madame Tussaud's waxworks and the Tower. *Mont Blanc* was an illustrated lecture interspersed with songs, jokes and comic impersonations, and although Smith was careful about the tone of his act, and gave a command performance for Prince Albert, he was widely scorned as a vulgar showman.[42] Dickens's readings differed substantially in form from Smith's entertainment, but the comparison was not without foundation. Not only did Dickens speak favourably of Smith in public (*Speeches*, pp. 175–6), he turned to Smith's brother Arthur when he sought a manager for his own first series of professional engagements. And after Arthur Smith's death Dickens contracted himself to the theatrical agents, Chappell, whose representative, George Dolby, promptly consulted the greatest humbug of the entertainment world, P. T. Barnum.[43] A shameless bid for popular approval, then, was only one of the grounds on which Dickens laid himself open to objection. The public readings had a number of close affinities with examples of showmanship far removed from the artistic accomplishment of his fiction.

Several possible arguments can be put forward to meet this challenge. First, one can argue, as Charles Kent and J. B. Van Amerongen do, that objection to Dickens's readings betrays a prejudice against the actor's craft in comparison to the written word, and that just valuation of the excellence appropriate to the stage leads inevitably to respect for the propriety of Dickens's undertaking. It is true, as Van Amerongen notes, that Forster speaks of 'higher' and 'lower' aims, but Dickens's friend was less concerned with the transient nature of stagecraft than with the temptations it offered to foresake duties, habits and principles. Forster, like Emlyn Williams and Philip Collins after him, was a devoted admirer of the theatre, but he felt that Dickens's particular kind of performance, especially at so unsettled a time in his life, was a diminution of his genius. It neglected the profundity of which Dickens's writing was capable, in favour of merely immediate sensation.[44] Even if one accepts the proposition that theatrical art is as worthy as literary art, that is, it is still entirely possible to see Dickens's readings as a limited accomplishment as stagecraft.

A second line of defence is to point to the professionalism with which Dickens approached the stage: his careful rehearsals; his insistence that the auditorium be properly set up for good acoustics and sight-lines; and, compared to the prevalent acting conventions of the time, the relative restraint, decorum and naturalness of his performances. Contemporary accounts suggest that all these things were true, and for us today, with only the texts of the readings and reported accounts of Dickens's stage presence available to us, there may be a temptation to judge the readings without full awareness of their actual impact in performance.[45] But again the defence is insufficient: a vulgar form of entertainment, no matter how skilfully presented, remains vulgar. If the texts do not reveal Dickens's creativity at its best, and if the theatrical effects predominantly sought lack the complexity and insight which his fiction achieves, then again the readings are a lesser achievement.

A third line of argument proposes that the development of a new mode of presentation, which the readings assuredly were, opens up possibilities for extending the audience which writings alone would not reach. It was argued at the time that readings had a distinct advantage in this regard over drama, because respectable people, whose consciences would never permit them to enter a theatre, went quite happily to a lecture-hall in which a highly theatrical reading was being given.[46] Dickens unquestionably attracted large audiences to the 472 or so readings he gave, but what is questionable is how many of his listeners were unfamiliar with his work beforehand. There are anecdotes of innocents in remote outposts such as Aberdeen and Boston who had never heard of Dickens, but accounts of audience behaviour, cheering at the first mention of Sam Weller and Sairey Gamp, suggest that most people who came to hear Dickens read had already encountered his work on the printed page.[47] The readings reinforced his fame, but it is doubtful whether they brought his art to any large, previously untapped, sections of the population. In any case, size of audience alone is no measure of intrinsic excellence in a performance.

A more satisfactory defence of Dickens's reading is to be found by suggesting a different sort of argument altogether, one which arises directly out of the themes of the present book. Evidence of Dickens's attitudes to popular entertainment which we have explored in previous chapters indicates that he undertook his public readings not because he desired to scale new heights of aesthetic accomplishment, but because he was profoundly convinced of people's need for direct, compelling entertainment. His choice to devote more time to reading aloud than to writing was not a matter of valuing performance more than creative writing; rather, it was a question of priorities. It was choice, conscious, concerned, heroic, even tragic: like Plato's philosopher-king, he felt the situation in society demanded not thought and words, but action, and he committed himself wholeheartedly to acting in the most immediate and constructive way within his power. By giving readings he was going out to people whose right to carefree, innocent amusement he had proclaimed all his life, and in his own person offering them a vital focus for their imaginations. He was, in short, enacting the values which his fiction and journalism propounded. To have done otherwise would have been to concede a less passionate conviction than he in fact held. After a reading of the *Carol* in Sheffield in 1855 he pledged:

> . . . that to the earnestness of my aim and desire to do right by my readers, and to leave our imaginative and popular literature more closely associated than I found it at once with the private homes and public rights of the English people, I shall ever be faithful, – to my death – in the principles which have won your approval. (*Speeches*, p. 209)

His reading career was the honouring of that pledge.

To argue thus is to reject the view which originated with Edmund Wilson and has been most recently propounded by Raymund Fitzsimons, that the readings were an unhealthy, even suicidal, manifestation of dark obsessions.[48] On the contrary, Dickens devoted himself to reading not because he was driven by unconscious forces to find some distraction for the turmoil seething inside him, but because he saw forces outside, in society, which required urgent attention. Judging that opportunities for wholesome amusement were inadequate, seeing little sign of progress in directions he approved, and knowing his own capabilities as an entertainer, he made a clear-sighted decision to deal directly with the situation. Assuredly at the time he began his first extended series of readings in 1858 he was personally unhappy over the breakdown of his marriage, and he was eager for activity which would require his concerted energy. It is even probable, as another modern commentator has proposed, that 'even if Dickens had never read a line of his works in public he would have thrown himself into some other activity which might have proved equally injurious to his health'.[49] But the fact that he chose to commit himself to public service, that he worked diligently to bring gaiety and happiness to others, and that his entertainments provided the very imaginative stimulation which he had long upheld as a human necessity, all stand in evidence against obsession as the root cause of the readings.

Nor did he embark on his career as a public reader, as R. H. Hutton suggested, merely because of a weak-willed craving for personal adulation. Without doubt the readings gave him intense personal satisfaction, but it is equally certain that they brought great joy to the many people who came to see and hear him. He knew that he was offering entertainment of an exceptionally high standard; that the tours also helped him personally to cope with his own need for love and respect does not in any way lessen their value as entertainment for his admirers. Altruistic as well as self-centred motives spurred him to create the readings. Dickens was a complex man, whose self-understanding always included blind spots and whose virtues were mixed with limitations and failings. But to call him 'ignoble' on account of the readings contradicts the evidence of a lifetime. Dickens cared genuinely about the imaginative health of his fellow human beings, and the readings were a specific for their well-being.

Furthermore, Dickens did not abandon fiction and journalism when he embarked on his readings. He tried not to take on heavy writing commitments at the same time that he was involved in a reading series, but it was in 1860, after he had toured the provinces twice, that he wrote one of the crowning achievements in English literature, *Great Expectations*, and five years later that he produced one of the great social panoramas of his maturity, *Our Mutual Friend*. Similarly, he retained his commitment to journalism throughout the years of his readings, and *All the Year Round*, the successor to *Household Words* (which he wound up following a breach with his publishers at the time of his separation from his wife) continued weekly publication for many years even after his death. *All the Year Round* is a less varied and interesting periodical than *Household Words*, partly because Dickens supervised its contents less closely than he did for *Household Words*, but a journal which contained in its pages original work by Wilkie Collins, Charles Reade, Elizabeth Gaskell – and Charles Dickens – is hardly without merit.

The readings were thus an extension of his other professional activities, not a substitution. Dickens always thought of art and entertainment in an integral relationship: good entertainment, in his view, required skill, preparation and thought in its presentation, just as good art had to be appealing to its audience. For him, the best entertainment aspired to aesthetic distinction, and the best art was richly entertaining. One may legitimately wish that Dickens had allowed more time during the last twelve years of his life, when he

Through his public readings Dickens enacted in his own person the values which he had spent his entire career as a novelist and journalist propounding. He is depicted here by an anonymous artist during his farewell series of readings in 1870 performing *Sikes and Nancy*.

was at the height of his artistic powers, for the writing of fiction, just as one laments that politics diverted Milton from creative writing for much of his adult lifetime. But for both writers a sense of higher public responsibility drew them from the artistic tasks to which they were supremely fitted, and led them to place human values above aesthetic ones. Milton, living in an age of political crisis, entered government; Dickens, facing what he saw as a cultural crisis, took the most direct step of which he was capable, to improve the quality of life for thousands of people, by providing for their need for imaginative entertainment. By practice and example he strove to make better quality of entertainment more widely available. We may, then, concede the lower artistic achievement of the readings (although clearly recalling that we are speaking of levels of excellence, not of good versus bad art), and we may regret the novels left unwritten, but at the same time we should admire the nobility of the choice which Dickens made in undertaking the readings. Having long urged the importance of popular entertainment, he dedicated the greater part of the last quarter of his life to creating splendid entertainment, in his own person, for crowded audiences on both sides of the Atlantic.

In *Doctor Marigold*, one of the most popular as well as one of the most typical of Dickens's public readings, the eponymous hero describes his acquaintance with a fairground giant. He is 'an amiable though timid young man' named Pickleson, but the cheap Jack is disposed – morally, at least – to look down upon his tall friend because his bid for popularity involves deception. The giant exhibits himself not simply as a human curiosity but in the guise of a Roman, under the sobriquet of Rinaldo di Velasco. Commenting on this practice, Doctor Marigold gives voice to a principle which serves admirably as the basis for a final assessment of Dickens's role as a popular entertainer. The cheap Jack finds Pickleson's exhibition unworthy: 'For the general rule is, going round the country, to draw the line at dressing up. When a man can't trust his getting a living to his undisguised abilities, you consider him below your sort.'[50] Dickens spent a lifetime providing popular entertainment by dint of his 'undisguised abilities'. We seriously misjudge this giant if we consider him below our sort.

NOTES

CHAPTER 1: INTRODUCTION: DICKENS AND THE CHANGING PATTERNS OF POPULAR ENTERTAINMENT

1 [Charles Dickens], 'The Queen's Coronation', *Examiner*, 1 July 1838, p. 403. Attributed to Dickens by the Pilgrim editors, vol. 1, p. 408.
2 'Lord' George Sanger, *Seventy Years a Showman* (London, 1927), p. 114. Other observers confirmed the successful nature of the Coronation Fair and the orderly behaviour of the crowds there; see, for example, *Bell's Life* for 1 July 1838.
3 Forster, bk 1, ch. 3, p. 39, and bk 11, ch. 3, pp. 833–4. Mamie Dickens, *My Father as I Recall Him* (London, 1897), pp. 41–2, 69–72.
4 Peter Burke, *Popular Culture in Early Modern Europe* (London, 1978), pp. 24–9, distinguishes usefully between 'great' and 'little' traditions of culture. G. K. Chesterton, *Charles Dickens* (London, 1906), p. 106, accurately identifies the key to Dickens's attitudes on these matters when he states: 'Dickens did not write what the people wanted. Dickens wanted what the people wanted . . . There was this vital point in his populism, that there was no condescension in it.' Similarly, Philip Collins, 'Dickens and popular amusements', *Dickensian*, vol. 61 (1965), p. 8, correctly judges that 'He wrote about and defended popular amusements not mainly out of a sense of public duty, or for want of a likely subject, but because he enormously enjoyed them'.
5 [Charles Dickens], 'A Preliminary Word', *HW*, vol. 1 (30 March 1850), p. 1; Nonesuch, vol. 2, p. 518 (to W. H. Wills, 17 November 1853).
6 James Walvin, *Leisure and Society, 1830–1950* (London, 1978); Peter Bailey, *Leisure and Class in Victorian England: Rational Recreation and the Contest for Control, 1830–1885* (London, 1978); Robert Malcolmson, *Popular Recreations in English Society, 1700–1850* (Cambridge, 1973); Morris Brooke Smith, 'The growth and development of popular entertainment and pastimes in the Lancashire cotton towns 1830–1870', MLitt thesis, University of Lancaster, 1970. For a dissenting view, cf. Hugh Cunningham, *Leisure in the Industrial Revolution* (London, 1980); Cunningham judges popular culture to have been in a more thriving condition in the first half of the nineteenth century than most historians claim, but even he is convinced that the vigour he sees is 'not a survival: so much in this culture was new, an invention of the Industrial Revolution'; rather than old communal pastimes, 'all these forms of entertainment were frankly commercial in nature', and 'a new phase in the history of leisure opens in the mid-nineteenth century' (pp. 35–6, 140).

7 Henry Grote Lewin, *The Early Railways: A Short History of Their Origin and Development, 1801–1844* (London, 1925), p. 186. Precise figures vary; Michael Mulhall, *Dictionary of Statistics* (London, 1884), p. 381, lists 838 miles of railway built by 1840; *Encyclopaedia Britannica* gives a figure of over 1,300 miles laid by 1841. In any case, a considerable amount of track had been built.

8 J. H. Plumb, *The Commercialisation of Leisure in Eighteenth-Century England* (Reading, 1973); Burke, *Popular Culture*, pp. 248–9.

9 Sanger, *Seventy Years a Showman*, p. 235.

10 See Paul Schlicke, 'A "discipline of feeling": Macready's *Lear* and *The Old Curiosity Shop*', *Dickensian*, vol. 76 (1980), pp. 78–90.

11 [Dudley Costello], 'History in Wax', *HW*, vol. 9 (18 February 1854), pp. 17–20, and 'Our Eye-Witness in Great Company', *AYR*, vol. 2 (7 January 1860), pp. 249–53; [H. Cole], 'London Musical Clubs', *HW*, vol. 3 (17 May 1851), pp. 179–81; [James Hannay], 'The Palace of Flowers', *HW*, vol. 3 (26 April 1851), pp. 117–20; [W. B. Jerrold], 'The British Museum a Century Ago', *HW*, vol. 3 (3 May 1851), pp. 130–1; [Charles Knight], 'Three May Days in London', *HW*, vol. 3 (19 April–3 May 1851), pp. 73–5, 105–9 and 121–4.

12 [Charles Dickens], 'Where We Stopped Growing', *HW*, vol. 6 (1 January 1853), pp. 361–3.

13 [Charles Dickens], 'A Preliminary Word', *HW*, vol. 1 (30 March 1850), p. 1.

14 'Where We Stopped Growing'. For a discussion of Dickens's ideas on the subject, cf. Philip Collins, 'Queen Mab's chariot among the steam engines: Dickens and "fancy"', *English Studies*, vol. 42 (1961), pp. 78–90.

15 Malcolmson, *Popular Recreations in English Society*, pp. 100–1, sums up the antagonism as follows:

> Evangelical sentiment was almost always at odds with the traditions of popular diversion. It was forward-looking, morally 'reformist', profoundly concerned with sin and salvation and the need for social and self-discipline, interested more in the individual's private life than in the affairs of the community (though the former assumed attention to the latter), suspicious of worldly pleasures (though nicely discriminating in its suspicions), and contemptuous of much of the culture of earlier generations (especially that of its immediate predecessors); on most counts its morality was completely inconsistent with the conservative, gregarious, and ritualistic morality which was represented in the pastimes of the common people. Evangelicalism could not accommodate itself to the traditions of popular leisure without abandoning its basic presuppositions; indeed, there was virtually no room for compromise.

For a thorough study of the Sabbatarian movement, see George Mark Ellis, 'The Evangelicals and the Sunday Question, 1830–1860: organized Sabbatarianism as an aspect of the Evangelical movement', PhD thesis, Harvard University, 1951.

16 Rev. Baptist Noel, *The Sanctification of the Sabbath and the Blessing Attached to It* (London, 1835), p. 13.

17 Peter McOwen, 'The Sabbath: the spirit and manner in which the day ought to be sanctified', *Wesleyan Methodist Magazine* (June 1842), p. 466.

18 Brian Harrison, 'State intervention and moral reform', in Patricia Hollis (ed.), *Pressure from Without in Early Victorian England* (London, 1974), pp. 289–90. The summary in this paragraph of opposition to popular entertainment in the nineteenth century draws on this and other work by Dr Harrison, who has written extensively and most illuminatingly on the subject. In addition to the article noted above, cf. 'The Sunday Trading Riots of 1855', *Historical Journal*, vol. 8 (1965), pp. 219–45; 'Religion and recreation in nineteenth-century England', *Past and Present*, no. 38 (1967), pp. 98–125; and *Drink and the Victorians: The Temperance Question in England, 1815–1872* (London, 1971).

CHAPTER 2: POPULAR ENTERTAINMENT AND CHILDHOOD

1 Dorothy Van Ghent, 'The Dickens world: a view from Todgers'', *Sewanee Review*, vol. 58 (1950), pp. 419–38; Peter Coveney, *Poor Monkey* (1957), revised as *The Image of Childhood* (Harmondsworth, 1967); Philip Collins, 'The rights of childhood', in his *Dickens and Education* (London, 1963), ch. 8; Angus Wilson, 'Dickens on children and childhood', in Michael Slater (ed.), *Dickens 1970* (London, 1970), pp. 195–227.

2 [Charles Dickens], 'Our School', *HW*, vol. 4 (11 October 1851), pp. 49–52.

3 Forster, bk 1, ch. 2, p. 31.

4 'Our School', *UT*, p. 148; 'A Christmas Tree', *HW*, vol. 2 (21 December 1850), pp. 289–95.

5 Aldous Huxley, 'The vulgarity of Little Nell', in *Vulgarity in Literature* (London, 1930), pp. 54–9.

6 George Henry Lewes, 'Dickens in relation to criticism', *Fortnightly Review*, vol. 17 (February 1872), pp. 141–54; F. R. Leavis, *The Great Tradition* (London, 1948), p. 19.

7 Denis Donoghue, 'The English Dickens and *Dombey and Son*', *Nineteenth-Century Fiction*, vol. 24 (1970), p. 384.

8 ['Dullborough Town'] 'The Uncommercial Traveller', *AYR*, vol. 3 (30 June 1860), pp. 274–8; 'Dullborough Town', *UT*, pp. 116–26.

9 Forster, bk 9, ch. 3, p. 733.

10 Forster, bk 1, ch. 1, p. 2. Dickens himself tells the story in one of the *Uncommercial Traveller* sketches, 'Travelling Abroad', pp. 61–2.

11 J. A. Langford, 'Warwickshire folk-lore and superstitions', *Transactions of the Archaeological Section of the Birmingham and Midland Institute* (1875); A. H. Wall, 'Warwickshire folklore', in William Andrews (ed.), *By Gone Warwickshire* (Hull, 1893), p. 244.

12 John Davidson, 'The Crystal Palace', in *The Poems of John Davidson*, ed. Andrew Turnbull, 2 vols (London/Edinburgh, 1973), pp. 427–33. Gissing devoted a chapter to the Crystal Palace in *The Nether World* (1889),

but he described it as a rural festivity, with old-fashioned attractions which emphasize aggression in a 'spirit of imbecile joviality' and lead at the evening's end to a drunken brawl, torn clothes, blood, weariness and 'utter misery' (ch. 12). His negative view is nearly as bleak as Wordsworth's famous denunciation of Bartholomew Fair as a microcosm of the wicked city in *The Prelude* (1805 version), bk 8, ll. 675–730.

CHAPTER 3: 'NICHOLAS NICKLEBY': THE NOVEL AS POPULAR ENTERTAINMENT

1 Louis James, *Fiction for the Working Man* (London, 1963; rev. edn Harmondsworth, 1973), p. 73. See Mary Theresa McGowan, 'Pickwick and the pirates: a study of some early imitations, dramatizations, and plagiarisms of *Pickwick Papers*', PhD thesis, University of London, 1975, and Michael Slater, *The Composition and Monthly Publication of 'Nicholas Nickleby'* (London, 1973), pp. 18–20.

2 The *Nickleby* 'Proclamation' is included in the part-issue edition of *Nicholas Nickleby* in the Dexter Collection, lodged at the British Library (Dex. 281); it is reproduced in Slater, *Composition*, facing p. 20.

3 Slater (*Composition*, pp. 13–15) points out how Dickens drew on his Yorkshire observations, recorded in a letter to his wife (Pilgrim, Vol. 1, pp. 365–6), in presenting the school episodes of *Nickleby*. Dickens stated his motives for going to Yorkshire in a letter to Mrs S. C. Hall dated 29 December 1838 (Pilgrim, Vol. 1, pp. 481–3), and years later, in the preface to the 1848 edition of *Nicholas Nickleby*, he publicly declared that he had gone to Yorkshire with the specific intention of seeing the kind of school he had resolved to write about.

4 Forster, bk 9, ch. 3, p. 734.

5 Dickens recorded in his diary that he wrote the preface to *Nickleby* on 15 September 1839, and that he finished the novel on the 20th (Pilgrim, Vol. 1, p. 642).

6 Pilgrim, Vol. 1, p. 463. For the context of popular literature preceding *Pickwick*, see George H. Ford, *Dickens and his Readers: Aspects of Novel-Criticism since 1836* (Princeton, NJ, 1955), ch. 1. Pierce Egan, whose *Life in London* is often mentioned as an influence on Dickens, reversed the process in his last novel, *The Pilgrims of the Thames*, when he wrote a chapter entitled 'The Pilgrims Turn Pic-nic-ians'.

7 In his important study of the development of Dickens's conception of the imagination, Garrett Stewart, *Dickens and the Trials of Imagination* (Cambridge, Mass., 1974), argues that Sam Weller is Dickens's best answer to 'how the imaginative life can really be lived', a problem which he was 'never to solve as well again' (p. 85). Although I agree with Stewart at many points and find his arguments stimulating at all times, it will be clear that my own view of the development of Dickens's ideas about these matters differs substantially from his.

8 Preface to the Cheap Edition of *Pickwick* (1847).

9 Pilgrim, Vol. 1, pp. 123–4 and n.

10 Forster, bk 1, ch. 5, p. 76. In recent years *Sketches by Boz* has attracted its
    share of scholarly attention, including two book-length studies. See John
    Butt and Kathleen Tillotson, *Dickens at Work* (London, 1957), ch. 2;
    Margaret Ganz, 'Humor's alchemy; the lesson of *Sketches by Boz*', *Genre*,
    vol. 1 (1968), pp. 290–306; J. Hillis Miller, 'The fiction of realism: *Sketches by
    Boz, Oliver Twist*, and Cruikshank's illustrations', in Ada Nisbet and Blake
    Nevius (eds.) *Dickens Centennial Essays* (Berkeley/Los Angeles, Calif.,
    1971), pp. 85–153; Virgil Grillo, *Charles Dickens's 'Sketches by Boz'* (Boulder,
    Colo., 1974); Duane DeVries, *Dickens's Apprentice Years: The Making of a
    Novelist* (Hassocks, 1976); Edward Costigan, 'Drama and everyday life in
    Sketches by Boz', *Review of English Studies*, NS, vol. 27 (1976), pp. 403–21.
11 Pilgrim, Vol. 1, pp. 83, 97, 98, 103, 123 n, 208.
12 Pilgrim, Vol. 1, p. 88.
13 [Charles Buller], 'The Works of Dickens', *London and Westminster
    Review*, vol, 27 (July 1937), p. 202.
14 Grillo, *Dickens's 'Sketches by Boz'*, ch. 4; Costigan, 'Drama and everyday
    life', p. 420.
15 Butt and Tillotson, *Dickens at Work*, pp. 45–6.
16 Steven Marcus, *Dickens from Pickwick to Dombey* (London, 1965), p. 63,
    tellingly notes that Dickens introduces two new characters – Wilkins
    Flasher and Mr Simmery – in ch. 55 of *Pickwick*, only some twenty pages
    from the end.
17 'Greenwich Fair', *SB*, p. 115. Butt and Tillotson, *Dickens at Work*, p. 65,
    suggest that Dickens's readiness to sign a contract with Macrone for a
    three-volume novel after two numbers of *Pickwick* had appeared indi-
    cates that 'he was still seeing *Pickwick* as journalism, as distinct from a real
    novel'. The announcement in number 10, invoking Richardson,
    supports this, and shows that, even if Dickens had begun to think of
    Pickwick as a 'real' novel by that stage, he certainly still saw it as popular
    entertainment. Dickens published an obituary article on John Richard-
    son in *Bentley's Miscellany*, vol. 1 (February 1837), pp. 178–86, when he
    was editor of that journal, and besides this and his own account of
    Richardson in *Sketches by Boz* there are scattered references to Richard-
    son throughout his writing. For Dickens the great 'Muster' Richardson,
    with his large portable theatre booth, in which he could stage thirteen or
    fourteen melodramas in a single day, epitomized the robust fun of the
    fair. For a modern account of Richardson, see Sybil Rosenfeld, 'Muster
    Richardson the great showman', in David Mayer and Kenneth Richards
    (eds) *Western Popular Theatre* (London, 1977), pp. 105–21.
18 Earle Davis, 'Dickens and the evolution of caricature', *PMLA*, vol. 55
    (1940), pp. 231–40, and *The Flint and the Flame: The Artistry of Charles
    Dickens* (London, 1964), pp. 37–53; Forster, bk 5, ch. 1, p. 380; *PP*, 2.
19 Pilgrim, Vol. 1, p. 133. Dickens meditated on the amusement of con-
    ceiving of all the world as a stage in his essay 'The Pantomime of Life',
    BM, vol. 1, pp. 291–7, published in March 1837, by which time *Pickwick*
    had reached number 12. The significance of the essay is discussed by
    William F. Axton, *Circle of Fire: Dickens' Vision and Style and the Popular
    Victorian Theater* (Lexington, 1966), p. 39 ff.

20 'The Young Dickens' (1950), *Collected Essays* (London, 1969), pp. 79–86.
21 Raymond Williams observes this contrast in his Introduction to the Penguin edition of *Dombey and Son* (Harmondsworth, 1970), pp. 13–15.
22 Kathleen Tillotson, '*Oliver Twist*', *Essays and Studies*, NS, vol. 12 (1959), pp. 87–105.
23 *Quarterly Review*, vol. 59 (October 1837), p. 518; *National Magazine and Monthly Critic*, vol. 1 (December 1837), p. 449.
24 [Charles Buller], 'The Works of Dickens', *London and Westminster Review*, vol. 27 (July 1837), p. 212. For comparisons with novelists who preceded him, cf. Philip Collins (ed.), *Dickens: The Critical Heritage*, (London, 1971), pp. 31, 32, 37, 55, 65 and *passim*.
25 Forster, bk 2, ch. 1, p. 91; bk 2, ch. 2, p. 109.
26 J. Hillis Miller, *Charles Dickens: The World of His Novels* (London 1958), pp. 89–90; Bernard Bergonzi, '*Nicholas Nickleby*', in John Gross and Gabriel Pearson (eds), *Dickens and the Twentieth Century* (London, 1962), p. 69; Michael Slater, Introduction to the Penguin edition of *Nicholas Nickleby* (Harmondsworth, 1978), pp. 15–16.
27 Pilgrim, Vol. 1, p. 42 and n.
28 Forster, bk 2, ch. 4, p. 125; Pilgrim, Vol. 1, pp. 459–60 and nn, pp. 463–4 and nn. Mrs Keeley's anecdote, originally printed in the [*Weekly*] *Westminster Gazette*, 13 March 1899, which I have not seen, is quoted in Pilgrim, Vol. 1, p. 460 n. Edward Stirling, *Old Drury Lane: Fifty Years Recollections of Author, Actor and Manager*, 2 vols (London, 1881), Vol. 1, p. 95, claims that his adaptation of *Nickleby* ran for 160 nights, and the Pilgrim editors accept this figure, but it is in fact considerably inflated. The play ran at the Adelphi from November 1838 to March 1839, and during February and March, while it was running four nights a week at the Adelphi, Yates took his company across the river to perform it twice a week at the Surrey Theatre as well. Early in the next season, beginning on 21 October 1839, the play was repeated at the Adelphi for a single week, after which it was replaced by an equally successful adaptation of Ainsworth's *Jack Sheppard*. On 2 March 1840, Stirling's sequel to *Nickleby, The Fortunes of Smike*, appeared at the same theatre, but it ran for only three weeks. The number of London performances of *Nickleby* at this time came to 104, an impressive run, but even including figures for the sequel, which was a different play, the total figure falls well short of 160 performances. Subsequently it was revived by Stirling at other theatres, including the Marylebone in January 1850 and the Strand in November 1855, but these performances were well removed in time from the play's original run.
29 Bernard Levin, 'The truth about Dickens in nine joyous hours', *The Times*, 8 July 1980. Leon Rubin, *The 'Nicholas Nickleby' Story: The Making of the Historic Royal Shakespeare Company Production* (London 1981), pp. 174–9, describes the responses of audiences and critics to the play.
30 Dickens did not confine role-playing to the characters of *Nickleby*, of course; it is a characteristic which he explored in a variety of ways throughout his career. For discussion of its use in social satire, see Paul

Schlicke, 'Bumble and the Poor Law satire of *Oliver Twist*', *Dickensian*, vol. 71 (1975), pp. 149–56.

31 Leman Thomas Rede, *The Road to the Stage* (London, 1827), pp. 22, 57–64 and *passim*. The advice to aspiring players is repeated in the 1835 edition.

32 Playbills for Sadler's Wells Theatre in the Percival Collection, 14 vols lodged in the British Library (Crach 1 Tab 4 b), Vol. 4.

33 Playbill in the British Library collection no. 302.

34 A Septuagenearian, 'The Old Circuits', *Theatre*, NS, vol. 1 (April 1880), pp. 193–9.

35 A copy of Frederic Coleman Nantz, *Pickwick; or, The Sayings and Doings of Sam Weller* is lodged in the Lord Chamberlain's Collection (BM Add. MS. 42947). There are playbills for the play in local studies collections in Ipswich, Norwich, Cambridge and Bury. A bill for Colchester dated 18 December 1837 is in the private collection of Dr Robin Alston. For discussion of the play, cf. McGowan, 'Pickwick and the pirates', pp. 138–45; for Nantz, cf. Paul Schlicke, 'The life of a strolling player: Frederic Coleman Nantz (1810–1844)'; *Theatre Annual*, vol. 34 (1979), pp. 5–24. The review cited is to be found in the Eyre MSS. (Ipswich Record Office), Vol. 4, p. 173.

36 Playbills for 1838–9 in the British Library collection no. 367.

37 For detailed discussion of popular attractions of the nineteenth-century theatre, see Michael Booth, *English Melodrama* (London, 1965), pp. 86, 100, 108 and *passim*. For discussion of the relation between circus and theatre, see Chapter 5 below. *Black-Eyed Susan* was staged in Portsmouth on 21 December 1835 (British Library playbill collection no. 302).

38 Forster, bk 1, ch. 1, p. 2; James G. Ollé, 'Where Crummles played', *Dickensian*, vol. 47 (1951), pp. 143–7; Slater, *Composition*, p. 26.

39 Charles Lander, the adopted son of Jean Davenport, affirmed that his mother was Dickens's model for the Infant Phenomenon in a letter to the *Daily Telegraph*, 3 December 1904, quoted by S. J. Adair Fitz-Gerald, *Dickens and the Drama* (London, 1910), p. 118. The claim was current well before this and has been widely accepted. William Henry Saunders, *Annals of Portsmouth* (London, 1880), p. 217, says that the playbills 'prove' that Billy Floyer is Mr Folair. In his manuscript notes lodged at the Theatre Museum at the Victoria and Albert Museum, Malcolm Morley records that W. Floyer took the part of Squeers in a production of *Nickleby* in Portsmouth on 17 May 1839.

40 Malcolm Morley, 'Where Crummles played', *Dickensian*, vol. 58 (1962), pp.23–9, and 'Dickens goes to the theatre', *Dickensian*, vol. 59 (1963), pp. 165–71. See also Morley, 'More about Crummles', *Dickensian*, vol. 59 (1963), pp. 51–6.

41 Walter Baynham, *The Glasgow Stage* (Glasgow, 1892), pp. 150–2.

42 The claim that Dickens acted with Davenport has been attributed to Edmund Yates, W. H. Pollock, W. A. Chapman, and to the Davenports themselves, but I have not been able to trace this legend, almost certainly apocryphal, to its source. See Charles Lander, 'Mr Vincent Crummles', *Daily Telegraph* (3 December 1904); 'The original of the Infant Phenom-

enon', *Dickensian*, vol. 11 (1915), p. 134; Otis Skinner, *Footlights and Spotlights: Recollections of My Life on the Stage* (Indianapolis, Ind., 1923), pp. 37–39; A. E. Brookes Cross, 'The fascination of the footlights', *Dickensian*, vol. 23 (1927), p. 86. Malcolm Morley, 'Where Crummles played', proposes that if Dickens played for Davenport at all 'the most likely opportunity would have been at the Westminster'. See also J. W. T. Ley's note in Forster, pp. 67–9.

43 Pilgrim, Vol. 3, p. 333.
44 [Leigh Hunt], 'Theatricals', *The News* (19 May 1805); [Gilbert Abbott Á Beckett], *Figaro in London*, vol. 1 (25 August 1832), p. 152, and vol. 1 (2 June 1832), pp. 103–4.
45 Playbills for Portsmouth and Portsea theatre in the British Library collection no. 302.
46 Dewey Ganzel, 'Patent wrongs and Patent theatres: drama and the law in the early nineteenth century', *PMLA*, vol. 76 (1961), pp. 384–96.
47 V. C. Clinton-Baddeley, 'Snevellicci', *Dickensian*, vol. 57 (1961), pp. 43–52.
48 William Charles Macready, *Diaries*, ed. William Toynbee, 2 vols (London, 1912), Vol. 2, p. 24.
49 Michael Baker, *The Rise of the Victorian Actor* (London, 1978), p. 16.
50 David Prince Miller, *The Life of a Showman* (London, 1849), pp. 1–10, 115 and *passim*. See also Baynham, *Glasgow Stage*, pp. 130, 138, 144–5, 153–4; and Thomas Frost, *The Lives of the Conjurors* (London 1876), pp. 225–7; S. T. Coleridge, *Table Talk*, 2 vols (London, 1835), Vol. 1, p. 24; Pierce Egan, *The Pilgrims of the Thames in Search of the National!* (London, 1838), p. 112. Both Egan's *Life of an Actor* (London, 1825), which is dedicated to Kean, and *Pilgrims* contain extended accounts of Richardson and describe Kean's days in the fairground theatre.
51 Playbills for Drury Lane from 22 October 1838 to 23 March 1839 in the British Library collection no. 76; 'Lord' George Sanger, *Seventy Years a Showman* (London, 1927), pp. 173–7.
52 Peter Paterson (pseud. James Glass Bertram), *Glimpses of Real Life* (Edinburgh, 1864), p. 49.
53 See [William Green], *The Life and Adventures of a Cheap Jack* (London, 1876).
54 'Strolling Players', *AYR*, NS, vol. 8 (25 May 1872), pp. 37–42.
55 Paterson, *Glimpses of Real Life*, pp. 167–8.
56 Marcus, *Dickens From Pickwick to Dombey*, p. 118, is a clear exception when he says: 'These plagiarized skits and patchwork pageants rehearse the universal subjects of folk art. They resemble the fair, the circus, and the carnival as much as they do the London theatre; something persists in them, vulgarized, insular, and dilapidated though it is, of an earlier imaginative power, of a popular imagination with which Dickens understood his own active connection.' This is admirable, but it is an insight which Marcus does not develop.
57 Edward Anderson, *The Life of Ann Moore of Tutbury in Staffordshire: Giving an Account of Her Wonderful Existence without Food for above Three Years Past* (Gateshead, 1810); Alexander Henderson, *An Examination of*

the *Imposture of Ann Moore, Called the Fasting Woman of Tutbury* (London, 1813); Anon., *A Full Exposure of Ann Moore, the Pretended Fasting Woman of Tutbury* (London, 1813). James Boswell, *Life of Johnson* (1791) (London, 1949), Vol. 1, pp. 252–3; [H. Morley], 'The ghost of the Cock Lane Ghost', *HW*, vol. 6 (20 November 1852), pp. 217–23; Sanger, *Seventy Years a Showman*, p. 115.

58 Michael Slater, notes to the Penguin edition of *Nickleby*, p. 961; Daniel Lysons, *Collectanea* (a five-volume scrapbook covering the years 1661–1840 and lodged in the British Library, c. 103.k.11), Vol. 1, p. 170, contains clippings from 1814–15 for Bidder and for a contemporary rival from America, Zerah Colburn, whose attractions included not only his calculating skills but also the allegation that he had six fingers on each hand and six toes on each foot – no doubt the cause of his superior ability in counting. There is a memoir of Bidder, who went on to become an eminent civil engineer, in *Minutes of the Proceedings of the Institution of Civil Engineers with Other Selected and Abstracted Papers*, vol. 57, no. 3 (1878–9), pp. 294–309.

59 *The Times* featured numerous reports on the Siamese twins from 17 November 1829 to 9 January 1830. Kay Hunter, *Duet for a Lifetime* (London, 1964), is a modern study of Chang and Eng.

60 See James C. Whyte, *The History of the British Turf from the Earliest Period to the Present Day*, 2 vols (London, 1840); Roger Longrigg, *The History of Horse Racing* (London, 1972), and *The Turf: Three Centuries of Horse Racing* (London, 1975); Wray Vamplew, *The Turf: A Social and Economic History of Horse Racing* (London, 1976).

61 Egan, *Pilgrims*, p. 153. See also Egan's *Book of Sports* (London, 1832 and 1836).

62 Vamplew, *Turf*, p. 133.

63 Forster, bk 2, ch. 2, p. 121; Peter Coveney, *Poor Monkey* (1957), revised as *The Image of Childhood* (Harmondsworth, 1967), p. 138, finds a 'deeply intended implicit comparison between the world of Vincent Crummles and the world of Squeers'; John Archer Carter, 'The world of Squeers and the world of Crummles', *Dickensian*, vol. 58 (1962), pp. 50–3, sees the theatrical episodes as an 'inversion' of the scenes at Dotheboys Hall; and Jerome Meckier, 'The faint image of Eden: the many worlds of *Nicholas Nickleby*', *Dickens Studies Annual*, vol. 1 (1970), p. 131, sees the novel as 'a series of circles', of which each is 'both a parody and a foreshadowing' of the book's conclusions. None of these views is as convincing as Philip Collins's assessment: 'Simply, Dickens wanted to write about Yorkshire schools and theatrical companies and the rest. Nicholas has virtually no character upon which these experiences might impinge; the novel has no theme to which they might be relevant. The plot is meaningless: the novel exists, like others of that period, as a compendium of items, some excellent and some inferior' (*Dickens and Education* (London, 1963; reprinted with alterations 1965), p. 110).

64 Slater, Introduction to Penguin *Nickleby*, p. 16.

65 Rede, *Road to the Stage* (1827 edn), pp. 79, 93.

66 See Joseph W. Donohue, Jr, *Theatre in the Age of Kean* (Oxford, 1975), pp. 67–73, and *Dramatic Character in the English Romantic Age* (Princeton, NJ, 1970), pp. 216–23.

67 Giles Playfair, *The Prodigy: A Study of the Strange Life of Master Betty* (London, 1967), pp. 41–3.

68 See Baker, *Rise of the Victorian Actor*, ch. 1. For a study of the reflection of class-consciousness in nineteenth-century fiction, see Robin Gilmour, *The Idea of the Gentleman in the Victorian Novel* (London, 1981).

69 F. G. Tomlins, *A Brief View of the English Drama* (London, 1840), p. 116; James Cooke, *The Stage in Its Present State and Prospects for the Future* (London, 1840); Dramaticus, *The Stage as It Is* (London, 1847); George Henry Lewes, 'The Old and Modern Dramatists', *Examiner* (3 August 1850), reprinted in *Dramatic Essays* (London, 1896), p. 101.

70 Michael Booth, 'The social and literary context', in Clifford Leech and T. W. Craik (eds), *The Revels History of Drama in English*, Vol. 6, *1750–1880* (London, 1975), p. 8.

71 William Charles Macready, *Reminiscences*, ed. Sir Frederick Pollock, 2 vols (London, 1875), Vol. 2, p. 23. Alfred Bunn, *The Stage both Before and Behind the Curtain*, 3 vols (London, 1840), Vol. 2, p. 33.

72 Population figures cited from *VCH, Hampshire*, Vol. 5, p. 450. For evidence of military patronage, see playbills for the Portsmouth and Portsea theatre in the British Library collection, no. 302. For a stimulating discussion of audience composition and the problems for the modern student of theatre history in achieving an accurate picture of theatre attendance, see Clive Barker, 'A theatre for the people', in Kenneth Richards and Peter Thomson (eds), *Nineteenth Century British Theatre* (London, 1971), pp. 3–24.

73 Press cuttings in Jean Davenport Lander's scrapbooks (Library of Congress MS 78–1738, containers 11 and 12) state that the Davenports left Cork on 4 April 1838 in the steamer *Sirius* and arrived on 24 April in New York, where Jean Davenport was promptly engaged at the National Theatre.

74 F. R. and Q. D. Leavis, *Dickens the Novelist* (London, 1970), p. 88.

75 Marcus, *Dickens From Pickwick to Dombey*, discusses *Nickleby* under the chapter heading 'The true prudence', but he does not make the connection between the exhilarating imprudence of Crummles and that of Micawber.

CHAPTER 4: 'THE OLD CURIOSITY SHOP': THE ASSESSMENT OF POPULAR ENTERTAINMENT

1 Noble Collection, Guildhall Library, collection relating to fairs.

2 Pilgrim, Vol. 2, p. 49.

3 Forster, bk 2, ch. 7, p. 117.

4 The history of the fair, *Memoirs of Bartholomew Fair* (London, 1859), was written by Henry Morley, a contributor to *Household Words*. William Hone's *Every Day Book*, 2 vols (London, 1826–7), includes a lengthy and

circumstantial survey of every show at the fair in the year 1825. Nearly every historical account of English fairs deals with 'Old Bartlemy' to a greater or lesser extent, as do many early nineteenth-century surveys of London amusements. Particularly useful is Sybil Rosenfeld, *The Theatre of the London Fairs in the Eighteenth Century* (Cambridge, 1960). There are copious scrapbook collections dealing with Bartholomew Fair at the Guildhall Library and a less full scrapbook at the British Library. In the Guildhall Record Office the Journals of the City Market Committee, commencing in 1835, and of the City Lands Committee prior to that date, have extensive entries relating to Bartholomew Fair.

5 Journal of the Market Committee, Guildhall Record Office, Vol. 2, pp. 328–9.

6 George Daniel, *Merrie England in the Olden Time* (London, 1842), Vol. 2, pp. 192–3.

7 Journal of the Market Committee, Guildhall Record Office, Vol. 2, pp. 295–300.

8 Journal of the Market Committee, Guildhall Record Office, Vol. 2, pp. 282–3.

9 Journal of the Market Committee, Guildhall Record Office, Vol. 2, pp. 360–1.

10 Noble Collection, Guildhall Library, C.26.5.

11 Noble Collection, Guildhall Library, Bartholomew and Frost Fairs scrapbook.

12 Bartholomew Fair scrapbook, British Library, C.70.h.6.

13 Pilgrim, Vol. 2, p. 40.

14 Malcolm Andrews, 'The composition and design of *The Old Curiosity Shop*: a study in the working of Dickens's imagination', PhD thesis, University of London, 1973, pp. 51–2.

15 Robert L. Patten, '"The story-weaver at his loom": Dickens and the beginnings of *The Old Curiosity Shop*', in Robert B. Partlow (ed.), *Dickens the Craftsman* (Carbondale, Ill., 1970), pp. 44–64.

16 Patten, '"Story-weaver at his loom"', pp. 44–64.

17 Pilgrim, Vol. 2, p. 45.

18 Pilgrim, Vol. 2, p. 49.

19 Daniel Lysons, *Collectanea* (a five-volume scrapbook covering the years 1661–1840 and lodged in the British Library, c.103.k.11), Vol. 2, p. 108; Richard D. Altick, *The Shows of London* (London, 1978), pp. 17–19; Fenwick Collection, Tyne and Wear County Council Museums, J/88 69–483.

20 Altick, *Shows of London*, pp. 420–30.

21 The classic account of this vital aspect of Dickens's style is Dorothy Van Ghent, 'The Dickens world: a view from Todgers'', *Sewanee Review*, vol. 58 (1950), pp. 419–38.

22 Edward Geoffrey O'Donoghue, *The Story of Bethlehem Hospital from Its Foundation in 1247* (London, 1914), p. 240; Anthony Masters, *Bedlam* (London, 1977).

23 Pilgrim, Vol. 2, p. 70.

24 Pilgrim, Vol. 2, pp. 131–2.

25 Walter Dexter, 'Little Nell's journey', *Dickensian*, vol. 20 (1924), pp. 196–201, and *The England of Dickens* (London, 1925), pp. 134–88.

26 Pilgrim, Vol. 1, pp. 447–8, 634–6.

27 Pilgrim, Vol. 1, p. 46; Forster, bk 2, ch. 8, p. 158.

28 Angus Easson, notes to the Penguin edition of *The Old Curiosity Shop* (Harmondsworth, 1972), p. 687.

29 John Alfred Langford, *A Century of Birmingham Life; or, A Chronicle of Local Events from 1741 to 1840* (Birmingham, 1868), Vol. 2, pp. 508, 519, 606, 608; Robert K. Dent, *Old and New Birmingham: A History of the Town and Its People* (Birmingham, 1880), pp. 385, 436, 485, 487; circus bills in the Local Studies Department, Birmingham Public Libraries.

30 Robert Gibbs, *Buckinghamshire: A Record of Local Occurrences* (Aylesbury, 1880), Vol. 3, pp. 144, 237.

31 Dexter, *England of Dickens*, p. 176; Clement Shorter, *Highways and Byways of Buckinghamshire* (London, 1910), p. 19; Robert Gibbs, *A History of Aylesbury* (Aylesbury, 1885), p. 554.

32 Gibbs, *Buckinghamshire*, Vol. 3, pp. 105, 200, 224; *VCH: Buckinghamshire*, Vol. 2, pp. 230–2; press cuttings in the Local Studies Department, County Library, Aylesbury.

33 J. T. Harrison, *Leisure Hour Notes on Historical Buckingham* (London, 1909), pp. 30–1; S. Jackson Coleman, *Treasury of Folklore*, no. 11, *Buckinghamshire* (Douglas, IOM, n.d.).

34 *VCH: Oxfordshire*, Vol. 10, pp. 15, 59; Alfred Beesley, *The History of Banbury* (London, 1841), p. 544; B. S. Trinder, 'Banbury Fair in the nineteenth century', *Cake and Cockhorse*, vol. 4 (Winter 1968), pp. 29–30.

35 J. Harvey Bloom, *Folklore, Old Customs, and Superstitions in Shakespeare Land* (London, 1929), pp. 106–7; Roy Palmer, *The Folklore of Warwickshire* (London, 1976), p. 109; S. Jackson Coleman, *Treasury of Folklore*, no. 19, *Warwickshire* (Douglas, IOM, n.d.); *VCH: Warwickshire*, Vol. 2, p. 386; Hone, *Every Day Book*, Vol. 1, pp. 978–99.

36 'Lord' George Sanger, *Seventy Years a Showman* (London, 1927), p. 30.

37 Walter Bagehot, 'Charles Dickens', *National Review* (October 1858), reprinted in Philip Collins (ed.), *Dickens: The Critical Heritage* (London, 1971), p. 394.

38 Una Pope-Hennessy, *Charles Dickens, 1812–1870* (London, 1945), p. 144; Anita Leslie and Pauline Chapman, *Madame Tussaud Waxworker Extraordinary* (London, 1978).

39 John Payne Collier, *Punch and Judy*, with illustrations by George Cruikshank (London, 1828; expanded edn also 1828), p. 27; Henry Mayhew, *London Labour and the London Poor*, 4 vols (London, 1861–2), Vol. 3, p. 44; George Speaight, *The History of the English Puppet Theatre* (London, 1955) revised as *Punch and Judy* (London, 1970); John Philip Stead, *Mr Punch* (London, 1950); Michael Byrom, *Punch and Judy: Its Origin and Evolution* (Aberdeen, 1972).

40 George Scharf, 'Sketch Book', British Museum Print Room, 198.A.25; Mayhew, *London Labour and the London Poor*, Vol. 3, pp. 148–51; Henrietta Ward, *Memoirs of Ninety Years* (London, 1924), p. 237.

41 Robert Chambers, *The Book of Days*, 2 vols (London, 1863), Vol. 1, pp. 293–5; John Johnson Collection, Bodleian Library, '*Animals on show*', box 1; Bob, *The Dog of Knowledge* (London, 1801), p. 35.

42 Frederick Reynolds, *Life and Times*, 2 vols (London, 1826), Vol. 1, pp. 261–4; Joseph Strutt, *The Sports and Pastimes of the People of England* (London, 1801), p. 186; Charles W. Montague, *Recollections of an Equestrian Manager* (London, 1881), p. 99; Sanger, *Seventy Years a Showman*, p. 207; James Lloyd, *My Circus Life* (London, 1925), p. 39.

43 In addition to Leslie and Chapman, *Madame Tussaud*, bills, advertisements and guidebooks to her exhibitions can be found in collections all over Britain, the most complete of which is in the Tussaud archive, on which the present account is based. See also Francis Hervé (ed.), *Madame Tussaud's Memoirs and Reminiscences in France* (London, 1838).

44 Advertisement on p. 55 of George Smeeton's 'Exhibitions of Mechanical and Other Works of Ingenuity' (1840), a scrapbook in the British Library; on p. 64 there is a verse advertisement for Madame Tussaud's, commencing, 'I stand amid a breathless throng . . .' Wilfred Partington, 'The blacking laureate: the identity of Mr Slum', *Dickensian*, vol. 34 (1938), pp. 199–202, claims one Alexander Kemp, who wrote jingles for Warren's Blacking, as the prototype for Slum. Warren's, so well known to Dickens, published verse advertisements all over Britain for many years, but none among the hundreds I have seen includes an acrostic suitable for conversion from WARREN to JARLEY.

45 Bill Smith, *Joe Smith and His Waxworks* (London, 1896), p. 95.

46 Smith, *Joe Smith and His Waxworks*, p. 119.

47 Thomas Frost, *The Old Showmen and the Old London Fairs* (London, 1874), pp. 257–9.

48 This paragraph is based largely on information to be found in Leslie and Chapman, *Madame Tussaud*; Lysons, *Collectanea*; Altick, *Shows of London*; and E. J. Pike, *A Biographical Dictionary of Wax Modellers* (Oxford, 1973).

49 Strutt, *Sports and Pastimes*, p. 78; Hone, *Every Day Book*, Vol. 1, p. 356; Mayhew, *London Labour and the London Poor*, Vol. 3, pp. 148–51.

50 Strutt, *Sports and Pastimes*, pp. 185–6; Reynolds, *Life and Times*, Vol. 1, pp. 261–4; Lysons, *Collectanea*, Vol. 2, p. 93; Anon., *Historical Account of the Life and Times of the Learned Dog Munito* (London, 1817); Bob, *Dog of Knowledge*.

51 Speaight, *Punch and Judy*; Byrom, *Punch and Judy*.

52 Quoted by Angus Easson, '*The Old Curiosity Shop* from manuscript to print', *Dickens Studies Annual*, vol. 1 (1970), p. 116.

53 Reynolds, *Life and Times*, Vol. 1, pp. 261–4.

54 Information from Tussaud archives. See [Dudley Costello], 'Our Eyewitness in Great Company', *AYR*, vol. 2 (1860), pp. 249–53.

55 *Gentleman's Magazine* (7 March 1837), pp. 326–7.

56 Collier, *Punch and Judy*, p. 27; Mayhew, *London Labour and the London Poor*, Vol. 3, p. 45.

57 Mayhew, *London Labour and the London Poor*, pp. 109, 148–51.

58 Mayhew, *London Labour and the London Poor*, pp. 45, 148–51, 181–2.

59 A. H. Saxon, *The Life and Art of Andrew Ducrow and the Romantic Age of the English Circus* (Hamden, Conn., 1978), pp. 335–46.

60 James R. Kincaid, *Dickens and the Rhetoric of Laughter* (Oxford, 1971), p. 89.

61 J. B. Priestley, *English Humour* (London, 1929), p. 16.

62 Forster, bk 2, ch. 1, p. 85.

63 Rose Caroline Paynter, *Sketches from the Diaries of Rose Lady Graves Sawle* (London, 1908), p. 19, quoted in Pilgrim, Vol. 2, p. 107 n; Robert Simpson Maclean, 'Putting Quilp to rest', *Victorian Newsletter*, vol. 34 (1968), pp. 29–33, and 'Another source for Quilp', *Nineteenth-Century Fiction*, vol. 26 (1971), pp. 337–9; Toby A. Olshin, '"The Yellow Dwarf" and *The Old Curiosity Shop*', *Nineteenth-Century Fiction*, vol. 25 (1970), pp. 96–9; G. M. Watkins, 'A possible source for Quilp', *Notes and Queries*, vol. 18 (1971), pp. 411–13; Rachel Bennett, 'Punch versus Christian in *The Old Curiosity Shop*', *Review of English Studies*, vol. 22 (1971), pp. 423–34; Paul Van Waters Schlicke, 'The grotesque puppet', in 'Comic characterization in Dickens's early fiction', PhD thesis, University of California, San Diego, 1971, pp. 93–133.

64 Collier, *Punch and Judy*, is the earliest text, but is not wholly reliable; Mayhew, *London Labour and the London Poor*, Vol. 3, pp. 43–60, prints a text by a showman who claimed to have been the original for Cruikshank's drawings; Speaight, *Punch and Judy*, pp. 146–55, the best modern history of Punch, reprints what Speaight calls the 'best script of the show ever written', by Robert Brough, first published anonymously in 1854 as *The Wonderful Drama of Punch and Judy*, by Papernose Woodensconce Esq.

65 Bennett, 'Punch versus Christian', pp. 427, 431.

66 As late as the 1820s the devil occasionally carried Punch off to hell, as was traditional in eighteenth-century marionette shows, but the normal nineteenth-century pattern was for Punch to conquer the devil. See Speaight, *Punch and Judy*, p. 89.

67 Henri Bergson, *Laughter* (1900), trans. Fred Rothwell in *Comedy*, ed. Wylie Sypher (Garden City, NY, 1956); Sigmund Freud, *Jokes and Their Relation to the Unconscious* (1905), in *The Standard Edition of the Complete Psychological Works*, trans. James Strachey (London, 1960), Vol. 8.

68 Collier, *Punch and Judy*, pp. 15, 45, 52 and 64.

69 Kincaid, *Dickens and the Rhetoric of Laughter*, p. 99.

70 Gabriel Pearson, '*The Old Curiosity Shop*', in John Gross and Gabriel Pearson (eds), *Dickens and the Twentieth Century* (London, 1962), p. 83, makes this connection.

71 Garrett Stewart, *Dickens and the Trials of Imagination* (Cambridge, Mass., 1974), devotes a full chapter to 'the pivotal Swiveller' (pp. 89–113). His analysis and mine touch, but I believe that Swiveller's creativity owes more to his imaginative response to entertainment than to language, as Stewart proposes; and, unlike Stewart again, I do not find Swiveller a less true poet than Sam Weller.

72 J. W. T. Ley, 'The songs Dick Swiveller knew', *Dickensian*, vol. 27 (1931), pp. 205–18.

CHAPTER 5: 'HARD TIMES': THE NECESSITY OF POPULAR ENTERTAINMENT

1 G. K. Chesterton, *Charles Dickens* (London, 1906), p. 264, suggests that this is a tendency of Dickens's treatment of character generally: 'Dickens did have a disposition to make his characters at all costs happy, or, to speak more strictly, he had a disposition to make them comfortable rather than happy. He had a sort of literary hospitality; he too often treated his characters as if they were his guests.'

2 Edgar Johnson, *Charles Dickens: His Tragedy and Triumph*, 2 vols (Boston, Mass., 1952), Vol. 2, p. 792.

3 Nonesuch, Vol. 2, p. 544.

4 Nonesuch, Vol, 2, pp. 543, 566, 602.

5 Forster, bk 7, ch. 1, p. 565.

6 Johnson, *Dickens*, Vol. 2, p. 795.

7 Nonesuch, Vol. 2, p. 567.

8 Nonesuch, Vol. 2, p. 542.

9 Pilgrim, Vol. 5, pp. 127–9.

10 Nonesuch, Vol. 2, pp. 630–1.

11 Nonesuch, Vol. 2, p. 439.

12 Pilgrim, Vol. 4, pp. 179–82; Vol. 5, pp. 89, 549–50; Nonesuch, Vol. 3, p. 386.

13 W. J. Thoms, 'A Chapter on Clowns', *BM*, vol. 3 (1838), pp. 617–24; [Peter Paterson], 'Town and Country Circus Life', *AYR*, vol. 6 (16 December 1861), pp. 181–6.

14 Peter Paterson (pseud. James Glass Bertram), *Glimpses of Real Life* (Edinburgh, 1864), p. 7. He is speaking here of the theatre, but the point has more general application.

15 Nonesuch, Vol. 2, p. 867.

16 Nonesuch, Vol. 3, p. 224.

17 Anon., 'In the Ring', *AYR*, vol. 13 (28 January 1865), pp. 18–24.

18 Nonesuch, Vol. 3, pp. 284–5.

19 Forster, bk 8, ch. 1, p. 628.

20 The most recent, informative and wide-ranging history of the circus is George Speaight, *A History of the Circus* (London, 1980), which the author generously allowed me to read in typescript before it was published. Thomas Frost, *Circus Life and Circus Celebrities* (London, 1875), M. Willson Disher, *The Greatest Show on Earth* (London, 1937), Antony Hippisley Coxe, *A Seat at the Circus* (London, 1951), A. H. Saxon, *Enter Foot and Horse: A History of Hippodrama in England and France* (New Haven, Conn., 1968) and *The Life and Art of Andrew Ducrow and the Romantic Age of the English Circus* (Hamden, Conn., 1978), are other essential studies. In dealing with the circus background to *Hard Times*, for primary materials I have relied principally upon the British Library playbills collection and the Fenwick Collection at the Tyne and Wear Museum in Newcastle-upon-Tyne. Among memoirs by circus performers, I have found particularly useful Paterson, *Glimpses*; W. F. Wallett, *The Public Life* (London, 1870); Charles W. Montague, *Recollec-*

tions of an Equestrian Manager (London, 1881); James Lloyd, *My Circus Life* (London, 1925); and 'Lord' George Sanger, *Seventy Years a Showman* (London, 1927).

21 Lloyd, *My Circus Life*, pp. 17–22; Montague, *Recollections*, p. 28; [Paterson], 'Town and Country Circus Life', p. 182. Montague claims (p. 90) that Dickens modelled Sleary on the asthmatic circus proprietor Jack Clarke, but Wallett's description of Clarke as 'a man of violent passions', who 'indulged in the strongest expletives' (*Public Life*, pp. 63–5), hardly accords with Dickens's genial ringmaster.

22 Playbills in the Preston District Central Library and in British Library playbill collection no. 298; Nonesuch, Vol. 2, p. 538. It is a tantalizing coincidence that in the same year as *Hard Times* Thackeray included a visit to Astley's in the novel he was then writing, *The Newcomes*.

23 George Orwell, 'Charles Dickens' [1940], *The Collected Essays, Journalism and Letters of George Orwell*, Vol. 1 *An Age Like This* (Harmondsworth, 1970), p. 493.

24 Playbills in British Library collection no. 173; James C. Whyte, *The History of the British Turf from the Earliest Period to the Present Day*, Vol. 1 (London, 1840), pp. 424–5; Roger Longrigg, *The History of Horse Racing* (London, 1972), pp. 54–5, 59–62, 75. Besides The Flying Childers, the statesman H. C. E. Childers (1827–96) was available to Dickens. Appropriately for Dickens's satiric purposes in *Hard Times*, H. C. E. Childers began his career as a school inspector – but in Australia; he did not enter the English political scene until his return in 1857 (see *Dictionary of National Biography*).

25 There is a memoir of Ducrow in *AYR*, NS, vol. 7 (3 February 1872), pp. 223–9, shortly after Dickens's death. Louisa Woolford is praised in *SB*, 'Astley's'.

26 Playbills for 23 August 1830 in British Library collection no. 170; for 10 January 1853 and for 29 August 1853 in British Library collection no. 173.

27 Playbill for 8 September 1828 in British Library collection no. 170 and, with slightly altered wording, on a playbill for Clarke's New Circus at the Green Dragon tavern, Stepney, for 18 December 1828, in British Library Theatre Cuttings no. 50.

28 *Billy Button's Journey to Brentford and Back* (London, n.d.), a chapbook in the British Library, pressmark ch.820/50 (13). For an account of this act, see George Speaight, 'Some comic circus entrées', *Theatre Notebook*, vol. 32 (1978), pp. 24–7.

29 Astley's pantomime of *Billy Button* ran from 26 December 1853 to the week of 6 March 1854; see playbills in British Library collection no. 173.

30 Playbills in British Library collection nos 170 and 173.

31 Undated playbill (*c.*1835) in British Library Theatre Cuttings no. 50. Speaight, *History of the Circus*, p. 67, notes that 'plates spun on canes don't really call for much skill if a small hole is drilled in the centre of the plate'.

32 Playbills for 16 August 1838 in British Library Theatre Cuttings no. 50 and in British Library collection nos 170 and 173.

33 Saxon, *Enter Foot and Horse*, p. 28.
34 Sleary's adaptation is much closer to the original ballad than was Morton's opera of *The Children in the Wood* in 1794. Powell's 1805 stage version approximates the ballad more nearly but has additional characters and a happy ending. The play appeared so frequently in theatres throughout the century that the lack of a hippodramatic text precisely like Sleary's is no evidence that Dickens simply invented it.
35 Playbills for 9 September 1833, 7 June 1824 and 31 August 1829 in British Library collection no. 170.
36 Frost, *Circus Lives*, pp. 64–72.
37 Playbills for Astley's in British Library collection nos 170, 173 and 352. Frost *Circus Lives*, pp. 111–15, discusses the balancing elephant; the *Theatrical Journal* for 1854 notes several times the 'extraordinary success' of Cooke's elephants; Cooke himself printed a large broadsheet containing press notices from a dozen newspapers marvelling at his elephants (in British Library playbill collection no. 173).
38 Playbills in British Library collection nos 170, 171, 173 and 352, and in A. D. Morice Collection, Aberdeen University Library.
39 Hughes Le Roux and Jules Garnier, *Acrobats and Mountebanks* (London, 1890), p. 130.
40 G. Van Hare, *Fifty Years of a Showman's Life* (London, 1888), pp. 61, 89, 103; Speaight, *History of the Circus*, p. 79.
41 Playbills in British Library collection no. 170; Speaight, *History of the Circus*, pp. 63, 89.
42 David Mayer, *Harlequin in His Element: The English Pantomime, 1806–1836* (Cambridge, Mass., 1969), p. 36. Joseph Butwin, 'The paradox of the clown in Dickens', *Dickens Studies Annual*, vol. 5 (1976), pp. 115–32, argues that Jupe derives from Grimaldi's legacy to clowning, but his case conflates quite separate traditions of stage and circus, and results in entirely too sombre a view of Dickens's attitude to clowns.
43 M. Willson Disher, *Clowns and Pantomimes* (London, 1925), p. 201.
44 W. J. Thoms, 'A Chapter on Clowns', *BM*, vol. 3 (1838), pp. 617–24; Disher, *The Greatest Show on Earth*, pp. 114–16.
45 Frost, *Circus Lives*, pp. 70–2.
46 Wallett, *The Public Life*; playbills in British Library collection no. 173; Disher, *Greatest Show on Earth*, p. 199.
47 Frost, *Circus Lives*, pp. 276–89.
48 'Pegasus' was a name inevitably linked with the equestrian circus; Ducrow had a favourite steed of this name, and there was a statue of the mythical winged horse atop Hughes's Royal Circus. See Disher, *Greatest Show on Earth*, pp. 41, 116.
49 Lloyd, *My Circus Life*, p. 16.
50 [Paterson], 'Town and Country Circus Life'.
51 Lloyd, *My Circus Life*, p. 77.
52 Frost, *Circus Lives*, p. 28, quoting *Gentleman's Magazine* on the size of the crowd.
53 Playbills for 24 January and 13 June 1853 in British Library collection no. 173.

54 Forster, bk 9, ch. 1, pp. 727–8.
55 Johnson, *Dickens*, Vol. 2, p. 813, sees the circus as a symbol of art, but I think that its implications are wider than this, and include the imaginative life generally.
56 Playbills for June 1823 at Davis's (as Astley's was called at this time) in British Library collection no. 170. For an earlier production, using a clown rather than pugilists, see, for example, the bill for 17 September 1821 in the same collection. In 1861 the pugilist Tom Sayers toured with Howe's and Cushing's Circus (Speaight, *History of the Circus*, p. 101).
57 Playbill for 17 September 1821 in British Library collection no. 170.
58 David Prince Miller, *The Life of a Showman* (London, 1849), p. 57.
59 Coxe, *Seat at the Circus*, pp. 17–18.
60 Playbills for 16 August 1838 in British Library Theatre Cuttings no. 50, and for 29 May 1841 in British Library collection no. 170.
61 *The Newcomes*, ch. 16.
62 Saxon, *Enter Foot and Horse*, p. 14. A bill for 27 April 1829 in British Library collection no. 171 claims that 22,864 spectators attended Astley's during the previous week and that there were 'thousands more turned away'. The *Theatrical Journal*, which regularly reviewed Astley's productions, often remarked on the capacity houses between 1839, the year it began publication, and 1854, when Dickens wrote *Hard Times*. Dickens himself was turned away from a full house at Astley's in 1865 when he tried to see Adah Isaacs Menken in *Mazeppa* (Nonesuch, Vol. 3, p. 439).
63 F. R. Leavis, *The Great Tradition* (London, 1948), p. 260.
64 John Holloway, '*Hard Times*: a history and a criticism', in John Gross and Gabriel Pearson (eds), *Dickens and the Twentieth Century* (London, 1962), pp. 159–74.
65 Sally Shapiro Vernon, 'The London theatre and the English novel, 1830–1865: a study of relationships', PhD thesis, Cambridge University, 1975, pp. 8–10.

CHAPTER 6: POPULAR ENTERTAINMENT IN DICKENS'S JOURNALISM

1 Harry Stone, 'Dickens "conducts" *Household Words*', *Dickensian*, vol. 64 (1968), pp. 71–85.
2 [Charles Dickens], 'A Preliminary Word', *HW*, vol. 1 (30 March 1850), p. 1.
3 [Charles Knight and Charles Dickens], 'The Tresses of the Day Star', *HW*, vol. 3 (21 June 1851), pp. 289–91.
4 [H. Morley], 'The Theatres of Paris', *HW*, vol. 6 (2 October 1852), pp. 63–9; [J. Oxenford], 'A French Audience', *HW*, vol. 7 (11 June 1853), pp. 349–52; [G. Murray], 'The Roving Englishman: Very Cold at Bucharest; The Theatre; The Terrible Officer', *HW*, vol. 11 (24 February 1855), pp. 82–5, and 'The Roving Englishman at the Pera Theatre', *HW*, vol. 10 (27 January 1855), pp. 570–2; [E. H. Michelsen], 'Chinese Players', *HW*, vol. 8 (19 November 1853), pp. 281–3; [W. Collins], 'A

Breach of British Privilege', *HW*, vol. 19 (19 March 1859), pp. 361–4; [A. M. Howitt], 'Bits of Life in Munich: The Fair', *HW*, vol. 2 (1 March 1851), pp. 535–8; [W. Allingham], 'Irish Ballad Singers and Irish Street Ballads', *HW*, vol. 4 (10 January 1852), pp. 361–8; [J. Capper], 'Number Forty-Two', *HW*, vol. 8 (3 September 1853),pp. 17–20; [G. Murray], 'The Roving Englishman: A Greek Carnival', *HW*, vol. 10 (9 September 1854), pp. 77–9; [A. M. Howitt], 'The May Festival at Starnberg', *HW*, vol. 3 (23 August 1851), pp. 511–16; [J. Hollingshead], 'The Great Pugilistic Revival', *AYR*, vol. 3 (19 May 1860), pp. 133–8; [S. Sidney], 'Fox-Hunting', *HW*, vol. 4 (31 January 1852), pp. 443–4; [J. Capper], 'The Art of Catching Elephants', *HW*, vol. 4 (20 December 1851), pp. 305–10; [E. Gaskell], 'Cumberland Sheep-shearers', *HW*, vol. 6 (22 January 1853), pp. 445–51; [Hale], 'Three Guns in Albania', *HW*, vol. 5 (20 March 1852), pp. 16–19; [G. Murray and H. Morley], 'A Roving Englishman. Benighted', *HW*, vol. 4 (29 November 1851), pp. 221–4; [Mrs G. Murray], 'A Gun among the Grouse', *HW*, vol. 6 (16 October 1852), pp. 115–18; [A. Mackay], 'How We Went Fishing in Canada', *HW*, vol. 1 (8 June 1850), pp. 243–5; [Charles Dickens and W. H. Wills], 'A Popular Delusion', *HW*, vol. 1 (1 June 1850), pp. 217–21; [E. S. Dixon], 'A Russian Singing Match', *HW*, vol. 12 (24 November 1855), pp. 402–5; [G. W. Thornbury], 'At a Bull-Fight', *HW*, vol. 18 (30 October 1858), pp. 457–63; [J. Hollingshead], 'Musical Prize-Fight', *AYR*, vol. 2 (12 November 1859), pp. 65–8.

5 [E. Ollier], 'Ghostly Pantomimes', *HW*, vol. 8 (24 December 1853), pp. 397–400; [G. A. Sala], 'Strollers in Dumbledowndeary', *HW*, vol. 9 (3 June 1854), pp. 374–80.

6 [G. A. Sala], 'The Sporting World', *HW*, vol. 6 (23 October 1852), pp. 133–9; [Browne], 'Early Days in Dulminster', *HW*, vol. 13 (16 February 1856), pp. 116–20; [H. Morley], 'Man as a Monster', *HW*, vol. 9 (17 June 1854), pp. 409–14; [D. Costello], 'Superstitions and Traditions', *HW*, vol. 16 (4 July 1857), pp. 1–6; [F. K. Hunt], 'How to Spend a Summer Holiday', *HW*, vol. 1 (6 July 1850), pp. 356–8; [O. Macpherson], 'Excursion Trains', *HW*, vol. 3 (5 July 1851), pp. 355–6; [R. B. Brough], 'An Excursion Train', *HW*, vol. 12 (20 October 1855), pp. 270–3; [J. Hollingshead], 'Two Trains of Pleasure', *AYR*, vol. 1 (17 September 1859), pp. 492–7.

7 [Charles Dickens and R. H. Horne], 'Shakspeare and Newgate', *HW*, vol. 4 (4 October 1851), pp. 25–7.

8 [Charles Dickens], 'The Uncommercial Traveller', ['Two Views of a Cheap Theatre'], *AYR*, vol. 2 (25 February 1860), pp. 416–21.

9 [Dickens], 'Preliminary Word', p. 1.

10 [Grenville Murray and W. H. Wills], 'Cheap Pleasures – A Gossip', *HW*, vol. 3 (24 May 1851), pp. 201–3; [E. S. Dixon], 'Holiday Times', *HW*, vol. 7 (4 June 1853), pp. 329–32.

11 [G. A. Sala], 'Things Departed', *HW*, vol. 4 (17 January 1852), pp. 397–401.

12 Anon., 'Dummy books at Gad's Hill Place', *Dickensian*, vol. 54 (1958), pp. 46–7.

13 [R. H. Horne], 'A Tower of Strength', *HW*, vol. 5 (3 April 1852), pp. 66–8; [Charles Dickens], 'The Amusements of the People', *HW*, vol. 1 (30 March 1850), pp. 13–15 and (13 April 1850) pp. 57–60; [G. A. Sala], 'The Sporting World', *HW*, vol. 6 (23 October 1852), pp. 133–9; Anon., 'Pinchback's Amusements', *AYR*, vol. 7 (29 March 1862), pp. 71–2; [W. H. Wills and D. Costello], 'The Pedigree of Puppets', *HW*, vol. 4 (31 January 1852), pp. 438–43; [J. Forster], 'Seventy-Eight Years Ago', *HW*, vol. 7 (5 March 1853), pp. 1–6 and (16 April 1853) pp. 157–63; [G. A. Sala], 'A Case of Real Distress', *HW*, vol. 8 (14 January 1854), pp. 457–60.

14 [Dickens], 'Amusements of the People'; Henry Mayhew, 'Vic Gallery', in his *London Labour and the London Poor* (London, 1861), Vol. 1, pp. 18–20, offers a similar vivid, if somewhat less sympathetic, account of the audience at the Vic. For the significance of the Britannia, see Harold Scott, *The Early Doors: Origins of the Music Hall* (London, 1946), p. 53. After the premises were rebuilt in 1858 and renamed the Britannia Theatre, Dickens paid another visit and reported his impressions in 'Two Views of a Cheap Theatre', *UT*, pp. 29–39. H. Barton Baker, *History of the London Stage and Its Famous Players* (London, 1904), pp. 379–80, describes the Britannia Theatre as 'perhaps the best paying in London but one unknown unless by name, to all except the residents in the immediate neighbourhood'.

15 [Andrew Halliday], 'Mr Whelks Revived', *AYR*, vol. 15 (16 June 1866), pp. 548–52; 'Mr Whelks at the Play', *AYR*, vol. 15 (23 June 1866), pp. 563–6; 'Mr Whelks Over the Water', *AYR*, vol. 15 (30 June 1866), pp. 589–92; 'Mr Whelks Combining Instruction with Amusement', *AYR*, vol. 15 (7 July 1866), pp. 610–13; 'Mr Whelks in the East', *AYR*, vol. 16 (21 July 1966), pp. 31–5.

16 [Dickens], 'Amusements of the People'; [Halliday], 'Mr Whelks at the Play'; [Murray and Wills], 'Cheap Pleasures – A Gossip'; [W. B. Jerrold], 'Ruins with Silver Keys', *HW*, vol. 3 (13 September 1851), pp. 592–4.

17 [G. A. Sala], 'Sunday Out', *HW*, vol. 10 (9 September 1854), pp. 73–7.

18 [W. Duthie], 'Some German Sundays', *HW*, vol. 13 (9 April 1856), pp. 320–5, and 'More Sundays Abroad', *HW*, vol. 13 (10 May 1856), pp. 400–4; [W. B. Jerrold], 'Deadly Lively', *HW*, vol. 9 (25 March 1854), pp. 138–40; [G. Murray], 'The Roving Englishman: Greek Easter at Constantinople', *HW*, vol. 8 (31 December 1853), pp. 415–18; Anon., 'Some Old Sundays', *AYR*, vol. 16 (21 July 1866), pp. 38–43; [E. S. Dixon], 'Holiday Times', *HW*. vol. 7 (4 June 1853), pp. 329–32; [A. Halliday], 'Latitude and Longitude of Sunday', *AYR*, vol. 13 (15 July 1865), pp. 589–91, and 'More Scotch Notes', *AYR*, vol. 14 (25 November 1865), pp. 421–3; [J. Payn], 'A Sabbath Hour', *HW*, vol. 18 (30 October 1858), pp. 470–2; Anon., 'Small-Beer Chronicles', *AYR*, vol. 8 (6 December 1862), pp. 295–8; *The Times*, 1 April 1853.

19 [G. A. Sala], 'Sunday Music', *HW*, vol. 12 (13 October 1855), pp. 261–4; *The Reasoner* (23 November 1856), p. 162.

20 [Charles Dickens], 'The Great Baby', *HW*, vol. 12 (4 August 1855), pp. 1–4. *The Report from the Select Committee of the Sale of Beer, Etc., Act*

(1854–5 (H. C. 407) X.339 and (H. C. 427) X.505), which occasioned Dickens's outburst, was published 20 and 26 July 1855, addressing itself to such questions as to whether it is possible to 'make people sober by Act of Parliament' (Q.557), and whether 'the working men of this country consider that they are so weak that they require to be protected from their own weakness' (Q.579). Both questions were answered by witnesses in the affirmative. The statement that workers were 'very much in the condition of children' was made by Rev. J. T. Baylee, *SCHC Public Houses* (1854 (367) XIV. Q.235).

21 [Charles Dickens], 'The Sunday Screw', *HW*, vol. 1 (22 June 1850), pp. 289–92.

22 [Charles Dickens], 'Cruikshank's "The Drunkard's Children"', *Examiner*, 8 July 1848; reprinted in *MP*, pp. 39–43.

23 Brian Harrison, *Drink and the Victorians: The Temperance Question in England, 1815–1872* (London, 1971), p. 84.

24 [Dickens], 'Cruikshank's "The Drunkard's Children"'.

25 [Charles Dickens], 'The Poor Man and His Beer', *AYR*, vol. 1 (30 April 1859), pp. 13–16.

26 [Charles Culliford Boz Dickens], 'The Great Drunkery Discovery', *AYR*, NS, vol. 2 (31 July 1869), pp. 204–9.

27 'The Great Baby', 'The Sunday Screw', and [Charles Dickens], 'Whole Hogs', *HW*, vol. 3 (23 August 1851), pp. 505–7.

28 [Charles Dickens], 'It is Not Generally Known', *HW*, vol. 10 (2 September 1854), pp. 49–52, 'The Great Baby', and 'Stores for the First of April', *HW*, vol. 15 (7 March 1857), pp. 217–22.

29 See Chapter 5; [Dickens], 'Preliminary Word', pp. 1–2; Forster, bk 9, ch. 1, pp. 727–8; *Speeches*, p. 96.

30 [Dickens], 'Preliminary Word'.

31 [Dickens], 'Amusements of the People'.

32 ibid. [Dickens], 'Amusements of the people'.

33 [G. A. Sala], 'Sunday Tea-Gardens', *HW*, vol. 10 (30 September 1854), pp. 145–8.

34 Anne Lohrli, *'Household Words', a Weekly Journal 1850–59 Conducted by Charles Dickens: Table of Contents, List of Contributors and Their Contributions, Based on the 'Household Words' Office Book* (Toronto, 1973), pp. 421–6, succinctly describes Sala's relationship with Dickens as a contributor to his periodicals, and she lists his contributions to *Household Words*. As she notes, Dickens found some pieces by Sala 'capital' but took exception to others. Sala's first essay for *Household Words*, 'The Key of the Street', Dickens found 'remarkable' (Nonesuch, Vol. 2, p. 337; to Wills, 13 August 1851), but a later piece, 'The Sporting World', he found 'very bad' (Nonesuch, Vol. 2, p. 421; to Wills, 13 October 1852). George Augustus Henry Sala (1828–95) collected many of his contributions to *Household Words* in volumes published under his own name; he wrote a memoir of Dickens, *Charles Dickens* (London, 1870), and included material about Dickens both in his reminiscences, *Things I Have Seen and People I Have Known* (London, 1894), and in his autobiography, *The Life and Adventures of George Augustus Sala Written by Himself* (London, 1896).

35 Nonesuch, Vol. 2, p. 548; to Knight, 17 March 1854.

36 [Dickens], 'Sunday Screw'.

37 [G. A. Sala], 'A Canny Book', *HW*, vol. 9 (29 April 1854), pp. 249–53; [Charles Dickens], 'Insularities', *HW*, vol. 13 (19 January 1856), pp. 1–4; [Murray and Wills], 'Cheap Pleasures – A Gossip'.

38 [J. Hannay], 'The Palace of Flowers', *HW*, vol. 3 (26 April 1851), pp. 117–20; [W. B. Jerrold], 'The British Museum a Century Ago', *HW*, vol. 3 (3 May 1851), pp. 130–1; *Sunday under Three Heads, RP*, p. 639; [G. A. Sala], 'Open-Air Entertainments', *HW*, vol. 5 (8 May 1852), pp. 165–9.

39 [Morley], 'Theatres of Paris'; [G. A. Sala], 'Getting Up a Pantomime', *HW*, vol. 4 (20 December 1851), pp. 289–96; [Charles Dickens], 'Gaslight Fairies', *HW*, vol. 11 (10 February 1855), pp. 25–8; [Browne and Morley], 'Perfectly Contented', *HW*, vol. 14 (13 September 1856), pp. 213–16.

40 *Sunday under Three Heads, RP*, p. 661. Published in June 1836, the pamphlet appeared too late to make any contribution to the Bill's rejection on 18 May by the House, which had been dismissing similar bills regularly since 1833. Walter Dexter, 'Early propaganda', *Dickensian*, vol. 32 (1936), pp. 272–4, demonstrates that *Sunday under Three Heads* attracted favourable attention when it was published, and Edgar Johnson, 'Dickens and the bluenose legislator', *American Scholar*, vol. 17 (Autumn 1948), pp. 450–8, discusses the political context out of which the pamphlet emerged.

41 *Sunday under Three Heads* is vigorously polemical, but hardly original. The arguments were familiar ones in the parliamentary debate over Sir Andrew's bills, which opponents repeatedly denounced as 'cant, humbug, and hypocrisy'. As part of their general campaign against privilege, Radicals in the reformed House attacked the Sabbath Observances Bills as class legislation. Joseph Hume, for example, urged that 'if there were to be restrictions on the poor, there ought also to be restrictions on the rich . . . If a poor man was to be prevented from getting his piece of beef or greens, let the rich man be prevented from getting his ices and other luxuries.' Hume declared that 'no legislation would compel the people to become pious', and that Sir Andrew's bills 'would not effect that object'. Edward Lytton Bulwer, later an intimate friend of Dickens, accused Sir Andrew of 'endangering religion itself by showing to what gloomy and tyrannical purposes the name of religion might be applied'. William Cobbett declared that a bill so bad 'would make such a revolution in the manners of the country that it never could pass', and yet another Member of Parliament predicted that enactment of the Sabbath Observances Bill 'would disorganise the whole social system in England and interfere with the most innocent recreations of the people on Sundays' (*Hansard*, 3 July 1832, 29 March 1833 and 30 April 1834). All of these were points which Dickens repeated in his pamphlet.

42 'Author's Preface to the Third Edition', *OT*, p. lxv.

43 *Sunday under Three Heads, RP*, p. 636.

44 [Dickens], 'Amusements of the People'. For studies of the role of the Lord Chamberlain in English theatre history, see Watson Nicholson, *The*

Struggle for a Free Stage in London (London, 1906), and Ernest Bradlee Watson, *Sheridan to Robertson: A Study of the Nineteenth-Century London Stage* (Cambridge, Mass., 1926). The situation is succintly summarized by Michael Booth, 'Public taste, the playwright and the law', Clifford Leech and T. W. Craik (eds), *The Revels History of Drama in English*, Vol. 6, *1750–1880* (London, 1975), pp. 39–44. The Pilgrim editors suggest that Dickens helped his friend Macready to draft a petition to Parliament regarding the 1843 bill, in which the Eminent Tragedian complained of the misuse of licensing:

> These persons have . . . used their trust as a mere piece of property, letting it out to any adventurer who would hire it . . . That by these means all kinds of degrading exhibitions, tending not to humanise and refine, but to brutalise and corrupt, the public mind, have been introduced upon the patent stage; with which practices of licentiousness and habits of debauchery, unknown at places of theatrical entertainment in any other civilised country, have also, by the same system, been connected as matters of profit and gain . . . (Pilgrim, Vol. 3, p. 521 n).

45 [J. A. Heraud], 'Crotchets of a Playgoer', *HW*, vol. 2 (16 November 1850), pp. 188–90.

46 [Halliday], 'Mr Whelks Revived'; [J. Hollingshead], 'An Official Scarecrow', *HW*, vol. 18 (24 July 1858), pp. 143–4; [G. Dodd], 'Music and Poor Neighbourhoods', *HW*, vol. 12 (8 September 1955), pp. 137–41.

47 [Halliday], 'Mr Whelks in the East'.

48 [H. G. Wreford], 'Lazzaroni Literature', *HW*, vol. 4 (7 February 1852), pp. 467–9; [W. Duthie], 'Licensed to Juggle', *HW*, vol. 7 (20 August 1853), pp. 593–4; [G. A. Sala], 'Powder Dick and His Train', *HW*, vol. 7 (7 May 1853), pp. 235–40; [J. Hollingshead], 'Vestiges of Protection', *HW*, vol. 17 (2 January 1858), pp. 70–2.

49 [Charles Dickens], 'Betting Shops', *HW*, vol. 5 (26 June 1852), pp. 333–6.

50 Thomas Carlyle, *Chartism* (1839), in *The Centenary Edition of the Works of Thomas Carlyle* (London, 1896–9), Vol. 29, p. 157.

51 [Dickens and Horne], 'Shakspeare and Newgate'.

52 Peter Bailey, *Leisure and Class in Victorian England: Rational Recreation and the Contest for Control, 1830–1885* (London, 1978), pp. 35–6.

53 Bulwer, *England and the English* (London, 1833); the quotation is taken from his preface to the 3rd edn (1934), p. xvii.

54 William Cooke Taylor, *Notes of a Tour in the Manufacturing Districts of Lancashire*, expanded edn (London, 1842), p. 132. For Dickens's cognizance of Taylor, see Pilgrim, Vol. 5, p. 661 and nn.

55 *Speeches*, p. 45.

56 [Charles Dickens], 'Some Account of an Extraordinary Traveller', *HW*, vol. 1 (20 April 1850), pp. 73–7; [R. H. Horne], 'The Hippopotamus', *HW*, vol. 1 (3 August 1850), pp. 445–9; [R. Owen], 'Justice to the Hyena', *HW*, vol. 6 (1 January 1853), pp. 373–7; [H. Morley], 'The Gardens of Rye', *HW*, vol. 6 (2 October 1852), pp. 55–60; [N. B. Ward and H. W. Wills], 'Back Street Conservatories', *HW*, vol. 2 (14

December 1850), pp. 271–5; [G. Hogarth and W. H. Wills], 'Music in Humble Life', *HW*, vol. 1 (11 May 1850), pp. 161–4; [H. Cole], 'London Musical Clubs', *HW*, vol. 3 (17 May 1851), pp. 179–81; [H. Morley], 'Playthings', *HW*, vol. 6 (15 January 1853), pp. 430–2; [T. Stone], 'A Shilling's Worth of Science', *HW*, vol. 1 (24 August 1850), pp. 507–10.

57 [Halliday], 'Mr Whelks Combining Instruction With Amusement'.

58 [Charles Dickens], 'Frauds on the Fairies', *HW*, vol. 8 (1 October 1853), pp. 97–100.

59 [Charles Knight], 'Three May-Days in London, iii: The May Palace (1851)', *HW*, vol. 3 (3 May 1851), pp. 121–4; [W. H. Wills and G. A. Sala], 'Fairyland in "Fifty-Four"', *HW*, vol. 8 (3 December 1853), pp. 313–17; *Speeches*, p. 134. For a discussion of Dickens's views on the Great Exhibition, see T. W. Hill, 'Dickens and the 1851 Exhibition', *Dickensian*, vol. 47 (1951), pp. 119–24.

60 [Charles Dickens], 'Mr Booley's View of the Last Lord Mayor's Show', *HW*, vol. 2 (30 November 1850), pp. 217–19.

61 Anon., 'Shoemakers' Holiday', *AYR*, vol. 16 (15 December 1866), pp. 544–6.

62 [Charles Dickens and W. H. Wills], 'A Curious Dance Round a Curious Tree', *HW*, vol. 4 (17 January 1852), pp. 385–9.

63 [Sala], 'Getting Up a Pantomime'.

64 The phrase is Bailey's: *Leisure and Class*, p. 54.

65 Forster, bk 2, ch. 4, p. 125.

66 'Birthday Celebrations', *UT*, p. 200; 'Shy Neighbourhoods', *UT*, p. 98.

67 [Horne], 'Hippopotamus'; [Charles Dickens], 'From the Raven in the Happy Family', *HW*, vol. 1 (24 August 1850), pp. 505–7; [Charles Dickens], 'Please to Leave Your Umbrella', *HW*, vol. 17 (1 May 1858), pp. 457–9.

68 [H. Morley], 'A Great Idea', *HW*, vol. 5 (21 August 1852), pp. 546–8, and 'Mr Gulliver's Entertainment', *HW*, vol. 8 (8 October 1853), pp. 142–4; [Dickens], 'From the Raven in the Happy Family', *HW*, vol. 1 (24 August 1850), pp. 505–7; [G. Meredith], 'A New Way of Manufacturing Glory', *HW*, vol. 4 (7 February 1852), pp. 472–6; [W. H. Wills], 'The Monster Promenade Concerts', *HW*, vol. 2 (19 October 1850), pp. 95–6; [J. D. Lewis], 'A Voice from a "Quiet" Street', *HW*, vol. 2 (2 November 1850), pp. 143–4.

69 Boz [Charles Dickens], 'Public Life of Mr Tulrumble, Once Mayor of Mudfog', *BM*, vol. 1 (1837), pp. 49–63; [Charles Dickens], 'Going into Society', *HW*, vol. 18 (Extra Christmas Number 1858), pp. 18–23; [Charles Dickens and Wilkie Collins], 'A Clause for a New Reform Bill', *HW*, vol. 18 (9 October 1858), pp. 385–7; [Charles Dickens], 'Proposals for Amusing Posterity', *HW*, vol. 6 (12 February 1853), pp. 505–7.

70 Anon., 'Death in the Latest Fashions', *AYR*, vol. 13 (18 March 1865), pp. 181–3; Pilgrim, Vol. 3, pp. 453–4; [Charles Dickens], 'Trading in Death', *HW*, vol. 6 (27 November 1852), pp. 241–5, and 'From the Raven in the Happy Family', *HW*, vol. 1 (8 June 1850), pp. 241–2; *MC*, vol. 19; *GE*, vol. 35.

71 [Charles Dickens], 'Lying Awake', *HW*, vol. 6 (30 October 1852), pp. 145–8.
72 [G. A. Sala], 'Travels in Cawdor Street', *HW*, vol. 4 (21 February 1852), pp. 517–21; [Charles Dickens], 'It is Not Generally Known', *HW*, vol. 10 (2 September 1854), pp. 49–52, and 'Stores for the First of April'.
73 Pilgrim, Vol. 5, pp. 644–5, 651–4, 656.
74 [Sala], 'The Sporting World' and 'Open-Air Entertainments'; [Dickens and Horne], 'Shakspeare and Newgate'.
75 [Dickens], 'Amusements of the People'.
76 Richard D. Altick, *The Shows of London* (London, 1978), p. 509; Bailey, *Leisure and Class*, pp. 167–8.

CHAPTER 7: DICKENS'S PUBLIC READINGS: THE ABIDING COMMITMENT

1 The scholarship of Professor Philip Collins, to which I have been indebted time and again in the development of themes and topics in this book, has been indispensable to the present chapter. Through his definitive editions of Dickens's reading-texts, his critical essays on many aspects of the readings, and his example as a public reader himself of Dickens's works, Professor Collins has constructed the solid foundation upon which all future studies of Dickens's readings must build. For relevant details, see the Select Bibliography below; for the immediate matters at hand, see *Readings*, p. lxii; also Field, p. 28, and Kent, pp. 91–4.
2 Forster, bk 4, ch. 6, p. 363; Dolby, p. 451; *Readings*, pp. xvii and xxix.
3 Philip Collins discusses the selection of reading-texts and emendations to them in detail. See especially *Readings*, pp. xxvii, xxxv–xxxvi, lxv–lxvi. For Mrs Raddle's maid, see Field, pp. 92–5.
4 *Readings*, p. lxvi. I have discussed the melodramatic nature of Dickens's conception of tragedy elsewhere, in my article 'A "discipline of feeling": Macready's *Lear* and *The Old Curiosity Shop*', *Dickensian*, vol. 76 (1980), pp. 78–90.
5 For particularly clear statements by Dickens of these views, see 'The Amusements of the People', *HW*, vol. 1 (30 March 1850), pp. 13–15, and *HW*, vol. 1 (13 April 1850), pp. 57–60; 'A Curious Dance Round a Curious Tree', *HW*, vol. (17 January 1852), pp. 385–9; 'Lying Awake', *HW*, vol. 6 (30 October 1852), pp. 145–8; 'Two Views of a Cheap Theatre', *AYR*, vol. 2 (25 February 1860), pp. 416–21; *Speeches* pp. 157–8.
6 Field, p. 21; Forster, bk 3, ch. 1, p. 38; G. A. Sala, *Charles Dickens* (London, 1870), p. 14.
7 Forster, bk 1, ch. 4, p. 59; William Charles Macready, *Reminiscences*, ed. Sir Frederick Pollock (London, 1875), Vol. 1, p. 112. For the *Morning Post* and Hunt remarks and for numerous other contemporary assessments of Dickens's acting, see J. B. Van Amerongen, *The Actor in Dickens: A Study of the Histrionic and Dramatic Elements in the Novelist's Life and Works* (London, 1926), pp. 19–29.

8 Kent, p. 244; Field, pp. 19–20.

9 Forster, bk 8, ch. 2, pp. 641, 646, 647.

10 John Butt and Kathleen Tillotson, *Dickens at Work* (London, 1957), p. 75; Forster, bk 8, ch. 4, p. 664; Field, pp. 1–11; Dolby, p. 257.

11 For Mechanics' Institutes, see Edward Royle, 'Mechanics' Institutes and the working classes, 1840–1860', *Historical Journal*, vol. 14 (1971), pp. 305–21. J. F. C. Harrison, *Learning and Living, 1790–1960* (London, 1961), p. 213, states that 'increasingly the view was propounded that what the working men needed after a hard day's toil was not the rigour of advanced study but amusement and recreation'. The effort to provide entertainment for the same audiences sought by the Mechanics' Institutes produced the penny readings movement, which offered programmes of amateur and professional elocutionists reciting a varied selection of poetry, prose and drama. Penny readings reached the peak of their popularity in the years Dickens was giving his readings. See [Thomas Wright], *Some Habits and Customs of the Working Classes* (London, 1867), pp. 168–83; H. P. Smith, *Literature and Adult Education: Pantopragmatics and Penny Readings* (Oxford, 1960); Victor E. Neuberg, *Popular Literature: A History and Guide* (Harmondsworth, 1977), pp. 242–6.

12 See Dolby, pp. 167–9, 210, 236–7 and *passim*. The announcement for Dickens's first series of professional readings in *HW*, vol. 17 (24 April 1858), p. 456, indicates that seats were sold at 5s, 2½s and 1s. See also *Readings*, pp. xxviii–xxx, and Forster, bk 11, ch. 3, pp. 829–33.

13 Dickens gave his first reading for his own profit on 29 April 1858; his first letter mentioning thoughts about public readings was written to Forster 11 October 1846 (Pilgrim, Vol. 4, p. 631). He read *The Chimes*, on 1 December 1844 to Macready; on 3 December to Forster, Fox, Harness, Dyce, Carlyle, Maclise, Stanfield, Blanchard, Jerrold, and Frederick Dickens; and on 5 December to Forster, Barnham, Fonblanque, Stanfield and Maclise (Forster, bk 4, ch. 6, pp. 355–6, 363–4; Pilgrim, Vol. 4, pp. 232–5 and nn; *Readings*, pp. xvii–xix).

14 Forster, bk 1, ch. 4, pp. 59–60; bk 4, ch. 1, p. 380.

15 Earle R. Davis, 'Dickens and the evolution of caricature', *PMLA*, vol. 55 (1940), pp. 231–40, and *The Flint and the Flame: The Artistry of Charles Dickens* (London, 1964), pp. 37–53; Ana Laura Zambrano, 'Dickens and Charles Mathews', *Moderna Sprak*, vol. 66 (1972), pp. 235–42; *Readings*, p. xxvii.

16 The account of Mathews's career is based principally on *Memoirs of Charles Mathews, Comedian*, written by his widow, Anne Mathews, in 4 vols (London, 1838–9), particularly useful for the large number of contemporary eye-witness accounts of Mathews's acting which she reprints; and on Richard L. Klepac, *Mr Mathews At Home* (London, 1979).

17 *Readings*, pp. lii–lxii; Forster, bk 8, ch. 2, p. 641; bk 8, ch. 4, pp. 661, 664, 665, 667; bk 8, ch. 6, p. 690; Kent, pp. 92–3.

18 Kent, p. 97.

19 Mathews, Vol. 1, pp. 453, 470.

20 Anon., 'Notices of the Acted Drama in London: English Opera House, Strand', *Blackwood's Edinburgh Magazine*, vol. 7 (June 1820), p. 311.

21 Field, p. 49.
22 Mathews, Vol. 1, pp. 453–4.
23 Anon., 'Mr Charles Dickens' Farewell Readings', *Scotsman* (8 December 1868), p. 2.
24 Mathews, Vol. 1, p. 449
25 Mathews, Vol. 3, pp. 109, 181, 182, 264.
26 Ernest Bradlee Watson, *Sheridan to Robertson: A Study of the Nineteenth-Century London Stage* (Cambridge, Mass., 1926), p. 325.
27 Kent, pp. 94, 135.
28 Anon., 'Readings', *Saturday Review* (4 October 1862), p. 411.
29 Field, pp. 29, 61, 103.
30 Mathews, Vol. 1, p. 452; Vol. 3, p. 59; Anon., 'Notices of the Acted Drama in London'.
31 Field, p. 50; Anon., 'Mr Charles Dickens' Farewell Readings'; see also *Readings*, p. 1x.
32 Klepac, *Mr Mathews At Home*, pp. 37–41.
33 Mathews, Vol. 3, p. 61.
34 [Charles Dickens], 'A Preliminary Word', *HW*, vol. 1 (30 March 1850), p. 1.
35 Pilgrim, Vol. 4, p. 631; *Readings*, pp. xlvi–liii; Philip Collins, *Reading Aloud: A Victorian Métier* (Lincoln, 1972); Klepac, *Mr Mathews At Home*, pp. 9–11.
36 Pilgrim, Vol. 4, p. 631.
37 Forster, bk 8, ch. 2 p. 641.
38 Dolby, pp. 136–9.
39 Emlyn Williams, 'Dickens and the theatre', in E. W. F. Tomlin (ed.), *Charles Dickens 1812–1870* (London, 1969), p. 192.
40 Philip Collins, 'Dickens's public readings: texts and performances', *Dickens Studies Annual*, vol. 3 (1974), pp. 182–4, and 'Dickens's public readings: the performer and the novelist', *Studies in the Novel*, vol. 1 (1969), p. 126. R. H. Hutton, 'From a review of Volume III of Forster's *Life, The Spectator*, 7 February 1874, xlvii, 174–6', in Philip Collins (ed.), *Dickens: the Critical Heritage* (London, 1971), p. 585.
41 Dolby, pp. 81, 175.
42 See Raymund Fitzsimons, *The Baron of Piccadilly: The Travels and Entertainments of Albert Smith, 1816–1860* (London, 1967).
43 Dolby, p. 125.
44 Kent, pp. 19–21; Amerongen, *Actor in Dickens*, pp. 32–4; Forster, bk 8, ch. 2, pp. 641–3.
45 See *Readings*, pp. lix–lx.
46 Anon., 'Readings', *Saturday Review* (4 October 1862), p. 411. Collins, *Reading Aloud*, pp. 1, 12, recounts an amazing anecdote about the elocutionist John Chippendale Montesque Bellew, who read *Hamlet* aloud while a company of players silently mimed the roles of the play, thus comforting his audience with the pretence that they were being preserved from the wickedness of theatrical entertainment.
47 Dolby, p. 36; Field, p. 127.
48 Edmund Wilson, 'Dickens: the two Scrooges' (1939), in *The Wound and*

the Bow (new corrected edn., New York, 1965), p. 56; Raymund Fitz-simons, *The Charles Dickens Show: An Account of His Public Readings, 1858–1870* (London, 1970).

49 Robert Woodall, 'The public readings of Charles Dickens', *Blackwood's Magazine*, vol. 326 (1979), p. 511.

50 *Readings*, p. 389.

SELECT BIBLIOGRAPHY

The literature on popular entertainment is vast, as is that on Dickens, and to attempt to offer a bibliography which remotely approached completeness would be unmanageable. The following list includes only those works which I have found most directly useful in the writing of this book. For further bibliographical information about popular entertainment, see:

Arnott, James Fullerton, and Robinson, John William, *English Theatrical Literature, 1559–1900: A Bibliography*, incorporating R. W. Lowe, *A Bibliographic Account of English Theatrical Literature* (1888) (London, 1970).
Stott, Raymond Toole, *Circus and the Allied Arts: A World Bibliography, 1500–1970*, 4 vols (Derby, 1958–71).
Wilmeth, Don B., *American and English Popular Entertainment: A Guide to Information Sources* (Detroit, Mich., 1980).

For bibliographical information about Dickens, see:

Cohn, Alan M., and Collins, K. K., *The Cumulated Dickens Checklist, 1970–1979* (Troy, NY, 1982).
Collins, Philip, 'Charles Dickens', in George Watson (ed.), *The New Cambridge Bibliography of English Literature* (Cambridge, 1969), Vol. 3, pp. 779–850.
Fenstermaker, John J., *Charles Dickens, 1940–1975: An Analytical Subject Index to Periodical Criticism of the Novels and Christmas Books* (London, 1979).
Gold, Joseph, *The Stature of Dickens: A Centenary Bibliography* (Toronto, 1971).

For convenience I have not distinguished between contemporary and modern sources, nor between book, article or manuscript sources, but have made only a broad division between works on popular entertainment and works on Dickens. For information about texts by Dickens used in the present study, see References and Abbreviations.

(I) POPULAR ENTERTAINMENT

Addison, William, *English Fairs and Markets* (London, 1953).
Aleph (pseud. W. Harvey), *London Scenes and London People* (London, 1863).
Alexander, Sally, *St Giles Fair, 1830–1914: Popular Culture and the Industrial*

Revolution in Nineteenth-Century Oxford, History Workshop Pamphlet no. 2 (Oxford, 1970).

Altick, Richard D., *The English Common Reader: A Social History of the Mass Reading Public, 1800–1900* (Chicago, Ill., 1957).

Altick, Richard D., *The Shows of London* (London, 1978).

Bailey, Peter, *Leisure and Class in Victorian England: Rational Recreation and the Contest for Control, 1830–1885* (London, 1978).

Baker, Michael, *The Rise of the Victorian Actor* (London, 1978).

Barnum, P. T., *Struggles and Triumphs; or, Forty Years' Recollections of P. T. Barnum Written by Himself* (Hartford, Conn., 1869).

Beer, Gillian, '"Coming wonders": uses of theatre in the Victorian novel', in Marie Axton and Raymond Williams (eds), *English Drama: Forms and Development* (Cambridge, 1977), pp. 164–85.

Blackmantle, Bernard (pseud. Charles Molloy Westmacott), *The English Spy* (London, 1825).

Booth, Michael, *English Melodrama* (London, 1965).

Bratton, Jacqueline, and Traies, Jane, *Astley's Amphitheatre* (Cambridge, 1980).

Briggs, Asa, *Mass Entertainment: The Origins of a Modern Industry* (Adelaide, 1960).

Burke, Peter, *Popular Culture in Early Modern Europe* (London, 1978).

Byrom, Michael, *Punch and Judy: Its Origin and Evolution* (Aberdeen, 1972).

Colburn, Henry, *Colburn's Kalendar of Amusements in Town and Country for 1840* (London, 1840).

Collier, John Payne, *Punch and Judy*, with illustrations by George Cruikshank (London, 1828; expanded edn also 1828).

Collins, Philip, *Reading Aloud: A Victorian Métier* (Lincoln, 1972).

Coxe, Antony Hippisley, *A Seat at the Circus* (London, 1951).

Cruikshank, Robert, *Cruikshank's Trip to Greenwich Fair: A Whimsical Record* (London, 1832).

Cunningham, Hugh, *Leisure in the Industrial Revolution* (London, 1980).

Daniel, George, *Merrie England in the Olden Time*, 2 vols (London, 1842).

Disher, M. Willson, *Clowns and Pantomimes* (London, 1925).

Disher, M. Willson, *Fairs, Circuses, and Music Halls* (London, 1942).

Disher, M. Willson, *The Greatest Show on Earth* (London, 1937).

Donohue, Joseph W., *Theatre in the Age of Kean* (Oxford, 1975).

Egan, Pierce, *Life in London* (London, 1820).

Egan, Pierce, *The Life of an Actor* (London, 1825).

Egan, Pierce, *Pierce Egan's Book of Sports* (London, 1832).

Egan, Pierce, *The Pilgrims of the Thames in Search of the National!* (London, 1838).

Ellis, George Mark, 'The Evangelicals and the Sunday Question, 1830–1860: organized Sabbatarianism as an aspect of the Evangelical movement', PhD thesis, Harvard University, 1951.

Fitzsimons, Raymund, *The Baron of Piccadilly: The Travels and Entertainments of Albert Smith, 1816–1860* (London, 1967).

Frost, Thomas, *Circus Life and Circus Celebrities* (London, 1875).

Frost, Thomas, *The Lives of the Conjurors* (London, 1876).

Frost, Thomas, *The Old Showmen and the Old London Fairs* (London, 1874).

Ganzel, Dewey, 'Patent wrongs and Patent theatres: drama and the law in the early nineteenth century', *PMLA*, vol. 76 (1961), pp. 384–96.

Grant, James, *Sketches in London* (London, 1838).

[Green, William], *The Life and Adventures of a Cheap Jack* (London 1876).

Grice, Elizabeth, *Rogues and Vagabonds; or, The Actors' Road to Respectability* (Lavenham, 1977).

Harris, Neil, *Humbug: The Art of P. T. Barnum* (Boston, Mass., 1973).

Harrison, Brian, *Drink and the Victorians: The Temperance Question in England, 1815–1872* (London, 1971).

Harrison, Brian, 'Religion and recreation in nineteenth-century England', *Past and Present*, no. 38 (1967), pp. 98–125.

Harrison, Brian, 'State intervention and moral reform', in Patricia Hollis (ed.), *Pressure from Without in Early Victorian England* (London, 1974), pp. 289–322.

Harrison, Brian, 'The Sunday trading riots of 1855', *Historical Journal*, vol. 8 (1965), pp. 219–45.

Hone, William, *Every Day Book*, 2 vols (London, 1826–7).

James, Louis, *Fiction for the Working Man* (London, 1963; rev. edn Harmonds-worth, 1973).

Klepac, Richard L., *Mr Mathews at Home* (London, 1979).

Leech, Clifford, and Craik, T. W. (eds), *The Revels History of Drama in English*, Vol. 6, *1750–1880* (London, 1975).

Leslie, Anita, and Chapman, Pauline, *Madame Tussaud Waxworker Extra-ordinary* (London, 1978).

Lloyd, James, *My Circus Life* (London, 1925).

Lysons, Daniel, 'Collectanea', five volumes of scrapbooks in the British Library (London, 1661–1840).

McKechnie, Samuel, *Popular Entertainments through the Ages* (London, 1931).

Macready, William Charles, *Diaries*, ed. William Toynbee, 2 vols (London, 1912).

Macready, William Charles, *Reminiscences*, ed. Sir Frederick Pollock, 2 vols (London, 1875).

Malcolmson, Robert, *Popular Recreations in English Society, 1700–1850* (Cambridge, 1973).

Mayer, David, *Harlequin in His Element: The English Pantomime, 1806–1836* (Cambridge, Mass., 1969).

Mayer, David, and Richards, Kenneth (eds), *Western Popular Theatre* (London, 1977).

Mayhew, Henry, *London Labour and the London Poor* 4 vols (London, 1861–2).

Miller, David Prince, *The Life of a Showman* (London, 1849).

[Mogridge, George], *Old Humphrey's Walks in London and Its Neighbourhood* (London, [1843?]).

Montague, Charles W., *Recollections of an Equestrian Manager* (London, 1881).

Morley, Henry, *Memoirs of Bartholomew Fair* (London, 1859).

Neuburg, Victor, *Popular Literature: A History and Guide* (Harmondsworth, 1977).

Palmer, Roy, and Raven, Jon, *The Rigs of the Fair: Popular Sports and Pastimes in the Nineteenth Century through Songs, Ballads, and Contemporary Accounts* (Cambridge, 1976).

Paterson, Peter (pseud. James Glass Bertram), *Glimpses of Real Life* (Edinburgh, 1864).

Playfair, Giles, *The Prodigy: A Study of the Strange Life of Master Betty* (London, 1967).

Plumb, J. H., *The Commercialisation of Leisure in Eighteenth-Century England* (Reading, 1973).

Rede, Leman Thomas, *The Road to the Stage* (London, 1827).

Reid, J. C., *Bucks and Bruisers: Pierce Egan and Regency England* (London, 1971).

Reynolds, Frederick, *Life and Times*, 2 vols (London, 1826).

Robson, J. P., *The Life and Adventures of the Far Famed Billy Purvis* (Newcastle-upon-Tyne, 1849).

Rosenfeld, Sybil, *The Theatre of the London Fairs in the Eighteenth Century* (Cambridge, 1960).

Sanger, 'Lord' George, *Seventy Years a Showman* (1908), with an introduction by Kenneth Grahame (London, 1927).

Saxon, A. H., *Enter Foot and Horse: A History of Hippodrama in England and France* (New Haven, Conn., 1968).

Saxon, A. H., *The Life and Art of Andrew Ducrow and the Romantic Age of the English Circus* (Hamden, Conn., 1978).

Smeeton, George, *Doings in London* (London, 1825).

Smeeton, George, 'Exhibitions of Mechanical and Other Works of Ingenuity', a scrapbook lodged in the British Library (London, 1840).

Smith, Bill, *Joe Smith and His Waxworks* (London, 1896).

Smith, Charles Manby, *Curiosities of London Life* (London, 1853).

Smith, Morris Brooke, 'The growth and development of popular entertainment and pastimes in the Lancashire cotton towns, 1830–1870', MLitt thesis, University of Lancaster, 1970.

Speaight, George, *A History of the Circus* (London, 1980).

Speaight, George, *A History of the English Toy Theatre* (London, 1969).

Speaight, George, *Punch and Judy* (London, 1970).

Stirling, Edward, *Old Drury Lane: Fifty Years Recollections of Author, Actor and Manager*, 2 vols (London, 1881).

Strutt, Joseph, *The Sports and Pastimes of the People of England* (London, 1801).

Timbs, John, *Curiosities of London* (London, 1855).

Traies, Jane, *Fairbooths and Fitups* (Cambridge, 1980).

Vernon, Sally Shapiro, 'The London theatre and the English novel, 1830–1865: a study of relationships', PhD thesis, Cambridge University, 1975.

Wallett, W. F., *The Public Life* (London, 1870).

Walvin, James, *Leisure and Society, 1830–1950* (London, 1978).

Watson, Ernest Bradlee, *Sheridan to Robertson: A Study of the Nineteenth-Century London Stage* (Cambridge, Mass., 1926).

[Wright, Thomas], *Some Habits and Customs of the Working Classes* (London, 1867).

(II) DICKENS

Amerongen, J. B. Van, *The Actor in Dickens: A Study of the Histrionic and Dramatic Elements in the Novelist's Life and Works* (London, 1926).

Andrews, Malcolm, 'The composition and design of *The Old Curiosity Shop: a study in the working of Dickens's imagination*', PhD thesis, University of London, 1973.

Axton, William, F., *Circle of Fire: Dickens' Vision and Style and the Popular Victorian Theater* (Lexington, Ky, 1966).

Bennett, Rachel, 'Punch versus Christian in *The Old Curiosity Shop*', *Review of English Studies*, vol. 22 (1971), pp. 423–34.

Butt, John, and Tillotson, Kathleen, *Dickens at Work* (London, 1957).

Butwin, Joseph, 'The paradox of the clown in Dickens', *Dickens Studies Annual*, vol. 5 (1976), pp. 115–32.

Chesterton, G. K., *Charles Dickens* (London, 1906).

Churchill, R. C., 'Dickens, drama and tradition', *Scrutiny*, vol. 10 (1942), pp. 358–75.

Clinton-Baddeley, V. C., 'Snevellicci', *Dickensian*, vol. 57 (1961), pp. 43–52.

Clinton-Baddeley, V. C., 'Wopsle', *Dickensian*, vol. 57 (1961), pp. 150–9.

Collins, Philip (ed.), *A Christmas Carol: The Public Reading Version* (New York, 1971).

Collins, Philip, *Dickens and Education* (London, 1963; reprinted with alterations 1965).

Collins, Philip, 'Dickens and popular amusements', *Dickensian*, vol. 61 (1965), pp. 7–19.

Collins, Philip, 'Dickens's public readings: the kit and the team', *Dickensian*, vol. 74 (1978), pp. 8–16.

Collins, Philip, 'Dickens's public readings: the performer and the novelist', *Studies in the Novel*, vol. 1 (1969), pp. 118–32.

Collins, Philip, 'Dickens's public readings: texts and performances', *Dickens Studies Annual*, vol. 3 (1974), pp. 182–97.

Collins, Philip (ed.), *Dickens: The Critical Heritage* (London, 1971).

Collins, Philip, 'The popularity of Dickens', *Dickensian*, vol. 70 (1974), pp. 5–20.

Collins, Philip, 'Queen Mab's chariot among the steam engines: Dickens and "fancy"', *English Studies*, vol. 42 (1961), pp. 78–90.

Collins, Philip (ed.), '*Sikes and Nancy' and Other Public Readings* (London, 1983).

Costigan, Edward, 'Drama and everyday life in *Sketches by Boz*', *Review of English Studies, NS*, vol. 27 (1976), pp. 403–21.

Coveney, Peter, *Poor Monkey* (1957), revised as *The Image of Childhood: The Individual and Society. A Study of the Theme in English Literature,* with an introduction by F. R. Leavis (Harmondsworth, 1967).

Darton, F. J. Harvey, *Vincent Crummles: His Theatre and His Times* (London, 1926).

Davis, Earle R., 'Dickens and the evolution of caricature', *PMLA*, Vol. 55 (1940), pp. 231–40.

Dexter, Walter, 'Little Nell's journey', *Dickensian*, vol. 20 (1924), pp. 196–201.

Dexter, Walter, 'Mr Charles Dickens will read', a series of articles published in *Dickensian*, vols 37–9 (1941–3).

Dickens, Mamie, *My Father as I Recall Him* (London, 1897).

Donaghue, Denis, 'The English Dickens and *Dombey and Son*', *Nineteenth-Century Fiction*, vol. 24 (1970), pp. 383–403.

Ellis, Julie Wren, Rothwell 'A critical analysis of Charles Dickens's *The Old Curiosity Shop*', EdD thesis, Ball State University, 1975.

Fawcett, F. Dubrez, *Dickens the Dramatist: On Stage, Screen and Radio* (London, 1952).

Fitz-Gerald, S. J. Adair, *Dickens and the Drama* (London, 1910).

Fitzsimons, Raymund, *The Charles Dickens Show: An Account of His Public Readings, 1858–1870* (London, 1970).

Ford, George, H., *Dickens and His Readers: Aspects of Novel-Criticism since 1836* (Princeton, NJ, 1955).

Garis, Robert, *The Dickens Theatre: A Reassessment of the Novels* (Oxford, 1965).

Gordon, John D., *Reading for Profit: The Other Career of Charles Dickens* (New York, 1958).

Harbage, Alfred, *A Kind of Power: The Shakespeare–Dickens Analogy* (Philadelphia, Pa., 1975).

Harbage, Alfred, 'Shakespeare and the early Dickens', in G.B. Evans (ed.), *Shakespeare: Aspects of Influence* (Cambridge, Mass., 1976). Harvard English Studies, no. 7, pp. 109–34.

Hewett, Edward, and Axton, William F., *Convivial Dickens: The Drinks of Dickens and His Times* (Athens, Ohio, 1983).

Hollington, Michael, 'Dickens the Flâneur', *Dickensian*, vol. 77 (1981), pp. 71–87.

Humphrey, Harold E., 'The background of *Hard Times*', PhD thesis, Columbia University, 1958.

Johnson, Edgar, *Charles Dickens: His Tragedy and Triumph*, 2 vols (Boston, Mass., 1952).

Kettle, Arnold, 'Dickens and the popular tradition', *Zeitschrift für Anglistik und Amerikanistik*, vol. 9 (1961), pp. 229–52.

Leavis, F. R., and Leavis, Q. D., *Dickens the Novelist* (London, 1970).

Ley, J. W. T., 'The songs Dick Swiveller knew', *Dickensian*, vol. 27 (1931), pp. 205–18.

McCarron, Robert M., 'Folly and wisdom: three Dickensian wise fools', *Dickens Studies Annual*, vol. 6 (1977), pp. 40–56.

Marcus, Steven, *Dickens from Pickwick to Dombey* (London, 1965).

Morley, Malcolm, 'Dickens goes to the theatre', *Dickensian*, vol. 59 (1963), pp. 165–71.

Morley, Malcolm, 'More about Crummles', *Dickensian*, vol. 59 (1963), pp. 51–6.

Morley, Malcolm, 'Where Crummles played', *Dickensian*, vol. 58 (1962), pp. 23–9.

Ollé, James G., 'Where Crummles played', *Dickensian*, vol. 47 (1951), pp. 143–7.

Paroissien, David, 'Literature's "eternal duties": Dickens's professional creed', in Robert Giddings (ed.), *The Changing World of Charles Dickens* (London, 1983), pp. 21–50.

Pemberton, Thomas E., *Charles Dickens and the Stage* (London, 1888).

Priestley, J. B., *The English Comic Characters* (London, 1925).

Schlicke, Paul, 'A "discipline of feeling": Macready's *Lear* and *The Old Curiosity Shop*', *Dickensian*, vol. 76 (1980), pp. 78–90.

Slater, Michael, *The Composition and Monthly Publication of 'Nicholas Nickleby'* (London, 1973).

Slater, Michael (ed.), *Nicholas Nickleby* (Harmondsworth, 1978).

Smith, Grahame, *Dickens, Money, and Society* (Berkeley/Los Angeles, Calif., 1968).

Stewart, Garrett, *Dickens and the Trials of Imagination* (Cambridge, Mass., 1974).

Stone, Harry, *Dickens and the Invisible World: Fairy Tales, Fantasy and Novel-Making* (London, 1979).

Stone, Harry, 'Dickens "conducts" *Household Words*', *Dickensian*, vol. 64 (1968), pp. 71–85.

Stone, Harry (ed.), *The Uncollected Writings of Charles Dickens: 'Household Words', 1850–1859* (Bloomington, Ind., 1968).

Tate, E., 'Dickens' Vanity Fair: the show image in *The Old Curiosity Shop*', *Hong Kong Baptist College Academic Journal*, vol. 4 (1977), pp. 167–71.

Van Ghent, Dorothy, 'The Dickens world: a view from Todgers'', *Sewanee Review*, vol. 58 (1950), pp. 419–38.

Wilson, Angus, 'Dickens on children and childhood', in Michael Slater (ed.), *Dickens 1970* (London, 1970), pp. 195–227.

Wilson, Angus, *The World of Charles Dickens* (London, 1970).

Zambrano, Ana Laura, 'Dickens and Charles Mathews', *Moderna Sprak*, vol. 66 (1972), pp. 235–42.

INDEX

Figures in *italic* type refer to illustration captions